Shanghai Gone

STATE AND SOCIETY IN EAST ASIA
Series Editor: Elizabeth J. Perry

State and Society in the Philippines
   By Patricio Abinales and Donna J. Amoroso
Revolution in the Highlands: China's Jinggangshan Base Area
   By Stephen Averill
Embattled Glory: Veterans, Military Families, and the Politics of Patriotism in China, 1949–2007
   By Neil J. Diamant
Marxism in the Chinese Revolution
   By Arif Dirlik
Sovereignty and Authenticity: Manchukuo and the East Asian Modern
   By Prasenjit Duara
A Chinese Economic Revolution: Rural Entrepreneurship in the Twentieth Century
   By Linda Grove
The Party and the Arty in China: The New Politics of Culture
   By Richard Kraus
Chinese Among Others: Emigration in Modern Times
   By Philip A. Kuhn
Webs of Smoke: Smugglers, Warlords, Spies, and the History of the International Drug Trade
   By Kathryn Meyer and Terry Parssinen
Patrolling the Revolution: Worker Militias, Citizenship, and the Modern Chinese State
   By Elizabeth J. Perry
Of Camel Kings and Other Things: Rural Rebels Against Modernity in Late Imperial China
   By Roxann Prazniak
Underground: The Shanghai Communist Party and the Politics of Survival, 1927–1937
   By Patricia Stranahan
Shanghai Gone: Domicide and Defiance in a Chinese Megacity
   By Qin Shao
Communication in China: Political Economy, Power, and Conflict
   By Yuezhi Zhao

Shanghai Gone

Domicide and Defiance in a Chinese Megacity

Qin Shao

ROWMAN & LITTLEFIELD PUBLISHERS, INC.
Lanham • Boulder • New York • Toronto • Plymouth, UK

Published by Rowman & Littlefield Publishers, Inc.
A wholly owned subsidiary of The Rowman & Littlefield Publishing Group, Inc.
4501 Forbes Boulevard, Suite 200, Lanham, Maryland 20706
www.rowman.com

10 Thornbury Road, Plymouth PL6 7PP, United Kingdom

British Library Cataloguing in Publication Information Available

Library of Congress Cataloging-in-Publication Data
Shao, Qin
  Shanghai gone : domicide and defiance in a Chinese megacity / Qin Shao.
     pages cm. — (State and society in East Asia)
  Includes bibliographical references and index.
  ISBN 978-1-4422-1131-5 (cloth : alkaline paper) — ISBN 978-1-4422-1132-2
(paper : alkaline paper) — ISBN 978-1-4422-1133-9 (electronic) (print) 1. City
planning—China—Shanghai—History. 2. City planning—Political aspects—China—
Shanghai—History. 3. City planning—Social aspects—China—Shanghai—History.
4. Wrecking—Social aspects—China—Shanghai—History. 5. Protest movements—
China—Shanghai—History. 6. Shanghai (China)—Biography. 7. Social change—
China—Shanghai—History. 8. City and town life—China—Shanghai—History. 9.
Shanghai (China)—Social conditions—20th century. 10. Shanghai (China)—Social
conditions—21st century. I. Title.
  HT169.C62S527 2013
  307.1'2160951132—dc23

                                                                              2012030732

♾™ The paper used in this publication meets the minimum requirements of
American National Standard for Information Sciences—Permanence of Paper
for Printed Library Materials, ANSI/NISO Z39.48-1992.

Printed in the United States of America

To the Undemolishable Human Spirit

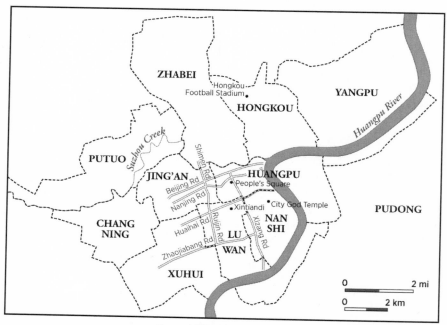

Central Shanghai, ca. 2000

Being has a memory.

—Vaclav Havel, *To the Castle and Back*

It is a deadened world, and its growth is sometimes unhealthy for want of air.

—Charles Dickens, *Bleak House*

If history is to be creative, to anticipate a possible future without denying the past, it should, I believe, emphasize new possibilities by disclosing those hidden episodes of the past when, even if in brief flashes, people showed their ability to resist, to join together, occasionally to win.

—Howard Zinn, *A People's History of the United States*

Contents

	Illustrations	xi
	Preface	xv
Introduction		1
	Housing: Reform and Conflict	6
	Patterns of Grassroots Resistance	16
	Domicide	24
Chapter 1	The Woman of a Thousand-and-one Petitions	39
	The Petition System	40
	Meet Zhou Youlan	50
	"I Stood There and Watched . . ."	52
	A Road with No Return	56
	Going Mental?	79
	Moment of Inertia	85
Chapter 2	Nightmares: Old and New	91
	Xintiandi—The New World	93
	From a "Fine Home" to a "Stuck Fish Bone"	101
	"You Destroyed My Home and You Now Own Me"	129
	Dream Team and Nightmares	138
Chapter 3	Waving the Red Flag	145
	The Deceit	146
	The Initial Conflict	151

	The Negotiations	156
	Cultural Resistance	159
	Mr. C	169
	A Mixed Ending	181
Chapter 4	A Barrack-room Lawyer	189
	Squatting in Shanghai	190
	The Transformation of a Shack	197
	A Nail Household	201
	The Education of Shi Lin	204
	The Formula	208
	The Political Arena	213
	Waiting for Nirvana	224
Chapter 5	Mr. Lincoln's Lane	229
	The Pretext	230
	The Issue of Preservation	232
	A Community Leader	236
	Discovering a Usable Past	239
	Letter Writing	242
	A Propaganda War	244
	The Involvement of Experts	249
	A Ghost Document	252
	The Peak and the Valley	255
	The Last Nail	259
	A Problematic Future	268
	Conclusion	275
	Bibliography	285
	Index	293
	About the Author	307

Illustrations

Central Shanghai, ca. 2000   vi

1.1:   Zhou Youlan treasured her house, which had two south-
oriented balconies, good for drying the laundry and keeping
the house warm in winter.   54

1.2:   The many petition forms Zhou Youlan filled out at the
district office and brought back home because the office
refused to receive her.   61

1.3:   Zhou Youlan was beaten during one of the detention
periods and suffered bruises.   75

2.1:   On July 19, 1997, the Shanghai Municipal Housing Bureau
signed this contract with the Hong Kong developer
Vincent Lo's Landton Ltd., for the land use rights of Lot 108.   97

2.2:   The street-front of He Chujin's home.   103

2.3:   The He family shortly after the house was built in 1925.   104

2.4:   On February 8, 1999, the Luwan District issued this
compulsory eviction notice to the He family.   113

2.5: On a Wednesday in June 2007, this group of five former residents of the Taipingqiao and its surrounding area who were petitioning the government for their lost homes gathered at a KFC restaurant next to Xintiandi to exchange documents and information about their cases. 126

2.6: During the 1950s socialist reform, the government nationalized several of Zhu Guangze's properties. In token compensation, it issued Zhu a certificate to collect "fixed rent," 23.37 yuan a month, for one of her properties, through the government, which was now the new manager. This certificate shows a stamp for every month from 1963 to November 1965, the onset of the Cultural Revolution, when the payments came to a halt. 133

2.7: Zhu Guangze (1922–), since her eviction in late 2005, has become a self-imposed hostage—she has insisted on staying in a Spartan apartment provided by the district government until her housing dispute is resolved. 137

3.1: In summer 2004, the remaining residents in East Eight Lots formed a Legal Study Forum in an abandoned apartment. 161

3.2: An evicted family left an antithetical couplet on their door. It reads: "Maintaining [my] rights led to eviction; today the Constitution looks hopeless"; the horizontal phrase gets to the point: "Illegal Demolition." 167

3.3: In the morning of June 9, 2004, neighbors watched as the authorities cordoned off Mr. C's apartment building and got ready to evict his family. 176

3.4: Mr. C on his balcony, holding a page of the *Renmin ribao* to protest, while the movers and their truck, arranged by the authorities, were ready to take away his family's belongings. 178

3.5: At the end of the five-hour eviction, Mr. C grasped the bars on the windows of his apartment as a last act of resistance. 180

4.1: Shi Lin's home. He rents the street-front of the house to peasant workers for a glass shop. 201

4.2: One of the cardboard signs Shi Lin made to carry in street protests. 218

4.3: Shi Lin assisted these eight residents with their cases. They took this picture together to appeal for help. 219

4.4: Shi Lin created this chart and printed it on the backs of the envelopes in which he sends petition letters to Beijing. 222

5.1: This "Housing Demolition and Relocation Permit," issued by the Hongkou District Housing Bureau, dated January 3, 2003, listed Lane 264, Xijiangwan Road (Lincoln Lane), as part of the M8 line road extension project and scheduled the demolition to be completed in two months. 233

5.2: The residents used the wall space in Lincoln Lane to campaign for their cause. 247

5.3: The residents placed this custom-made plaque at the entrance of Lincoln Lane to rally public support for the preservation of their lane. 248

5.4: On June 30, 2004, the authorities convened an expert panel, ostensibly to review the Lincoln Lane case but essentially to retract an earlier document that proposed to preserve it so as to allow the Hongkou District government to demolish the lane. 264

5.5: The destruction of Lincoln Lane in March 2005. 269

Preface

It was a pair of sandals: blue soles and pearl-like translucent stripes, with the characters *xinshiji*, "the new millennium," in cheerful red printed on the sole. My sister let me wear them during my visit to Shanghai in the summer of 2002. On the eve of my return to the United States, my sister, who was helping me with the packing, asked if I would like to bring the sandals with me. "No," I replied, as I preferred to travel light. "But isn't it pretty? It is a handmade present from my friend Youlan," my sister said. I was mildly curious as to why anyone in Shanghai still made anything by hand when cheap goods of every kind imaginable flooded the city. My sister explained: "Poor Youlan! She lost her home and job, and now petitions all day long. When she has time, she makes sandals for her friends."

That was how I began to learn about Zhou Youlan's story. A reticent and polite former kindergarten teacher, Youlan was evicted from her home in 1996. She has since become a full-time petitioner with the mouth of a truck driver. My sister and I talked until dawn and by then I wished I could have cancelled my trip because I could not wait to meet this Youlan.

The timing was perfect. I was in China that summer on my last research trip to gather material for the publication of my book on China's urbanization in the late nineteenth and early twentieth centuries, focusing on the small city of Nantong in the lower Yangzi region. I was looking to launch a new project. While studying Nantong, I was mindful of the impact of the post-Mao reform on the city, and the conflict between the construction of new projects and the preservation of past landmarks. I was also reminded by the degree of change in Shanghai, as I often got lost in the city of my birth. But it was Youlan's experience and my sister's vivid account that night that provided me with an immediate, personal link to the urban transformation in post-Mao China. I was convinced that there were compelling stories to tell and important issues to explore. That my work until that point had little to do with contemporary China made such a new project daunting, but also exciting.

This book is meant for both the scholarly community and the public. Other than the introduction and conclusion, all the chapters are written without extensive scholarly references, a deliberate choice to make the book accessible to anyone who is interested in the vicissitudes of contemporary China.

Many people have helped with this project. Perry Link, David Strand, Lynn T. White, III and the late Stephen Averill supported my initial grant proposal. Zhang Jishun accommodated my stay in Shanghai during my first field trip. Members of the Shanghai Foreign Correspondents Club and the Shanghai Historic House Association offered leads to some of my case studies. Perry Link kindly read parts of the manuscript and shared his critical insights. David Strand introduced me to scholarship that challenged me to think in new ways. His thoughtful reading of the manuscript and unfailing encouragement are invaluable. Benjamin Read reviewed the manuscript for the press and offered very helpful suggestions. Benjamin Wood, the architect for the Xintiandi project in Shanghai, granted me interviews and provided me with crucial material about the project. Richard Gunde, with his abundant knowledge and kindness, has been simply indispensible in improving my work in every way. Roderick MacFarquhar came up with titles for some of the chapters over a lunch, one of the most productive and stimulating lunch breaks I have had. Susan McEachern and Rick Baum helped shape the book title. Jayne Cohen offered tips on the fine points of writing. I benefited tremendously from the rich knowledge of Deborah Davis, Henrietta Harrison, Judith Herman, and Hanchao Lu on many issues: housing reform, grassroots protest, the history of Shanghai, and trauma and recovery. Gary Cohen contributed to this work with his many talents and much patience. He improved the quality of every image used in this book and served as an astute sounding board for my ideas. I owe all of them my heartfelt gratitude.

I have enjoyed ongoing discussions about China—for instance, is corruption in China best described as "particle decay" or "moment of inertia"?—and beyond with my son, Songsong, who has grown from a college freshman to a published research scientist during the years I have worked on this book. I look forward to celebrating his graduation from his doctoral program next spring, which coincides with the publication of this book; Songsong makes my heart sing.

For a historian who works on post-Mao China, one could not have found a better mentor and friend than Elizabeth Perry. Liz's consistent and enthusiastic support of my work made all the difference. She helped to keep me focused and never lost sight of the heart of the book, which is the stories of the people. Liz read the entire manuscript and offered critical comments. Her extraordinary kindness and generosity is only matched by her exceptional knowledge and scholarship on China and beyond; I am deeply grateful to have benefited from both.

It has been a pleasure to work with Susan McEachern, my acquisitions editor at Rowman & Littlefield, and her staff. I thank her for guiding me through the publishing process with her expertise, and for our many engaging exchanges. Alden Perkins, my production editor, was patient, understanding, and supportive.

This project would not have been possible without the generous support of many institutions. The American Council of Learned Societies, with a contribution from the National Endowment for the Humanities, funded my initial six-month field research in China. A residential fellowship from the Radcliffe Institute for Advanced Study at Harvard University and a Scholar Grant from the Chiang Ching-kuo Foundation provided the much-needed time for writing. The unique, interdisciplinary environment at Radcliffe was most thought-provoking. I thank Judith Vichniac and her dedicated staff and my fellow fellows for an unforgettable year there. I was also awarded a residential fellowship by the Woodrow Wilson International Center for Scholars in Washington, DC, and a Weatherhead Residential Scholar Fellowship from the School for Advanced Research on the Human Experience at Santa Fe, New Mexico—both for the 2007–2008 academic year while I had the Radcliffe Fellowship. I deeply regretted that I was unable to be part of those celebrated institutions, but my appreciation toward them is no less profound.

The College of New Jersey has consistently supported my research with mini grants, research equipment, reduced teaching load, and a sabbatical. Benjamin Rifkin, the current Dean of the School of Humanities and Social Sciences, and Susan Albertine, the previous dean, have enthusiastically supported my work. I counted on Chris Larthey, the History Department's IT liaison, to help solve technical problems when I worked in the field. Megan Ayers, the extremely capable and kind program assistant of the History Department, and her staff, especially Beth Amicucci, always cheerfully attended to my needs as I worked on the book. I thank all of them for their support and kindness.

Over the years, I have shared my work-in-progress at various venues and learned much from lively scholarly exchanges. They include the Centre of Oriental Studies at Vilnius University, Lithuania; Stockholm University, Sweden; a number of institutes at Harvard University: the Radcliffe Institute for Advanced Study, the Fairbank Center for Chinese Studies, the Law School, the Harvard Asia Center, and the Harvard-Yenching Institute; the annual meeting of the Association for Asian Studies; the Political Forum at The College of New Jersey; the East Asian Studies Seminar at Princeton University; the Center for Chinese Studies at the University of California, Los Angeles; the US-China Institute at the University of Southern California; and the Modern China Seminar at Columbia University. I wish to thank William Alfred, Robert Barnett, Clayton Dube, Benjamin Elman, Andrea Goldman, Henrietta Harrison, Michael Herzfeld, Jennifer Leaning, Miriam Lowi, Elizabeth Perry, Lynn T. White, III, Chuck Wooldridge, and Yunxiang Yan for their very kind invitations to present my work. The two Asian Neighborhood Research Group workshops organized by Michael Herzfeld and supported by the Harvard-Yenching Institute were most stimulating and useful in thinking about my own work.

Parts of the book have been published as articles. I thank *Future Anterior*, *China Currents*, and *Modern Chinese Literature and Culture* for permission to reprint them here.

I owe my innermost debt to the people in Shanghai. At the onset of the project, I thought about studying the experience of "ordinary people" in China's reform. As soon as I started interviews, I abandoned that concept and was convinced that no one, absolutely no one, was "ordinary." Everyone I met in China is remarkable in his or her own right. Lin Weihang helped with my research in many ways. His enthusiasm for culture and historic architecture is contagious. I thank Dai Lixiang, Mr. C, He Yidong, Shi Lin, Zhang Xiaoqiu, Zhou Youlan, Zhu Guangze, Zhu Jianjun, and many others and their families for opening their homes to and sharing their experiences with me, sometimes under difficult circumstances when their personal freedom was at stake. They have allowed me to interview them regularly throughout the years in person and via the Internet and telephone and to observe and study their lives in their own environment. They have also provided me with much-needed source material that they collected and documented—in the struggle for justice, they have become researchers and writers themselves.

Most of these residents suffered from domicide—the destruction of home against the will of its dwellers—that has taken place globally in the name of economic growth. Domicide has shattered their lives in so many ways that it has led me to question whether it is a crime against humanity. But these residents are also agents of change. Their courage and unyielding pursuit of justice is inspirational. This book is dedicated to their spirit. I hope someday there will be a monument to commemorate their struggle.

Q. S.
Newtown, Pennsylvania
August 2012

~

Introduction

Holes—immense, tiny, and multidimensional—everywhere. Holes where an entire street block was knocked down; holes in skeletal buildings where the shards of shattered windows thrust out like exclamation marks; holes in abandoned sofas and shoes scattered everywhere in the debris. Holes, too, in the eyes of those few residents in nearly every neighborhood who had decided to hold out against demolition, some of them for months or even years. The haunting void and silence of those holes were only accentuated by the shimmering skyscrapers and the bustling city life that surrounded them.

This was Shanghai, or rather, the Shanghai in the shadow of high-rises, that I saw in 2004 when I started my field research. Rising to become one of the world's most economically powerful cities, Shanghai has undergone a profound transformation since the late 1980s. Led by a massive building boom and housing reform as part of a grand economic agenda to introduce a market economy to a pre-capitalist society, this transformation has altered the cityscape beyond recognition. Shanghai looks more and more like what the Dutch architect Rem Koolhaas has termed the "generic city" that is fast popping up, especially in the developing world.[1]

Not since the forced opening of Shanghai as a treaty port in 1843 after the Opium War had the city experienced such a rapid and drastic change. Massive construction went hand in hand with massive destruction. In the 1990s alone, Shanghai built nearly 3,000 skyscrapers, with more of them planned; each tried to top the other in a never-ending chase to be China's, if not the world's, tallest.[2] The construction of those high-rises came at a price. By 2004, over 70 percent of the alleyway houses, which accounted for 80 percent of Shanghai's residential housing prior to 1980, were wiped out.[3] Also gone were the millions of residents and the pattern of everyday life that had defined the city for more than a century.[4]

This process is known in Chinese as *chaiqian*: demolition and relocation— demolishing existing structures to make space for new projects, and relocating residents to the ever-expanding suburbs. *Chaiqian* has been taking place all over China, in cities small and large. Since *chai*, demolition, implies *qian*, relocation, for more than two decades since the late 1980s this term, often written in big red characters, has flooded the public space of Shanghai on structures slated for demolition. The sign has only recently vanished as there is little left in the city to be razed.

The impact of this large-scale *chaiqian* on Shanghai and its residents is complex. Most visible are the newly erected dense clusters of high-rises and the related dramatic improvement of housing conditions for millions of residents. The average living space per person increased from four square meters in 1979 to fifteen square meters in the early 2000s,[5] an accomplishment unimaginable only a few decades ago. This improvement, however, has left behind human wreckage, often invisible, unquantifiable, and absent from China's official discourse. This human cost is an integral part of China's march toward a market economy.

Demolition and relocation have caused massive destruction to the patterns of daily life, especially for the economically disadvantaged—people with few resources for coping with the fast-paced change. Such destruction recalls the brutal impact of the early Industrial Revolution on the working poor in the West. As was the case in that early stage of capitalism, economic development in China has gone much farther and faster than regulatory institutions could govern; lawlessness and predatory behavior have ruled the day. Some in China consider demolition and relocation to be a new wave of "enclosures"—the single-minded pursuit of profit, which is at the heart of the blistering capitalism in China, has driven people out of their homes and off their land. This geographic displacement has led to emotional, economic, and social dislocations as people were uprooted, some unnecessarily and violently, from their homes, refuges imbued with family history and community memory.

Most important and least recognized of all, demolition and relocation have been violent, and the violence has been sanctioned by the state. Such violence is mostly carried out through domicide, the "murder of the home," against the owners' will,[6] as detailed below. It is also perpetrated against residents in the form of physical abuse, imprisonment, murder, and suicide as they resist demolition and relocation on the government's terms.

Central to the conflict is the loss of home and the practical and emotional challenges it poses, a topic to which we will return. Suffice it to say here that issues surrounding the home and housing are often at the center of politics within nations and on the global stage. For a prime example, one only needs to look at the thorny settlement situation in the long-standing Israeli-Palestinian conflict. Elsewhere, some of the most important news in the eventful month of August 2011 alone involved housing—in London, the British government considered evicting protesting rioters and their families from their public housing as punishment,[7] and in Israel, standing out from the demands of the 300,000 tent-city protesters was the issue of affordable housing, which underscored, more than anything else, the widening gap between the rich and poor that had spurred the unrest in that country.[8]

Housing issues also play a crucial role in global economy. China's recent economic growth has by and large been fueled by real estate development. The ruinous financial crisis of 2008, on the other hand, started with widespread subprime-lending abuses in the United States that capitalized on the kind of risky behavior underlined by the irrepressible human desire to own a home, the bedrock of the American dream. In a recent study on gender and racial equality, Anita Hill highlights the role of home in access to opportunities in America—an insight that rings true universally.[9]

The importance of both the physical and symbolic home to human life can hardly be overstated. Home is thus a vital subject in almost every major field of the humanities and social sciences. Human history generally and social change particularly are often examined through issues of housing and home. Most fiction revolves around the physical and emotional home, family dynamics, and the struggle of the self. According to the literary scholar Rosemary Marangoly George, "The search for the location in which the self is 'at home' is one of the primary projects of twentieth-century fiction in English" and, in that sense, "all fiction is homesickness."[10] Numerous poems and songs, East and West, ancient and contemporary, are about home. Philosophy, too, is said to be really "homesickness"; metaphysically, "it is the urge to be at home everywhere."[11]

Indeed, the home is a unique and fundamental physical and emotional space for fulfilling the essential human need for attachment and identity. This attachment is not merely to the physical space of the house; rather it is attachment also to the intangible—love, emotional bounds, family values, routines, rituals, and memories. As a Chinese saying goes, "Gold house, silver house, nothing tops my thatched house." The emphasis here is on what is mine, a unique and special sense of belonging to a place that one calls one's own and in which one plants one's roots from which the rest of life grows.

The home, simply put, is "where the heart is." To be sure, the situation at home may not always be rosy. Domestic abuse can be as devastating as any trauma caused by outside forces.[12] But even the dark side of the home underscores its irreplaceable importance in our lives.

The loss of one's home, therefore, is often life shattering. While natural disasters are a common culprit in destroying homes and communities, it is domicide that inflicts the most profound grievance, because it results from human intention. The conflict generated in domicide in China is compounded by an arbitrary compensation policy, prevailing corruption, and weakness in the law and in its enforcement. For more than a decade, Chinese authorities have consistently identified demolition and relocation as one of the top factors that has contributed to heightened popular grievance and social instability in urban China, much as illegal land taking has been the main source of unrest in the countryside. The severe challenge this and other tensions have posed to Beijing is reflected in a new state budget category termed "Stability Maintenance." At 514 billion yuan annually, it is second only to the 532 billion yuan allocated for the military budget.[13]

Reform in post-Mao China has provided a fascinating laboratory for scholarly inquiry. Urban housing reform, central to both the development of a market economy and to its success, has become a growing field in contemporary China studies. To date, scholars have mainly explored the economic, regulatory, spatial, and social dimensions of the issue. Studies include the transition of housing as a socialist welfare program to a commodity; the development and functions of a real estate market; investment in and construction of housing; the impact of property issues on marriage and class status; urban planning and infrastructure building; housing and globalization; housing and consumer and popular culture; the formation of new, gated communities and the rise of China's middle class as both powerful consumers and a potential political force.[14] Scholars have also focused more on construction, from the new city to the new community, than destruction. They have paid less attention to those who have been stuck in limbo for years after their homes were destroyed, without any resolution of their demands in sight. Moreover, housing reform has had a far-reaching impact on all aspects of Chinese society; yet current studies have emphasized its economic and social consequences, with insufficient attention to its human effects.

The accelerated urbanization and gentrification and its impact on community life worldwide have attracted scholarly interest. Michael Herzfeld's *Evicted from Eternity* on the restructuring of the Monti District of Rome is an exemplary work in this regard.[15] Yet there have been relatively few in-depth studies of *chaiqian* in China, where rapid urbanization has been most notable.[16]

Unlike the new cities and new communities with their concrete presence and evolving implications, demolition and relocation are a fleeting moment between the past and present. Though they are a recent phenomenon, they have already been erased from the public face of Shanghai by the imperative of new construction and the deliberate effort of official amnesia. Today, visitors will find few traces of the scarred, "phantom" city Shanghai was at the height of demolition only a few years ago.[17] But invisible and buried phenomena often hold the key to understanding some of the central issues of our time. Demolition and relocation have generated some of the most intense struggles that signify both the problems and promises of China's reform era. These struggles, profoundly personal because they involve the home, increasingly the most intimate and private space of all to the Chinese family,[18] have had and will continue to have complex repercussions for Chinese society.

This book considers domicide—demolition and relocation against the dwellers' will—as a human experience. Based on years of field research and primarily oral history, the book puts a human face on the conflicts through an in-depth study of five family and neighborhood cases in Shanghai. It investigates the interaction between the residents, the government, the courts, the developers, the media, and other agencies in dealing with the conflicts. The struggle of these forces—residents' protest for justice and property rights, government's prioritization of economic growth and social stability, developers' pursuit of access and profits, and the media's split identity as the mouthpiece of the Chinese Communist Party (CCP) and the conscience of society—has characterized much of the housing conflict.

Shanghai has been a trendsetter in housing reform.[19] This has had a concentrated impact on its cityscape and residents. Real estate values in Shanghai are the highest in China,[20] a powerful incentive not only for developers and officials alike to maneuver for their own gain, but also for residents to hold out for the highest compensation. The city has also grown so wealthy and powerful that the municipal government often ignores Beijing's repeated, albeit half-hearted, appeals for a more rational approach to development, which has further frustrated the residents. But Shanghai is also China's window to the world, and social stability is of paramount importance and political control is strict. At the same time, the city has among the most resourceful, pragmatic, and politically savvy residents in China. These factors have combined to produce a determined, inventive, and measured resistance that defines the urban movements there.

Examining both the human scale of a rapid, globalizing economic change locally and its implications for the post-Mao transition broadly, the book explores questions such as: What else was demolished along with old neighborhoods?

What else was built in their ruins? What does the struggle in housing reform tell us about the nature of China's reform era?

Housing: Reform and Conflict

In the late 1970s, the Chinese government, under the leadership of Deng Xiaoping, launched its opening and reform policy to introduce a market economy that inaugurated the post-Mao era. Housing reform took place in this large context. In a span of two decades from 1980 to 1999, the reform transformed urban housing from a state welfare program to a commercialized market. As a result, state and public ownership of housing property has given way to private ownership, which is at the heart of the reform and a watershed departure from a central policy of the CCP since 1949.

At the onset of the housing reform, however, the pressing concern was not so much about the issue of ownership as about alleviating the severe housing shortage in urban China and the crushing financial burden it inflicted on the government. The housing problem was historical. During the Guomindang (GMD, Nationalist Party) period (1927–1949), private property ownership was customary and public housing was almost nonexistent. The GMD—controlled by propertied interests and haunted by the instability inherited from the late Qing dynasty, the constant fighting with the CCP since the late 1920s, and a protracted war against the Japanese invasion until 1945—simply had neither the intent nor the resources to address urban housing needs. The Civil War between the GMD and the CCP (1945–1949) only made this situation worse. War refugees crowded in cities, colossal inflation, and business speculation that led to drastic rent increases made the housing problem a catastrophe waiting to happen. With a small number of large landlords controlling the majority of the urban housing stock, the burden of the housing crisis predictably fell on the urban poor—the working class, the unemployed, peasant migrants, refugees, and urban pariahs.[21]

In 1949, to the newly established CCP government, this housing crisis not only challenged its political and ideological convictions, but also undermined social stability that the new ruling party desperately tried to establish. Consistent with its belief that private ownership was the root cause of all social ills, its hostility toward the propertied classes, and its support of the working poor, the CCP launched a series of measures to take charge of urban housing problems. It tried rent control to stabilize the market, confiscation of "enemy" property to increase the housing supply, and finally, starting in 1956, a decade-long, massive socialist transformation that effectively replaced the dominant private property ownership with state ownership.

To be sure, the socialist transformation did not completely eliminate private ownership in urban China. The CCP made a distinction between the means of production, such as factories and rental properties which were undisputed targets of nationalization and the means of livelihood, and usually spared residences, especially if they were the only houses the families themselves lived in. What it eradicated was the housing market. By 1966, the state, through municipal housing bureaus and *danwei*, the various work units that employed most urban residents, was in full control of urban housing, from its construction and allocation, to its management. Most residents became tenants of either the municipal and district housing bureau or their workplaces and paid a low rent. Housing effectively became part of the state welfare system.[22]

This program, like the rest of the socialist welfare system, was unsustainable. For one thing, the low rents did not yield any profit to cover even the cost of maintenance, much less investment in public housing. The Chinese government simply lacked the financial means to sustain the welfare housing program. Also, the constant, demoralizing political campaigns, the stagnant economy worsened by man-made disasters, and the rapid population increase made housing improvement under Mao impossible.[23]

Indeed, the problem of the housing shortage in Shanghai was compounded by a population explosion: on average in each of the first three decades from the 1950s to 1970s, one million additional people had to be housed. By 1985, Shanghai had more than seven million residents, compared to four million in the 1940s. Population density in the central districts reached 40,000 per square kilometer and in the busy downtown area, 160,000 per square kilometer. A 1985 survey indicates that of the 1,800,000 households in the city, half suffered from a housing shortage and other difficulties—216,000 households had an average of less than four square meters of living space per person, and 15,000 of them had less than two square meters. There were also 3,650,000 square meters of slums and another 11,000,000 square meters of old alleyway houses built in the early twentieth century that were frozen in time—they had no basic modern amenities and sanitary services to speak of. Millions of residents lived in substandard conditions. It was not uncommon for three generations of a family to live in one room, and for several married couples to share one room, and still, they were the envy of the many more married couples who had no housing at all.[24] In Shanghai, the collapse of this socialist welfare housing program made housing the "number one difficult issue under heaven" for officials.[25] After three decades of the socialist state, housing remained on the verge of a catastrophe, much like that on the eve of the CCP takeover in 1949.

This housing crisis, on the other hand, explains the early success of demolition and relocation in Shanghai, which was carried out under the rubric of urban renewal (*jiuqu gaizao*). Urban renewal then was understood by the Chinese as a government-sponsored, not-for-profit project to bring down entire neighborhoods and build better, high-rise apartments for the residents, as opposed to for-profit, commercial, real estate development (*shangye kaifa*). This distinction between urban renewal and commercial development was important in the Chinese context at the time when the housing welfare system remained the norm and the introduction of the market economy was tentative. The former meant that residents were more willing to move out and to support a government program that offered them improved and affordable housing, while the latter put the residents in a business relationship with the developer, a relationship governed by market forces, at least in theory. Years later, the end of welfare housing and the deepening of market reform essentially changed the meaning of urban renewal to commercial development and gentrification, a process that has taken place across China. Tension rose when the government continued to use the term "urban renewal" in its original meaning as a pretext to force residents out to promote for-profit commercial real estate development.[26]

The first wave of a decade-long urban renewal in Shanghai, started tentatively in 1980 and gradually accelerated in the late 1980s, was to help households with four square meters per person or less. The city government redeveloped dozens of dilapidated neighborhoods by building multistory apartments, a project supported by the residents. Capitalizing on this achievement, the second wave of urban renewal, started in 1990, was even more ambitious. Termed a "365 Project," the plan was for the Shanghai government to eliminate not only the 3,650,000 million square meters of slums but also another 3,000,000 square meters of dilapidated, old alleyway housing in the inner city by the end of the twentieth century, another ten-year project.[27] This "365 Project" was supposed to fulfill the UN-Habitat goal of a "city without slums."[28] The early stage of the process was successful. Up until the mid-1990s, hundreds of thousands of residents, mostly from the worst neighborhoods, grabbed the first opportunity in their lifetimes to better their housing situation and moved to newly built apartments, some of which were in the suburbs.[29]

However, the "365 Project" was soon hijacked and, from mid-1990s onward, neighborhood resistance to demolition and relocation became increasingly open and intense. Several factors contributed to this change.

Commodification of Housing

First, the deepening of the commodification of real estate and the privatization of ownership rights altered the nature of urban housing redevelopment.

In the early 1980s the central and local governments gradually took steps to experiment with the marketization of real estate assets. In 1986, the first legal land sale took place in Shenzhen, one of the Special Economic Zones that led China's opening and reform campaign.[30] Shanghai closely followed the trend and had its first lot of land leased to a Japanese company in 1988, which opened the door for land transactions.[31] The commodification of land laid the foundation for commercial housing development.

In the meantime, the government took measures to encourage a shift from public housing to the private purchase of homes. For instance, it sold welfare flats to sitting tenants at discounted prices. Most important of all, it gradually implemented the necessary financial instruments to facilitate home purchases. In 1991, Shanghai initiated the first provident fund that made it possible for individuals to enter the housing market. Throughout the 1990s, the central government issued a series of policies to promote the full commodification of urban real estate. The process was completed with the issuing in May 1999 by the Ministry of Construction of a document to legalize the sale and resale of previously subsidized public housing. As Deborah Davis points out, "May 1999 marked the point at which the central government fully legitimated privatization of this former public good on a nationwide scale and thereby commodified rights of transfer or alienation."[32]

This marketization of urban housing had a profound impact on the subsequent housing development. Market forces now took over. Urban renewal, like any other real estate project, became profit-driven commercial development, though the government continued to capitalize on its earlier meaning. Urban land, state property that had been taken for granted as free in building welfare housing, was now a hot commodity. Its cost had to be figured into housing prices, which drove up the real estate market. Promoted by the government and driven by developers, real estate development has since become one of the most powerful engines in China's phenomenal economic growth.

Changing Regulations

This shift in priority from improving residential housing to pursuing economic growth was shaped by and reflected in government policies. A brief comparison of the "Regulations on Urban Housing Demolition and Relocation" issued by the State Council in 1991 and its revised version in 2001 demonstrates the point.[33] The 1991 document was the first systematic guideline for demolition and relocation in urban China. Its purpose was to "ensure the smooth undertaking of urban development."[34] A decade later, the 2001 revisions, issued as Document 305, were to meet "the demands of the market economy" and to "ensure the smooth undertaking of construction projects."[35] This reflects a narrower, pro-growth and business approach compared with that of the 1991 Regulations. Also, the 1991 Regulations explicitly required a "written contract" between the demolisher and the resident about a compensation and settlement plan before demolition. Document 305 omitted the crucial word "written,"[36] which created loopholes for some developers and officials to use vague, casual exchanges as the bases for settlements, imposing them on residents.

Additionally, Document 305 expanded on some of the punitive measures against residents included in the 1991 Regulations and thus further strengthened the government's power. For instance, item 15 of the 1991 document stated that local government could force residents out if they refused to relocate "without justifiable reasons." Yet item 17 of Document 305 simply allowed the authorities to evict such residents, regardless of whether or not they had valid reasons to stay. More specifically, Document 305 stipulated that in cases where residents disagreed with the demolisher on a settlement, relevant authorities could make an administrative ruling on demolition. If the residents objected to that ruling, they could, within three months, appeal their cases in court. But during the three-month period, the government could implement the demolition, by force if necessary.[37] Document 305 failed to address the obvious absurdity of this ruling, which completely ignored the question of if—granted a big if, since it hardly ever happens—the court did, in fact, rule in favor of residents by granting their appeal, what would be the point if the house had already been destroyed? Clearly, Document 305 legitimatized the use of force, which opened the floodgates to domicide. It is in this sense that the Chinese party state is responsible for the violent nature of demolition documented in this book. While scholars have studied violence in China, there has been little attention to violence against the people as a result of the recent economic reform policy.[38]

As Beijing called the tune, provincial and municipal governments followed suit. Some of the documents on demolition and relocation issued by the Shanghai government in the 1990s emphasize the importance of a signed agreement between the parties involved before any action is taken.[39] Yet immediately after Document 305 was issued, the Shanghai government announced Document 111, titled "Detailed Regulations on Shanghai City Housing Demolition and Relocation Management," which fully reflects the same hardline approach toward residents.[40] Furthermore, while previous documents set a limit on the number of applications for administrative compulsory ruling on demolition at 5 percent of all households involved in any given two-year period,[41] Document 111 had no such limit. As a principal guideline for future demolition and relocation in Shanghai, it took a step backward from protecting residents' interests.[42]

With the liberty to use force, the local government hired demolition squads to beat up resident protesters, vandalize their property, cut off their utilities, drag them out of their homes, and set their houses on fire to force them out—all of this led to more cases of domicide. In August 2005, a demolition squad in Shanghai committed arson that claimed the lives of a couple in their seventies. A subsequent investigation revealed that the demolition squad had already committed arson five times in this neighborhood since 2004, when it was slated for demolition. But the district government did nothing to stop it until the loss of the two lives caused public outrage.[43] Many residents in Shanghai condemned Documents 305 and 111 as "evil laws" and petitioned for years to have them rescinded. Finally, in January 2011, after a decade-long trail of violence, the Chinese State Council issued Document 590 to replace Document 305. The new Document eliminated some of the most oppressive and punitive measures against residents discussed above.[44]

Administrative Decentralization

When it came to the issue of demolition and relocation, administrative decentralization, once considered an antidote to the previously highly centralized Chinese state, turned out to be a double-edged sword. In the past, the use of land as state property was controlled by the central and municipal/provincial governments and was off limits to lower-level administrations. In the late 1980s, with increased initiative granted to local-level administrations, the Shanghai municipal government gradually shifted some of the authority over land use rights to the lower levels to improve administrative efficiency. In 1992, it assigned full authority for the approval of land transactions to the district and county levels, with the municipal government continuing to control the total amount of land allocated annually for development.[45]

This decentralization in controlling land use rights was a nationwide phenomenon and led to widespread chaos. According to statistics issued by the Bureau of National Land Resources, by the end of 2003, there were 1,780,000 cases of illegal handling of land use. An investigation of 124,000 such cases resulted in fines totaling 12,200,000 yuan.[46] In 2004, Beijing started a nationwide investigation into illegal land taking, trying to reclaim its declining authority over this most important and nonrenewable resource. But this did not stop the illegal seizure of land, especially in the Yangzi delta, of which Shanghai is a part, where the construction of various industrial parks, resorts, factories, and high-tech districts meant an infinite appetite for land. Many construction projects were initiated at local levels—county, municipal, township, and village—without proper procedures. In Zhejiang Province, for instance, a city of 54 square kilometers had taken control of

734.61 square kilometers from the surrounding countryside. Such predatory behavior not only caused a shortage of agricultural land, but also severely challenged the power supply in the region—all of these projects consumed huge amounts of electricity. As such, the priority of city mayors in the Yangzi region was to hunt for sources of energy, such as coal, in other provinces.[47]

The issue of land shortage was more acute in some cities than others. Shanghai was blessed with a large rural area—Pudong—across the Huangpu River to the east of downtown. Since the early 1990s, the development in Shanghai has turned the sleepy villages in Pudong into a sprawling new city which now houses the visual spectacle of the Oriental Pearl Television Tower that has come to represent the new Shanghai. But among Shanghai's various districts and counties, land resources were uneven.[48] Typically, downtown districts had less land than those on the periphery.

It was therefore crucial, in 1992, when the decentralization finally allowed districts to freely use land, that they find available land to make a profit and grow the economy; otherwise their newly gained authority would be meaningless. Moreover, the promotion of local officials was based on how much they grew the GDP. Here, land sales were a vital source of local revenue.[49] With the shrinkage of urban land and rising real estate prices, downtown and other districts started indiscriminately designating even well-maintained and historically significant neighborhoods and other recently built structures for demolition. Wholesale destruction became such an expected norm that in one case, a ten-room family house in a suburb of Shanghai with a sign that read "Not to be demolished" was knocked down.[50] Both the district governments and the developers stood to reap a huge profit in this large-scale demolition—the former by selling neighborhoods to the highest bidder to boost local revenue and the GDP figure and the latter by replacing the regular two- to five-story buildings with high-rises to increase the marketable floor area per square meter of land and therefore maximize profit. This decentralization and unchecked power led to extensive domicide, turning more residents into protesters.

Corruption

In myriad ways, this process was infested with corruption. The most common scheme was to use a public project as a pretext to push residents out. Since land in China has been a nationalized asset, the concept of eminent domain was foreign to the Chinese. It was simply taken for granted by both the government and the citizens that public projects took precedent over private needs. Unlike commercial projects, where compensation was often a point of contention, set compensation for public projects was more likely to be accepted by residents, which made demolition and relocation a much easier task. That is in part why the Chinese government was able to relocate millions of people in quick order for some mega-projects such as the Three Gorges Dam.

Leveling a neighborhood for a legitimate public project is one thing, but doing so for an illegitimate project is quite another, at least on paper. The procedure for demolition and relocation started with an application by the developer to the District Housing and Land Management Bureau (hereafter, district housing bureau) for a demolition permit. This permit was issued based on a number of conditions that included the approval of the construction project; permission to use the land for this particular project; and plans that included a time table and budget for demolition and relocation of the neighborhood. Once these documents were presented and the permit was issued, the district housing bureau would announce the demolition and relocation to the neighborhood in question. In other words, the residents were to be informed as to the purpose, scope, and timeline of the demolition. It was illegal, according to Chinese regulations, for the developer to change the use of the land once the demolition permit was granted.[51]

Midway changes, however, were routine, as the cases studies in this book illustrate. The root cause was in the district government and the profit it stood to gain by supporting business interests, often at the expense of residents and at the risk of breaking the law. On the surface, demolition and relocation for commercial real estate development was a matter between the developer and residents—the former provided a compensation package and the latter decided whether to accept it. The district government, together with its housing bureau and the courts, was supposed to serve as impartial monitor of the process and handle disputes, should they arise, between the developer and residents. In reality, however, most developers had district governments in their pocket. Using a public project as a ploy to get a commercial project was only possible because of conspiracy between the two. Often the district government sold a certain neighborhood to a developer with the full knowledge that the latter intended to develop it into a commercial project. But the government would tell the public otherwise, just to speed demolition and relocation and to keep the cost low. The residents targeted by the scheme were thus kept in dark.

The reason local governments were concerned about the cost of demolition pointed to another major corruption of the process. Item 10 in Document 305 and other regulations explicitly prohibit local governments that administer urban demolition and relocation, such as the district housing bureau, from carrying out the demolition or acting on behalf of the developer. But that is exactly what local governments have done. In fact, in many cases, local governments and developers were partners in commercial development, from investment to profit sharing. Additionally, in the face of intensifying popular resistance, demolition became extremely difficult. It often took the full weight of government—its administrative, police, and judicial forces—to clean out a neighborhood; the developer on his own was not equipped to do the job. Therefore, the most common practice was for a developer to commission the district housing bureau to carry out the demolition and relocation, together with, as was widely assumed and has been proven in publicized corruption cases, a large bribe. The district housing bureau, in turn, would form its own company to do the deed. In other words, the developer hired the government to do the dirty work of cleaning out the residents, which was illegal to begin with.

This created a zero-sum game between the district and the residents—the less the district compensated the residents, the greater its profits. This game resulted in widespread arbitrary compensation. Typically, residents who agreed to move out early were considered easy targets and got the least payment, while those who held out longer often compelled the local government to offer more. But residents quickly learned this pattern and became deeply distrustful of the government. They collectively held out, aiming for a higher compensation. In some cases, realizing that they had been cheated, people who moved out earlier came back to demand more. As the local government gamed the system for its benefit, so did the residents; the former enabled the latter.

As a hired hand of the developer, the local government could not possibly be impartial in dealing with any disputes between the developer and the residents. When such disputes arose, the residents were on their own, while the developer was joined by the local government and its courts. Thus the government became a teammate of developers rather than acting as a referee. This power structure invariably deprived residents and privileged developers. As a result, in most housing disputes, residents were doomed to lose. Indeed, the combined force of power in the government and money in the business sector has relentlessly pushed forward the shared agenda of pursuing growth and profit, crushing everything else, most of all justice, along the way. One can argue that since state regulations forbid those that administrate demolition, such as local housing bureaus, from being the demolisher and since such bureaus have been routinely involved in demolition, much of the urban real estate development in China in the past two decades has been against Beijing's own regulations and is thus illegitimate.

Such violation of regulations in demolition has to be understood in the context of the infectious culture of corruption in China. Corruption has been a twin brother of the reform policy.[52] This ugly twin has become more predacious as the reform has deepened, generating more opportunities and wealth. Phrases such as "corruption by design," "institutional corruption," and "systematic corruption" are frequently used to describe what has been happening in China.[53] In 2007, a report produced by the Carnegie Endowment for International Peace indicated the "astonishing" level of corruption in China. According to the report, the cost of corruption, the money illegally taken by officials annually, is about $86 billion—0.65 percent of China's GDP and more than China's annual education budget. In some cases, "collusion has transformed entire jurisdictions into local mafia states."[54] In fact, popular sentiment characteristically compares local party bosses to gangsters. Among the well-connected and powerful in China, illicit loans, the illegal taking of land and other property, and money laundering through foreign banks are so common that they are taken for granted.

Most damaging is that corruption costs lives. China's notorious "fake world" goes beyond imitations of Ikea and Dairy Queen.[55] Tainted baby formula has caused deaths and sickened 300,000 babies.[56] Adulterated food is so pervasive that Chinese consumers now accept it as part of everyday reality and rely on their own vigilance as the only defense. Shoddy construction— "tofu projects" as the Chinese call them—has imperiled many lives.[57] More than five thousand children died in the 2008 Sichuan earthquake because of the poor quality of their schools, built by local officials who cut corners to line their own pockets.[58] In November 2010, a towering inferno in a residential building under renovation in Shanghai claimed fifty-eight lives and injured scores of people because officials took bribes to allow unlicensed subcontractors to do the work; nearly a dozen of the officials are now in prison.[59] After the fatal high-speed train wreck in July 2011 in eastern China, the Chinese public immediately suspected corruption as the cause.[60] China's Ministry of Railways conceded that the construction of the railroad was substandard.[61]

Beijing's perennial "anti-corruption" campaign is part of the problem.[62] This campaign is mostly used as a temporary damage-control mechanism, such as in the case of the tainted baby formula, and as a weapon in internal power struggles within the party. In 2006, corruption charges against the powerful Shanghai party boss Chen Liangyu and his subsequent long prison sentence are widely believed to be Beijing's effort to eradicate the influence of the "Shanghai clique" built up by the former CCP chairman Jiang Zemin.[63] The recent Bo Xilai scandal indicates that while Bo, the ambitious former Chongqing party chief, used corruption as a weapon to attack his own political enemies, he himself was purged by Beijing on charges of corruption after he became a threat to the party's agenda and unity.[64] In these as in many other cases, people are used to Beijing's "doublespeak"—saying one thing and meaning another—and are highly cynical about its anti-corruption rhetoric.[65]

The default mode of Beijing's response to corruption is to cover up. Anyone who questioned the inferior quality of school construction and demanded accountability in the Sichuan earthquake case was silenced, by force if necessary. The outspoken artist Ai Weiwei, who tried to look into the situation, was beaten by the police in Chengdu, the provincial capital of Sichuan. His involvement in this matter probably also contributed to his three-month detention in spring 2011.[66] Days after the train accident, when millions of furious Chinese demanded answers on the blogosphere and when even the officially controlled media embarked on an enraged scrutiny, the Chinese authorities imposed a complete blackout of news on the tragedy.[67] During sensitive times, postings on relevant topics are wiped out and microblogging and other social network sites are frozen. Such media suppression only protects and encourages official wrongdoing.

The corruption in demolition and relocation takes place in this fertile culture where vicious abuse of power is so pervasive as to barely attract attention. The epidemic of corruption has contributed to a pessimistic public view that the CCP is in an inevitable state of decay.[68] Beijing's ongoing "new anti-corruption" campaign has only betrayed the permanent and grave state of the situation.

These factors combined—the marketization of real estate assets, the privatization of housing ownership, the development of pro-business and pro-growth public policies, the state-sponsored use of force, the decentralization in the governing of land use rights, and rampant corruption—have been responsible for the increased tension and violence in demolition and relocation in Shanghai and elsewhere in China since the mid-1990s.

Patterns of Grassroots Resistance

Grassroots resistance to forced demolition and relocation, individually and collectively, began to intensify from the mid-1990s onward and has not stopped since. Collective action has sometimes involved just a few households and sometimes an entire neighborhood block or several adjacent neighborhoods. *Dingzi hu*, or "nail household," one of the many new terms that has entered China's reform-era lexicon, captures the tenacity of individual resistance—families holding on to their homes, in the midst of the debris from the neighborhood that has been demolished around them, like a nail driven into the ground. While collective neighborhood holdouts have often lasted from months to a few years, single nail households can persevere for decades. There are various reasons for such a lengthy holdout. Some families were happy with their homes, either privately owned or otherwise, and the locations, and refused to give them up and move elsewhere; others, mistreated by the authorities in the initial negotiation, held out as an act of defiance; but most of them aimed for fair treatment and compensation. Residents have often continued to protest for justice and compensation long after eviction put an end to their holdout. Some of them have become seasoned petitioners and even policy entrepreneurs; very few of them have quit before reaching their goal.

These protesters constitute an apparently elusive but active social movement in China—elusive because, to avoid government suppression, mostly they act as individuals without leadership and headquarters, and active because they are aware of their large numbers, millions nationwide, and they network with and draw strength from each other, exchanging information and launching signature drives. Like participants in any contentious social movement where issue-framing is crucially important, Chinese protesters have developed certain frames to interpret their struggle, to identify culprits responsible for their plight, to articulate their demands, and to rally support. Rights—property and human—and injustice serve as generic, inclusive, and flexible master frames.[69] Such frames are logical to and resonate with the majority of these protesters, who are either under siege, facing demolition, or who have suffered eviction and various other injustices. Within these master frames are case-specific frames, such as the historic preservation frame, whereby residents use the history of their buildings to resist demolition. These master and specific frames are reflected in the means by which the residents protest.

The Law

One of these means is the law. In the past three decades, the Chinese government has built a legal infrastructure demanded by the reform era. It has created a large body of law in criminal, civil, and other domains. Lawyers, whose profession did not exist under Mao, are now flourishing. The government has also established legal aid centers to meet the increasing need for legal services.[70]

The most profound step in establishing rule of law in the reform era was the implementation of the Administration Litigation Law (ALL) in 1990. The ALL allows Chinese citizens to defend their interests by suing corrupt officials. Obviously, this could be a giant step forward in China's legal reform. Residents in housing disputes often invoke this law. Some of them have pursued their cases for years, taking them from the local district government to the higher courts. In reality, however, most residents in Shanghai who have resorted to the ALL because of domicide have not won their cases. As Minxin Pei pointed out in a 1997 study, when it comes to ALL cases, the dismissal rate is high and the likelihood of winning is low.[71]

One reason for ALL's ineffectiveness is a lack of judicial independence. District judges answer to the same district party bosses who administrate demolition and are responsible for the abuse in the first place. No judge in his right mind would rule against the bosses even if the evidence overwhelmingly indicates that he should. Another reason that ALL hardly ever works in favor of residents is that the government and the courts take it for granted that economic growth trumps everything else, including justice. In some cases, the government has banned class-action lawsuits against illegal land taking.[72] The fact that Document 305, which was implemented as law, openly permitted the use of force against residents preempted any chance for the latter to employ ALL or other legal protection.

Laws, much like traffic signs, are treated as something optional in China. Their enforcement is essentially pragmatic, to serve the interest of the enforcers themselves—the local governments in most cases. When China finally passed the long-debated Property Law in 2007 that provided legal protection to both public and private property rights, residents thought they had a new legal weapon to wield against domicide. Some of them re-launched their lawsuits, hoping for a different result under the new law. But they were once again disappointed—the Property Law contradicts Document 305. Local governments exploited this loophole, thus rendering the Property Law useless in most cases by overriding it with Document 305. The powerlessness of ALL and the Property Law in protecting people's interests is demonstrated by the consistent abuse of residents-turned-protesters documented in this book. To a great degree, rights in China are still based on what policy will allow rather than what the law permits or prohibits. Besides, corruption has eroded the impact of even just policy and law.[73]

The failure of the law and the courts to defend citizens' rights is further demonstrated by the rise of a peculiar Chinese brand of attorneys called *weiquan*—or rights-protection—lawyers. These legal experts are among the very few who have been willing to represent residents in housing disputes. Why are there so few of them? Because they know they are fated to lose their cases, sometimes together with their law licenses and even their personal freedom, as documented in chapter 3. China's Minister of Justice openly stated that the priority for lawyers must be to obey the party. He once threatened to send party cadres to all law firms to "guide their work."[74]

A number of brave rights-protection lawyers have disappeared into police stations, been abused, and suffered from extralegal house arrest and even long jail sentences. What the blind activist lawyer Chen Guangcheng experienced prior to his escape from his farmhouse arrest in March 2012 is a case in point.[75] Chinese activists' protests and international media attention have not changed the conditions under which these lawyers work and live.[76] Until recently, the perennial alleged "crime" of these lawyers has been "stealing state secrets." Perhaps this pretext has become dull and predictable, or perhaps the Chinese police state has learned from its counterpart in Putin's Russia,[77] since in some recent cases against rights activist dissidents, Chinese authorities have cited supposed tax evasion as a new cover for illegal detention.[78]

Petitions

The weakness in the law has made *xinfang*, petition by letter and in person to local and higher authorities, a most popular channel for residents seeking justice.

In China, the idea that aggrieved people suffering from official wrongdoing can bring their complaints to higher authorities can be traced to ancient times. It is rooted in two key concepts in age-old Confucian statecraft. One is *minben*, the people as the foundation of the state and the notion that their concerns must be attended to.[79] The other is rule by man—the benevolent and wise emperor, the "son of heaven," and his upright officials would correct the abuses of lower-ranking officials and render justice to the people if only they learned about their suffering. Such officials were called *qingtian*, "blue sky"; they opposed the forces of darkness: corrupt officials. Chinese history offers glowing stories of legendary "blue sky" officials who battled corrupt colleagues and occasionally even the emperor on behalf of the people. Such stories did not just project an image of rectitude, but also revealed the rarity of upright officials in the vast imperial bureaucracy. Frequently, such champions of justice were disgraced because their high moral principles almost inevitably clashed with the entrenched interests of the court and the emperor at whose pleasure they served. These stories indicate the arbitrary and fragile nature of justice in a society ruled by man. Regardless, the idea of petitioning appealed to both the ruler and the ruled—it was supposed to check and restrain local officials, provide the people with a sense of justice from above, and thereby reinforce the emperor's absolute authority and legitimacy.[80]

The CCP launched its own petition system in 1951. The party intended it to be a bridge to the people. Responding to the stress generated from the structural change in the economic and political system under the new regime, Chinese used the petition system, individually and collectively, for a variety of causes, from employment to divorce. Labor disputes had led to a mass of petitions with complaints about abusive supervisors and local party bosses.[81] But under Mao, petitioning by letter was much more prevalent than in-person petitioning. Also, not all the petitions were about grievances and injustice. Some of the letters were to report on the behavior of those targeted by Mao's many mass movements. Others made suggestions about certain policies. Still others simply wrote to ask for employment.[82] Petitioning under Mao also came in waves during some of the key moments of social change, in 1956–1957 at the onset of the socialist reform movement, for instance, and again in 1966–1967 at the beginning of the Cultural Revolution.[83]

The Chinese petition system, however, has taken a new and disturbing turn in the current reform era. Since the 1990s, there has been an ever intensifying, nationwide, though uncoordinated, active petition movement heretofore unseen that involves more than ten million Chinese annually.[84]

Economic reform has dramatically widened the gap between the rich and the poor in China. While the Chinese economy is the second largest after the United States, China's per capita GDP is ranked 124th, behind Albania and Ecuador.[85] The pervasive belief, from miners and peasants in interior China to residents in coastal cities alike, is that a system that has produced millionaires in quick order—reportedly 236,000 of them in 2005—and left the majority in poverty is unjust and that the rich have gamed the system and taken advantage of the poor.[86] At the same time, the reform has allowed more personal and political freedom and has fostered an acute consciousness among the people about their own interests as separate from and in conflict with those of the state. Moreover, the numerous laws and regulations to "protect" the citizenry and the CCP's continuous anti-corruption campaign rhetoric give people hope that the injustices they have endured will be set right if only "blue sky" officials learn of their plight. Also, those who are displaced from their homes lose their attachment to their community and to their routine in life. In searching for justice, they find a new focus in petitioning and, by joining the army of petitioners, a new sense of community.

All the residents documented in this book have petitioned, often from the first instance when their homes were threatened with demolition to long after their evictions. Their lengthy battles reflect the failure of the petition system. The petition offices from the county level to the State Council function more as an ear to popular grievances. They have no resources or authority to solve any of the issues brought before them. A 2004 survey reports that of the 2,000 cases studied, only three of them were resolved, due to individual "blue sky" officials' intervention.[87] In addition, local officials often take revenge on petitioners by detaining and beating them. The ineffectiveness of the petition system and the violence it has generated have made the system itself a source of popular frustration.

Some scholars have considered the current petition system to be a continuation of the ancient Chinese system of rule by man.[88] One scholar points out that the prevalence of the petition system has resulted in one of the "greatest dilemmas" in China's legal framework, threatening its integrity.[89]

However, neither petitioning nor a "blue sky" mentality is uniquely Chinese. Kenneth Feinberg, the compensation czar who has been entrusted with handling several high-profile victim funds, is perhaps one such "blue sky" official in American society. Reviewing David Vine's book on the forced eviction of an island people in Diego Garcia by the US military, Jonathan Freedland expects President Barack Obama, after reading the book, to "instantly realize that a great injustice has been done—one that could easily be put right."[90] Freedland essentially treats President Obama as the sort of "blue sky" official that many wronged Chinese petitioners hope for in their own society. Indeed, such a mentality, together with petitioning, is evident in many societies throughout time. Daniel Carpenter points out that in the United States, petitioning has been one of the "staple features" in some of the most important political movements throughout the nineteenth and twentieth centuries.[91] A petition system similar to the one under Mao also existed in the Soviet Union, Bulgaria, and other Communist countries. Across time and political landscapes, petitioning has served as a vehicle for the powerless, activists, and special interest groups to voice their concerns, seek redress of their grievances, and participate in the political process.

Cultural Memory

Grassroots protest also unfolds in the symbolic universe of cultural repertoires, especially from the Mao era. For instance, throughout China, nail households often fly the Chinese national red flag on their property. At evictions, residents frequently sing "The Internationale," the Communist party's anthem, in public. Most pervasive is the "language game"—protesters use the CCP's official language to mock, pressure, and criticize local officials and to support their own causes.[92] In fact, protesters from urban residents to unemployed workers and peasants throughout China have employed the rich Maoist cultural memory and revolutionary myths in their struggle against corrupt officials, part of what O'Brien and Li term "rightful resistance."[93] Such re-appropriation of the past is neither uniquely contemporary nor specifically Chinese. Elizabeth Perry points out that the CCP's own success in the 1920s in mobilizing the labor movement was due to its "cultural positioning"—the "strategic deployment of a range of symbolic resources . . . for [the] purpose of political persuasion."[94] Elsewhere, popular protests have utilized familiar, and sometimes also innovative, cultural repertoires to frame their struggle and carry their message.[95]

A key question is the meaning of such re-appropriations. Some China scholars have identified among disgruntled workers and peasants outside China's most developed coastal cities—people who have been marginalized by the reform—a genuine belief in some of the dominant Maoist values, such as class divisions and socialist egalitarianism. This has been described as nostalgia for the Mao era.[96]

While the construction of meaning in recasting Maoist or other familiar symbols is often complicated and even contradictory, fundamentally, it is local. As Charles Maier reminds us, memory does not occur in a "social or political vacuum." Rather, we must investigate "the interests of the stakes involved in memory."[97]

A quarter century of penetrating and widespread economic reform has made Shanghai the center of China's consumer culture and turned even those who are disadvantaged by the market economy into its willing subscribers. This changed socioeconomic context has brought a paradigmatic shift in the value system among Shanghai's residents. The distressed workers in interior China have been disempowered net losers in the reform with a shrinking and also more demanding job market, suspended pay, vanished welfare programs, reduced status, and limited resources as a result of the collapse and subsequent privatization of state-owned enterprises (SOEs). They may indeed remain committed to the values represented in Maoist cultural repertoires. However, the residents in Shanghai, who have a new identity as homeowners or aspiring homeowners, can become net winners in the reform if they play their cards right.[98] Far from being merely passive victims of the reform, they have become entrepreneurs. They have chased—by holding out and other means—the moving target of the property market and refused to settle for less than the maximum. Such an uncompromising sense of entitlement and persistent pursuit of their own interests, as well as justice for that matter, are clearly a departure from Maoist revolutionary values. Instead of protesting the loss of Maoist egalitarianism, these Chinese, as stories in the book and elsewhere demonstrate, employ the Maoist repertoires tactically to protest corruption and achieve potential upward mobility for themselves.[99]

Historic Preservation

Rapid economic development and urbanization have inevitably made historic preservation an urgent and tension-charged issue globally. Though compelling arguments have been made about the role historic preservation plays in improving the quality of city life,[100] preservation is a low priority, especially in developing countries. China is no exception, where significant historic landmarks and heritage sites have been disappearing at an alarming rate.

Complicating the matter in China is that urban residents have used historic preservation as a way of resisting demolition when other means fail. Despite its less significant status compared with economic growth, preservation nevertheless is a legitimate issue that projects moral uprightness and has popular support. Since 1991, the Shanghai government has issued a number of documents on historic preservation. In response to a public outcry over the city's vanishing past, it has also identified some four hundred buildings for protection.[101] In 2002, a municipal government document allowed residents' involvement in preservation. As owners and users, they could identify and recommend their buildings for preservation, with approval subject to review by experts and officials.

This document gave birth to a citizen preservation movement in Shanghai. It initially brought much hope to those who were looking for a way to legitimately resist demolition. Those citizen preservation enthusiasts filled out relevant forms, rallied experts for support, attended workshops, and researched the history of their property. Some of them worked like historians, anthropologists, and writers all rolled into one. They searched for material in libraries, conducted interviews, and compiled literature and lengthy chronicles of events relevant to their buildings, hoping to construct a useful past to save them for the future.

But they ended up disappointed. The politics and economics of historic preservation simply are not in their favor. Local governments have no incentive to spend money conserving old buildings. They are much more eager to simply demolish them for new projects that will yield an immediate profit.

The difficulty with such citizen activism and in historic preservation generally also has much to do with the prevailing misunderstanding and mishandling of the issue, in China and beyond. Historic preservation in China is often used as an excuse for commercial and tourist developments. It routinely leads to gentrification. In that it is motivated by profit and causes displacement of the residents, it is no different from any other commercial enterprise. Furthermore, such preservation has nothing to do with history. Often an entire, authentic traditional neighborhood is torn down to build new malls that, to attract tourists, are made to look old. This is certainly the case with Shanghai's famed City Temple, where the fake old buildings hold no historical value whatsoever. As Rem Koolhaas points out, such "preservation" is a destruction of history that threatens the collective heritage of mankind.[102]

In China, this commercial preservation impulse means that even if residents provide indisputable evidence of the historical significance of their buildings, and even if their recommendations are approved by the municipal government, they still have to give up their homes and relocate. The local government can then sell their property to developers to start a "preservation" project to turn it into, for instance, a profitable tourist attraction. In Shanghai and elsewhere in China, the record of successful citizen preservation projects is predictably poor.

Suing and petitioning the government, invoking Maoist cultural remains, and resorting to historic preservation are some of the common strategies resident protesters have used to defend their interests. Framing their struggle as rights protection and injustice, these residents convey both their determination to pursue their rights and their defiance of the authorities. While they have suffered from abuse and defeat, they have also become a pressure group that holds the government accountable. Just as grassroots environmental campaigns in China have successfully forced some policy shifts,[103] resident protests have won government concessions in some cases, as detailed in the book.

Domicide

The uncaged emotions and tenacious resistance documented in the book are largely the result of domicide. Porteous and Smith define domicide as "the murder of home," and "the planned, deliberate destruction of home causing suffering to the dweller."[104] They point to two kinds of domicide. One is "extreme": caused by war, colonization, military installment, and ethnic cleansing; the other is "everyday": the result of economic development, urbanization, and infrastructure, energy, and irrigation projects.[105]

While extreme domicide continues to take place in war-torn zones of the world, everyday domicide is much more widespread. Because it takes place mostly in the name of economic growth and public interest, its impact attracts little attention, or it is taken for granted as "creative destruction" necessary for progress. But both types of domicide, the extreme and the everyday, share some common features. In both cases, decisions are made by a few in power and the majority of people, often the disadvantaged in society who bear the greatest burden of domicide, have no voice in the process. Both types of domicide lead to the destruction of homes and communities and the displacement of their inhabitants.

The domicide that has occurred in post-Mao China is "everyday." Rapid urbanization and sprawling suburban development are responsible for the loss of homes and farmland. The unrelenting hunger for energy to fuel the ever-demanding economic growth in China and beyond has become such an all-consuming national agenda that the term "energy and resource nationalism" has been coined to describe it.[106] In China, this hunger has led to eco-altering projects such as the Three Gorges Dam on the upper Yangzi River, known as the "mother of all dam projects." The construction of this dam alone involved resettling 1.3 million people. Their homes and communities—some 320 villages and 140 towns and cities, together with more than 1,200 historic sites—were sunk under the Yangzi forever.[107] "Image projects," a by-product of the rise of China that was epitomized by the 2008 Beijing Olympic Games and the 2010 Shanghai World Expo, have been another cause of domicide. The Beijing Olympics led to the displacement of over one million residents.[108]

Such displacement has a negative impact on the targets. The victims often lose their customary livelihood and are forced to learn new skills with which they may not succeed. Children have to change schools and the elderly have to look for new care facilities. The problem in China is that most people are pushed to the distant suburbs where adequate facilities such as schools and hospitals may take years to develop. It is also common for evictees in China to lose their personal belongings because they refuse to move to government-assigned apartments where the demolition squad has dropped off the possessions taken from their homes against their will. In one case documented in the book, a man who was evicted in 1998 has not seen any of the family's belongings accumulated through four generations and seventy-five years. Being forced to give up one's belongings comes at a cultural and psychological cost. "Take away our things and something in us dies," the literature scholar Andre Aciman says, because we humans are defined by "the things we call our own."[109]

Another issue is about memory. The loss of home represents the permanent vanishing of the physical embodiment of the inhabitants' memory of family life, ancestral history, culture, tradition, and community ties. Memory is a highly contested subject. In extreme domicide, the perpetrator often deliberately imposes amnesia or memoricide by wiping out or radically altering the built environment of its intended target, as in ethnic cleansing.[110] Although everyday domicide, driven by the pursuit of economic interest, does not primarily aim to impose amnesia, it nevertheless achieves the same effect. The demolition of homes and communities inevitably destroys the memory the inhabitants invested in the physical structure of their lives. The Chinese government has shown complete disregard for the memory of the displaced. There is no monument, for instance, to remember the more than one million people in Beijing whose lives were permanently altered for the Olympic Games that lasted sixteen days. In some cases, as the book demonstrates, everyday domicide can also lead to the deliberate suppression of memory. The two types of domicide and a number of other issues are responsible for an epidemic of amnesia and the extinction of tangible cultural heritage in our time.

To be sure, not all those affected by demolition and relocation are its victims. As pointed out earlier, many residents have moved willingly and resettlement has improved their living conditions. But those who suffered from domicide, in China and elsewhere, have certain shared experiences. One is their intense response. The loss of home can trigger a radical reaction. Some displaced people have committed homicide—killing those they hold responsible for their suffering.[111] In China, eviction often provokes immediate, radical resistance that causes arrest, injury, and even death. In fact, the government's violent tactics have driven some residents to take extreme action. In 2007, a Beijing woman was determined to "use my life to protect our house" from being knocked down for the Olympic Games. The house was a bakery run by her ancestors in the mid-nineteenth century.[112] Incidents such as residents staging or committing suicide on the site of demolition—burning themselves with gasoline for instance—have taken place in various parts of China.[113]

The other characteristic is the extraordinary tenacity the inhabitants demonstrate in their struggle to return home and obtain justice. Apparently, the passing of time does not necessarily diminish the longing for one's lost home and for justice. The earliest victims of domicide in the post-Mao era date back to the mid-1990s, and some of them have been petitioning since that time. In Boston, the West Enders who lost their neighborhood to an urban renewal project in the 1950s have continued to remember their past with passion.[114] The same is true with the former residents of Chavez Ravine in Los Angeles. Their community was destroyed in the 1950s; Dodger Stadium is now in its place. These former residents remain deeply attached to the memory of their vanished neighborhood and, to honor it, some of them, despite their love for baseball, never go to a Dodgers game.[115]

The anthropologist David Vine has provided perhaps the most illuminating example in this regard. He studied the Chagossians of Diego Garcia, a British colonial island in the Indian Ocean. From the late 1960s onward, in the midst of the Cold War era and in order to control the Indian Ocean and the Persian Gulf, the British and American governments deceptively and forcibly expelled the local inhabitants, the Chagossians, to make way for a US military base. Soldiers simply packed them in cargo ships and dumped them on "neighboring" islands, some 1,200 miles away, with neither compensation nor resettlement assistance. The Chagossians have since scattered to various locations, including Britain, and have endured extreme poverty, unemployment, and health problems.[116] In a span of more than half a century during which many of the Chagossians who suffered from the eviction firsthand have passed away, this displaced community has continued to fight for the right to return home. In an uphill battle against a world power, the Chagossians have recently sued the British government, and brought their case to the European Court of Human Rights.[117]

Such persistent struggle of the displaced is related to another common characteristic among the victims of domicide: emotional stress, or the "grief syndrome."[118] Being forcibly thrown out of one's home is a traumatic experience that can result in heightened emotional reactions—shock, grief, anger, distress, and even chronic depression and long-term post-traumatic stress disorder, or PTSD. The victims are uprooted from the life they know and thrown into uncertainty without a mooring; they simply lose part of themselves. The emotional impact of the dislocation caused by domicide is more devastating than that by other factors, such as a natural disaster, because of the deliberate human effort and violence involved. There is, therefore, an injustice to be redressed and someone to be charged with responsibility.[119]

The acute and potentially chronic emotional damage resulting from the loss of one's home has been documented in a number of works.[120] Vine's study of the Chagossians, again, provides perhaps one of the most compelling examples. Shortly after their expulsion, some of the homeless and country-less Chagossians died, others committed suicide, and still others were treated for psychiatric problems. The common causes were said to be unhappiness, difficulty in adapting to life in exile, and poverty.[121] The victims suffer from a disease previously unknown to them, which they call *sagren*, profound sorrow. They are simply "dying of sorrow." According to Vine's study, 60 of 396 Chagossians died "in part or wholly due to 'sadness' and homesickness." He quotes an eighty-year-old female islander as saying: "Many people have died like that . . . *Sagren*! Yes! When one has *sagren* in your heart, it eats you. No doctor, no one will be able to heal you!"[122] In other words, those islanders died of broken hearts, literally, because of homesickness. *Sagren* has been recognized by the World Health Organization (WHO) as a legitimate medical problem. Vine considers *sagren* to be an example of "root shock"—"the traumatic stress reaction to the destruction of all or part of one's emotional ecosystem."[123] Clearly, one's home, neighborhood, and community are at the center of that ecosystem. In China, the mental state of some of the evictees-turned-long-term petitioners, as chapter 1 indicates, has become an issue of public debate. The Chinese authorities and health professionals, however, have not made any effort to study the impact of domicide on those petitioners, aside from—to provide a rationale for dismissing their cases—accusing them of being crazy. But the Chagossians' case has established a clear link between the dispossession of home and mental disease, a potentially deadly one at that.

The study by Porteous and Smith highlights domicide as a global phenomenon, with an estimated 30 million people worldwide "suffering its ravages" at the beginning of the twenty-first century.[124] In terms of everyday domicide, they locate its source in the various forms of capitalism and its representatives—a small, transnational group of the political and corporate power elites—who promote short-term economic interest at the expense of humanity. The authors consider domicide to be a "moral evil" and suggest broad public participation in the decision-making process and a makeover of capitalism with a more humanistic bent as part of the solution to domicide.[125]

Clearly, everyday domicide is as systematic and widespread as the pursuit of economic interest. It has affected and will continue to affect large numbers of mostly powerless people, especially in the developing world. The murder of homes is an intentional act. Domicide violates and terrorizes its victims as bulldozers and cranes reduce their homes to rubble. It severs its victims' lifetime attachment to homes and community and deprives them of the built environment that has shaped their tradition and identity. It also wounds their sense of dignity. Everyday domicide, in other words, in many ways cruelly redefines the existence of its victims and severely diminishes, if not destroys, the quality of their lives. Considering all of the immediate and lingering damage it causes, perhaps it is time to think of domicide as something beyond mere "moral evil."

This book presents the following cases:

Chapter 1 focuses on the transformation of a woman from a timid kindergarten teacher into a diehard petitioner as she was first victimized by domicide and then again by the petition system through which she was seeking justice. She is but one of the ten million Chinese who resort to the petition system annually to redress their grievances and who are frustrated by its ineptitude. This chapter explores the relationship between domicide and petition and the dynamic of the petition system that has perpetually generated and sustained its own clients, vast in both their numbers and their outrage.

Chapter 2 is about two families who lost their homes to the construction of Xintiandi, or the New World, one of the infamous sites of gentrification in recent Shanghai. Both families, one a Chinese Muslim whose ancestors include a seventeenth great-granddaughter of Zheng He, the famed maritime explorer of the Ming dynasty in the early fifteenth century, and the other with close ties to top GMD officials in Taiwan, lost their homes during the Cultural Revolution, and then again in the post-Mao reform. The chapter suggests that the New World was built on the old nightmare of property deprivation under the CCP.

Chapter 3 details a high-profile case of neighborhood resistance to domicide in downtown Shanghai. One of the prominent features in this case is the residents' use of Maoist cultural repertories in their protests. The case involves a corruption scandal that implicated the Shanghai CCP party boss and a star businessman, a Christian lawyer who ended up in prison for representing the evictees, a Hong Kong retailer who turned the tale of her family's eviction into a best seller, and a politically detached worker who emerged as a savvy community leader. The story ends with the surprising reconfiguration of a public space in downtown Shanghai which simultaneously represents a government concession to the residents and its attempt to repress their collective memory.

Chapter 4 documents one of the most tenacious nail households in Shanghai. The husband, a descendant of gangsters and squatters, has been empowered by the demolition and relocation. He has defied the government not only by holding on to his own home since 1998, aiming for a multimillion yuan payout, but also by providing legal service to other residents and moonlighting as a policy entrepreneur. He plays with the system and hopes to beat it at its own game.

Chapter 5 follows a neighborhood in Lincoln Lane through its years of struggle for historic preservation. Convinced that their lane, built in the 1920s, was named after the American president, the residents launched a global propaganda campaign to preserve it against demolition. This chapter examines community grassroots actions, the roles of the media and law in dealing with housing conflict, the politics and economics of historic preservation, the link between local protest and the impact of globalization, and the hypocrisy of some of the renowned Chinese preservationists who sided with the government in destroying the city's past when the going got tough.

A note on the research: In January 2004 I started six months of field research in Shanghai for this book. It was during that period that I first studied the cases in chapters 1, 3, and 5. Since then and until 2011, I returned to China for field work every summer except 2008 and 2009, both to follow up on the three initial cases and to conduct new research—I began to study the cases for chapter 2 in 2005 and for chapter 4 in 2007. Needless to say, I have encountered and studied many more cases than the five included in the book. I have also maintained frequent email and phone exchanges with the residents throughout all those years as their cases have evolved.

During my field trips, I have spent countless hours in person with the residents, not only to interview them, but also to observe and experience their lives first hand. For instance, I was on the site of a five-hour eviction of a family that I have documented in chapter 3. I participated in some of the residents' meetings that strategized their resistance, got to know the entire families that I wrote about, and have been inside the apartments and houses I have described, with exception of those that had been demolished before my study. I have recorded my interviews with both sound and visual devices, filmed the sites and the people I studied, and gathered a considerable amount of material from the residents—petition letters; court papers; family photographs; contracts, floor plans, and other documentation on their properties; and artifacts they made and used in their protests. The book is largely based on their oral history, lived experience, and the material they have gathered and produced, and on my own observations. I took all the pictures used in the book, unless otherwise indicated. The quotes in the book either come directly from residents' own writings or from my interview notes. My attempts to contact some of the officials and developers were met with silence. The residents mentioned in the book, except Mr. C in chapter 3, insisted that I use their real names. Regarding Internet material, whenever possible, I have cited multiple sources as some sensitive Chinese web links disappear due to censorship and other reasons. The elimination of such web links—if and when they are eliminated—is part of the reality depicted in this book.

Forced demolition and relocation have changed and will continue to reshape the lives of all these people and the society in which they live. While the book presents them as a set of urban lives, it focuses on them as unique individuals. My research centered on the following aspects: personal history; family history; community history; the history of their residences; and their experience in demolition and relocation. It was extremely important to me to learn first who they are, what their families are like, and how they came to live in their particular homes. Such information provides insight to their behavior in their struggle against domicide. After all, not every resident and neighborhood has resisted or resisted in the same fashion. Their behavior has much to do with their self-perceived identity, their values, their relationships to their homes, and their understanding of the reform.

In his study of the transformation of Paris into the capital of modernity in the second half of the nineteenth century, David Harvey points out that "the most interesting urban writing is often of a fragmentary and perspectival sort," if such writing conveys "some sense of the totality of what the city was about."[126] I hope this book, while depicting these individuals and communities and their perspectives, provides a unique entrance to understanding the complexity of China's reform era.

Notes

1. Rem Koolhaas and Bruce Mau, *S, M, L, XL* (New York: The Monacelli Press, 1998), 1239–264. For Koolhaas's life and work, and some critical takes on his work, see http://www.acturban.org/biennial/doc_planners/koolhaas_generic_city. htm; http://www.nybooks.com/articles/archives/2012/may/10/master-bigness-rem-koolhaas/?page=1, accessed 28 October 2012.

2. http://news.bbc.co.uk/2/hi/asia-pacific/3105948.stm, accessed 22 April 2009. The obsession to possess the world's tallest building seems to be particularly prominent in Asia and the Middle East, http://www.huffingtonpost.com/2011/08/02/ kingdom-tower-tallest-building _n_916207.html, accessed 2 August 2011.

3. Shanghai zhengda yanjiusuo (Research Institute of Shanghai Zhengda), ed. *Shanghai ren* (Shanghai People) (Shanghai: Xuelin chubanshe, 2002), 278.

4. For one of the best studies on the alleyway houses and patterns of everyday life in Republican Shanghai, see Hanchao Lu, *Beyond the Neon Lights: Everyday Shanghai in the Early Twentieth Century* (Berkeley: University of California Press, 1999).

5. http://www.urban-age.net/10_cities/02_shanghai/shanghai_overview.html, accessed 28 June 2011.

6. Douglas J. Porteous and Sandra E. Smith. *Domicide: The Global Destruction of Home* (Montreal & Kingston McGill-Queen's University Press, 2001).

7. http://www.nytimes.com/2011/08/13/world/europe/13britain.html?nl=todays headlines&emc=tha22, accessed 13 August 2011.

8. http://www.nytimes.com/2011/08/12/world/middleeast/12israel.html?_r=1&n l=todaysheadlines&emc=tha2, accessed 12 August 2011.

9. Anita Hill, *Reimagining Equality: Stories of Gender, Race, and Finding Home* (Boston: Beacon Press, 2011).

10. Rosemary Marangoly George, *The Politics of Home: Postcolonial Relocations and Twentieth-Century Fiction* (New York: Cambridge University Press, 1996), 3.

11. Novalis, quoted in George, *Politics of Home*, 1.

12. See an insightful analysis of the idealization of home in George, *Politics of Home*, 19–23.

13. http://www.nybooks.com/articles/archives/2011/jan/13/china-famine-oslo/, accessed 4 October 2011.

14. Deborah S. Davis has written extensively on housing reform in China, covering a wide range of issues. Deborah S. Davis and Hanlong Lu, "Property in Transition: Conflicts over Ownership in Post-Socialist Shanghai," *European Journal of Sociology* XLIV, 1 (2003): 77–99; "From Welfare Benefit to Capitalized Asset: The Re-Commodification of Residential Space in Urban China," in *Housing and Social Change: East-West Perspectives*, eds. Ray Forrest and James Lee (London: Routledge, 2003), 183–96; "My Mother's House," in *Unofficial China: Popular Culture and Thought in the People's Republic*, eds. Perry Link, Richard Madsen, and Paul G. Pickowicz (Boulder: Westview Press, 1989), 88–100. Also see Jean C. Oi and Andrew G. Walder, eds., *Property Rights and Economic Reform in China* (Stanford: Stanford University Press, 1999); Xiaowei Zang, "Urban Housing Reform in China," in *China in the Reform Era*, ed. Xiaowei Zang (Commack, NY: Nova Science Publishers, 1999),

53–80; Min Zhou and John R. Logan, "Market Transition and the Commodification of Housing in Urban China," in *The New Chinese City: Globalization and Market Reform*, ed. John R. Logan (Oxford, UK: Blackwell Publishers, Ltd, 2002), 137–52; Fulong Wu, "Real Estate Development and the Transformation of Urban Space in China's Transitional Economy, with Special Reference to Shanghai," in *The New Chinese City*, 153–66; Yongshun Cai, "China's Moderate Middle Class: The Case of Homeowners Resistance," *Asian Survey* 45.5 (2005): 777–99; "Civil Resistance and the Rule of Law in China: The Defense of Homeowners' Rights," in *Grassroots Political Reform in Contemporary China*, eds. Elizabeth J. Perry and Merle Goldman (Cambridge, MA: Harvard University Press, 2007), 174–95; Li Zhang, *In Search of Paradise: Middle-class Living in a Chinese Metropolis* (Ithaca, NY: Cornell University Press, 2010), among many other scholarly works.

15. Michael Herzfeld, *Evicted from Eternity: The Reconstructing of Modern Rome* (Chicago: University Chicago Press, 2009).

16. The urban transformation of Beijing is better documented than that of Shanghai in works such as Wang Jun: *Beijing Record: A Physical and Political History of Planning Modern Beijing* (Singapore: World Scientific Publishing Co. Pte. Ltd., 2011); Fang Ke, *Dangdai Beijing jiucheng gengxin, diaocha, yanjiu, tansuo* (Contemporary Redevelopment in the Inner City of Beijing: Survey, Analysis, and Investigation) (Beijing: Zhongguo jianzhu gongye chubanshe, 2000); and Ian Johnson, *Wild Grass: Three Portraits of Change in Modern China* (New York: Vintage Books, 2004), chapter 2. Also see a number of books about Beijing reviewed by Ian Johnson: http://www.nybooks.com/articles/archives/2011/jun/23/high-price-new-beijing/?page=1, accessed 28 October 2011. Other studies on demolition and relocation include Li Zhang, "Forced from Home: Property Rights, Civic Activism, and the Politics of Relocation in China," *Urban Anthropology* 33 (2004): 247–81.

17. See some of the spectacular images in Greg Girard, *Phantom Shanghai* (Toronto: The Magenta Foundation, 2006); Howard W. French, "Disappearing Shanghai," in *China in 2008: A Year of Great Significance*, eds. Kate Merkel-Hess, Kenneth L. Pomeranz, and Jeffrey N. Wasserstrom (Lanham, MD: Rowman & Littlefield, 2009), 117–31.

18. Davis, "My Mother's House," 88–100.

19. Zang, "Urban Housing Reform in China," 76. Also, for an introduction to literature on Shanghai's past and more recent developments, see Jeffrey N. Wasserstrom, *Global Shanghai, 1850–2010: A History of Fragments* (New York: Routledge, 2009), 141–46.

20. For instance, in the first quarter of 2004, Shanghai housing prices increased by 28 percent compared to the same period in the preceding year, while the average increase in other major cities was 8 percent. *Qingnian cankao* (Elite Reference), 12 May 2004, B20.

21. Xing Quan Zhang, "Chinese Housing Policy 1949–1978: The Development of a Welfare System." *Planning Perspectives*, 12 (1997): 433–455.

22. Zhang, "Chinese Housing Policy," 433–455; Zang, "Urban Housing Reform in China," 53–58.

23. Zang, "Urban Housing Reform in China," 59–71.

24. *Shanghai gaige kaifang ershi nian* bianjibu (Two Decades of Opening and Reform in Shanghai Editorial Committee), ed. *Shanghai gaige kaifang ershi nian: chengjian juan* (Two Decades of Opening and Reform in Shanghai: City and Construction) (Shanghai: Shanghai renmin chubanshe, 1998), 239.

25. *Shanghai gaige kaifang ershi nian* bianjibu, *chengjian juan*, 7.

26. Cui Zhuolan, ed., *Fangwu chaiqian weiquan zhinan* (Legal Guidelines in Rights Maintenance in Housing Demolition and Relocation) (Changchun: Jilin renmin chubanshe, 2004), 107–108.

27. Luo Xiaowei, et al., *Shanghai Xintiandi: jiuqu gaizao de jianzhu lishi, renwen lishi yu kaifa moshi de yanjiu* (Shanghai Xintiandi: A Study of Architectural and Human History and Developmental Models in Urban Renewal) (Nanjing: Dongnan daxue chubanshe, 2002), note 1, 73; http://www.ucl.ac.uk/dpu-projects/Global_Report/pdfs/Shanghai.pdf, accessed 28 June 2011.

28. http://www.ucl.ac.uk/dpu-projects/Global_Report/pdfs/Shanghai.pdf, accessed 28 June 2011.

29. *Xinmin wanbao* (Xinmin Evening News), 9 August 2003: 4.

30. Davis, "From Welfare Benefit to Capitalized Asset," 187.

31. *Shanghai gaige kaifang ershi nian* bianjibu, *chengjian juan*, 213–14.

32. Davis, "From Welfare Benefit to Capitalized Asset," 189. For the process of housing reform, also see Zang, "Urban Housing Reform in China," 71–79.

33. See also a comparison of the 1991 and 2001 regulations in Jianshe bu zhengce yanjiu zhongxin (The Center for Policy Research at the Ministry of Construction), ed., *Zuixin chengshi fangwu chaiqian zhinan* (Newest Guidelines on Urban Housing Demolition and Relocation) (Beijing: Zhongguo jianzhu gongye chubanshe, 2004), 88–92.

34. http://house.focus.cn/news/1991-06-01/4326.html, accessed 26 August 2012.

35. Falü chubanshe fagui zhongxin (The Center of Law and Regulations at the Law Press), ed., *Fangwu chaiqian fagui zizhu* (Self-help in Laws and Regulations on Housing Demolition and Relocation) (Beijing: Falü chubanshe, 2004), 27.

36. Falü chubanshe fagui zhongxin, ed., *Fangwu chaiqian fagui zizhu*, 22.

37. Falü chubanshe fagui zhongxin, ed., *Fangwu chaiqian fagui zizhu*, 23.

38. A 1990 study of violence in China covered conflict and violence in a number of arenas with little on violence due to economic development. See Jonathan N. Lipman and Stevan Harrell, eds., *Violence in China: Essays in Culture and Counterculture* (Albany, NY: State University of New York Press, 1990).

39. http://zhidao.baidu.com/question/171835460.html, accessed 26 August 2012; Falü chubanshe fagui zhongxin, ed., *Fangwu chaiqian fagui zizhu*, 103–109.

40. Zhongguo fazhi chubanshe, ed., *Chaiqian buchang shiyong falü shouce* (Compensation in Demolition and Relocation: A Practical Legal Handbook) (Beijing: Zhongguo fazhi chubanshe, 2007), 281–91.

41. Falü chubanshe fagui zhongxin, ed., *Fangwu chaiqian fagui zizhu*, 105.

42. Wang Cailiang, *Fangwu chaiqian jiufen jiaodian shiyi* (Guide to Solving Disputes over Urban Housing Demolition and Relocation) (Beijing: Falü chubanshe, 2004), 415, 424.

43. *Fazhi ribao* (Legal Daily), August 25, 2005.

44. http://www.gov.cn/zwgk/2011-01/21/content_1790111.htm, accessed 6 August 2012.

45. *Shanghai gaige kaifang ershi nian* bianjibu, *chengjian juan*, 219–20.

46. *Baokan wenzhai* (Digest of Newspapers and Magazines), 19 April 2007: 1.

47. *Yangzi wanbao* (Yangzi Evening News), 28 June 2004: A3.

48. For the changes of districts and counties in Shanghai in the 1990s, see Duo Wu and Taibin Li, "The Present Situation and Prospective Development of the Shanghai Urban Community," in *The New Chinese City: Globalization and Market Reform*, ed. John Logan (Oxford, UK: Blackwell Publishers Ltd., 2002), 22–36.

49. http://www.time.com/time/magazine/article/0,9171,2096345-2,00.html, accessed 17 October 2011.

50. *Xinmin wanbao*, 23 May 2011: 3.

51. Zhongguo fazhi chubanshe, ed., *Chaiqian buchang shiyong falü shouce*, 282–83.

52. Yan Sun, *Corruption and Market in Contemporary China* (Ithaca, NY: Cornell University Press, 2004).

53. Melanie Manion, *Corruption by Design: Building Clean Government in Mainland China and Hong Kong* (Cambridge, MA: Harvard University Press, 2004).

54. http://news.bbc.co.uk/2/hi/asia-pacific/7039383.stm, accessed 15 October 2007.

55. Laurie Burkitt and Loretta Chao, "Made in China: Fake Stores." *Wall Street Journal*, 3 August 2011: B1.

56. http://topics.nytimes.com/top/reference/timestopics/subjects/m/melamine/index.html, accessed 5 August 2011.

57. See a list of collapsed new bridges and roads and other construction projects and their human and monetary cost in Sun, *Corruption and Market*, 223–24.

58. http://www.nytimes.com/2011/08/22/world/asia/22china.html?nl=todaysheadlines&emc=tha24, accessed 22 August 2011.

59. http://www.nytimes.com/2011/08/04/world/asia/04shanghai.html?ref=bribery, accessed 5 August 2011.

60. http://www.nytimes.com/2011/02/13/world/asia/13china.html?_r=2&scp=9&sq=china%20sentence%20officials,%20construction%20workers%20for%20shanghai%20fire&st=cse, accessed 5 August 2011.

61. http://www.nytimes.com/2011/08/17/world/asia/17trains.html?scp=7&sq=china%20high%20speed%20rail%20crash,%20aug.%202011&st=cse, accessed 22 August 2011.

62. For a list of corruption cases in China and the government's effort to deal with them, see http://factsanddetails.com/china.php?itemid=303&catid=8&subcatid=49, accessed 3 June 2011.

63. http://www.nytimes.com/2006/09/26/world/asia/26china. html?pagewanted=all; http://www.nytimes.com/2011/02/13/world/asia/13china.html?scp=9&sq=china%20sentence%20officials,%20construction%20workers%20for%20shanghai%20fire&st=cse, accessed 5 August 2011.

64. http://www.nytimes.com/2012/03/27/world/asia/bo-xilais-china-crime-crack down-adds-to-scandal.html?pagewanted=1&_r=1&nl=todaysheadlines&emc= tha22_20120327, accessed 27 March 2012.

65. Kerry Brown, *Struggling Giant: China in the 21st Century* (London: Anthem Press, 2007), 68–74.

66. http://www.nytimes.com/2011/07/07/world/asia/07artist.html?emc=eta1, accessed 7 July 2011.

67. http://www.nytimes.com/2011/08/01/world/asia/01crackdown.html?emc =eta1, accessed 12 August 2011.

68. Jeffrey C. Kinkley, *Corruption and Realism in Late Socialist China: The Return of the Political Novel* (Stanford: Stanford University Press, 2007), 170–71.

69. See a discussion on the core function of framing and master frames in Robert D. Benford and David A. Snow, "Framing Processes and Social Movements: An Overview and Assessment," *Annual Review of Sociology* 26 (2000): 615–16, 618–19.

70. http://unpan1.un.org/intradoc/groups/public/documents/apcity/unpan017813. pdf, 3–5, accessed 1 October 2011.

71. Minxin Pei, "Citizens v. Mandarins: Administrative Litigation in China," *China Quarterly* 152 (December, 1997): 832–62.

72. http://www.nybooks.com/articles/archives/2011/jun/23/high-price-new-beijing/?page=1, accessed 3 October 2011.

73. http://unpan1.un.org/intradoc/groups/public/documents/apcity/unpan017813. pdf, p. 4, accessed 1 October 2011.

74. http://www.nytimes.com/2009/08/10/world/asia/10rights.html?th&emc=th, accessed 10 August 2009.

75. http://www.nytimes.com/2012/05/01/opinion/chen-guangcheng.html, accessed 8 May 2012.

76. http://www.nytimes.com/2009/08/10/world/asia/10rights.html?th&emc=th, accessed 10 August 2009; also see Jerome A. Cohen's testimony at a congressional hearing on November 1, 2011 at http://www.nybooks.com/blogs/nyrblog/2011/nov/08/chinas-lawyers-under-siege/?utm_medium=email&utm_campaign=NYRblog+November+15+ 2011&utm_content=NYRblog+November+15+2011+Version+B+CID_3f7a37e5b1cb 8baedcb56e950a458798&utm_source=Email+marketing+software&utm_term=Chinas +Lawyers+Under+Siege, accessed 16 November 2011.

77. "Tax evasion" is a routine excuse used to jail dissidents in Russia. http://www. nytimes.com/2011/06/04/opinion/04nocera.html?nl=todaysheadlines&emc=tha212, accessed 4 June 2011.

78. http://www.nytimes.com/2009/08/10/world/asia/10rights.html?th&emc=th, accessed 10 August 2009; http://www.nytimes.com/2011/04/20/opinion/20Rushdie. html?emc=eta1, accessed 4 June 2011.

79. For a study of the ancient Chinese concept of *minben*, see Qin Shao, "Xi 'Minben': due xian Qin zhi xi Han 'minben' sixiang de kaocha" ("Minben": An

Investigation of the Changing Statecraft from the pre-Qin to Western Han Periods) *Lishi yanjiu* (Historical Study) 6 (1985): 3–16.

80. For a study of the complaint system in imperial China, see Qiang Fang, "Hot Potatoes: Chinese Complaint Systems from Early Times to the Late Qing (1898)," *Journal of Asian Studies* 68.4 (November, 2009): 1105–135.

81. Elizabeth J. Perry, "Popular Protest in China: Playing by the Rules," in *China Today, China Tomorrow: Domestic Politics, Economy, and Society*, ed. Joseph Fewsmith (Lanham, MD: Rowman & Littlefield, 2010), 14–18.

82. Diao Jiecheng, *Renmin xinfang shilue* (A Brief History of People's Petitioning) (Beijing: Beijing jingji xueyuan chubanshe, 1995), 31, 55–57.

83. Perry, "Popular Protest in China," 14–18.

84. According to a study, there were 11.5 million cases of petitioning in 2002. Zhuoyan Xie, "Petition and Judicial Integrity," *Journal of Politics and Law* 2.1 (March 2009): 25. The situation has been no better in following years. See http://query.nytimes.com/gst/fullpage.html?res=9C01E0D61031F93AA35751C1A9639C8B63, accessed 8 July 2011.

85. http://www.indexmundi.com/g/r.aspx?v=67, accessed 15 August 2011.

86. Elizabeth J. Perry, *Anyuan: Mining China's Revolutionary Tradition*, cited from unpublished manuscript, 382, 385–87 (Forthcoming: Berkeley: University of California Press, 2012); Deborah S. Davis and Wang Feng, eds., *Creating Wealth and Poverty in Postsocialist China* (Stanford: Stanford University Press, 2009), especially chapters 1, 8, 13, and 14.

87. http://news.sina.com.cn/c/2004-11-17/15374946096.shtml, accessed 5 October 2007.

88. http://news.sina.com.cn/c/2004-11-17/15374946096.shtml, accessed 22 April 2009.

89. Xie, "Petition and Judicial Integrity," 25.

90. http://www.nybooks.com/articles/archives/2009/may/28/a-black-and-disgraceful-site/, accessed 25 September 2010.

91. Daniel Carpenter, "The Petition as a Recruitment Device: Evidence from the Abolitionists' Congressional Campaign," unpublished manuscript, 2004. Cited with the author's permission; http://people.hmdc.harvard.edu/~dcarpent/petition-recruit-20040112.pdf.

92. "Language game" is a concept Perry Link borrowed from Ludwig Wittgenstein to describe the situation in China (Perry Link, email messages to author, 28 August 2011 and 14 January 2012). For an in-depth study of the topic, see Perry Link, *An Anatomy of Chinese: Rhythm, Metaphor, Politics* (Cambridge, MA.: Harvard University Press, 2012).

93. Kevin J. O'Brien and Lianjiang Li, *Rightful Resistance in Rural China* (New York: Cambridge University Press, 2006), 3.

94. Perry, *Anyuan*, 6.

95. Sidney Tarrow, *Power in Movement: Social Movements and Contentious Politics* (New York: Cambridge University Press, 1998), especially chapter 7; Charles Tilly, *The Contentious French* (Cambridge, MA.: Belknap Press of Harvard University Press, 1986).

96. Elizabeth J. Perry, "'To Rebel is Justified': Cultural Revolution Influences on Contemporary Chinese Protest," in *The Chinese Cultural Revolution Reconsidered: Beyond Purge and Holocaust*, ed. Kam-yee Law (New York: Palgrave Press, 2003), 270–72; *Anyuan*, 379–81; *Patrolling the Revolution: Worker Militias, Citizenship, and the Modern Chinese State* (Lanham, MD: Rowman & Littlefield, 2006), 275–303; Ching Kwan Lee, "What Was Socialism to Chinese Workers? Collective Memories and Labor Politics in an Age of Reform," in *Re-Envisioning the Chinese Revolution: The Politicis and Poetics of Collective Memory in Reform China*, eds. Ching Kwan Lee and Guobin Yang (Stanford: Stanford University Press, 2007), 141–65; Feng Chen, "Worker Leaders and Framing Factory-based Resistance," in *Popular Protest in China*, ed. Kevin J. O'Brien (Cambridge, MA: Harvard University Press, 2008), 88–107.

97. Charles Maier, "A Surfeit of Memory? Reflections on History, Melancholy and Denial," *History & Memory* 5.2 (Fall/Winter 1993): 136.

98. Urban and coastal residents are generally perceived as winners and factory workers and residents of the interior as losers in China's reform. See Chunping Han and Martin King Whyte, "The Social Contours of Distributive Injustice Feelings in Contemporary China," in *Creating Wealth and Poverty in Postsocialist China*, eds. Davis and Feng, 195.

99. O'Brien and Li, *Rightful Resistance*, 120.

100. Eric W. Allison and Lauren Peters, *Historic Preservation and Livable City* (Hoboken, NJ: John & Wiley, 2011).

101. http://sh.focus.cn/news/2003-03-13/42523.html, accessed 13 March 2003.

102. http://www.nytimes.com/2011/05/24/arts/design/cronocaos-by-rem-kool-haas-at-the-new-museum.html?_r=1&emc=eta1, accessed 25 May 2011.

103. Andrew C. Mertha, *China's Water Warriors: Citizen Action and Policy Change* (Ithaca, NY: Cornell University Press, 2008), 15.

104. Porteous and Smith, *Domicide*, 3, 19.

105. Porteous and Smith, *Domicide*, 64–150.

106. http://www.nbr.org/publications/issue.aspx?id=236, accessed 25 September 2011.

107. Porteous and Smith, *Domicide*, 139–40.

108. http://www.nytimes.com/2008/04/13/opinion/13bissinger.html?_r=1&scp=1&sq=buzz+bissinger&st=nyt&oref=slogin, accessed 13 April 2008.

109. http://www.nytimes.com/2009/06/09/opinion/09aciman.html?th&emc=th, accessed 9 June 2009.

110. Porteous and Smith, *Domicide*, 198–99.

111. Porteous and Smith, *Domicide.*, 5–6.

112. http://www.nytimes.com/2007/08/09/world/asia/09china.html?pagewanted=all, accessed 29 September 2011.

113. *Xinmin zhoukan* (Xinmin Weekly), 1–7, 2003: 26–29; *Zhongguo jingji shibao* (China Economic Times), 19 November 2003: 9.

114. Thomas H. O'Connor, *Building a New Boston: Politics and Urban Renewal, 1950–1970* (Boston: Northeastern University Press, 1993), 136–39; http://www.wickedlocal.com/somerville/town_info/history/x1091748953#ixzz1W6tqCtB2;

http://www.boston.com/news/local/massachusetts/articles/2010/03/14/west_ends_
old_guard_reaches_out_to_instill_passion_for_cause/, accessed 2 October 2011.

115. http://www.nbclosangeles.com/news/sports/Name-Change-Seen-as-Another-
Insult-for-Former-Chavez-Ravine-Residents.html, accessed 1 October 2011.

116. David Vine, *Island of Shame: The Secret History of the US Military Base on
Diego Garcia* (Princeton, NJ: Princeton University Press, 2009).

117. http://www.newstatesman.com/human-rights/2010/04/160-mauritius-brit-
ish-chagos, accessed 11 January 2011.

118. Porteous and Smith, *Domicide*, 191–94.

119. Porteous and Smith, *Domicide*, 19–20.

120. Porteous and Smith, *Domicide*, 191–98.

121. David Vine, "Dying of Sorrow: Expulsion, Empire, and the People of Diego
Garcia," in *The War Machine and Global Health: A Critical Medical Anthropological Examination of the Human Costs of Armed Conflict and the International Violence
Industry*, eds. Merrill Singer and G. Derrick Hodge (Plymouth, UK: AltaMira Press,
2010), 185–86.

122. David Vine, "Dying of Sorrow," 182.

123. David Vine, "Dying of Sorrow," 192.

124. Porteous and Smith, *Domicide*, 210.

125. Porteous and Smith, *Domicide*, 22, 237–42.

126. David Harvey, *Paris, Capital of Modernity* (New York: Routledge, 2003), 17.

CHAPTER ONE

~

The Woman of a
Thousand-and-one Petitions

Equity sends questions to Law, Law sends questions back to Equity; Law
finds it can't do this, Equity finds it can't do that; neither can so much as
say it can't do anything . . . And thus, through years and years, and lives
and lives, everything goes on, constantly beginning over and over again,
and nothing ever ends. We can't get out of the suit on any terms, for we
are made parties to it, and *must* be parties to it, whether we like it or not.

—Charles Dickens, *Bleak House*

In late March 2008, I called Zhou Youlan from my office in Cambridge,
Massachusetts, to interview her—one of the many phone interviews I have
conducted with her over the years. She immediately recognized my voice and
said, "My phone is bugged; I've just returned from Beijing." Before I could
respond, she quickly added, "But everything I have to say is true," which was
a message to both the invisible listener that she was innocent and me that
she still wanted to talk to me.

Zhou Youlan is a Shanghai resident whose case I have studied since 2004.
The Beijing trip she referred to was yet another petition trip she made during what is known in China as the annual "two meetings" in March: the
National People's Congress and the People's Political Consultative Conference. She went to the capital before the meetings in early March to avoid
the heightened security during the events, but was immediately corralled and
sent back to Shanghai. To prevent her from returning to Beijing, the authorities put her in detention for two weeks until the end of the "two meetings."

This was not the first or the last time that Zhou went to Beijing to petition and got into trouble with the authorities. In fact, being caught petitioning in the capital and sent back to detention in Shanghai has become a routine in Zhou Youlan's decade-long experience as a full-time petitioner.

Since Zhou Youlan's home was demolished against her will in 1996, she has been petitioning at every level of the government, from the district and municipal to Beijing. A petite, frail woman of five feet, Zhou used to be a timid, soft-spoken kindergarten teacher—never a troublemaker. When she started petitioning, she was frightened by the sight of the authorities and eager to settle her case. But in the span of a decade, she has quit her job to petition full time, insisted on her ever-changing demands being met and, in the process, developed the mouth of a truck driver. The web of resentment, anger, and despair that has resulted from more than a decade of unvaryingly humiliating and frequently violent interaction with the authorities has simply become too dense and complex to be unraveled. She holds the authorities in utter contempt, as indicated by the fact that she would still talk to me despite knowing she was under surveillance.

To the officials, Zhou Youlan has become shameless and willfully rude. Even some of her family members and friends have been surprised by her transformation. Her husband is among those who have given up any hope for getting their housing issue resolved and wants her to quit. Frequent petition trips have not only taken her away from home but have also caused the rest of the family constant stress as they worry about her fate on the road. Her trips involve elaborate, underground plotting to avoid the attention of the authorities. They also expose her to other dangers on the road—she was almost raped once at an overnight stop. But the possibility that Zhou will give up petitioning anytime soon is slim. She is among hundreds of thousands of "occupational petitioners" for whom petitioning has become a way of life. Among them are also "petition specialists" who have become experts on all things regarding the Chinese petition system, even more knowledgeable than the officials who handle their cases. Zhou's experience is symptomatic of the failure of a petition system that was supposed to provide one of the few channels for evictees to have their grievances redressed. But because the system rarely resolves anything, it has not only failed to ease tensions, it has also both re-victimized those it was meant to serve and empowered them to intensify the pursuit of justice. Zhou, like other long-term petitioners, is a product of this system.

The Petition System

Responding to the mounting pressures that resulted from the reform, in October 1995, the State Council issued a forty-four item document entitled

"Regulations on Petitioning" which was to serve as a detailed nationwide guideline. But new conflicts quickly brought about a need to update the Regulations. In addition, numerous documents and directives, variously called "petition specifics," "petition methods," "urgent notice on petitioning," and "rules on orderly petitioning" were issued by government agencies in Beijing. Provincial and municipal governments also supplied their own rules and regulations.[1]

In the following years, petition offices were gradually established at every level of the government, from the county, district, and province, to the State Council. Petition offices have also been set up by different departments and bureaus at the same administrative level. For instance, while the petition office of the State Council is the main central government organ that handles petitioners from all over the country, various ministries in Beijing, such as Construction and Planning, also have their own petition offices. The proliferation of petition-related documents and institutions testifies to the seriousness and persistence of popular grievances.

Not surprisingly, in 2005, the State Council issued a new version of the Regulations, with fifty-one items, 90 percent of which were either completely new or significantly different from the 1995 version.[2] At that point, books and pamphlets under such titles as "Supplemental Reading on 'Regulations on Petitioning,'" and "Questions and Answers to 'Regulations on Petitioning'" were rushed to bookstores and classrooms of the nation's law schools.

The 2005 Regulations were meant to fix the petition system in two ways. One was to better "regularize," that is, control, the petitioners; the other was to improve officials' response to petitioners. At the time, it was all too evident that the system was close to the breaking point—petitioners were out of control and petition offices were failing miserably at their tasks.

There were a number of indicators of this failure. One was that most petitioners were resorting to what they call *shangfang* ("in-person petitioning to higher authorities") as opposed to *xinfang* (officially defined as petitioning by "letter, e-mail, fax, telephone"),[3] resulting in a flood of petitioners inundating petition offices. While the government prefers written petitions and includes a "walk-in petition" template in the Regulations as just one of several forms appropriate for use in *xinfang*, people no longer believe anything short of persistent in-person presence can resolve their cases. The revised 2005 Regulations were by and large prompted by the dramatic increase in the number of in-person petitions as well as repeat petitions for the same cases. Also, all of these petitions were concentrated in five areas: urban housing demolition and relocation, rural land seizure, health care, education, and the legal system. In the first eight months of 2004, for instance, petition cases in those five areas increased by 125.6 percent, compared to the same period a year earlier.[4]

Another issue was the rise of group petitioning, termed *jifang* or *qunfang*. In the first eight months of 2004, compared to the same period in 2003, the number of people involved in group petitions increased by more than 20 percent nationwide.[5] The government is adamantly opposed to group petitioning since it perceives any collective action as threatening. Indeed, angry protesters have joined together to occupy local government offices, block traffic, hold up official transportation, and stage open, sometimes prolonged, demonstrations. This has often resulted in violent clashes with the police, with protesters being detained and arrested—which turns them into even more zealous petitioners.

Some of these petitioners have resorted to desperate tactics as their cases have dragged on for years and even decades and their hopes have been dashed time and again. In an extreme case, in 1991, after a twenty-year-old man in Henan Province was beaten to death by the local police and thugs working for mine bosses, his mother petitioned for justice, but to no avail. After local authorities repeatedly dismissed her case, she cut her son's head off, wrapped it up, and carried it all the way to Beijing. Thirteen years later, in 2004, she had received a mere 5,000 yuan in compensation and was still petitioning. The local government, meanwhile, had reportedly spent 40,000 yuan in efforts to stop her from petitioning.[6] Distressed petitioners have also employed other radical means. Some of them have taken the law into their own hands by killing corrupt officials or hiring someone to do the job. In 2008, a villager in northern China paid a nineteen-year-old man 1,000 yuan ($146) to stab a local party official to death, because in 2003 the official seized his land without compensation and then repeatedly beat him when he petitioned for redress. Apparently, the party official had been bullying the villagers for years. Their petitions against him, both individually and collectively, had led nowhere. The villagers thus celebrated his death and regarded the teenage assassin as a hero. More than twenty thousand people petitioned a court to spare the teenager from the death sentence.[7] Other petitioners have staged hunger strikes and suicide attempts as a last resort, which in some cases has led to their deaths. The bereaved families then blame officials and continue their quest for justice through petitioning.

Such roiling conflict, often generated at the local level, has spilled over into Beijing as more and more petitioners have engaged in *jingfang*—coming to Beijing to appeal their cases. In 2004, for instance, the petition cases received by county, district, province, and the state petition offices grew 11 percent, 13.9 percent, 17 percent, and 19.5 percent, respectively, forming an upside-down pyramid.[8] This scale shows the failure of the petition system at the local level. The large number of aggrieved people swamping the streets of Beijing represents a logistic and political nightmare for the authorities. Their need for transportation, lodging, and other necessities must be met but they cannot afford the expense involved. Various government agencies have tried to accommodate them. Some motels, subsidized or operated by the government, supply rooms (shared by multiple petitioners) for a token amount of ten yuan a night. Petitioners who are able but unwilling to pay for their accommodations also rely on such subsidies because they believe that the government is ultimately responsible for their plight. Many petitioners try to cut corners whenever and wherever they can, even refusing to pay bus fare and arguing with bus conductors, "I'm a petitioner and I've nothing. I've come to ask the government to return my property so that I can live."[9]

Many petitioners camped on the streets and in other public spaces and formed the notorious *shangfang cun*, petitioners' villages, in Beijing. A particularly favorite space was near Beijing South Railway Station, with a number of petition offices in the vicinity. For years thousands of petitioners from all over China got off the train and simply squatted there.[10] Such "villages," the new shantytowns in China's capital, were an eyesore and a public relations disaster for the government. Yet they became "home" for the petitioners. Zhao Liang's documentary film, years in the making and simply titled *Petition*, captured the plight of such petitioners.[11] The film, which one review called "an unblinking record of human suffering" and which was acclaimed overseas, was banned in China.[12] These petitioners made a mockery of the official claim of a "harmonious society." In preparation for the 2008 summer Olympic Games, China's most elaborate image project and coming-out party on the world stage, the Chinese government made a concerted effort to clean out these villages.

But the biggest nightmare for the central government is that more and more Beijing-bound petitioners, Zhou Youlan among them, have become "event petitioners."[13] They choose to come to Beijing during the CCP's landmark festivals such as National Day on October 1 and the Party's birthday on July 1, or during special events such as the Olympic Games and the annual "two meetings" in March, as well as at other sensitive times, such as when dignitaries visit or on June 4, the anniversary of the massacre of the 1989 Tiananmen Square protesters. They especially target the two meetings in March—the National People's Congress and the People's Political Consultative Conference. The meetings are meant to represent the people and check the Party. Petitioners feel they are entitled to exercise their right to hold their representatives responsible and to have their voices heard. Also, while the "people's representatives" and the petitioners may live in the same city or county, the former are inaccessible to the latter back home because of the security apparatus that surrounds them. However, once these representatives arrive in Beijing for the meetings, their whereabouts are public information and they are under close media scrutiny designed to show that they "listen to the people." Petitioners thus feel they may have a real chance to confront them in Beijing, by waiting for them for hours at the meeting venues and their hotels. They also protest outside those meeting locations both to embarrass the government and to get an opportunity, they hope, to meet an incarnation of a "blue sky" official who will finally set things right.

Every year on June 4, the anniversary of the massacre in 1989, perhaps the darkest stain in the CCP's recent history, the government nervously beefs up its security in public spaces, especially Tiananmen Square, the symbolic site of modern China's struggle for democracy and the center of the 1989 massive student protest. Knowing how vulnerable the government is at such times, petitioners often purposefully wander around Tiananmen Square, and some of them look for opportunities to publicly challenge the authorities and air their discontent by, for instance, pulling out a white banner, a sign of mourning in Chinese culture, or handing out leaflets with protest messages, all meticulously prepared beforehand. As such, in recent years, Tiananmen Square has literally become a police square—plainclothes police, that is—during sensitive dates. They often appear from nowhere and, within a matter of minutes, they drag those who dare to pull a stunt into a van and whisk them away.

To better control petitioners, especially group and event petitioners who squat in Beijing, the revised 2005 Regulations specifies that petitioners are protected by the law only when they go to designated offices during scheduled hours, and that group representatives are limited to no more than five people; those who continue to press "abnormal petitions," such as those who come to the sites of the two annual March meetings and Tiananmen Square, are subject to prosecution.[14]

The other main goal of the 2005 Regulations is to compel local officials to improve their dealings with petitioners. It connects their performance in this regard with their overall assessment for promotion. The stated purpose is to assure that petitioners receive the same treatment from local officials as they do from those in Beijing so that their problems are solved locally.[15]

Considering the large number of Beijing-bound petitioners as indicative of failure on the part of local governments, Beijing punishes local officials in charge of petition with demotions and fines. Such measures are taken based on statistical information about the home districts of petitioners gathered through the registration system in petition offices in Beijing. To receive a hearing in any of the petition offices in Beijing, each person has to register using his/her personal identification card which, much like a driver's license in the United States, has the person's name and address, and an identifying number. Beijing thus learns which regions produce the most petitioners and applies pressure on those local governments accordingly. The Shanghai municipal government is reportedly fined 6,000 yuan for every petitioner that comes from that city.

But such pressure has not improved the performance of local officials. Instead, to please Beijing and protect their own careers, local government officials redirect the pressure onto the petitioners. As in dealing with other cases of popular grievances and resistance, the main response of local governments is suppression.[16] They usually keep petitioners under tight surveillance to prevent them from going to Beijing. If that fails, they bring them back as quickly and quietly as possible and, upon their return, they use whatever means they see fit to keep them at home. Each of the cities, provinces, and even counties in China with regular Beijing-bound petitioners has set up a bureau with a team of retrievers in the capital. Their task is to deal with diehard petitioners from back home. These bureaus have an almost unlimited budget and also regularly hire peasant workers to help—the deportation process can be violent when kidnapping is necessary as some petitioners refuse to go home. Cadres in the offices in Beijing closely coordinate with their counterparts back home and are informed immediately if any petitioners have evaded the surveillance system. They will then try to catch them at train and bus stations before they manage to register at petition offices in Beijing. Their plan B is to round them up at the petition offices where they inevitably come and send them back home by bus or train. This process has become so predictable that petitioners usually do not budget for their return trip because it is nearly always courtesy of their local government.

On the other hand, petitioners understand that by registering at the petition offices in Beijing they become part of the official record and an embarrassment to the local cadres. Therefore, petitioners consider their mere registration at those offices to be a victory even if they are caught and forced back within hours of their arrival.

But that is as far as their satisfaction goes. In this hide-and-seek game, petitioners often pay a huge price. Back home, some of them have been detained, put under house arrest, and beaten. If some of the violence against petitioners was illegal in the past, the new 2005 Regulations document changed that by mandating that "abnormal" petitioning be punished, which allows local officials to arbitrarily accuse people of "abnormal" petitioning, sometimes even making them *shizhong* or "missing." *Shizhong* is a euphemism for kidnapping coined by the Chinese to refer to their government, which shares certain traits with notorious dictatorships elsewhere. Roger Cohen wrote of Muammar el-Qaddafi and Hosni Mubarak: "Disappear is a transitive verb for dictators. That's what they do to foes, disappear them in the night for questioning" that sometimes "becomes a nameless forever."[17] Indeed, the Chinese do not always report a missing person in the way Westerners do. When petitioners, outspoken lawyers, and dissidents go missing—some of them have periodically and predictably gone missing—their families and friends usually know what has happened. The authorities themselves are behind such incidents, and most likely their loved ones have vanished into one of the numerous "black jails" in China.[18]

Black jails are extralegal detention centers where people can be imprisoned for months without access to any legal protection. As widely reported by the media and denied by the Chinese government, these jails are prevalent in China and have been experienced by many petitioners, including those I have interviewed.[19] The sites of such black jails vary. They can be an isolated house in a remote rural area, an abandoned warehouse or factory in the suburbs, a vacant building in a partially demolished city neighborhood, a basement of a newly erected and yet-to-be fully occupied high-rise building, a motel, and even one's own home, as was the case with the blind activist lawyer Chen Guangcheng. Some petitioners are delivered to such sites directly after the train ride from Beijing, without a chance to contact their families, with their cell phones confiscated. They lose their freedom yet their crime is never openly pronounced, nor are they allowed to seek legal aid or any other help. Their jail time ranges from one week to months or even years, depending on their "attitude"—they are often forced to sign a note promising to quit petitioning and to keep quiet about the abuse they have suffered as conditions for their release. The authorities provide guards in three shifts to watch them twenty-four hours a day, including bathroom breaks, and to deliver their meals. Those who are punished with long-term incarceration are often leaders of petition groups and repeat petitioners whom the local governments want to intimidate most, or they may be petitioners who have been injured in the rounding-up process. Violence is commonplace as petitioners often refuse to get on the homebound bus; cadres and their hired hands do not hesitate to use force against them to accomplish their mission, and it may take time for the bruises to disappear. While the authorities prefer not to let injured petitioners appear in public or be photographed, they will not treat their injuries either. After being beaten and denied proper medical care, some petitioners with health issues have died in black jails and incidents of rape by guards have also been reported. But officials take little responsibility as they continue to deny the very existence of black jails.[20]

The violence that is an integral part of the petition process also causes death in other ways. A petitioner in Hubei reportedly risked his life to burn down the black jail that imprisoned him.[21] The documentary film *Petition*, mentioned above, records the story of two petitioners who were hit by a train as they were running away from security forces.[22] The 2010 death of Qian Yunhui, a fifty-three-year-old man in Zhejiang Province in east China, crushed under the tires of a truck, is widely suspected by Chinese netizens as a hit job by the local government. Qian was one of the leaders of four thousand villagers in a six-year campaign against the local government for illegally taking their land. He had gone to Beijing to petition and was arrested many times. This conflict led to a riot in 2004 in which hundreds of villagers were beaten and arrested by the police.[23] In December 2011, thousands of villagers in Wukan, Guangdong Province, revolted against local authorities as their petition against land grabbing achieved no results. After the death of one of their leaders in police custody, the angry peasants blockaded their villages and drove out the security forces.[24]

These incidents, which took place years after the issuing of the new petition Regulations, illustrate the continuing failure of the system. Clearly, the new Regulations have not been effective at better controlling petitioners or at improving the performance of local governments. While the new Regulations also suggest other channels for petitioning, such as via email and telephone, and broader participation by lawyers and volunteers in the petition process,[25] these new measures have not provided much-needed relief to the overburdened system.

The reason is that the new Regulations, like the previous ones, focus on the petitioners and the petition offices instead of the root cause of popular grievances, the prevailing corruption that has made the petition system a necessary evil. The 2005 Regulations also fail to address an inherent flaw in the system. The numerous petition offices have no authority or resources to resolve any of the specific issues they handle daily. They are often presented with overwhelming evidence of officials' wrongdoing, but they have no authority either to investigate or punish those officials. Sometimes petitioners make specific requests for compensation that the petition officials recognize as reasonable. But since the petition offices have no resources to meet such requests, all they can do is simply listen, record, and then refer those cases back to the local governments that caused the grievances in the first place. Clearly, rampant institutional corruption has both enabled and disabled the petition system.

Also, the petition system itself has become a reason for increased and repeated petitioning. It frustrates petitioners all the more when they think that the petition offices at the higher levels have recognized their plight and sympathized with them yet have done nothing to help them. As a result, they return to those offices repeatedly to extract more sympathy, a precious emotion sorely lacking at the local level, and to reinforce their sense of righteousness.

Moreover, petitioning often invites revenge. One study indicates that among the 632 petitioners surveyed, 56.2 percent kept petitioning because local government, as an act of retribution, attacked and arrested them and thus created additional grievances.[26] The 2008 case mentioned above where a villager paid a teenager to murder a local official was precisely caused by cadres' exacting retribution. Situations like these build resentment, anger, and despair, and make even initially minor and solvable problems difficult to resolve. As many cases linger for years and even decades and turn some people into full-time "professional petitioners," the system has become a trap that consumes enormous energy and the resources of both petitioners and the government without serving its stated purposes.

Daniel Carpenter, in his study of the high tide of antislavery petitions in 1837–1839 in the United States, wonders why petitions flourished while they were largely ignored. The same question can be asked about the current Chinese petition system. Carpenter's study shows that people petition for various reasons, not always about the most immediate issues that prompt their petitioning. For instance, the process of gathering signatures for petitions was a useful recruitment device for activists to build and strengthen their organizations and networks.[27] In China, the petition system has also gained a life of its own; it has become a ritual for petitioners in search of information, community, and a new focus in life.

Take Shanghai as an example. There, in-person petitions are most prevalent. The main municipal petition office is conveniently located downtown, on People's Square, with a central subway station and many bus stops nearby. Of all the petition offices in Shanghai, this one is the most popular. Its address, 200 People's Square Boulevard, is widely known among Shanghai petitioners simply as "Number 200." In the cases of housing disputes involving eviction and loss of property that I studied, for instance, some of the residents would head to this office straight from their demolished homes, often carrying elderly or sick family members on stretchers; others would come to show their fresh bruises and hospital records in the aftermath of a violent encounter with a government-hired demolition squad.

Part of the attraction of this office, interestingly enough, is in the petitioners themselves. The office is open on weekdays. But those who have housing disputes all come on Wednesday by a tacit agreement and they form a kind of community with a shared plight and purpose. One clothing retailer with her own shop and a flexible schedule, for instance, chooses Wednesday as her day off so that she can come to join her fellow petitioners. As such, this petition office is extremely busy on Wednesdays. It opens at 9 a.m., but by 10:30 a.m. it is already crowded with more than a thousand people, each with a number in hand. Petitioners are issued numbers according to the order of their arrival—and each waits in line to be received.

Some residents have been coming to this office for more than a decade and have earned the nickname "petition specialists." They are the stars among petitioners and take it upon themselves to study the most relevant and up-to-date official documents in order to come up with new strategies and demands. They are highly recognizable, and in fact, are an institution at this petition office, with much to offer to newcomers. These seasoned petitioners have been crucial in building an information infrastructure for their comrades. For instance, they have quietly issued a list of major petition offices in Beijing—the State Council, *Renmin ribao* (People's Daily), Xinhua News Agency, and CCTV—complete with addresses, phone numbers, and bus routes that they have compiled and printed. Such lists are updated and thus some of the lists are titled, "The newest contact information on central government petition offices." Petitioners have also circulated among themselves jingles, poems, and essays that expose corruption, which have always helped boost their morale. They have launched signature drives to protest certain housing policies, such as Document 305, that affect all of them. They are very aware that their number in and of itself is their strength and it is in their best interest to muster a robust petition army.

Collectively, these petitioners are well-informed, resourceful, and tenacious. Any nervous newcomer who steps into Number 200 will immediately get a briefing from fellow petitioners—a sort of "Petition 101" tutorial—and feel energized. These petitioners learn from each other how to fight for their cause, keep each other up to date on new developments, and draw strength from and support one another. The municipal petition office thus has become a gathering point and self-support center for petitioners who have built a community there. That the petition office has been turned into an organizational locus for scattered individual petitioners and a politically charged institution of sociability with its own veteran clients is perhaps the most telling evidence of its failure.

The nationwide petition movement, or more accurately, the nationwide failure of the petition system, has undercut the Party's claimed highest priority—social stability and harmony—and caused grave concern to Beijing. In an extraordinary move, on January 24, 2011, Chinese Premier Wen Jiabao visited the petition office of the State Council. He listened to petitioners' complaints and promised to solve their problems. As the first and only such high-ranking CCP official to ever stop at the office, Wen's visit generated headlines across the globe but little else.[28] Then, as the CCP approached its ninetieth anniversary on July 1, 2011, and prepared a nationwide celebration, hundreds of thousands of event petitioners flooded Beijing to push for their causes. All the efforts by local governments to stop them from reaching the capital failed, and a massive number of petitioners from all over China inundated relevant institutions and infrastructure: petition offices, government-run motels, and temporary shelters. Beijing was forced to act. For more than a week in early July, several petition offices of the central government combined their resources and sent their agents to receive all of the petitioners in the shelter in Jiujingzhuang, Beijing, where the government set up facilities to keep them all in one place so as to control them.

The shelter in Jiujingzhuang was dreaded by petitioners in the past, because it was used to detain "abnormal" petitioners until their respective local governments came to retrieve them. Some Chinese activists called the place a "concentration camp" for the petitioners.[29] But this time, many petitioners came to stand in line as early as 2 a.m. for a chance to meet officials. Concerned about what would happen with thousands of agitated people in scorching and humid heat, the authorities provided tents and doctors on site, but also armored vehicles and soldiers. The security force was overburdened. One guard reportedly said that he had only had two days off since May. The petitioners were treated with a meal, a hearing, and then sent home—thousands of official vehicles with license plates of various provinces awaited them in the parking lot. The event was news only among the petitioners; expecting few results and trying not to attract more people to Beijing, the official media by and large ignored it. In the end, the extravaganza was only another event that dashed petitioners' hopes.

It is this systematic failure of the petition system and corruption in the housing reform that has transformed Zhou Youlan from a kindergarten teacher into a committed petitioner. Let us now turn to her story.

Meet Zhou Youlan

Born in 1952, Zhou Youlan was the youngest of six children, five girls and one boy. Her family had lived for generations in Shanghai. Before 1949, her father worked as a telegrapher for several GMD newspapers in Shanghai. Afterward, his skills earned him a job with *Jiefang ribao* (Liberation Daily), a leading CCP newspaper in Shanghai. During the Cultural Revolution, his prior association with the GMD came back to haunt him. Red Guards searched his home repeatedly, forcing him to write one confession after another about his past and the people he knew. An introvert, Mr. Zhou suffered in silence, and often poured out his sorrow by playing the pipa, a traditional Chinese string instrument, in a loft at night in the dark.

Zhou Youlan was her father's favorite daughter. While her brother and sisters were afraid of their father, Zhou Youlan played hide-and-seek with him. Her father would chase after her to make sure that she drank milk, which was precious then. Mr. Zhou had a special soft spot in his heart for his youngest daughter, in part because he thought she was disadvantaged; her mother was paralyzed for three years after Zhou Youlan's birth and could not nurse her. For that same reason, Zhou's mother considered her a curse and resented her. Her mother often yelled at her to vent her frustration, while her father always tried to protect her. If there was a special dish on the table and Zhou tried to help herself, her mother would kick her under the table while her father would serve her. Growing up between a tempestuous mother and a loving father, as well as five older siblings, Zhou Youlan developed a great capacity for enduring mistreatment, but also expected her abuse to be compensated and her grief validated. This character trait has been severely tested in her decade-long journey as an evictee and petitioner.

Like many of her contemporaries, Zhou Youlan's education was interrupted by the Cultural Revolution. Thanks to her older siblings, who had already been sent into the countryside, Zhou was able to stay in Shanghai but had no good job prospects. In the mid-1970s, Zhou became a teacher in a neighborhood kindergarten. Through a friend, she began to date a man with the surname Chen. At the time, it was a great match any way one looked at it. Chen, a junior high graduate, worked in the Shanghai Port Office. A job in a state-owned enterprise with a stable salary and benefits was usually considered far superior to one in a neighborhood enterprise, such as Zhou's employment at the kindergarten. Chen was said to be well mannered and also a bit dull, which often inspires a sense of trust. But Chen's most attractive asset was the apartment his family had, which happened to be just a short walking distance away from Zhou Youlan's home. With his two younger siblings living outside Shanghai, Chen's parents wanted Chen to stay with them, even after marrying. In other words, Chen and his bride would have their own room in his own house, a rarity for newlyweds in those days.

Moreover, the Chens' place was not the kind of cramped, government-supplied rental where many of the Shanghai residents lived. The Chen family owned the apartment. Chen's father, an engineer at a textile factory, bought the apartment in 1949 just before his wife gave birth to their first child. The apartment, together with the new son born soon after, gave the couple a sense of family and a source of lasting pride. The apartment consisted of two parts, the main room of 17.6 square meters, which was divided into two after Chen's marriage, with one part as the newlyweds' bedroom and the other as the family dining room, and a loft of 8 square meters for Chen's parents. An additional advantage was that the house had two balconies, both facing the sunny south, a desirable feature for hanging out the laundry and keeping the house warm in winter, since no family had a washing machine or heating system then.

The apartment was located in what was then the Nanshi District of the city.[30] While the Chens' neighborhood was densely populated and conditions were generally poor, it had some redeeming qualities. The neighborhood was on the immediate outskirts of an upscale and once-gated community known as *Longmen Cun* (Dragon Village). The area was vibrant, with many small shops and some decent schools, and it was only two bus stops away from the renowned city temple and five bus stops away from Nanjing Road in downtown. It was also close to the work units of both Chen and Zhou. Moreover, the Chens' apartment was in a much better condition than those of their immediate neighbors, which made them feel special. Needless to say, Zhou Youlan and her family were delighted. There was no doubt that Zhou's marriage to Chen had much to do with the apartment, something that made this otherwise average man attractive. Years later, Zhou still talked about how special it was at the time to find a husband with an apartment and how all her friends envied her.

Zhou Youlan married in 1981, when her father was very ill. The idea was for the father to see his youngest daughter getting settled for life before he passed away. Married life for the new couple was content, if uneventful. Zhou was almost a model worker. Other than a maternity leave when she had a daughter, she never took a day off from work, nor did she ever come late or leave early, a record she was proud of. Hardworking and easygoing, she got along with her colleagues. She liked handcrafts, such as knitting and shoe-making, perfect skills to forge friendships with her mostly female co-workers.

"I Stood There and Watched . . ."

However, Zhou Youlan, this kindergarten teacher, would go through a transformation that neither she herself nor her co-workers could have foreseen. It was all because of the apartment that had for years given her and her family much comfort and pride. In spring 1995, four years after her in-laws' deaths, the Nanshi District launched a project to expand the office building of the district court. According to the district's plan, the expansion would take up Zhou's neighborhood area, which included about eighty households. The district delivered a letter of demolition to each of the families, with a compensation policy and deadlines spelled out. In August 1995, demolition and relocation formally started. This was in the earlier days of urban renewal and the Shanghai residents generally did not question the government because much of the corruption that has plagued the system was yet to be exposed. Since most of the neighbors lived in poor housing, they moved out quickly, heading for the outskirts of the city.

Zhou's family was fully prepared to move out as well, since there seemed to be no point in resisting a government project. But they wanted their terms to be met, which seemed simple enough. They asked for an apartment with two south-oriented balconies, just like that of their own home, located in the vicinity of their work units and Zhou's childhood home, where her sister's family still lived. Unlike many of her contemporaries who had been uprooted and sent to the countryside in their teenage years, thereby experiencing the world outside their hometowns, Zhou had remained a homebody. Prior to the demolition, she had never even set foot outside Shanghai. She was deeply rooted in the place where she had spent her childhood, experienced coming of age, enjoyed adult friendships, and cherished the comfort of family life. All this was practically her entire world and without it she could not quite imagine life.

However, the district demolition office would not even consider her request. It wanted to relocate her family across town on the western side of Shanghai, where the real estate was cheap. For Zhou Youlan, that was a foreign land. "What can I do in that remote corner? How can I get to work and see my family from so far away?" she asked. An official responded that she could ride a bicycle. "But I don't know how," Zhou replied. "Well, go learn," the official advised. While many residents hoped to improve their living conditions through the demolition and relocation process, Zhou was happy with what she had, and only asked for comparable housing nearby.

After some exhausting negotiations, Zhou tried to compromise and resigned herself to moving to the suburbs, but she still requested two south-facing rooms, much like her current home with its balconies. The demolition office deemed that to be out of the question and offered her a 19-square-meter apartment with one south-facing room. As far as she was concerned, including its balconies, her current home had a total area of 35 square meters, so Zhou could not figure out why she should move to a place that was smaller and worse than her current home, not to mention its distance and other inconveniences.

When the negotiations failed, cash compensation was an option, which Zhou Youlan was open to considering. The demolition office offered 80,000 yuan. When Zhou learned that a neighbor with only 15 square meters was given 180,000 yuan because of some alleged bribe of the demolition officials, she rejected the offer outright. Besides, she believed that her home was the best on the block, which even the demolition office recognized. When the

Figure 1.1. Zhou Youlan treasured her privately owned apartment, which had two south-oriented balconies, good for drying the laundry and keeping the house warm in winter. Since she could not resist demolition, Zhou agreed to move and requested an apartment with two south-oriented balconies. The district's rejection of her request was part of the deal breaker that has led her to petition since 1996. Courtesy of Zhou Youlan.

officials tried to persuade other neighbors to accept their offer, they reportedly used Zhou as an example: "We'll only give 80,000 yuan to Zhou Youlan and her apartment is much nicer than yours." At one point, the demolition office raised the cash offer to 100,000 yuan, which Zhou again rejected.

But what hardened Zhou's heart was the demeaning way the district treated her and her family. She believed that her family, without power, money, and connections, was trodden upon and stripped of any dignity. In the rounds of negotiations and in neighborhood gossip, she was constantly insulted. The head of the demolition office allegedly told a neighbor, "That woman is like a small bird that can be easily pinched to death, and her husband is simply a fool." As such, the local authorities were even more puzzled and irritated that they could not bully Zhou, this apparently helpless woman, to accept their conditions and simply go away.

And they made her pay for her stubbornness. At one point, a staff member of the demolition office told her that since she refused to move, the office punished her by assigning the family to an apartment as far away as possible from her husband's work unit, located on the worst floor, the sixth, the highest in a building, without an elevator, and the hottest in the summer. It was in a newly developed area on the western edge of the city and did not even have a bus line yet. Her husband would have to walk and change buses four times to cross the city to get to work; the commute would take three hours each way. At another point the demolition office had an apartment in Pudong with two south-oriented rooms in which Zhou expressed an interest. But it gave that unit to one of Zhou's neighbors instead, which Zhou considered to be an ugly provocation.

In the meantime, the demolition office took more punitive measures to make sure that Zhou's family suffered daily. Its hired demolition squad piled up a two-meter high mound of debris in front of Zhou's home to block the entrance. She and her family had to get help from the neighbors and climb out, which surprised a demolition official who asked, "How did you get out?" "I flew through the air!" an exasperated Zhou replied. The demolition squad also stuffed the key hole on Zhou's door with dirt. Worse yet, they paid peasant workers to defecate in front of her house; the family had to wash the place every morning. There was pressure at work and within the family as well. The authorities contacted the work units of both Zhou and Chen, criticizing the couple as "legally blind"—that they did not understand the law and were unreasonable. They also came to Zhou's sister's home and tried to damage her reputation by telling the neighbors that she was bringing an eviction on herself.

As Zhou Youlan's family became a "nail household" standing in the way of the district court's expansion, the district housing bureau in August issued an administrative ruling for the family to move. Two months later, the Nanshi District government issued an ultimatum, posted on Zhou's door and also delivered to her work unit for her signature. It ordered the family to relocate to the government designated apartment in days or the district housing bureau, security bureau, and the court would forcibly evict them. Soon after, an eviction notice was posted on Zhou's door for the public to see, "just like the 'big character posters' in the Cultural Revolution," a humiliated Zhou declared.

Facing eminent threat of domicide, Zhou was afraid. Resistance to demolition had been a learning process for Shanghai's residents. At the onset of urban renewal, they did not even know that they could hold out; it was not an option and there was no precedent. In the following years, forced demolition and relocation gradually became common when the public learned more about the corruption and residents' rights. They began to applaud the "nail households" for standing up for their rights. Also, when more people or a whole neighborhood collectively stood firm, they had less to fear. But in the mid-1990s, the initial urban renewal projects in Shanghai enjoyed some public support as they started with the worst housing areas, where residents were often eager to move out. There were few nail households and those who got evicted did not speak out either. Holding out was looked down upon by the public, and "nail household" was used as a derogatory term to imply that those families were impervious to reason. It is in this regard that Zhou compared the eviction notice to the "big character posters" during the Cultural Revolution which were also meant to expose and humiliate the target, whose guilt was automatically assumed. Eviction under such circumstances was much more intimidating as the families involved felt hopelessly isolated. But even when Zhou feared an eviction, she was deeply convinced of its injustice and refused to cave in. She stood fast in the face of the ultimatum.

In early April 1996 this stalemate was predictably resolved by force; the threat of eviction became a reality. Days before, Zhou, sensing the end was near and feeling unsafe at home, had taken her family to live with a relative but dispatched her nephew to keep an eye on the apartment. That day Zhou stood on a friend's balcony and looked on as the demolition squad arrived. The domicide Zhou witnessed left an indelible impression on her, which she has since recounted numerous times, often with a cold resolution to hold back her tears:

> My home was demolished on April 9, 1996. At noon that day, two trucks and two hundred some policemen were on site, blocking traffic on Shangwen Road. They broke into my home, loaded my belongings onto the two trucks, and drove away to Huicheng Xincun, an apartment of 19.4 square meters on the western side of the city, and leveled my home. . . . They couldn't see me, but I stood there and watched . . . in silence; I was at a loss for words and couldn't breathe. Because of my holding out, they [district demolition office] punished me by assigning me the 19.4 square-meter apartment. They told me that they wanted my family to cross the entire city to get to work. . . . I refused to go [to the assigned apartment] to get my belongings. How could they destroy my 35 square-meter apartment in the city with double balconies and give me a smaller one in the suburbs? Why should my living space be reduced while everyone else's seems to have increased? What kind of housing reform is this for me? . . . The police were the helpers of the demolition squad; they are the "heroes."

A Road with No Return

That was the end of Zhou Youlan's home and the beginning of her struggle for justice. Zhou found temporary housing among her relatives and friends, and eventually moved in with her sister in a 10-square-meter room in their childhood home. At the time her daughter was graduating from junior high with college in mind, which meant that she had to enter a quality high school first. But there was no space for her to study, and the family decided that she would go to a vocational school instead. The family had no peace either. Often in bad moods, Zhou and her husband argued frequently over their unsettling situation. No one knew what was coming next or what they should do. Zhou was sure of one thing, though, that she was not going to lose her home without a fight.

Prelude

The first step Zhou Youlan took was writing petition letters, the officially preferred form of petitioning. Zhou took this route because she felt apprehensive—she was just an apprentice in the trade and did not know any other means of petitioning. For an entire year in 1996, she wrote hundreds of letters to Jiang Zemin, then the CCP chairman, and relevant government agencies in Beijing and Shanghai. If the government truly wanted to encourage petition by letter, then it should have tried to solve the issues brought by those letters so as to make the system credible. But during a year of letter writing, all Zhou received was a routine acknowledgement of her letters, without any specific response. The only place that bothered to respond was the local demolition office, which was not good news at all. The office had not contacted her at all after the eviction, but now it came to warn her that her letters were a complete waste of time, because they all ended up in that office. It also insisted that the original settlement was a government decision that would not be revised. As mentioned earlier, one of the factors that has contributed to the failure of the petition system is that the culprits responsible for causing the grievances in the first place, in this case the district demolition office, are also put in charge of addressing them—this has rendered people like Zhou Youlan helpless.

That petition-by-letter was useless was the first lesson Zhou learned in the process. The next year, she changed her strategy to petitioning in person at the district office. At the time, the district had not even set up a petition office yet and the guards there refused to let her in. She resorted to making noise in front of the office building to attract attention and also to vent her frustration. Gradually she began to shout abuse, call officials names, curse, and cry in the street while striking a rice bowl—she reduced herself to a harpy, and she knew it. But it worked. As she created a scene and attracted a crowd of passersby, she was allowed into the office. But the officials there simply told her that the eviction was legal and correct and that she had no case. They then called her supervisor at the kindergarten to take her home. Such a humiliating fight, accompanied by a disappointing result, was both physically and mentally crushing. Zhou was often exhausted after such an episode. She would rest for a few days and then start all over again.

By chance, Zhou once saw the head of the district demolition office on the street and tried to follow him, but he was on a motorcycle and she was only able to identify the general direction he was heading. Next time she had a friend follow him on bicycle and finally found out where he lived. Since the district office took no responsibility for her case, Zhou wanted to talk to this man who had been directly involved in her eviction. But how to approach him? One friend suggested going nice, visiting him with a present. Before the National Day celebration on October 1, 1998, her kindergarten gave its employees a holiday gift certificate; Zhou bought a cake with hers. She carried the cake to the neighborhood where the official lived. But she paced back and forth, consumed by both anger and shame as she was acutely aware that she was at his mercy. "Where is justice when I have to bring a present in order to approach the man who evicted my family? How could something like this happen? It was all too much to bear." She turned back without knocking on the door.

Without knowing where else she could go or who else to turn to, the next day, Zhou gathered her courage and swallowed her pride, and went to visit the head of the demolition office. There she discovered that his wife was a casual acquaintance of hers who worked at another kindergarten. With this layer of connection, Zhou was able to talk to the wife and the husband. The husband explained that the demolition was not his fault and that he was in no position to help her. But Zhou kept visiting him. The fact was that before the eviction, officials often tried to contact her, to threaten her and push her out, while she tried to avoid them. But after the eviction the officials disappeared when she wanted to revisit her case. To Zhou, the head of the demolition office became the only person who at least knew of her ordeal firsthand. She tried to hold on to him as a tangible link to her plight and also directed her anger and frustration at him—Zhou was mourning her loss and wanted her grief to be heard and validated. She also took her husband to visit him when the couple had a fight over the housing issue. Sometimes the two would continue their argument there before the official.

Such constant, often volatile visits were certainly unwelcome and the host made it known. The last visit by Zhou and her husband went especially badly. After Zhou once again blamed the official for the eviction and things escalated into a shouting match between the two, the official called 110, the emergency number in Shanghai, and the police came. They accused Zhou of breaking into his home. Zhou defended herself by pointing to the obvious: "He opened the door to let us in." But the police insisted that since the host no longer welcomed them, they should leave. "But we have no place to go!" "Ok, then come with us," a policeman said. Being detained by the police is never something a Chinese takes lightly. Years earlier, merely the threat of police custody would have silenced Zhou. But at this point, she had come to the end of her rope and had nothing more to lose. "So be it!" she said. She and her husband were put in a police car and brought to her neighborhood police station. Overcome by fear and humiliation, Zhou was reduced to tears.

Unexpectedly, this ride to the police station became a turning point on Zhou Youlan's transformation to a full-time petitioner. Neither Zhou nor her husband had ever been in a police car, which in the popular imagination is for criminals or those suspected of crimes who are usually handcuffed on the way to jail. It was therefore a surprise to the couple that their ride in the police car involved nothing extraordinary—they were not abused. In fact, at the police station, an officer even listened to their experience. But they were in for an even bigger shock: the policeman deemed Zhou's petitioning so far to be too mild to have any effect. He had tips to offer: "You have to take your case to a higher and even the highest level and make a big fuss, or you'll never get a settlement." "Really? But will I be in trouble with the law?" Zhou was not convinced. "No, nothing bad will happen to you," the officer reassured her.

Keith Richards, a cofounder of the Rolling Stones, writes with his characteristic irreverence about his first arrest and appearance in 1967 in a British court: "It was only by getting busted that we realized how fragile the structure really was."[31] The same can be said about Zhou's 1998 encounter with this particular police officer. In Zhou's own words, it was "enlightening." She found out that riding in a police car was a cakewalk; that being brought to a police station was survivable; and more important, that she had been too restrained in her petitioning efforts. The officer simply shared with Zhou a basic fact that he had observed while doing his job, which was that local petitioning was useless and one must appeal to the higher authorities. Indeed, using higher authorities, especially the central government and its policy and rhetoric, to press local cadres for a solution is at the heart of "rightful resistance," something that Zhou and other veteran petitioners would all learn. In any event, this meeting with the officer marked the beginning of a much feistier Zhou and led to many rides to police stations and detention centers over the next ten years, usually with much harsher results than the first time; it also marked, according to Zhou herself, the beginning of her "formal path" to becoming a committed and full-time petitioner.

The Hell-Raising Petitioner

The district officials who were troubled by Zhou Youlan's previous behavior had seen nothing yet. Over the next four years, Zhou would become, in the eye of the officials, a repulsive shrew in white—she often wore a man's white shirt with the sleeves cut off and the characters "Return my house; return my human rights" written on the front and back. She wore that custom-made shirt underneath a jacket that she would take off in front of the district office. Zhou still placed her hope for a solution mainly in the district, which by then had set up a petition office. She not only visited the office regularly but also camped outside and waited for the district director to come out. Whenever she spotted him, she would throw off her jacket and rush to grab ahold of his legs. On her knees, Zhou would cry out for help until the guards came out to drag her away. Sometimes she would try to block or follow the director's car, insisting on a hearing. During the four years that Zhou visited the district office regularly, the district directorship changed four times and, according to Zhou, she had grabbed the legs of every director.

As such, the district petition office deemed Zhou to be hysterical and refused to hear her case. More than once when forcing her way into the building she was beaten by what she referred to as the "dogs"—the district guards and staff. "But the 'dogs' won't beat me outside the building and they're afraid of the public," she said. She went there every week. The district provided a form for all petitioners to fill out with name, address, and reasons for petition. Zhou always filled out that form but then brought it back home. She now has a collection of hundreds of such forms with various stated reasons such as "I was evicted and have been without a home for three years," "I demand a reasonable settlement!" and "Return my home; return my belongings; return my basic rights as a human being." Asked why she has kept all those forms, Zhou said: "I filled in the forms but no one wanted to take them and take my case. So I brought them back and kept them, as historical evidence, witnesses of my journey, how I've gone through this period of time, a reminder of my struggle."

Zhou Youlan also used props in her street protest. Once she and her husband brought a wooden board to the district office which they used to support a broken bed the family slept on. One day she was sitting home and looked at that "bed": "I felt so pathetic and sad. How come this is my bed? How come this is my home? And I decided to show that 'bed' to the officials." And so she did. "Look at this! Look at this! This is my bed!" She cried out while striking a bowl in front of the district office. The guards threw that board on top of a pile of trash and accused her of "creating a disturbance." Another time, she brought her quilt to the office to demonstrate her determination to camp there until her case was settled, only to be removed again.

By then Zhou had gotten to know some of the other petitioners, thanks to her many trips to the district office. She was particularly close to a determined mother who fought for the release of her daughter, jailed for petition-

Figure 1.2. The many petition forms Zhou Youlan filled out at the district office and brought back home because the office refused to receive her.

ing over a housing dispute. The mother broke one of her legs during a petition trip and got a wheelchair for herself, and became more ruthless afterward because she believed that even if the authorities wanted to arrest her, they still had to keep her out of prison for medical reasons. Zhou exchanged tips with her. The mother's persistent attempt to follow the vehicles of major municipal officials, while in a wheelchair, led to a direct audience with the chief of the city's security bureau and eventually also the desired amount of compensation, a random case of a "blue sky" official reincarnated. Zhou referred to this mother's case often because it set an example as to what ruthless and determined petitioning might accomplish.

However, Zhou was about to be exposed to a much wider circle of experienced petitioners. Since the district office repeatedly dismissed her complaints, she started visiting the municipal petition office, at 200 People's Square. While she had become a veteran petitioner at the district office, she was still intimidated by Number 200. After all, it was in the imposing municipal building complex for the highest authorities in Shanghai, protected by armed police and guards. But Zhou was soon at ease: "I no longer fear, knowing so many people there are all petitioners, just like me," Zhou said.

The fact that the petition office is located right on People's Square, the heart of downtown Shanghai, crowded with local residents and tourists from all over China and the world, provided an extended theater for street protest. Zhou would often wear a regular jacket to the square and, when no one noticed her, take it off and kneel down in that white, shredded shirt with its protest message. She soon learned that plainclothes police were everywhere—as soon as she kneeled down, the police, once thirty of them, would "jump out magically," Zhou said. "I don't know where they came from; they were nowhere to be seen." Those policemen would tear off her shirt and drag her inside a room in Number 200. She was beaten when she resisted, and once was thrown against a wall and shed blood. The police confiscated or otherwise destroyed a number of her white shirts, which some of her friends and colleagues had donated to support her. Zhou also attempted to block traffic downtown and stop the mayor's car, like the mother in wheelchair did, but was unsuccessful.

Like many other seasoned petitioners, Zhou Youlan gradually became an event petitioner—one of those who petition during major official events, landmark anniversaries, and national holidays. She learned about those events—dates, places, official presences, and other relevant information—from her fellow petitioners at the municipal petition office at Number 200. They passed on such information and encouraged each other to participate, because the bigger their crowd, the stronger they appear to be and the more protected they are. While such event petitions often involve some behind-the-scenes organization and coordination, the petitioners nevertheless all arrive as individuals, so as to avoid the appearance of collective action.

Once Zhou joined others petitioning at the site of the Municipal People's Congress annual meeting downtown on Nanjing Road. They demanded that the people's representatives serve the people's interests by coming out to listen to them. As usual, Zhou's oversized white shirt was visible underneath her jacket, which by then had become a known sign of pending trouble for the security forces. Sometimes representatives would come out to meet with people, mostly as a public-relations gesture. Zhou got ahold of such a representative and poured out her story. "It will be resolved," the representative assured her. "Could you write that down for me?" Zhou pressed, but the representative declined.

Behind the scenes, however, the authorities made sure those who dared to publicly pressure them were taught a lesson. Shortly after Zhou returned home from that encounter, the neighborhood authorities called her in for an "urgent meeting" and threatened to lock her up for "illegally disrupting" the Municipal People's Congress meeting, which was said to warrant fifteen days of detention. "Why is that illegal? Those who robbed me of my home are the real criminals!" Zhou shook with rage and showed them the pictures of her apartment that she carried with her all the time. They also asked where she got the information about the meeting in an effort to uncover her network: "From television reports," Zhou said.

Visits by foreign dignitaries, which are frequent in cities like Beijing and Shanghai, are always favored occasions for the petitioners to pressure and embarrass the government. One of the best known such visits was by Mikhail Gorbachev, the former head of Soviet Russia, in spring 1989. Student protesters in Tiananmen Square tried to use that visit as leverage to get the government to heed their demand for democracy. The authorities have since developed a series of measures to prevent open challenges like this. In June 1998, President Bill Clinton was to visit Shanghai, with a stop at the City Temple, which is close to Zhou's neighborhood. The police put Zhou under surveillance and her work unit delivered four watermelons to her as a bribe for her to stay home. Zhou still jokes about it: "Thanks to Clinton I got free watermelons." The officials' concern was well warranted; Zhou and other petitioners had been preparing to grab Clinton's attention—their efforts were thwarted only by the dense security surrounding the visit.

An Intermission

A turning point came in fall 1999 when Zhou Youlan once again had a chance to stop the district director and convince him to call a meeting. The director, in fact the entire district office, was familiar with one of the district's most tenacious petitioners. They were ready to resolve her case for good. The negotiations went through several rounds. The district proposed a plan of compensation according to a 1995 policy that was based on the size of the property in question. According to Zhou's own math, the compensation for her home should amount to more than 200,000 yuan. But the district ignored the balconies and loft in calculating the floor area. Zhou objected: "Would you get a balcony and loft for free when you purchase an apartment on the market?"

In the end, the district offered 195,000 yuan—which Zhou decided to accept—subject to two conditions. One was that Zhou had to sign a paper stating "This settles all of the matters concerning the demolition and relocation." Its purpose was to preempt any future complaints or demands. After discussing this with her petition comrades, she stated that "This settles the matter concerning the demolition and relocation" and left out "all of." For Zhou, this was an important distinction. But the authorities added those two words against her will anyway. The other condition was that Zhou had to move her furniture out of the district-assigned apartment in the suburbs to which she had refused to relocate. The first installment, 30 percent of the 195,000 yuan, came in November 1999 and the rest arrived the next month, when Zhou moved out all the furniture. Not surprisingly, several pieces of furniture were damaged. In 1996, the demolition squad and the district officials took her belongings out in a rage and carelessly piled them up on top of one another in an abandoned apartment where they sat for nearly four years. Her request for compensation for the damaged goods was denied.

Zhou was fully aware that accepting the 195,000 yuan payment was a compromise. But she was in no position to refuse it. The four-year ordeal had taken a toll on her and her family. The 1996 domicide was disruptive in every way. It not only deprived the family of their home, it also distracted Zhou from her work since she often took days off to petition. Unable to hold a full-time job and at the same time seek justice, she had to quit her job. As a condition for approving her resignation, her work unit made her submit a written statement that she quit her job on her own initiative, not because of the eviction. The family then depended on Chen's monthly income of 600 yuan alone. But in 1998, as the deepening of the economic reform and intensified market-based competition caused many state-owned enterprises to decline or close down, Chen also lost his job. The family had no choice but to depend on the mercy of others by borrowing money to live.

Then there was the issue of the family. Zhou's elder sister was the most supportive. This sister has stood by her in street protests and contacted their friends and fellow petitioners for support when Zhou was abused by the local officials.

But the rest of the family was losing faith in Zhou's campaign. Her daughter was initially on her mother's side. Before 1998, Zhou even brought her daughter with her to petition; each was dressed in a white shirt, which often attracted more attention. But local police together with the officials in the daughter's school had a talk with the girl, threatening severe consequences for her future if she joined her mother again. School officials warned her with the examples of student protesters in the 1989 Tiananmen Square demonstration: some were arrested; some went into hiding and exile; and others lost jobs. From that point on, she no longer went out petitioning with Zhou, but she still sometimes helped with computer work in writing petition letters. Zhou also felt sorry for her daughter, who suffered with her family during this trying time. Her school tuition cost 3,800 yuan a year, mostly borrowed from friends and relatives. The family could not afford her lunch money, so Zhou would make lunch and bring it to school. But this was rare among those growing up as an only child in China, targeted as they have been by the increasingly consumer-oriented society as an important market for expensive, "cool" food, drink, and snacks. Her daughter, embarrassed by her family's poverty, did not want her classmates to see her mother carrying a lunchbox to school. Zhou had to hide nearby and wait for her daughter to come out.

Zhou's husband is another issue. In time he lost any hope for a fair settlement and grew more disappointed with Zhou's actions. As far as he was concerned, Zhou was married to the apartment more than to him, and he resented her frequent absence. As such, her petitioning was all done behind her husband's back. Sometimes she could not answer the phone at home when her husband was around, and she had to go upstairs to her sister's room to talk. Zhou would not tell her husband if she had been beaten and abused, because then her husband would say, "Why do you keep on doing this? Just stay home and behave!" Once when Zhou was detained after a petition trip, she called her husband to let him know. Without a word of comfort, her husband asked, "When are you coming home to make dinner?" "But will anyone deliver a house to us if I don't fight? No! And what are my choices?" Zhou responded.

Zhou Youlan herself was exhausted physically and emotionally. "I cook at home, petition outside and am often abused by officials, and then I'm criticized by my husband at home. Friends and even some security guards told me that I'm so thin and I must take care of myself. They said that the housing thing isn't worth it and I can't win. But who will fight for me if I don't? Will a house all of a sudden fall on me from the sky?" she said. She weighed a mere 75 pounds, down from her usual 90-some pounds. "During the four years I have washed my face with tears. My body and mind are broken; my suffering is beyond words," Zhou wrote in one of her petition letters. Once during the Chinese New Year, she had no money to celebrate the most important holiday in Chinese culture. She swallowed her pride and asked for help at her previous work unit, and was given 50 yuan. With her family in deep debt and with survival at issue, she, in her own words, "was forced to accept the 195,000 yuan." She needed a break and also a tangible validation of her four-year struggle; the payment provided both.

The settlement that came in the winter of 1999 finally allowed Zhou and her family to celebrate the Chinese New Year for the first time in four years. It was the largest sum of money the family had ever seen. Had it come during the initial demolition, the family would have used it to buy an apartment unit and get settled, and that would have been the end of the matter.

Almost four years later, however, things were quite different. First of all, the real estate market had risen, which devalued the 195,000 yuan. Also, Zhou was now a seasoned petitioner who had learned that if one is persistent and resourceful enough, the government will give in. That the district doubled the initial settlement proved that point. She just needed to hang in there and keep going. After all, she had not gone to petition in Beijing as others had done. In other words, Zhou understood that she was far from having exhausted all channels of appealing for a better settlement.

More important, Zhou did not believe the settlement of 195,000 yuan was fair and should be final. With the rising real estate market, especially in downtown Shanghai, she knew that her previous apartment would have been worth much more had it not been demolished. In the meantime, years of petitioning had greatly sharpened her sense of justice, and now she was concerned with more than her lost home. She figured in her suffering from the eviction, which she believed also needed to be compensated, an issue we will return to shortly. Indeed, as far as Zhou was concerned, the dispute over her eviction was far from over. She had no doubt that her family needed a home and she would eventually get one, but not now, not with the 195,000 yuan. She counted on future concessions from the government to solve her housing problem once and for all.

For the moment, Zhou found better uses for the money. After repaying debts, she invested part of the money in the stock market and became one of the millions of retail shareholders in China. The Chinese stock market that emerged in the early 1990s has become a remarkable force that seduced almost everyone, with or mostly without any experience in stock trading. Neighborhood stock market branch offices grew rapidly, and by 2004, there were about five hundred such offices spread across Shanghai. Millions of people, who were retired, unemployed, or unemployable, found a new outlet for their time and energy, and also a new routine in their daily life. They go to the stock market in their neighborhood daily and form their own community. Some of these communities have sustained themselves for more than a decade. These small-time investors exchange information, compare notes about the market, discuss current affairs, or simply gossip to kill time. They are known as *gumin*, people of the stock market.

The stock market has politicized urban Chinese as never before. Because the market is influenced by many often fast-changing domestic and international developments, urban Chinese have become greatly interested in economic and legal policies and regulations, leadership changes at various levels of the government, new trends in the global market, and international affairs. They closely follow the news online and in the press and are well informed. But they are far from passive consumers of media. Because certain policy issues directly affect the value of their investments, shareholders constantly take a stand on what is right and wrong in policy and freely vent their discontent about the government, especially when the market is down. In short, they have developed an acute awareness of their own interests. The stock market office has thus become another new and politically charged institution of social interaction in urban China, where people form and share their critical opinions on the state.[32]

Zhou Youlan, well-informed on political matters from years of petitioning and certainly rights conscious, soon found she was right at home at the stock market office. With the 195,000 yuan payment, Zhou joined the ranks of the day traders, managing not only her own account but also those of her relatives. She had a fixed desk and computer in a room with about twenty other day traders at her neighborhood stock market branch office. Zhou kept her tea cup and other small personal things in the desk drawers, which somehow gave her a tangible sense of belonging there. "This is my desk, and these are my things that I keep here," she told me when I visited. The day traders in that room all knew each other. Zhou was comfortable with this environment where she spent most of her day. The job of a day trader is perfect for someone like Zhou who also happens to have other priorities in life. She was her own boss and could go and come as she wished, without any schedule issues. In fact, since 2001 Zhou has been both a day trader and a petitioner. She usually stays in the trading office when the market is up and petitions more frequently when it is down, a pattern even the local security office has found useful—they do not worry too much about Zhou's whereabouts if the market is doing well, but they watch her more carefully when the market heads south.

The Perpetual Petitioner

With an added routine in her life and her basic living expenses covered, Zhou Youlan restarted her petitioning in 2001. In a sense, the 195,000 yuan recharged her petition campaign. While the authorities were appalled that Zhou continued to make demands after accepting a settlement, she saw the matter differently. She considered the statement she signed for the 195,000 yuan to be a receipt, not a contract to settle everything. She argued that the payment was only for the "demolition and relocation," not for the "eviction," an unusual violation imposed on her family. Moreover, she pointed out that the amount was no longer enough to buy an apartment equivalent to the one she had lost. A common problem in housing redevelopment is that local government and developers often offer a below-market price for property that is to be demolished. If the residents refuse and the cases linger, the matter becomes complicated. As the market goes up, even the best offer from years ago is insufficient to purchase a comparable apartment unit. The problem is that the government argues that compensation should be based on the market price at the time the building was demolished and the residents insist on the market price when the case is settled, which can be years apart.

Besides, there are other matters to consider. For instance, Zhou argued that there should be a price tag attached to all her suffering caused by the eviction—her loss of job, salary, time, and peace at home, and her enduring the humiliation, abuse, violence, and emotional anguish involved in petitioning. Petitioners have developed a term for this emotional consideration: *xinli jiawei*, "psychological price mark" or "internal price mark." This "psychological price mark" is what petitioners believe to be a necessary part of a fair settlement. It figures in all of their losses directly and indirectly caused by the demolition, which could include all the costs of petitioning, from bus fare to meals and lodging expenses. It also includes emotional damage, especially when domicide is involved. In one of Zhou's petition letters, she made three requests as a condition for ending her petitioning, one of which was to "vent my years of grievances." But a monetary compensation for emotional distress is hard to estimate. Chinese culture and the legal system usually do not consider emotional suffering as a compensable damage. Suffering is part of life in the widespread teaching of Buddhism, and even a welcome necessity for character molding in the more pervasive doctrine of Confucianism.

Complicating the matter is that this "psychological price mark" is a moving target—if someone takes another petition trip or suffers another beating by the authorities, this price mark will go up. This is one of the reasons most petitioners have become meticulous in keeping a record of their experience, or a petition log, if you will, in the hope that someday every step in their journey as a petitioner will be acknowledged and validated by an all-inclusive compensation package.

For petitioners, the "psychological price mark" is also a bargaining chip not to be carelessly revealed to the authorities. To avoid being accused of "unreasonably demanding an exorbitant price," residents rarely volunteer their own price mark even when the authorities ask about it; they may hint at it but never give a clear amount, in order to see how far they can push. They feel that withholding their "psychological price mark" will give them an advantage as it keeps the authorities guessing and trying harder to meet their demands.

While petitioners consider this "psychological price mark" fully justified, the authorities reject it, fearing that there will be no end in sight once this

Pandora's Box is opened. This is one of the reasons that often keeps local officials and residents from reaching a final settlement, which has in turn produced long-term petitioners like Zhou Youlan. However, in some recent settlements, the authorities have been forced to accept the "psychological price mark" as a reality and include it in the compensation, without openly admitting its legitimacy. Such cases are common knowledge among petitioners. It is a game that both sides have learned to play.

The fact of the matter remains that residents are more likely to negotiate in good faith if treated fairly in the first place and are much more resistant to compromise once they suffer domicide and become seasoned petitioners. If they can sustain themselves, they often walk away from negotiations with the belief that the market will continue to go up and their continual petitioning will eventually yield a greater return, even a windfall. In this sense, for people like Zhou, petitioning, like stocks, is an investment expected to yield a return that will ensure them a future income and even a comfortable retirement. As long as they hold off from a final settlement, they believe their homes, though long demolished, are still on the market and that their market values will increase with each passing day. In cases like this, petitioners are very much in the driver's seat and the government loses the initiative unless it is willing to meet their psychological price mark.

The concept of "psychological price mark" essentially reflects a broader and deeper sense of justice that has emerged among petitioners. Educating themselves for years on issues concerning law and justice, including the justice system in the West, has taught them to value not only their property but also their dignity and other intangible but essential qualities as human beings that have been long repressed in Chinese society. Moreover, they have learned to connect their sense of justice with their own interest; thus they demand that the government pay for the damage it has done to them physically and emotionally.

In 2001 when Zhou restarted petitioning, this psychological price mark was very much on her mind. The district and municipal government offices considered her case closed and refused to reopen it, which did not surprise Zhou. But by this point she had become a less desperate and more resourceful petitioner, with a new take on justice. She states her logic for continuing to petition:

> I quit my job and petitioned full time, and held every district director's legs for four years. I petitioned weekly, three times a week, and struggled for four years. That's why in late 1999, they gave me 195,000 yuan; I signed a receipt, not a contract.

But now they say that the receipt is a contract, meaning that I agreed to give up my apartment for 195,000 yuan—but I didn't. Are all of the false contracts out there with signatures legal now? Cheating and lying to get a contract is legal?

Now they say that I've already got money, and that I'm just being unreasonable and making trouble. Is it ok if someone robs a bank and then returns the money? Is it ok if Chen Liangyu [former CCP party boss of Shanghai who is serving an eighteen-year prison sentence on corruption charges] returned all the money; will he be free and innocent? How is it ok that they demolished my house and then paid me so little after all my petitioning? Did the fact that they paid 195,000 [yuan] make it legal for them to destroy my home without my consent? What kind of law is that?

With this justification Zhou took her petition to another level. She had long ago learned about petitioning to the highest authorities in Beijing but had never tried it herself until September 2003. She has not stopped since. In the past nine years, Zhou has made it to Beijing at least five times a year, usually in March during the "two meetings," in early May on Labor Day, in July during the CCP's birthday, and in early October for National Day, as well as on other likely occasions, such as the CCP's Seventeenth National Congress in mid-October 2007. With few exceptions, those trips have led to detention and house arrest. Zhou has completed a full journey of petitioning through the Chinese bureaucratic hierarchy from the bottom to the top: the district, the municipal office, and finally to the State Council in Beijing, a predictable pattern for most long-term petitioners in China, with a predictable result: she has further hardened as her complaints go unresolved and as she has been repeatedly threatened and abused.

Zhou's journeys to Beijing are an elaborate adventure, full of plotting, covering up, detours, danger, and apprehension. The ordeal often lasts for two weeks to a month. Timing is everything. For instance, in order to reach the capital for the October 1 National Day, Zhou has to depart Shanghai in mid-September. Surveillance and checking is especially severe right before holidays and thus the earlier one goes the better one's chances of making it to Beijing. To avoid being picked up and sent back before the holidays, sometimes petitioners arrive in advance at small towns and cities around Beijing and then enter the city right before or during the holidays.

The first challenge, however, is to leave home without being detected. Ever since her initial petition trip to Beijing in 2003, the local authorities have identified Zhou as a target to keep an eye on. During sensitive dates when most petitioners flock to Beijing, the authorities intensify their surveillance of Zhou by sending guards to hold a stakeout in a small room across from her sister's home twenty-four hours a day and follow her every move; she is practically a prisoner in her own home. Under the circumstances, it is out of the question for her to leave home with any sign of a long-distance trip, such as a suitcase. Her trips have been arranged days earlier. Sometimes her daughter or sister will bring what she needs on the road in small installments to a friend's home for Zhou to gather, or they will deliver her stuff in a small bag to her at a meeting point in the city, and then Zhou can sneak out, usually at night.

Once Zhou manages to leave home, many things can still go wrong, derailing her trip. Fearing being intercepted on the way, she hardly ever takes the direct, most convenient train from Shanghai to Beijing. She studies train and bus schedules to work out the different legs of the trip. Often she takes a train or bus to one of the small cities near Shanghai from where she catches a train to a small station near Beijing where security is lax. At every stop, Zhou disappears among the travelers and spends a day or two to make sure she is not followed before embarking on the next leg. In time, as the Shanghai-Beijing railway line became intensely guarded by the authorities, some petitioners from Shanghai started to take more circuitous routes to places such as Wenzhou in Zhejiang Province, a relatively wealthy city with a vibrant mercantile culture where official surveillance is said to be relaxed since it has few petitioners. Poor areas such as those in Shandong Province are not ideal for detours or stopovers because the large number of local petitioners there keep the authorities on high alert.

Zhou Youlan's life on the road has been full of hardship. Getting to Beijing sometimes takes days, and Zhou gets little sleep or rest, not only because she has to stay alert all the time but also because she can only afford cheap motels where she shares a room with several people, sometimes without hot water in winter. Making a stop in small towns in rural areas, often purposefully arranged at midnight to avoid the authorities, is risky. Zhou also has had to prepare for unplanned stops in case she is followed. The thought that her life is in danger has never been far from her mind. She could also become a victim of crime—robbery, rape, even murder. Zhou trusts only her sister with her itinerary and calls her at every stop, "so that my family will at least know where and when I have disappeared if I stop calling," Zhou explains.

During her earlier trips, Zhou would look for a partner but never joined a group so as to avoid attention. The first time she went with a woman who had lost her job and home. The second time she identified a poverty-stricken man in the municipal petition office at Number 200 who had just returned from a trip to Beijing. Zhou offered to help with his travel expenses on their next trip in exchange for his companionship. She thought in this way if something happened to her, the man would report to her family, and also that a man would keep her safe. But when they stopped in a small city before their last leg to Beijing, the man attempted to extort money from Zhou, asking her to buy him a large quantity of expensive tea. Zhou's refusal caused a quarrel and the man then attempted to rape her. "I would rather die than give in to that," Zhou said. Eventually, Zhou was able to throw him off and found herself a separate motel for the night. But that encounter raised enough of a red flag that she has been content to travel alone on subsequent trips.

Once Zhou has arrived in Beijing and found herself an inexpensive motel, she first goes out to copy her material—her petition letter, pictures of her home, documents about the demolition, and previous responses from various petition offices—and then she sends that information via registered mail to all relevant government offices. Originally, she had sent those materials from Shanghai but became convinced that local authorities were blocking delivery. She then kills some time, waiting for her letters to arrive before going to those offices in person. In fact, she has to protect herself to make sure that she will eventually be able to register at the various petition offices in the capital before being sent back.

Petitioners all know that the moment they show up in petition offices in Beijing is the moment that their home authorities will catch them and take them back. There are a variety of ways this takes place. Zhou's first trip to Beijing was in the middle of September 2003, prior to the National Day of October 1. She and other petitioners from Shanghai found a motel for 15 yuan a night, but the price was hiked to 40 yuan on the eve of the National Day. Zhou and other petitioners sent representatives to the Ministry of Construction to ask for reasonable lodging arrangements. The ministry put them up in another motel specially reserved for petitioners, which was in fact a mechanism to control their whereabouts, and which also meant that their whereabouts were known to the retrievers from their respective hometowns. Not surprisingly, Zhou and the others never got to spend the night at that motel. By 9:30 p.m., their hometown police came to round them up. Those from Shanghai, a total of eight-five people, were loaded into five buses and driven back to Shanghai overnight in a twenty-hour journey. The second time, Zhou and other petitioners were "invited" to lunch by Shanghai officials while waiting outside a petition office in Beijing. Again, they were put on a bus and taken to the railway station to board an evening train back to Shanghai. After those two incidents, Zhou learned to refuse any official arrangement for lodging and meals in Beijing before she reached the petition offices.

Petitioning in Beijing is an eye-opening experience for first-timers like Zhou. On Zhou's first trip, for instance, she joined hundreds of petitioners from all over China, with about two hundred from Shanghai, in a sit-in in the front of the petition office of the Ministry of Construction. They sang "The Internationale" and shouted slogans such as "Down with corruption! Down with corrupt officials! Long live people united from around the world!" As curious Beijing residents approached them, the petitioners tried to rally their support by shouting slogans such as "We salute the people of Beijing!" On another trip, Zhou went to the petition office of the State Council and witnessed thousands of people lined up on either side of the road leading up to the office. In the office, Zhou met about two hundred fellow petitioners from Shanghai. Some officials from Shanghai were waiting inside and asked Zhou and others to talk outside the office—they will not use force openly outside petition offices in the capital. But the petitioners insisted on registering in the office first which, as mentioned earlier, they consider to be a small victory in their war with local governments. Since the possibility of real success—having their grievances addressed—is so remote, they have to settle for whatever satisfaction they can get.

Earlier on, all of the Shanghai petitioners who were brought back from Beijing were kept at one site. But the authorities soon realized that having a large group of mostly ornery people in one place spelled trouble. Once, the detainees started a hunger strike. The government's new strategy was to divide them by sending them back to their respective districts, which would then decide where to keep them. After they were released, these petitioners would again meet at Number 200, where they would compare notes about their experiences. The fact that some districts with more resources put their detainees up in decent motels while other, poorer districts held their detainees in rundown basements often generated new complaints.

Indeed, when people are transferred into the custody of their neighborhood police, the conditions under which they are detained and the length of detention can vary. On her first trip to Beijing, Zhou was brought back to Shanghai and kept for almost a month. The reason petitioners like Zhou are detained for such a long time is that many of them are so defiant and determined that, if not closely watched, they will turn around and catch the next train back to Beijing. Also, for week-long events such as the two March meetings, officials want to hold petitioners until the events are over. The first time Zhou was kept in a basement where each of the petitioners, watched over by guards in three shifts, had his or her own room. She was followed even when she went to the toilet. She was given food but had no shower for days at a time. On one occasion, Zhou and others at a detention site were awakened at night by the police who wanted them to watch as seven of their fellow petitioners were handcuffed and taken away for more severe punishment, a tactic intended to intimidate the rest of them.

Zhou herself has been beaten while in detention and has also been kidnapped several times. In a letter to the United Nation's Human Rights Council, she recounted two incidents that took place in 2006:

> On May 30, 2006, when I was petitioning in Beijing, retrievers from the Shanghai government kidnapped me from my motel and took me to a hotel in Yonganmen, Beijing. This hotel has been used by the retrievers to detain petitioners from Shanghai, and thirty-six of them were there on that day. I saw several retrievers holding a woman's hands and beating her. I could not help but shout: "Don't press her hands!" Immediately, two special task policemen dragged me to a vehicle with the license plate of [Bei]Jing HR-6359 parked outside. They handed me to a man named Xu. Xu claimed to be from the petition office of the State Council. In his twenties, he is big and strong. Xu started slapping my face hard left and right about a dozen times while forbidding me from screaming and crying. He is so young that he could have been my son. But he beat me, a fifty-five-year old woman who is 150 cm [4'11"] tall. Where's the justice? I was sent back to Shanghai and detained for two more days.

> I was kidnapped on the eve of the Shanghai Cooperation Organization Summit on June 15. At 23:15 while I was sleeping, seven people, four men and three women, broke into the house and took me from my bed to a police car, without showing any identification. My family told them that kidnapping was illegal. One of the men responded, "We are carrying out an order." This incident took place in this so-called "harmonious society." They kept me on the fourth floor of Nanya Hotel near the Nanpu Bridge. The fourth floor is specially set up for detaining petitioners. The floor was barred with a locked iron door on either end. Six security guards watched us. They did not release me until the Summit was over.[33]

Officials usually try to take advantage of petitioners in detention as their freedom is at stake. Once Zhou was detained for two weeks during which time the authorities took turns intimidating her. They wanted to know about her activities in Beijing. "I told them what I did. I didn't do anything illegal and I have nothing to hide," she said. As a condition for her release, they demanded she sign a statement that she would never again go to Beijing to petition, which Zhou refused. She often watched other petitioners leaving for home after signing such statements, but she herself did not give in. Zhou understood that it was a test of willpower and that the officials could not hold her forever and would eventually release her.

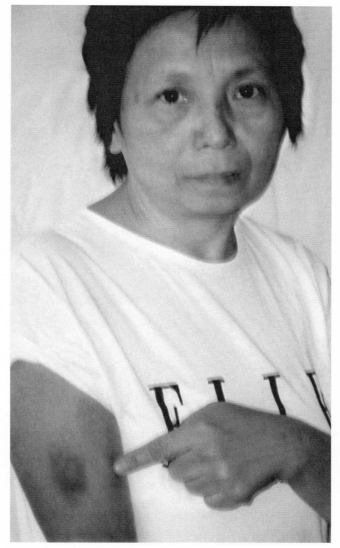

Figure 1.3. Zhou Youlan was beaten during one of the detention periods and suffered bruises.

Such encounters almost always present an opportunity for negotiations. When Zhou was in detention, the authorities posed some deceptively innocent questions: "What do you want? How much do you want?" Zhou has nothing but contempt for such questions: "Don't they know what I've gone through?" Instead of giving them a straight answer, she would say, "Compensation for all my losses resulting from your illegal eviction," and "Treating my case fairly, reasonably, and legally." These were the code words for the ever-elusive psychological price mark. In time, such exchanges became an all too familiar game that only intensified mutual distrust and made a potential solution even more remote.

Because of Zhou's persistent petitioning in Beijing, the local authorities have been under pressure from their superiors to deal with her case. Once after one of her Beijing trips, a dozen officials from the municipal petition office, the district court, lawyers, the district housing bureau, the demolition office, and the neighborhood committee gathered to meet with her. Zhou presented her case, and as usual she accused the district of illegally evicting her family and leveling her home. Throughout the meeting, what Zhou wanted first was for the authorities to admit their mistakes and apologize to her, but she never got that. In the end, all the officials present signed a paper to testify that a meeting with Zhou had indeed taken place and asked Zhou to do the same, so that they could report to their superiors that they had fulfilled their responsibility, but Zhou refused. "They continued to gang up on me and deny their mistakes. Why should I accept such a meeting?" As a result, Zhou continues her petitioning.

Hide and Seek

Zhou Youlan's repeated petition trips to Beijing have become a major headache for the local authorities who are primarily responsible for keeping her at home. They use a carrot and stick approach.

Around sensitive holidays, the authorities watch her all day and night, sometimes in a comic way. In the morning when Zhou went out to empty her chamber pot—the family lives in an old neighborhood without indoor plumbing—the guards immediately approached her to check on her schedule for the day: "Where are you going today? What are your plans?" "I don't know yet," Zhou replied. Then they followed her to the market when she did her daily grocery shopping, and sometimes even offered to do the shopping for her to make sure that she did not slip away. The guards would also follow her in a car and offer to give her a ride when she went out: "Where are you going? We can take you there." The surveillance might also be in the form of telephone calls. The minders would call her every half hour asking her whereabouts. "Is this 'asking for instructions in the morning and reporting in the afternoon'?" Zhou Youlan would reply. This reference is to a ritual during the Cultural Revolution that reinforced the Mao cult, often carried out collectively at work units, where groups of people bowed to Mao's portrait and recited Mao's quotations in the morning and afternoon. At the end of sensitive periods, officials call to inform her that the surveillance is over.

If the minders do not see Zhou for a day or two, especially in the afternoon when the stock market closes and Zhou is expected to return home, they come to knock on the door, insisting on information about Zhou. If the family claims it does not know where she is, the authorities harass her husband to investigate when and how his wife has left home.

Hounded by these "dogs," who sometimes park their car outside her home, which often invites the neighbors' gossip and unwanted attention, Zhou tries to confuse the surveillance team by going out randomly—and the "dogs" follow. Often when Zhou went to her neighborhood stock market, the car would park outside and one of the "dogs" would come inside with her. The same thing happened when she went to Number 200. When other petitioners greeted her, she would signal that she was followed to warn them. Those petitioners, most of whom have had the same experience, would try to help her get rid of her "tail." Once Zhou met another petitioner on the street and both of them were being followed. They greeted each other by saying "We now have our own body guards." Even the staff at Number 200 advised Zhou to elude her minders.

Once a group of petitioners accompanied Zhou to a busy taxi stand and tried to get her a taxi to throw off the minders. But three men who had been following her grabbed the door and got in despite her protests. On that occasion Zhou asked to go to the Shanghai municipal library where she entered with her identification card but the "dogs," who did not carry their identification cards, were stopped by the doormen. "They're following me!" Zhou shouted in the library. "I wanted everyone at the library to know that I don't have personal freedom," Zhou told me. The men eventually showed their security passes and got in; one watched Zhou in the reading room while the other two stayed in the hallway. At the library Zhou read materials on law and regulations, and copied relevant pages to study at home. She stayed in the library until dark to avoid being seen by the neighbors when she returned with the "dogs." During lunch time, the three men took turns having lunch yet offered Zhou nothing. She later complained to the staff at Number 200 that she was deprived of lunch while under surveillance. Her logic was that the officials were responsible for her lunch since they forced her to wander around. But another time Zhou refused when offered lunch. "I was afraid of eating their food. Who knows? What if there was poison in it?" Zhou had good reason to be concerned. After the library visit, the surveillance team gave her a ride to her home. But she no longer accepts such rides after the authorities tried once again to kidnap her. They would have succeeded if not for her sister rushing out and screaming for help. Zhou now insists that a taxi take her home, and that the surveillance team pay for the taxi. Zhou said that her aim is to escape and if that fails, then she wants to make the officials pay a price, whether with a taxi fare or their time, which gives her a sense of being in control.

One thing Zhou now always carries with her is her personal identification card, which allows her to get into the library or rent a hotel room. One of the "carrots" the neighborhood committee has offered is to reimburse her travel expenses, which requires her to produce her bus and train tickets. Zhou has declined: "Those tickets would reveal the routes and the detours I took. I can't let that happen. I've got to protect my routes for future trips."

Ironically, as adamant as Zhou is about petitioning in Beijing, she is realistic enough to understand that it is not Beijing, but the local district and the Shanghai government that can solve her problem. The fact is that petitioners like Zhou have no leverage against the local governments that have abused them. The only way they feel they can exert some pressure on them is to go to Beijing. They hope that their petitioning in Beijing will send a message to both the local and central governments that their cases need to be solved.

After more than fifteen years of struggle, Zhou feels as strongly as ever about her rights and has found even more reason to continue petitioning:

> Asked what my demands are, I would say: I want my house. My family of three has no place to live. Early in spring 2007, my daughter slept on the small loft above my bed. One night she fell down and broke a rib. She is now afraid of going up there. So my husband slept there instead. But on September 23, 2007, he also fell from the stairs leading up to the loft; he was bruised all over his body. Three days later he suffered a stroke and became incontinent. He was hospitalized for fifteen days, which cost 10,669.30 yuan . . . I've got records of all this.

> For more than a decade I've petitioned every week, often three times a week. I had no income after quitting my job until I retired when I was fifty years old, and then I got 800 yuan a month retirement pay.

> On September, 29, 2007, prior to the National Day and the CCP's Seventeenth National Congress, the deputy director of the neighborhood police brought me to the station and videotaped me as soon as I walked in. They gave me a notice to read and asked me to promise not to go to Beijing during the meeting, or I would be detained.

> I said that petitioning is my right; if I want to go, I don't need to tell you, and I can go any time I want. Since the petition offices in Beijing are open, why can't I go? Do the petition offices have handcuffs waiting at the door to lock up anyone who walks in? Are the petition offices there a trap? I don't think so. Then why can't I go? My petition has nothing to do with the meeting; it's a normal petition!

Going Mental?

In spring 2009, a small storm of words touched down in the media in China involving a renowned professor and petitioners. In an interview with *Zhong-guo xinwen zhoukan* (China News Week) published on March 23, Sun Dongdong, a psychology professor at the Law School of Beijing University who served on the advisory board of China's Ministry of Health and also on court cases to evaluate defendants' mental status, made some comments about petitioners:

> I can state responsibly that 99 percent of long-term occupational petitioners suffer from obsessive-compulsive behavior . . . They are mentally disabled and delusional. They keep petitioning at all costs, including their family. If you look into their cases, you would find their issues have been solved or they never had any case to begin with. But they stubbornly insist on their position and keep making trouble, regardless of how well you explain [the situation] to them. The media's concern about whether the rights of those petitioners are violated is in fact a reflection of its lack of basic knowledge about mental health issues.[34]

When asked what to do with those "obsessive-compulsive" people and whether it was appropriate to force them into treatment like other mental patients since they otherwise seem to be entirely normal, Sun responded that not all crazy people "look crazy," but "since their behavior disturbs social order, treatment needs to be imposed upon them,"[35] which Sun emphasized was the best way to protect their "human rights."[36]

Sun's remarks quickly spread through the media like wild fire, with provocative headlines such as "Beijing University Professor Sun Dongdong: 99% Petitioners Are Mentally Ill."[37] The blogosphere had a field day. Some well-known authors, lawyers, social activists, media commentators, scholars, and bloggers criticized Sun for "abusing petitioners and disrespecting their dignity." They questioned whether Sun is a "normal person" himself with "a basic sense of legal justice and human rights protection."[38] Sun became a laughingstock. One blogger wrote: "Petition offices have checked petitioners but found few mental patients among them. For instance, there are no mentally disabled among the six thousand petitioners in Xuzhou [a city in Jiangsu Province] or among the three thousand petitioners in Changsha [a city in Hunan Province]." Bloggers demanded Sun apologize, called for his resignation from Beijing University, and even suggested having him committed to a mental hospital so that he would not further "trash innocent people."[39] Since Sun was also one of the members of the committee entrusted by the Chinese

Ministry of Health with drafting the Law on Mental Health, some bloggers deemed that Sun was tainted and should be stripped of his position on the committee.[40] While a few bloggers tried to defend Sun's right to express himself, they also pointed out that Sun had become a scapegoat for corrupt officials who were truly responsible for the petitioners' and general public's anger.[41] But the blogosphere is unanimous in recognizing the distortion in Sun's remarks.

However, as one might expect, the strongest protest to Sun's comments by far comes from the community of petitioners themselves. Various petition offices were flooded with letters condemning Sun's remarks. On April 1, around forty petitioners marched to the campus of Beijing University and demanded a "dialogue" with Sun on the issue of "whether long-term petitioners are mentally ill." Some of them were stopped at the gate and others were dragged off of the campus by security guards, who, incidentally, denied that Sun was on the faculty. These petitioners thought about holding a sit-in on the campus, and mobilizing petitioners nationwide to sue Sun for damaging their reputations. What they wanted was for Sun to provide evidence for his statement. One angry petitioner declared, "If your home is being demolished, you're being robbed, and you had death in the family [as a result of the demolition], you have to be crazy not to petition. Sun Dongdong must be crazy [to think anything is wrong with our petitioning], and we should evaluate *his* mental state instead."[42]

Under tremendous pressure, Sun on April 6 broke his silence and issued a brief apology via the Chinese official Xinhua News website, stating that he was deeply sorry for the uproar and misunderstanding caused by his inappropriate remarks. He apologized for hurting "some people's feelings" and hoped they would "solve their issues through the legal channels." Sun promised to reflect on this incident, and be careful about his words in the future so that he could contribute to "social stability and harmony."[43] His apology satisfied neither the media nor the petitioners; both groups questioned its sincerity and substance.[44]

While the definition, diagnosis, and treatment of the mentally ill have historically been arbitrary and political charged, in fact an instrument of the powerful against the powerless, the volatile reaction to Sun's comments had deep roots in the public awareness that authorities often use mental illness as an excuse to ignore petitioners or forcibly commit them, a fact that had been exposed but not critically examined in the media.

A telling fact in this regard is that the public security bureau in various cities has its own mental institutions mainly to deal with people identified as a threat to social stability, including petitioners. Such facilities are not independent, professional care centers. A major difference between a public security bureau–run mental institution and a professional one is that the former can commit a person without the consent of that person or his/her family and without going through the court procedure. Such institutions are also closed to the media and public and are completely under the control of the security apparatus as part of its mechanism for maintaining social order—they have license to do anything in the name of social order.[45] Some online reports indicate that public security bureau–run mental institutions are dark and dirty places where illegal handling of and violent crime against petitioners routinely take place.[46]

Such incidents sometimes are reported. For instance, in October 2008, a villager in Xintai County, Shandong Province, named Sun was seized by the township government during one of his petition trips and sent straight to a mental facility for twenty days. He was released only after he promised to end his petitioning. Apparently several of Sun's fellow petitioners were also kept in the same facility.[47] In Heilongjiang Province, local authorities put a female petitioner in a mental institution for two years where her three roommates were accused of murder. The condition for her release, according to the local authorities, was for her to give up petitioning.[48] Zhou Youlan herself was often called "crazy" by the authorities, and she also knows personally some petitioners who were treated as mental patients. One of them, named Liu, is a divorced woman who happens to have a family history of mental illness. After her eviction, she started petitioning together with other evictees from her community and was detained regularly. In October 2007 after one of her petition trips to Beijing, the authorities declared Liu mentally ill and detained her in an isolated site in Pudong for more than a month.

The other issue underlining the strong reaction to Sun Dongdong's remarks is that the mentally disabled are generally discriminated against in Chinese society, especially by the government. That mental illness is considered dismissible is evidenced by the fact that sometimes the government uses it to cover up other issues in order to avoid dealing with them. For instance, in summer 2009, 1,200 workers in a textile mill in the industrial city of Jilin in northeastern China fell ill with the same symptoms—nausea, vomiting, blurry vision, muscle spasms, convulsions, and partial and temporary paralysis—and they came to the hospital in droves. The textile mill was located downwind from a chemical plant. Since the outbreak of the symptoms began shortly after the plant opened, many people suspected chemical poison as the culprit. But a team of public health experts from Beijing concluded that instead of actual pollution, it was the fear of pollution that caused the illness. With this diagnosis of a communal outbreak of mass hysteria, these experts closed the case with their prescription: "Get a hold of your emotions."[49] It did not occur to the experts and the authorities that even if this illness was indeed mass hysteria, it was still a serious public health issue to be investigated and that the 1,200 patients needed more help than being left to just tough it out on their own.

Because of the Chinese government's approach to mental illness—dismissing the real patients yet using mental illness as a means to forcibly commit petitioners—some bloggers believe that Sun's characterization of petitioners was used to help justify the government's illegal handling of them.[50] Authorities certainly welcomed Sun's comments. Yu Jianrong, the director of the Institute of Rural Development at the Chinese Academy of Social Sciences in Beijing, revealed in an open critique of Sun's comments a letter from some petition officials in support of Sun's view. According to Yu, Sun's remarks pandered to the official position. For years Yu himself and his Institute have actually investigated the petition issue, especially among rural Chinese, which we will return to shortly, and he challenged Sun's findings: "How exactly have they [petitioners] threatened social stability? Their only stubbornness is in that they carry their petition material and go to the petition office daily." Yu considered the impact of Sun's remarks on the socially disadvantaged: "What if now the authorities [based on Sun's 'expert opinion'] openly arrest and commit petitioners as a legal act? Many people could end up in jail." He emphasized that scholars have a social responsibility to be partial to the powerless, especially when the issue is as complicated as petitioners' mental states.[51]

To be sure, while Sun Dongdong's remarks were inflammatory, he certainly was not the only or the first one to raise the issue of petitioners' mental health. There is a general public perception that persistent petitioners are somewhat mentally problematic, which is reflected in a new phrase, *lao shangfang jingshenbing*, literally "long-term petitioners' mental illness."[52] However, similar to the way Americans use the phrase "you're crazy" as just a joke or even as a term of endearment, Chinese often use the term *jingshenbing*, mental illness, in casual conversation to refer to any behavior one does not quite like. But the term can also refer to serious mental illness. The phrase "long-term petitioners' mental illness" thus is popular psychology at best and certainly not a professional diagnosis, which is part of the problem—a public perception that may reflect a degree of reality with regard to a mental health condition that affects a disproportionate number of disadvantaged people in Chinese society has received scant official and professional attention. The questions therefore remain: Are there any real issues about the mental state of petitioners, such as Zhou Youlan? If there are, then what are they and what is the relationship between petitioners' mental issues and their petitioning? Did the former lead to the latter or the other way around?

Although addressing these issues fully requires an elaborate study, suffice it to point out that the forcible destruction of one's home, as in the case of domicide, is a traumatic experience. It is one of the most legitimate sources of emotional distress and can lead to chronic depression and PTSD. That petitioners themselves have developed the term "psychological price mark" is telling in studying their emotional state. They are deprived of the life they know—a familiar built environment, social and cultural roots, community ties, and often personal belongings—factors that are essential to a stable and meaningful life. They become rootless and lose their routine and focus. The emotional impact of such dislocation is compounded by the injustice generated in domicide where deliberate human effort and violence are involved.[53]

As mentioned in the introduction, the acute and potentially chronic emotional damage resulting from eviction has been documented in the anthropologist David Vine's study of the Chagossians of Diego Garcia, a British colonial island in the Indian Ocean. They have suffered from *sagren*, the deep melancholy associated with the loss of a homeland.[54] But they have never given up their hope of returning home and have brought the British government to court to appeal for justice.

Despite the differences in the specifics, the Chagossians' case sheds light on that of long-term Chinese petitioners in at least two respects. First, these Chagossians have waged a marathon, uphill battle against a powerful nation for reparations with the ultimate goal of returning home. Time—more than half a century in this case—and the tremendous difficulty of the struggle have not eroded either their longing for their home or their demand for justice, much like persistent Chinese petitioners. Second, the pain of being dispossessed of their homeland has caused the islanders to suffer from a potentially deadly depression. Whether some of the Chinese petitioners suffer from as severe a mental disease as *sagren* remains unknown. But petitioners like Zhou Youlan are clearly under constant emotional stress. They are entrapped by their initial traumatic experience of domicide and then re-traumatized by government's prolonged stonewalling. Yet their mental health has largely been ignored.

Appropriate treatment of emotional stress and PTSD varies from person to person. Experts differ on whether dwelling on one's problems or quickly moving on with life is the best coping mechanism. But they all share the understanding, which has in fact become common sense, at least in most Western cultures, that those who suffer from trauma should have a chance to mourn, express their grief, and repair the harm in order to restore their lives. Judith Herman, a Harvard M.D., for instance, points out in her classic study of trauma and recovery that recognition—public acknowledgment of the trauma—and restitution—assigning responsibility for the harm to repair the injury—are essential steps to recovery.[55]

Long-term Chinese petitioners are denied both. Take Zhou Youlan for example. After watching her home being destroyed and her belongings being shipped elsewhere, she hardly had any opportunity to mourn the loss, much less to repair the injury. What she wanted at the time was for the authorities to listen to her grievances and admit their mistakes. That was why initially she kept going to the home of the district demolition head; she just wanted to vent and to have her feelings validated. Instead, she came away not only disappointed, but further humiliated. More than a decade later, the authorities still insist that the eviction was legal and therefore just. Zhou never got an acknowledgment of the injustice done to her. As such, there is no restitution either—no one takes responsibility for what happened to her. Her sense of justice and trust in the system has been crushed.

Furthermore, after her eviction, she lost not only her home but all of her belongings, with nothing "normal" or familiar to restart life. She stayed in temporary housing and then moved in with her sister in a tiny room, with a broken bed and a damaged loft. Such a situation was hardly a starting point to normalcy, as everything around her reminded her of her "pathetic life." With few positive things to focus on, she began petitioning as a way of mourning. In time, petitioning became a new focus and routine in her life. The violence the government inflicted on her through detention and beating has taken a toll on her and she has become increasingly aggressive herself. All this has led her to pursue an even deeper path of petitioning, which in turn has resulted in more abuse—a vicious cycle. This repeated traumatization is not uncommon for many victims because, as Herman points out, the legal system is often partial to the powerful.[56] By the time in 1999 that Zhou received some compensation and established a new routine as a day trader, she had already gone too far as an ardent petitioner. The long-term psychological damage was done and the traumatic effects perpetuate themselves. According to Herman, "a hostile or negative response may compound the damage and aggravate the traumatic syndrome."[57] Indeed, if Zhou is obsessed with petitioning, it is because the hostile environment surrounding her has provided little incentive for her to heal.

That the petition system is responsible for petitioners' mental stress is reflected in one of the numerous popular jingles that the Chinese regularly create with "burning satire and freezing irony" to attack corruption and other deplorable social phenomena in today's China. The jingle is built on the words "in" and "out" and uses analogy to illustrate how the Chinese system has inherent deficiencies that ruin people's lives. For instance, on education, one "goes in with hope and comes out with despair"; on hospitals, one "goes in with minor discomfort and comes out with deadly diseases"; for official posts, one "goes in as Hai Rui [an exemplary 'blue sky' official of the Ming dynasty] and comes out as He Shen [a notoriously crooked official in the Qing dynasty]." As for petitioners, the jingle describes that they "go in as Dou E and come out as madmen."[58] Dou E is a tragic character in one of Guan Hanqing's famous plays written in the Yuan dynasty (1271–1368). The play, *The Injustice to Dou E*, is about a young woman named Dou E who, falsely accused of murder, was executed by a corrupt official. The Dou E analogy effectively portrays how the petition system has driven innocent petitioners into madness. A blogger also sheds light on the phenomenon of "long-term petitioners' mental illness": "Most petitioners, when they started, were just regular people. But the government pushes their problems around without any resolution and, in time, those issues become a huge headache no one wants to handle. Petitioners have no place to appeal their cases. Naturally, they are exhausted physically and mentally. Such a long struggle will of course have a psychological impact on petitioners."[59]

Amen to that.

Moment of Inertia

Yu Jianrong, the director of the Institute of Rural Development whom we mentioned earlier, has done an in-depth investigation of the petition system through surveys and other means, mainly because prominent among the petitioners are peasants. In late 2004, his officially sponsored research project produced a report that recommended the elimination of the petition system altogether. His argument is both compelling and obvious: the system simply does not work. Among the 2,000 cases he studied, only three were resolved, no thanks to the institutional mechanism but because certain powerful individuals, "blue sky" officials, took an interest in them. He further points out the inherent flaw in the petition system that renders it useless—the lack of the authority needed to resolve the issues brought to the petition offices. And according to Yu, the petition system highlights the failure of the law and thus severely diminishes the authority of the law, since the legal system is supposed to deal with most of the issues raised by petitioners. In other words, the petition system reinforces the notion that China continues to be a society ruled by man, not by law.[60] Thus Yu deems the petition system to be not only useless, but also harmful.

Yu's research was part of the process the State Council initiated to review and revise the 1995 Regulations on Petitioning. As the publication of the 2005 Regulations indicates, the central government rejected Yu's suggestion to abolish the system. In fact, his proposal caused a heated debate in China. In the face of the continuing spread of corruption and weak enforcement of the law, the petition system at least channels popular complaints and gives the illusion of hope to people—airing social grievances helps defuse destructive emotions and providing an illusion of hope is a way to sustain hope. That so many petitioners have patiently appealed their cases for years to no avail is evidence of this point. In other words, the petition system, while it does not solve these cases, has nevertheless helped absorb the tension generated by the reform, at least temporarily. Also, the hundreds of thousands of officials and staff involved in the petition system depend on it for their positions and jobs. Many of the petitioners I talked to are convinced that those officials and staff are in no rush to resolve their cases.

Opposition to ending the petition system has also come from unlikely sources, such as petitioners themselves, who have complained about and suffered from its failure. The meaning of petitioning for petitioners is a subject that deserves more attention. Many petitioners have endured not only domicide, but also the loss of loved ones, family, jobs, and other sources of focus in life that are imperative to their physical and emotional well-being. Their quotidian lives have been shattered as has their sense of dignity, trust, and justice. Yet society has refused to even acknowledge their loss, and thus has denied them the necessary space and opportunity to openly and legitimately mourn that loss and heal. It is often out of utter despair that they embark on a petition trip, which many of them refer to as "a road with no return," a reflection of both their determination to pursue justice and the ineptitude of the system.

For many of them, petitioning has become not only a channel to seek justice but also an interactive ritual for mourning, and a passage to restoring normalcy in life, or the hope of it. They have incorporated petitioning into their daily routine. On certain weekdays they go to visit local petition offices; and during certain times of the year, March for instance, they go to Beijing. They have formed their own community where they meet and chat with friends and acquaintances. In this long journey, some of them have given up hope but cannot admit defeat. They cannot afford to lose yet another focus in life. So they press on. Asked about the idea of abolishing the petition system, Zhou Youlan answered with a question, "Then what do I do?"—they have no alternative, much less a valid alternative; the petition system has become a trap from which they see no way out.

Indeed, people petition for various reasons in addition to seeking a solution to their immediate grievances. Petitioning takes place in different political systems, including Western democracy. Petitioning itself may not necessarily compromise the law, as some scholars have pointed out; it could be a complement to the legal framework and a channel for political participation. Chinese petitioners, collectively and individually, have, as we will see from the chapters to follow, achieved some results. But there should be little doubt that the epidemic of institutional corruption in China has created a dysfunctional petition system that has left both parties involved—the government and the petitioners—frustrated but dependent on it and on each other. This co-dependence perpetuates a life of its own. The system will either be improved by a determined, thorough reform within the political machine to rid itself of corruption or else corruption will erode the machine itself. Until then, the system will find abundant institutional debris to sustain its inertia and justify its existence as a futile but necessary outlet for popular discontent in this transitional period of Chinese society.

Notes

1. See a selected list of more than thirty such documents and directives issued between 1996 and 2005 in Zhongguo fazhi chubanshe (Law Press of China), ed. "*Xinfang tiaoli*" *yibentong* (Comprehensive Reading of "Regulations on Petitioning") (Beijing: Zhongguo fazhi chubanshe, 2005), 276–80.

2. Cao Kangtai and Wang Xuejun, eds., *Xinfang taoli fudao duben* (Supplemental Reading to "Regulations on Petitioning") (Beijing: Zhongguo fazhi chubanshe, 2005), 21.

3. Cao and Wang, *Xinfang taoli fudao duben*, 349.

4. Cao and Wang, *Xinfang taoli fudao duben*, 16.

5. Cao and Wang, *Xinfang taoli fudao duben*, 16.

6. *Qingnian cankao* (Elite Reference), 12 May 2004: A13–14.

7. http://www.azcentral.com/news/articles/2010/01/20/20100120china-killer-hero.html, accessed 21 January 2010.

8. Cao and Wang, *Xinfang taoli fudao duben*, 15.

9. That petitioners in Beijing try to ride on public transportation without paying is well-known. I witnessed such an incident on a trip to Beijing in mid-June 2010.

10. http://www.ce.cn/bjnews/zhengzhi/news/200701/25/t20070125_10206365.shtml; http://blog.sina.com.cn/s/blog_47010341010007gd.html; http://tt.mop.com/read_242264_1_0.html, accessed 27 August 2012.

11. http://ent9.com/forum.php?mod=viewthread&tid=267591&highlight=, accessed 27 August 2012.

12. http://www.nytimes.com/2011/08/14/world/asia/14filmmaker.html?pagewanted=2, accessed 14 August 2011.

13. Cao and Wang, *Xinfang taoli fudao duben*, 15–16.

14. Cao and Wang, *Xinfang taoli fudao duben*, 19, 23, 27–30.

15. Cao and Wang, *Xinfang taoli fudao duben*, 25–27.

16. Yongshun Cai, "Local Governments and the Suppression of Popular Resistance in China," *China Quarterly* 193 (March 2008): 24–42.

17. http://www.nytimes.com/2011/03/08/opinion/08iht-edcohen08.html?nl=todaysheadlines& emc=tha212, accessed 8 March 2011.

18. "Seeking Gao Zhisheng," *Wall Street Journal*, 11 January 2011: A16.

19. http://www.hrw.org/en/news/2009/11/02/china-secret-black-jails-hide-severe-rights-abuses; http://www.time.com/time/world/article/0,8599,1938515,00.html; http://news.bbc.co.uk/2/hi/8356095.stm; http://www.spectator.co.uk/essays/all/247856/the-terrible-secrets-of-beijings-black-jails.thtml, accessed 12 May 2010.

20. http://www.time.com/time/world/article/0,8599,1938515,00.html, accessed 14 January 2011.

21. http://globalvoicesonline.org/2011/02/18/china-petitioner-burns-down-his-black-prison/, accessed 18 July 2011.

22. http://www.nytimes.com/2011/08/14/world/asia/14filmmaker.html?pagewanted=2, accessed 14 August 2011.

23. http://www.nytimes.com/2010/12/29/world/asia/29china.html?_r=1&emc=etal, accessed 3 January 2011.

24. http://www.nytimes.com/2011/12/17/world/asia/wukan-revolt-takes-on-a-life-of-its-own.html?pagewanted=2&emc=etal, accessed 20 December 2011.

25. Cao and Wang, *Xinfang taoli fudao duben*, 25, 351–52.

26. http://news.sina.com.cn/c/2004-11-17/15374946096.shtml, accessed 20 December 2011.

27. Daniel P. Carpenter, "The Petition as a Recruitment Device: Evidence from the Abolitionists' Congressional Campaign," unpublished manuscript, http://people.hmdc.harvard.edu/~dcarpent/petition-recruit-20040112.pdf.

28. http://news.xinhuanet.com/english2010/china/2011-01/26/c_13707506_2.htm; http://www.guardian.co.uk/world/2011/jan/26/wen-jiabao-visits-china-complaints-department, accessed 28 January 2011.

29. http://www.blogchina.com/authorEdit/articleCommentAll.php?id=1015228, accessed 10 August 2011; http://blog.sina.com.cn/s/blog_99d8ddff01016iex.html, accessed 3 September 2012.

30. Nanshi District became part of Huangpu District in 2000.

31. Keith Richards, *Life* (New York: Little, Brown, 2010), 225.

32. For a detailed analysis of neighborhood stock market offices and their political implications, see Qin Shao, "A Community of the Dispersed: The Culture of Neighborhood Stock Markets in Contemporary Shanghai," *Chinese Historical Review* 14.2 (Fall, 2007): 212–39.

33. On the summit meeting, see http://www.gov.cn/misc/2006-06/16/content_312429.htm, accessed 22 April 2009.

34. http://wuxizazhi.cnki.net/Search/XWZK200910014.html, accessed 1 November 2012.

35. http://news.163.com/09/0404/05/561IOQ950001124J.html, accessed 22 April 2009.

36. http://www.wefweb.com/news/200946/1001386501_4.shtml, accessed 22 April 2009.

37. http://news.163.com/09/0404/05/561IOQ950001124J.html, accessed 22 April 2009.

38. http://www.wefweb.com/news/200946/1001386501_4.shtml, accessed 22 April 2009.

39. http://www.wefweb.com/news/200946/1001386501_0.shtml, accessed 22 April 2009.

40. http://epaper.oeeee.com/A/html/2009-04-08/content_753020.htm, accessed 22 April 2009.

41. http://focus.cnhubei.com/original/200904/t645442.shtml, accessed 22 April 2009.

42. http://www.dw-world.de/dw/article/0,4149437,00.html, accessed 22 April 2009.

43. http://www.wefweb.com/news/200946/1001386501_1.shtml, accessed 22 April 2009.

44. http://epaper.oeeee.com/A/html/2009-04-08/content_753020.htm; http://www.caijing.com.cn/2009-04-07/110134134.html, accessed 22 April 2009.

45. http://www.wefweb.com/news/200946/1001386501_4.shtml, accessed 22 April 2009.

46. http://epaper.oeeee.com/A/html/2009-04-08/content_753020.htm, accessed 22 April 2009.

47. http://news.163.com/09/0404/05/561IOQ950001124J.html, accessed 22 April 2009.

48. http://blog.sina.com.cn/s/blog_506e26770100e3tz.html, accessed 28 August 2012.

49. http://www.nytimes.com/2009/07/30/world/asia/30jilin.html?_r=1&th&emc=th, accessed 30 July 2009.

50. http://epaper.oeeee.com/A/html/2009-04-08/content_753020.htm, accessed 22 April 2009.

51. http://www.caijing.com.cn/2009-04-07/110134134.html, accessed 22 April 2009.

52. http://gb.cri.cn/27824/2009/04/07/2165s2477576.htm, accessed 22 April 2009.

53. Porteous and Smith, *Domicide*, 17.

54. http://www.nybooks.com/articles/archives/2009/may/28/a-black-and-disgraceful-site/, accessed 10 January 2011.

55. Judith Lewis Herman, *Trauma and Recovery* (New York: Basic Books, 1997), 70.

56. Herman, *Trauma and Recovery*, 72.

57. Herman, *Trauma and Recovery*, 61.

58. A friend from Beijing who wishes to remain anonymous emailed me this jingle, 28 May 2011.

59. http://gb.cri.cn/27824/2009/04/07/2165s2477576.htm, accessed 22 April 2009.

60. http://news.sina.com.cn/c/2004-11-17/15374946096.shtml, accessed 22 April 2009.

CHAPTER TWO

~

Nightmares:
Old and New

The Lord High Chancellor looks into the lantern that has no light in it
. . . This is the Court of Chancery . . . which gives to monied might, the
means abundantly of wearying out the right, which so exhausts finances,
patience, courage, hope, so overthrows the brain and breaks the heart,
that there is not an honourable man among its practitioners who would
not give—who does not often give—the warning, "Suffer any wrong
that can be done you, rather than come here!"

—Charles Dickens, *Bleak House*

In the last two decades, showing family and friends one's newly purchased and
decorated home has been a happy fad, in fact, almost an obsession, among
urban Chinese. Such gatherings are often followed by exhaustive discussions
and exchanges of information on the housing market, decorating tips, and life
in the new home, ending in a celebratory banquet. In short, it is an event.

In the summer of 2007 I was invited to visit a new apartment of a friend's
friend off Huaihai Zhong Road in Luwan District in downtown Shanghai. A
spacious elevator took us to the eighth floor into a private hallway with two
units on either side. The friend's apartment of about 200 square meters had
two bedrooms and a large living room with a balcony overlooking the bustling city. And then came a surprise. Outside a small, dark, closet-like space
behind the kitchen, said to be the maid's bedroom, was a narrow, separate
elevator built specifically for all of the maids who served the families in this
prestigious apartment complex.

While the owner of the flat, a middle-aged Chinese man who was once among the sent-down youth but now ran a restaurant business in Spain, marveled about his life in this new flat and swore about the fabulous experience of having a maid—"Trust me! It just feels different when everything, even your underwear, is ironed"—I was thinking about the extra elevator and the cost of the building.

But this is the very heart of downtown, next to Xintiandi, or the New World, known as the SoHo of Shanghai, a high-end commercial and entertainment center. The best-known example of gentrification in recent Shanghai, the Xintiandi area is dotted with trendy cafes, bars, restaurants, high-fashion boutiques, and international brand-name shops. Luxury, not affordability, is the concern. The real estate values in this area are among the highest in Shanghai, at about 60,000 yuan per square meter at the time and counting.

He Yidong, a man in his mid-forties, should have been ecstatic about the booming value of this area, because his ancestral home, a three-story, upscale old-fashioned alleyway (*shikumen*) house of more than 300 square meters, is located right in the center of Xintiandi. Given the choice, however, he would rather not have been caught up in the boom—the soaring value of the Shanghai real estate market and the gentrification of this area were the very reason his family was evicted from their home and now live some 20 kilometers away, on the edge of Shanghai.

The He family has lost their home twice. The first time was in 1966, at the onset of the Cultural Revolution when the family, who belonged to the propertied class, was "swept out the door." The He family thought that the nightmare of arbitrary property seizures under the CCP was over when in 1992 the government finally allowed them to return to their house. But in 1998 the redevelopment of Xintiandi led once again to their eviction. This time their home was converted into one of the many trendy restaurants there.

Still, the He family was lucky in that their house itself has survived. Its very existence has given the family some hope of reclaiming it once again someday. For thousands of families in this area, many of whom were once He's neighbors and were also homeowners, no trace of their properties is left.

One such homeowner is Zhu Guangze, an eighty-three-year-old, English-speaking, retired teacher who refused to relocate on the government's terms. One November morning in 2005, a district demolition squad broke into her home, kidnapped her, and then razed her home, another case of domicide. Zhu Guangze attempted suicide, in protest and despair, but failed. This was the last home the Zhu family had lost under the CCP after the government took over several of their properties in the 1950s.

In both of the He and Zhu cases, the nightmare of property confiscation, old and new, continues, ensuring that a clear and timely solution to their housing conflict cannot be reached.

Xintiandi—The New World

Xintiandi, a two-block area in downtown Shanghai, was part of a larger development project in the Taipingqiao (Peace Bridge) area of Luwan District. The district encompasses an area of about 8 square kilometers, and as of the early 2000s, had a population of 357,000, about 44,600 persons per square kilometer.[1] It is blessed with a central location, including Huaihai Zhong Road, the middle section of commercially vibrant Huaihai Road, second in fame only to Nanjing Road. While Nanjing Road, with its historic department stores, is perhaps the best-known tourist attraction in Shanghai, most Shanghainese consider Huaihai Road more culturally sophisticated. Previously part of the French Concession, Huaihai Xi Road, the western section of Huaihai Road, features some of the city's most charming and elegant homes, buildings, and landscapes.

In the reform era, the district has capitalized on its historical heritage to attract outside capital, technology, and human resources. Huaihai Zhong Road and its surrounding area have become a highly sought-after international business district. Dozens of Fortune 500 companies, such as IBM, and about two thousand other major Chinese and international companies have their offices on and around Huaihai Zhong Road. Real estate development has been the powerhouse of the district's economic expansion. Its fashionable, high-end apartments and offices have been in great demand for those who can afford them. Since the early 1990s, the real estate market in Luwan District has consistently grown at 10 percent annually.[2]

The development of the Taipingqiao area, which started in 1996, was one of the earliest and most ambitious real estate projects in Shanghai. The area of about 52 hectares, located immediately south of Huaihai Zhong Road, is highly desirable. Historically, the area had a unique character. With Huaihai Zhong Road immediately to the north, the slums of Zhaojiabang to the south, the old city to the east, and the exclusive foreign quarter to the west, the Taipingqiao area was a transitional zone between the rich and poor. It became a Chinese enclave in Shanghai's foreign concessions, attracting mostly Chinese from the lower-middle to middle classes. The area was densely covered with old-style and new-style alleyway houses. By 1948 there were nearly two hundred alleyways in Taipingqiao. Varied in size, they accommodated from twenty to sixty families each. Houses that fronted the street were often used for businesses of all sorts, from shops to inns, to meet the needs of the residents. In 1948, one such middle-size alleyway block had more than eighty shops. Alleyways were also homes to various institutions, especially kindergartens and elementary schools. The seamless mix of commercial, educational, and residential culture was at the very heart of the vibrant community life in Shanghai's alleyway neighborhoods.[3]

The dense population and the busy commercial activities in the alleyways provided ideal anonymity for radical and secret activities. Several houses in the Taipingqiao area became landmarks of the CCP's underground history from the 1920s to the 1940s. Most historically significant was a house on Xingye Road (then Wangzhi Road) where in July 1921 about a dozen early CCP activists, including Mao Zedong, held a meeting representing the fewer than one hundred members of the CCP nationwide. This event was later construed as the CCP's First National Congress, which gave birth to the party. The house that hosted the meeting has become a sacred site for the CCP.[4] In addition, in the late nineteenth and early twentieth centuries, many prominent Chinese once lived and worked in the Taipingqiao area, including Chiang Kai-shek, the future president of the GMD, Chen Duxiu, a CCP pioneer and professor at Beijing University, and Ding Ling, one of the most prominent female writers of modern China.

From the late 1930s to the 1940s during the Japanese occupation, the Taipingqiao area saw little significant development. Yet its central location continued to draw in people. Overcrowding and neglect inevitably led to decay. By the end of the 1940s, the area was considered a "lower corner"—Shanghaiese for an undesirable area. A stagnant economy and the population boom under Mao helped speed its deterioration. While some privately owned alleyway houses were well maintained, many were allowed to fall into disrepair.

Before the development activities in the mid-1990s, the Taipingqiao area included twenty-four neighborhood blocks, which were numbered from Lots 108 to 132, more than eight hundred various work units, such as schools, factories, and stores, and a population of about 70,000. Long overdue for a makeover, it was an ideal candidate for urban renewal.

A major question was what to do with the site of the CCP's First Congress, which had become a museum, a shrine to the party. There were other issues to be considered, such as what to do with the privately owned houses in the area. Some of them were in good condition. The area also had a mixture of housing styles—old-style alleyway houses, built in the late nineteenth and early twentieth century without modern amenities, and new-style alleyway houses, three- and four-story apartment buildings constructed later with a varied degree of modern amenities. For instance, in Lot 108, more than 13 percent of the houses were privately owned, and 22 percent were of the new-style alleyway type. Should the development of this area be carried out in the same fashion as that in slums, by indiscriminately knocking down entire neighborhoods? Should private property owners be consulted if the development involved their homes?

In December 1996, the Luwan District government, "assisted" by Hong Kong based Shui On Land Ltd., proposed a "Taipingqiao Area Specific Plan." The idea was to gentrify the area into a mix of high-end commercial, residential, and entertainment facilities. Other than spaces allocated to new roads and green land, the area was to be divided into four zones. One zone encompassed Lot 109, which included the Museum of the CCP's First Congress, which was to become the Xintiandi project. It was designated, predictably enough, for historic preservation. The model for this zone was the gentrified neighborhoods of Georgetown in Washington, DC, and the Marais in Paris. New construction was to be compatible with the traditional housing, since the site of the CCP's First Congress would remain in that style. The plan was to have culturally oriented businesses, such as art galleries, antique shops, and bookstores, in this zone to complement the dignity of the CCP's historic site. The other three zones included residential housing to the south, offices and hotels to the north, and business and entertainment facilities to the east. The plan included a man-made lake on the east, next to the historic preservation area. The purpose of the overall development, the plan stated, was to make Shanghai an international metropolis, to establish a model for urban renewal, and to create an environment for all to enjoy. Six months later, on June 16, 1997, the Shanghai Municipal Urban Planning Bureau (hereafter, municipal planning bureau) approved the plan.

The major player in this plan, which was listed as only an "assistant" in the district's proposal and not even mentioned in the municipal planning bureau's approval, was Shui On Land Ltd. Its participation in the Taipingqiao project was not an accident. Shui On Land Ltd. belongs to the flagship property company of the Shui On Group, Hong Kong. Vincent Lo (born 1948), its founder, chairman, and CEO, has been ranked by Forbes as among the world's richest people in recent years. Heir to a real estate fortune in Hong Kong, Lo was among the earliest developers to jump into the almost virgin and thus vastly profitable real estate market in China and became one of the most powerful developers there, especially in Shanghai. In fact, he is known as "Mr. Shanghai."[5] But his most telling nickname is "King of Guanxi"—the King of Connections. Lo had contacts within the highest ranks of Shanghai's leaders as early as 1985, when he helped build a hotel for the Communist Youth League in Shanghai.[6] Years later, Han Zheng, the

League's secretary, became the director of Luwan District, and, in 1998, was appointed acting mayor of Shanghai, and then mayor in 2003.[7] This crucial connection opened a web of invaluable contacts for Lo, which explains why he was given the exclusive right to develop the Taipingqiao area.

Vincent Lo himself was most frank about the ins and outs of connections in China. In an April 2007 interview with CNN, Lo summarized the importance of guanxi in business in the Chinese context. The rule of law in China, he noted, is "not as strong as in the West so a lot would rely on personal relationships," Lo emphasized, "because China is one party rule, so if you work with certain officials within a city when they move elsewhere they are actually bringing that relationship with them. And also other party members can always call up their comrades to check on you and that would be a very good reference." His advice for those who are interested in doing business in China is to "get someone who can make decisions on the spot."[8] Clearly, that China remains a one-party state with weak enforcement of the law is an advantage for someone like Lo, who happened to know precisely that particular "someone" who could make decisions beyond any check-and-balance mechanism.

In fact, in late 1996 when the Luwan District government proposed the Taipingqiao development plan, Shui On had signed a "Letter of intent with Luwan District government to acquire the development rights for the Taipingqiao Redevelopment Project; first phase of the project was Shanghai 'Xintiandi.'"[9] Things moved quickly thereafter, with a series of transactions and license applications to grant Shui On and other parties involved the legal right to develop the Taipingqiao area. The documents indicate that while the Taipingqiao area was treated as one large project acquired by Shui On, each zone in the area had an individual contract for land transactions at different times with different companies—different in name, all under Shui On, a confusing situation explained below.

Let us take Lot 108 as an example. On July 19, 1997, one month after the municipal planning bureau approved the district plan, the Shanghai Municipal Housing and Land Management Bureau (municipal housing bureau, hereafter) represented by the then bureau director Cai Yutian as Party A, signed a Contract for the Transfer of Use Rights of State Land in Shanghai with Party B—Landton Ltd. of Hong Kong, which was another company under the Shui On Group with Vincent Lo listed as its legal representative, and Fuxing Construction Development Company (Fuxing Co., hereafter) of Shanghai, which was operated by the Luwan District Housing Bureau.

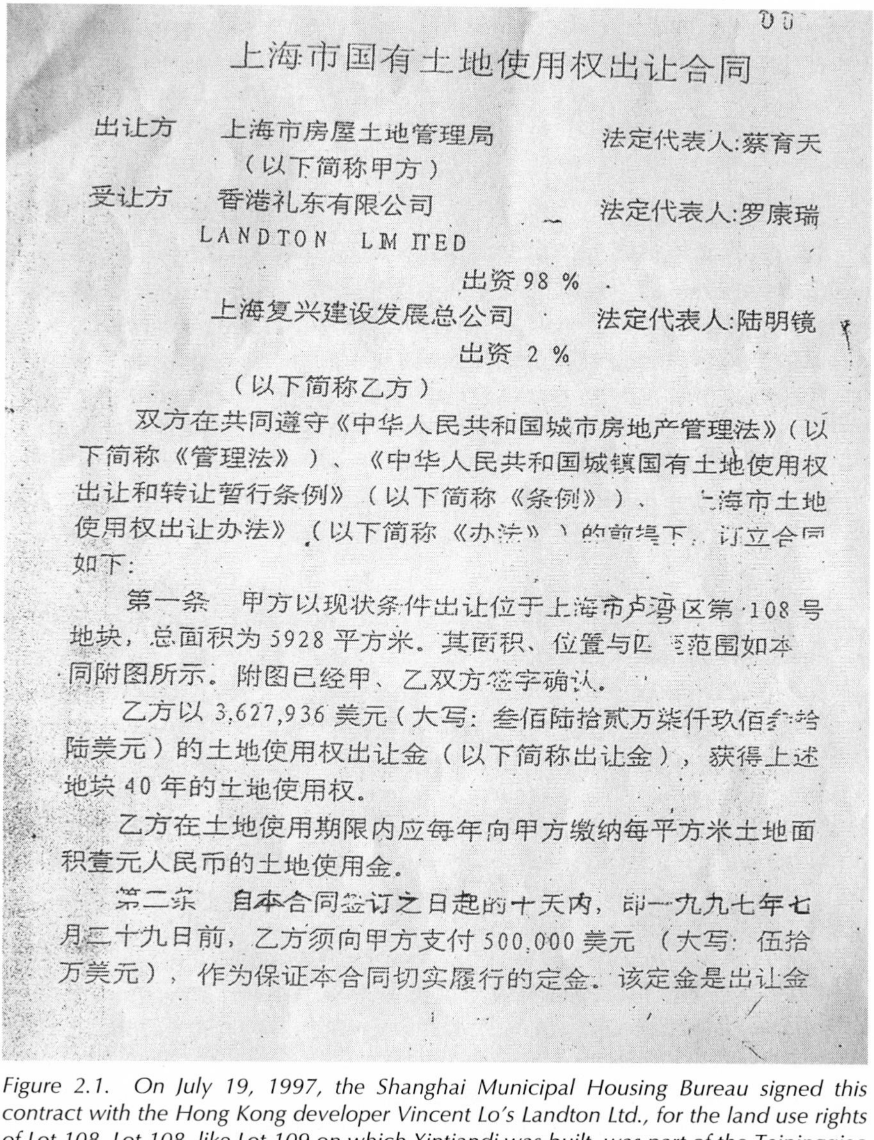

上海市国有土地使用权出让合同

出让方　上海市房屋土地管理局　　　　法定代表人:蔡育天
　　　　（以下简称甲方）

受让方　香港礼东有限公司　　　　　　法定代表人:罗康瑞
　　　　LANDTON LM ITED
　　　　　　　　　出资98 %
　　　　上海复兴建设发展总公司　　　　法定代表人:陆明镜
　　　　　　　　　出资 2 %
　　　　（以下简称乙方）

　　　双方在共同遵守《中华人民共和国城市房地产管理法》（以下简称《管理法》）、《中华人民共和国城镇国有土地使用权出让和转让暂行条例》（以下简称《条例》）、上海市土地使用权出让办法》（以下简称《办法》）的前提下，订立合同如下:

　　　第一条　甲方以现状条件出让位于上海市卢湾区第 108 号地块，总面积为5928 平方米。其面积、位置与四至范围如本合同附图所示。附图已经甲、乙双方签字确认。

　　　乙方以 3,627,936 美元（大写：叁佰陆拾贰万柒仟玖佰叁拾陆美元）的土地使用权出让金（以下简称出让金），获得上述地块 40 年的土地使用权。

　　　乙方在土地使用期限内应每年向甲方缴纳每平方米土地面积壹元人民币的土地使用金。

　　　第二条　自本合同签订之日起的十天内，即一九九七年七月二十九日前，乙方须向甲方支付 500,000 美元（大写：伍拾万美元），作为保证本合同切实履行的定金。该定金是出让金

Figure 2.1. On July 19, 1997, the Shanghai Municipal Housing Bureau signed this contract with the Hong Kong developer Vincent Lo's Landton Ltd., for the land use rights of Lot 108. Lot 108, like Lot 109 on which Xintiandi was built, was part of the Taipingqiao area development plan. But the residents were kept in dark about this plan. The He family on Lot 109 renovated their house in 1997 without knowing about the deal between the government and developer which, in early 1999, cost them their home. Lo signed the contract with his Chinese name: Luo Kangrui.

The key content of the contract is that both parties agreed that Party A would transfer the use rights of Lot 108, an area of 5,928 square meters, for forty years to Party B at a price of US$3,627,936, which amounts to $612 per square meter for the duration of forty years. In addition, during the forty years, Party B would pay Party A a land-use fee of one yuan per square meter per year as a token payment.

The relationship between the two companies in Party B—Landton Ltd. and the Fuxing Co.—however, needs some explanation. According to the contract, Landton Ltd. would contribute 98 percent of the capital for the development of Lot 108 and the Fuxing Co. 2 percent. This unequal partnership in terms of capital investment was mutually beneficial—by partnering with the district-owned Fuxing Co., Landton Ltd. would have the unconditional backing of the district government, while the Fuxing Co., therefore the district, would benefit financially from the development. They were essentially on the same team, with a shared interest in seeing the project through.

The other lots in the Taipingqiao area were leased in a similar fashion, except Shui On kept coming up with new company names for each contract. For instance, for the contract for Lot 114 in 2001, the Hong Kong company was named Baijing Ltd., yet its legal representative was once again Vincent Lo, who, as in the case of Lot 108, signed the contract with his Chinese name, Luo Kangrui, while its Chinese partner remained the Fuxing Co. The reason for this breaking up of the whole Taipingqiao area into parts and contracting it to apparently different companies at different times is that relevant regulations limit the amount of land local governments can transfer to a single company at any given time as a way of controlling state property. By breaking up the Taipingqiao area into small lots and inventing different company names for the contract for each lot, the district government and Shui On created the illusion of complying with the law while actually evading it.

The close relationship between the Luwan District government and the developers is further illustrated in the next, crucial step, which was to demolish the existing houses and relocate the residents, often a difficult task by any means. Who would do the dirty work and who would pay for it? The Contract for the Demolition and Relocation of Lot 114 in Luwan District, dated February 28, 2001, provides a clear picture of this process. The contract was signed between the developer, Baijing Ltd. of Shui On and Fuxing Co. as Party A, and the Luwan District government as Party B. According to the contract, Lot 114 of 32,603 square meters was destined for the development of commercial housing. In this contract, Party A commissioned Party B to "appoint a relevant professional company to execute the demolition and relocation" of that lot, for which Party A would pay Party B 501,380,000 yuan, 50 percent of which, 250,690,000 yuan, would be paid within fifteen days before demolition started on the lot. The contract also stipulated that Party B should complete the demolition and relocation by the end of February 2002 and, in the process, report monthly to Party A on the progress. The "relevant professional company" that the district "appointed" was Wuxin ("Five Hearts") Real Estate Demolition and Relocation Company (Wuxin Co. hereafter), a subsidiary of the Fuxing Co. of the district housing bureau— it was all in the family, so to speak.

As the district government became part of the developer and its interests were closely tied to Shui On's, it was impossible for it to check either Shui On's business practices or the behavior of the Wuxin Co. in dealing with the demolition and relocation, even if they acted outside the law. Also, because Shui On provided the overwhelming majority of the capital for the project and paid for the district to demolish the lot on its behalf, the district government practically became a hired gun for Shui On. Such involvement of the district housing bureau as both a business partner of Shui On and as a hired demolisher is unequivocally disallowed in housing regulations. In light of this, the massive redevelopment project of the Taipingqiao area was a fraud from the very beginning.

With the stage set for the Xintiandi project, the first phase for the gentrification of the Taipingqiao area, the next step, which would have a profound impact on the character of the project, was the selection of an architect. Shui On initially retained the services of the US-based architecture firm of Skidmore, Owings & Merrill LLP (SOM), which designed the 1996 Taipingqiao plan discussed above. But Shui On eventually settled on Benjamin Wood, a Boston architect trained at the Massachusetts Institute of Technology.

In May 1998, Wood was among five architects interviewed by Shui On in Hong Kong for the project. To prepare for the interview he flew to Shanghai for the first time and made his decision in twenty-four hours to take on the Xintiandi project, because he was "blown away" by "the magic of the place." He gushed, "It was amazing. There was laundry hanging everywhere, all these people, parents with kids flying kites, the whole litany of human experience."[10]

Wood wrote a letter to Shui On in which he highlighted his vision for the Xintiandi project. He warned against the general approach of development for such a project: "Saving a few historic structures while clearing the rest of the site for new buildings that need modern standards and conventions for retail and entertainment space, all over a continuous level of underground parking, is both ambitious and wrong." Instead, Wood suggested a "more incremental, and in many ways, a more efficient, responsive approach to the project." His inspiration came from the hill towns of Italy: "If someone gave you an Italian hill town you probably would not tear it down and then rebuild a modern facsimile of it atop a parking garage. Any hope you had at attracting people would be over. No matter how hard you try you will never recapture the scale, the ambiance, and the character." At the time Wood happened to have just returned from a vacation in Siena where he saw the success of "adaptive re-use": "An entire town re-used down to the last cobblestone. So many visitors in the summer months that you virtually need an advance reservation just to walk in one of the five gateways." He predicted a "remarkable transformation" of the Taipingqiao area from the "obvious, the dirt, the decay, the crowded, unsanitary conditions" to "a cultural artifact that could for generations to come symbolize the meeting of East and West on the vast delta of the Yangtze River." Mindful of the importance of profit for Shui On, Wood promised to find "creative ways to make old buildings into profitable retail, commercial, and residential space" and, given the "right 'tools,'" he would help Shui On "make the Taipingqiao French Quarter the leading retail and entertainment attraction in China."[11]

According to Wood, Vincent Lo knew exactly what Wood was proposing, for Lo happened to have also just returned from a visit to the hill towns of Italy. In competing for the project, Wood was interviewed by both the board of directors of Shui On and Vincent Lo himself. Wood said that he only got one vote, but the most important vote of all, from Lo. It is the shared vision of the two men that made Xintiandi what it is today. After all, while building glittering high-rise apartments, office spaces, malls, and parking garages has been the mainstream of urban development in Shanghai and elsewhere, what Wood specializes in are boutique structures that project something unique, historic, and aesthetic. In a time when the modern mall has become a boring norm, Wood's vision was appealing to both the rising middle class and the nostalgic masses in China.

Ironically, while Xintiandi has been widely proclaimed as a successful example of historic preservation, preservation was the last thing on Wood's mind in his plan for Xintiandi. In fact, Wood "disdains preservation." He explains, "I don't believe you should proclaim things dead and turn them into museums. I believe you should breathe life into places. That's my goal. I want to make living areas, where people can eat, drink and enjoy themselves."[12]

Of course, Taipingqiao before Xintiandi, while overcrowded, was far from dead: it was its very "litany of human experience" that inspired Wood to take on the project. The alleyway houses, while crying out for repair, were not in themselves a failure either. Wood recognized that and his approach of "adaptive re-use" has allowed 80 percent of the original buildings in Lot

109 to survive, which includes the house of He Yidong's family. As Wood promised, Xintiandi has indeed become a successful project in terms of both profit and image-making for Shui On, which now considers the project a milestone in its history.

What is missing from the apparent successful story of Xintiandi, however, is the price many families were forced to pay. The $170 million Xintiandi project wiped out the kind of neighborhood life that so excited Wood in the first place. The gentrification of the Taipingqiao area did not take into consideration the private property and homes there. While the plan would uproot thousands of families, neither the district government nor the developer sought any input from any of the residents; in fact, the residents were kept in the dark about the plan until long after they were relocated. Therefore, coincident with Shui On's milestone of success were milestones that marked the displacement of many families from their homes, some by force, and their subsequent, prolonged struggle to deal with that loss. The Hes and the Lus are two cases in point.

From a "Fine Home" to a "Stuck Fish Bone"

"Chujin's Fine Home"

The He family's misfortune—their eviction—and good fortune—the survival of their home—is solely because their house happens to be in a typical alleyway shikumen style and is located in Lot 109 (330 Huangpi Nan Road), the same block as the Museum of the CCP's First Congress, the ultimate preservation target.

All this thanks to the family's patriarch whose life journey started more than a century ago. The Hes are of the Hui ethnic group, or Chinese Muslims, with centuries-long roots in the Muslim communities of Suzhou, Nanjing, and Shanghai in the lower Yangzi delta. Their house in question was built in 1925 by He Yidong's great-grandfather, He Chujin. He Chujin (1880?–1943) was a self-made man who, during his youth, did all sorts of odd jobs from pulling a rickshaw to trading in fur. Eventually, he sold Western medicine in Shanghai and worked his way up to a senior position in a German pharmacy, a background the CCP later labeled as "comprador bourgeois."

Also in the small Muslim community in Shanghai was a renowned artist, art collector, and appraiser, Ha Shaofu, known by his literary name, "Well-Watching Old Gentleman" (*Guanjing laoren*) whose oldest daughter He Chujin had married—the Hui tradition was to marry within its own group. The Ha family was cosmopolitan by any standards of the day. Ha Shaofu was invited to visit Japan as an art appraiser. He brought his daughter with him on some of his trips. While Ha Shaofu was reasonably content with his son-in-law's respectable job in a foreign pharmacy, he was not happy that he lived in a rental. With his own private villa in Shanghai, Ha Shaofu never once came to visit the married couple, even after their first son was born in 1906—he did not recognize He Chujin as a proper son-in-law. He Chujin took this humiliation to heart.

Finally, in 1923, He Chujin accumulated enough savings to purchase a piece of land in Taipingqiao and built a house in 1925. It was a labor of love. He Chujin himself supervised the construction and his wife came to deliver lunch on the site. The structure was built in the then popular style of alleyway houses but took advantage of both its earlier and more updated versions. Alleyway houses in Shanghai, when they first appeared in the mid-nineteenth century, were often spacious—two-story, multi-bay, and multi-wing structures—but of poor quality with wooden frames that were prone to fire and without modern sanitary fixtures. Since the late 1910s, because of increasing population and rising property values in Shanghai, most of the alleyway houses built were smaller—two-story, single-bay, and without wings—but of better quality. They were constructed with brick, cement, and wood.[13] The He house was in the style of the most advanced alleyway houses of the day, and combined the merits of both the old and new styles. It was spacious, with three stories, three bays, and two wings. Initially, no expense was spared. The house was of reinforced concrete, with imported French windows, fireplaces, carved eaves, printed German tiles for the first floor and waxed hardwood for the two upper levels, modern amenities that included a bathtub, and a black double wooden door framed in stone in the front. The last feature, the door, is important. Alleyway houses in Shanghai made of brick and wood are known as shikumen—"stone gate"—houses, because of this kind of stone-framed wooden doors.[14] He Chujin spent 6,000 taels of silver on this house and ran out of money in the end. He had to compromise by denying the third floor a flush toilet.

Still, this house, while not a grand villa, was certainly distinct enough. Within its 307 square meters were a total of eighteen rooms ranging from 27.4 to 6 square meters. There were four fireplaces, two courtyards on the ground floor, in the front and the back respectively, and two balconies on the second floor extending from the two wings. To commemorate its completion, "AD 1925" was inscribed on the top of the two wings, still there to this day. In keeping with the Chinese literati tradition of endowing their residences with poetic and literary names, He Chujin simply named the house "Chujin jingshe"—"Chujin's Fine Home."

Figure 2.2. The street-front of He Chujin's home. The sign of "AD 1925" indicating when the house was built is visible on either side of its wings. The stone-framed black wooden doors were typical of Shanghai alleyway houses.

The father-in-law, Ha Shaofu, finally came for a visit. He took an inspection tour and was apparently satisfied. Soon after, a photograph was taken to mark the rare togetherness of the family that the house had brought about. In the photograph Ha Shaofu, seated in the center on the only decorated arm chair with a high back, wore a reserved but contented smile on his face, with his daughter on his left and his son-in-law, He Chujin, on the right, with folded arms and a remote and stiff expression on his face, perhaps a reflection of his complicated feelings about his father-in-law's years of snubbing him. Nevertheless, there was no question that Ha Shaofu had finally accepted his son-in-law. One of his friends, the celebrated Chinese artist Wu Changshuo, blessed the couple with his own painting of peonies, a symbol of love and happiness. Painfully aware of how the house represented his dignity and also the fruit of his decades of hard work, He Chujin laid down a rule for his offspring: "This house will forever remain in the He family and will never be up for pawn, sale, or rent."

Apparently, He Chujin had little to worry about as far as his children were concerned, because they were mostly successful by any measure. In keeping with the family's tradition, his two daughters became pharmacists and his

Figure 2.3. The He family shortly after the house was built in 1925. At the center in the armchair is the artist Ha Shaofu, with his daughter on the left and son-in-law, He Chujin, on the right. The two young women on the left are He Chujin's daughters. The young couple on the right is He Chujin's son He Shuhong and his wife Zheng Huifang, the seventeenth great-granddaughter of Zheng He, the Ming dynasty maritime explorer. Ha Shaofu never visited his son-in-law until he built this house. Courtesy of He Yidong.

son, He Shuhong, educated at Tongji University in Shanghai, became an engineer. He Shuhong (1906–1968) once worked at a water company in Nanjing where he was introduced to a girl from a prominent Hui grain merchant family named Zheng, whom he later married.

The girl, Zheng Huifang, was the seventeenth great-granddaughter of Zheng He. Zheng He (1371–1433), a eunuch of the Ming dynasty, is best known for leading the Ming imperial fleets seven times into the South Seas and reaching as far as the east coast of Africa, the most important maritime adventurer before the modern era. Late in his life, Zheng He apparently adopted a son of his brother (a common practice among childless Chinese families). Each generation of his descendants had a number of children, which allowed the Zheng family to spread to several dozen branches.[15]

Once again, the He family's elegant house in Shanghai was helpful in cementing this marriage with a distinguished merchant family. The young couple lived together with He's parents, along with a maid Zheng Huifang brought as part of her dowry. In the mid-1940s, He Shuhong and a few of his friends started a steel company in Shanghai. The family, while not super rich, nevertheless enjoyed a comfortable, middle-class lifestyle, with a chartered rickshaw service. Clearly, it had come a long way since the days when He Chujin himself was a rickshaw puller.

This comfortable domestic life became a source of contempt for the rebellious next generation of the He family. He Shuhong's son, He Liming (1928–2007), came of age in the tumultuous 1940s and, like many of his contemporaries, became a radical. Early on, he attended some of the best schools in Shanghai and was admitted in 1948 to a university to major in English. But he wanted none of it. The intimidating black door of his family's shikumen house and the live-in maid were all part of the backward "feudal family" from which he wanted to escape. A family tragedy only further alienated him. At the time, one of his aunts, the oldest pharmacist daughter of He Chujin, grew to become an active young woman. She ran a Muslim women's association from her home and herself fell in love with a non-Muslim doctor, something her mother adamantly opposed. Lovesick and yet bound to her mother's will, the aunt fell ill and died in her thirties in 1943. Both her activism and unfulfilled love had an impact on the impressionable Liming. During that period, many of the young Chinese who left home to join the CCP did so not always because of their faith in the revolution itself but because of suffocating family circumstances that deeply offended their growing sense of individual identity and social justice; Liming was one of them.

Restless and discontented but without any clear political and ideological convictions, He Liming first tried to run away from home to join a CCP army but failed. He was then admitted to a Nationalist military school to be trained as an officer. After Japan's defeat in August 1945, Liming, in part because of his English-language skills, was among those sent by the Nationalist government to Okinawa to oversee the transferring of some wartime materiel to the Chinese government.[16] He stayed there for two years and moonlighted as an English interpreter before returning home. Barely twenty years old and still adrift, Liming then joined the CCP's People's Liberation Army and, subsequently was sent to Korea after the Korean War broke out in 1950. He worked as an interpreter during the negotiations for the armistice and witnessed the celebration in Pyongyang at the conclusion of the war.

After braving the world, casting off his old self as a spoiled young master, and witnessing the death of many of his comrades in the war, He Liming finally came back to Shanghai in 1955, to a somewhat different home. While the door of his family shikumen house remained heavy and black, his father had lost his company in the CCP's socialist reform and now worked at a sewing machine factory. Liming himself was offered a job at a linens factory. Soon he got a taste of Mao's radical politics. In 1957 during the CCP's rectification movement in which people were encouraged to criticize the party and its officials, Liming questioned, with perfect common sense but fatal naivety, the rationale of the popular slogan, "Long Live Chairman Mao!" That criticism earned him the label of Rightist, along with some 300,000 other Chinese intellectuals.[17] He lost his job and was forced to labor for a construction company, transporting building material on a pedicab. This continued until 1962 when he was cleared of his Rightist label and allowed to return to his factory. The same year he also got married. The next year, his son, Yidong, was born; the roaming son finally settled down.

Only years later did He Liming realize how attached he was to the very home that he tried to break away from. In the late 1940s after the Okinawa mission, he declined the opportunity to drift further to Taiwan by joining many of his colleagues as the GMD retreated from the mainland in the face of the CCP's advance, simply because, in his own words, "My home is in Shanghai and I grew up here." Throughout the Rightist ordeal, that he could go back to that familiar home at night helped calm him. The home his grandfather built had kept the family together and soothed the wounds inflicted by the rough world beyond.

The Old Nightmare

Ironically, as He Liming was finally ending his youthful rebellion in the early 1960s, the People's Republic of China had only just begun its juvenile recklessness that culminated in the Cultural Revolution, known as the ten years of chaos, which would wrest from him the home that he had rediscovered.

The Hes' large house itself was evidence that they were a target of the revolution. The house escaped the 1950s socialist reform that nationalized private property only because it was the family's only residence.

Regardless, the family and its house would suffer from the madness of the Cultural Revolution. In the late summer of 1966, the Red Guards from He Shuhong's sewing machine factory searched the home and took away hundreds of the family's belongings. These included more than two hundred priceless paintings and calligraphy by some of China's most illustrious artists, numerous pieces of jewelry, gold bars, old china, antiques, fur coats, sets of rosewood and marble furniture, and many other family heirlooms accumulated by the first two generations of the Hes, including the considerable dowries their brides brought. Unlike the routine searches of the past when the Red Guards left after looting a house, this group of about forty Red Guards took a liking to the Hes' house, especially the telephone, which was a rarity at the time, and decided to invite themselves in. They confined the He family to a small room so that they could watch them closely and, in the meantime, helped themselves to what the house had to offer. They stayed for twenty days and hiked the family's monthly phone bill from its usual 4 yuan to over 100 yuan.

Things got progressively worse for the Hes. By the end of 1966, when the fighting among various Red Guard factions in Shanghai and the arrival of millions of Red Guards and fugitives from other regions almost paralyzed the city,[18] the neighborhood committee came to order the Hes out so that the authorities could use their house to lodge traveling Red Guards. The family of three generations was given a 30-square-meter space on a third floor of a house in the same neighborhood, vacated by a medical doctor whom the neighborhood committee had sent elsewhere. The family was not allowed to bring anything from their home with them.

The worst, however, was still to come. In May 1968 He Shuhong, who could no longer bear the frequent physical abuse and humiliation by the Red Guards in his factory, sneaked out of Shanghai and took refuge with his in-laws in Nanjing. But that only further infuriated the Red Guards, who brought him back for intense "struggle sessions." Only a day after his forced return, Shuhong collapsed in the factory and was left to die because as a "reactionary expert" his life was deemed not worth saving. It would take more than a decade and countless petitions from the family to get the authorities at the factory to admit that Shuhong had died of abuse at the hands of the Red Guards.

As for their home, the family was told that the Red Guards would only use it temporarily and, as soon as they left, the Hes would be able to return. But that did not take place until 1992, more than a quarter century later. What happened was that after the Red Guards' departure, the district housing bureau allowed eleven families who had some back-door connections with local officials to settle into the Hes' house, from whom the district collected rent. The He family, on the other hand, continued to live in that 30-square-meter space, without knowing if and when they would be allowed to return home. Since they were living in someone else's home, the district also charged them rent. The three children—He Liming had two more daughters by then—Yidong and his two sisters, grew up in a small loft above the bedroom their parents and grandmother shared.

There was, however, light at the end of the tunnel. After Mao's death in 1976, the CCP started to gradually correct some of Mao's mistakes. Yet the issue of restoring private property ownership, a low priority for the CCP to begin with, did not come up on the agenda of the Shanghai government until 1984. Also, after the decade-long chaos where housing was arbitrarily switched and occupied, it took time for the government to sort out often confusing property issues. Moreover, in this case, the task of relocating eleven families was no small matter due to the chronic shortage of housing in Shanghai. In 1988, the district issued a title to reconfirm the Hes' ownership of the house. Finally, in 1992, the district housing bureau resettled all of the eleven families and the Hes were given the green light to return.

The house was in near ruin after twenty-six years of abuse. To accommodate the eleven families, some of the original walls had been torn down and partitions set up. The colorful tile floor on one part of the ground level had been so damaged that it was replaced with concrete. One of the fireplaces was smashed. The large-scale construction of underground air-raid shelters under Mao—his response to the Cold War and Sino-Soviet tensions—had also destroyed the sewer system in the neighborhood, rendering the flush toilets, which the house was built with in 1925, useless; the families resorted to depending on night stools, like millions of urban Chinese in poorer quality housing did; "Chujin's Fine Home" had retrogressed decades back into the dusty past.

The family spent 50,000 yuan repairing, re-wiring, painting, and restoring the house, from the roof, the walls, the toilets, to the floors—the family poured their hearts, as well as their savings, into the renovation and restoration. The work was completed in 1997. By then, He Yidong's paternal grandmother from the Nanjing Zheng family had passed away. But it was comforting to the family that she at least saw the return of the house. After a quarter century of uncertainty, the Hes' faith in the government was somewhat restored; the family considered the repossession of their house to be a miracle. Moreover, the district documents that authorized the return of the house clearly indicated that what was returned to the family was not only the house itself but also their *chanquan*, that is, their ownership rights to the house, and the documents addressed the Hes as *yezhu*, property owner. Being able to regain their home as its rightful owner, more than anything else, convinced the Hes that the Cultural Revolution was only an aberration and normalcy had now returned.

The New Nightmare

In post-Mao China, the concept of a "normal" life, however, like everything else, was being redefined, and often destabilized, especially when it came to urban housing. Realizing that Shanghai's widespread redevelopment could pose a problem, the Hes, before committing to renovating their home in 1992, specifically inquired at the district office about whether their neighborhood was also a target for demolition. They were reassured that it was not, because, convincingly enough, the area with the Museum of the CCP's First Congress would not be touched. The Hes thus went full-force into the renovation.

Little did they know, of course, that the official promise meant nothing. Nor were they aware that in the midst of their ambitious renovation project, the Luwan District government and Shui On had already sealed their fate. By the time the Hes completed the renovation in 1997, the municipal government had leased to Shui On the use rights of Lot 109 on which the Hes' house stood.

Being in the dark did not spare the He family concern as their house continued to invite dubious inquiries. The neighborhood committee, a product of the Mao era to control urban residents, came to ask if their home could be used for neighborhood recycling and other functions. A state-owned enterprise also wanted to buy part of the Hes' house as offices. A Chinese television crew came to film the interior for a family drama about old Shanghai.

To forestall any further intrusion, the Hes decided to make good use of their house themselves. In spring 1998, they opened a small teahouse in the living room on the first floor and hung red lanterns to attract customers. With its central location and cozy setting, the teahouse thrived, which reflected not so much the Hes' business acumen but the general cultural interest in the city's past. The combination of a newly restored shikumen house, a type that had increasingly become a rarity in the city, and the teahouse, a traditional, popular Chinese institution of sociability that was making a comeback after the depressing years of the Mao era, was a winning formula.[19]

Outside interest in their house, however, only grew more aggressive. Throughout 1998, the family found people photographing and sketching their house from the street. While some of them were curious tourists, others acted suspiciously. Eventually, the neighborhood committee brought two people from Hong Kong to videotape the interior, which was followed by repeated inquiries whether the family would sell the house. Having barely warmed up to the home they had been forced to part with for decades, selling it was the furthest thing from the Hes' minds. The Hes read these inquiries as evidence of curiosity, because the construction of Xintiandi, so prominent a project, initially was concealed from the residents who would bear its impact the most.

When demolition on Lot 109 started in 1998, the district told the residents that it was for an urban renewal project—one of the examples where the government used "urban renewal" to clear people out for a commercial development. The Hes, reassured by the district early on, believed their proximity to the CCP Museum would spare their house from demolition. The other thing the Hes banked on was that they were the only family on Lot 109 to have full ownership of their home, with the ownership rights of other private properties either divided among siblings or shared with the district. The

Hes thus considered their case unique. Besides, it made more sense for urban renewal to target poor quality housing, which was exactly the official rhetoric. The Hes thought their house was too good to be "renewed." In any event, they failed to imagine that the government, which had just performed the miracle of returning their home, would once again take it away from them.

Reality soon set in. In August 1998 the Hes received a letter from the Wuxin Co. The letter, titled "Consultation on the Demolition and Relocation of Private Homes," informed the family that "according to the needs of city development, your home must be demolished in the near future," without spelling out what exactly the city's needs were. This letter of "consulting" offered the family a choice between two settlement plans. Plan A was for them to give up their ownership rights and take a cash payment, 151,140 yuan for the house's 307 square meters—about 492 yuan per square meter. According to the Wuxin Co., the house was too old to be worth much. Plan B was for the family to move to a few assigned apartments in the suburbs to which they would have ownership rights.

The letter indicated that the new apartments in the suburbs were priced at 2,350 yuan per square meter and thus the He family had to pay an additional 323,788 yuan in order to make up the difference in value if they chose Plan B. That payment, the company demanded, had to be made in one installment. "With utter seriousness, we have sent you this letter. Please make a decision before October 17, 1998, and bring your property title and other relevant documents to complete the process," the letter stated. It went on to say, "Failure to reply by the deadline means you have agreed to Plan A and have given up your ownership rights." Clearly, this last point and the demand that the Hes pay over 300,000 yuan in a single installment for Plan B were meant to force the family to accept plan A, that is, take the 151,140 yuan, relinquish their ownership rights, and go away for good.

The Hes were not ready to surrender the family house, not to mention that its market value far exceeded the offer and that they had just invested 50,000 yuan renovating it. They tried to delay the inevitable for as long as they could. On October 16, one day before the deadline set by the Wuxin Co. for a reply, they sent the Luwan District Housing Bureau a simple statement signed by all the members of the family: "We as the owners of the house on 330 Huangpi Nan Road want to retain our property rights and live in the same area. Additional payments either way, if any, should be resolved on a fair and reasonable basis." The letter represented the family's first acknowledgment that they might lose their home again. Should that be inevitable, they preferred Plan B, except with a crucial modification—they refused to relocate to the suburbs but insisted on exchanging their house for another one nearby with the full right of ownership intact. In essence, the Hes rejected both plans. Furthermore, they subtly indicated that their house would be worth more than the one they might move into and, if that was the case, they should be paid the difference, not the other way around. In short, they insisted on their rights to ownership and to a fair financial settlement.

From this point on the Hes were continually pressured to surrender. During the two months from December 1998 to January 1999, the district held five meetings with the Hes to negotiate a contract, and by early February the family was forced out. Of all the cases I have studied, the Hes were among those who were given the shortest time to deal with the conflict over their house, a privately owned and unusually fine and large house at that.

A series of documents reveals the intense pressure the district exerted on the Hes. In December 1998, while negotiations were still going on, the Wuxin Co. applied to the district housing bureau for an administrative compulsory ruling to force the family out in order to "ensure the smooth process of the nation's urban development." The district government, working in sync with the company, issued the ruling a month later, on January 26, 1999. It reemphasized that the Hes' house was on a site designated for demolition. The ruling allowed the Hes five days to move to the proposed apartments in the suburb. The Hes' response was consistent: they wanted to "maintain their property rights" and "stay in the same area."

But they were also concerned about their own safety. The overall situation did not look good as more of their neighbors left and some houses were leveled. The demolition squad stepped up its harassment. They frequently visited the family, often banging on the door after dark, to demand "talks." Twice they cut off the Hes' utilities for days at a time. As the Chinese New Year, which in 1999 fell on February 16, was approaching, the family asked the officials if they could spend the New Year, which for them could be the very last one in the family house, in peace and continue the "talks" afterward; the answer was "no." The demolition squad even escalated the threats. They surrounded the house and demanded He Yidong, the only young man in the family, to come out, for they wanted to "handle" him and teach him a "lesson." This often attracted gawkers. Among them were former evictees itching for a fight. They would laugh at, jeer, or otherwise taunt the demolition squad. On one such occasion, the demolition squad beat up a man in the crowd and caused a big scene. The family, with He Yidong's maternal grandmother, who lived with them, in her nineties, and his parents in their seventies, were not equipped to deal with such drama right in front of their home.

On February 3, the district issued a second compulsory ruling, stating that the family's refusal to obey the January 26 ruling and its continuing stay in the house were "unreasonable" and "unjustified." It ordered the family to relocate before February 7 to the assigned apartments, or else the district would "force you out according to the law." "If you disagree with this ruling," the document stated, "you can require the municipal government to reevaluate the case or bring a lawsuit in the Luwan District People's Court within three months." It all sounds reasonable, until the last sentence: "But neither a reevaluation nor a lawsuit will stop the implementation of this ruling." In other words, the Hes would lose their home no matter what they did. Then, on February 8, the district indeed followed up with an eviction notice. It "informed" the family to "wait by the house" at 8:30 a.m. on February 10 when the eviction would take place and, it added, "The eviction will proceed even in your absence."

Specifying a time and date, the district clearly meant business. The He family was now confronted with the certainty of domicide. They could stay and wait to be thrown out, as some other evictees had done, which meant that they would risk being injured or arrested, or they could stay away to avoid a confrontation and protect themselves. While the Hes valued their home, they valued their own lives more. He Liming, in particular, offered the perspective of his experience in the Korean War where he witnessed how lives were destroyed in an instant. He emphasized that their lives were infinitely more valuable than any material possession. The three generations of the family were concerned about each other. The elderly were most worried about the safety of Yidong, their only male heir, who was targeted by the demolition squad.

Moreover, the relevant regulations in Shanghai at the time required that the demolition of a housing property could not take effect until there was a contract with mutually agreeable terms and signed by both parties—the family involved and the demolition office.[20] In some cases when a family refused to sign a contract, authorities had grabbed the family and obtained their fingerprints by force, a desperate, illegal scheme, but one the Luwan District government was not above resorting to. The He family wanted to avoid such an encounter—if they had to lose their home, at least they did not want to be forced into giving their permission.

In light of all this, the family decided to walk out. To prepare for the impending departure, they invited their relatives to take whatever furniture or anything else they wanted, since the family did not have a storage place. At the time, the family, anticipating the children's future marriages, had bought two sets of custom-made furniture. But now they had to give that

上海市卢湾区人民政府

执 行 通 知

何礼明户:

区政府以卢府拆限字（ 99 ）第 2 号《限期拆迁决定书》

限你户于 1999 年 2 月 7 日前迁至本市梅陇□村141号602室、142号102、143号601室、143号602室、152号102、

174号302室，但你户至今未迁。为此，定于 2 月 10 日上午时

依法予以强制拆迁，特通知你于 2 月 10 日上午8:30时到

黄坡南路一弄330号你住处等候，拒不到场，不影响拆

迁的执行。

特此通知

（上海市卢湾区人民政府 拆迁专用章）

1999年 2 月 8 日

Figure 2.4. On February 8, 1999, the Luwan District issued this compulsory eviction notice to the He family. It stated that the family must relocate to government-assigned apartments before February 7 or suffer the consequence of eviction on the 10th. It instructed the family to wait at home on the 10th but stated that demolition and relocation would be carried out in their absence. On February 10, the district demolition squad came to take over the house, evict the family, and transport their belongings—which the family has not seen since—elsewhere.

up as well. He Yidong, assisted by his friends, managed to save a few pieces as memorabilia. He removed the four bedroom doors, each more than two meters high. Later, those four doors were installed in their new apartment, a tangible reminder of their other life.

On the night of February 7, the deadline in the district's second ruling, He Yidong and his sisters quietly moved their parents and grandmother, together with the family's two cats, to Yidong's office in the city for temporary lodging. He Yidong spent the last three nights alone at the home. On February 9, the eve of the pending eviction, He Yidong brought his girlfriend, whom he had only been dating a month, to the house. He gave her a tour of the house and then they sat in a bedroom on the second floor which Yidong's paternal grandmother had long ago promised to give him when he got married. Yidong had not seen the girl long enough to know if she would become his wife (she did), but just in case she would, he wanted her to see the house his great-grandfather built, for it could be destroyed tomorrow. At midnight, he sent away his girlfriend and stayed alone for the last night.

At 7 a.m. the next day, Yidong locked the door behind him and left. That morning, the demolition squad of more than a hundred, or the "army" as Benjamin Wood referred to it, arrived. Since the house was locked, the "army," which was instructed not to damage the house, called the architect to seek advice as to how to break in. Wood, who had had several conversations with He Liming in the previous months and was aware that the family did not want to leave, was concerned about the human aspect of the saga and in turn contacted Vincent Lo.

Lo reportedly responded with two points: first, he and Shui On had no control over evictions because they were handled by the district government and, second, if the Hes got to stay, then the government would not be able to relocate other families; therefore the Hes must go. Lo was disingenuous, to say the least, on the first point. Since it was his company that commissioned the district to clear out the residents and since the "army," the Wuxin Co., belonged to the Fuxing Co., partner of Shui On, Lo surely had control over the matter. In fact, at one point, Lo himself stated that he had "moved about 2,000 families from the site to relocate them."[21] But his second point was dead on. Indeed, the Hes' house, the first on the north end of the block, could have stayed as it was, without affecting the rest of the Xintiandi project. But if the Hes got to stay, then the relocation of other families, especially other homeowners, would have been difficult. Since Xintiandi was the first project in the Taipingqiao development plan, both the district and Shui On could not back off in the face of residents' resistance.

In the end, the "army" managed to get inside the house and shipped six truckloads of the Hes' belongings to the apartments in the suburbs assigned to them, and then sealed the house. The family has not seen any of their possessions, which include many pieces that had been passed on from generations ago. When the Hes moved out, rumors had it that they must have accepted a large payment to give up such a fine house. But, to this day, they have not taken a penny. As He Yidong said, "Taking any payment will mean that we've accepted the eviction and renounced our ownership rights. But we can never do that."

However, the house was to be spared demolition—except the family did not know it at the time. They thought the leveling of their home was only a matter of time. For through it all, the district and the Wuxin Co. conveyed in writing to the Hes in no uncertain terms that their home would be leveled.

A Son's Burden

The Hes became homeless on the eve of the 1999 Chinese New Year. They also lost their maternal grandmother, who died shortly after the eviction because of a fall that broke her pelvis. The family temporarily lodged in He Yidong's office. During the day when the office was used for business, Yidong's retired parents wandered outdoors while his sisters went on to work. The family would reunite in the evening, with a borrowed gas stove for cooking and folding beds and desks for sleeping. Though there was a toilet in the office building, there were no bathing facilities. They managed to stay there for six months before they purchased an apartment in the suburbs.

The task of dealing with the Hes' housing dispute now fell on the shoulders of He Yidong, who was thirty-six years old then. The post-Mao reform has created uncertainty as well as opportunities. By 1999, Yidong had already worked at several jobs and gained a measure of success as an entrepreneur in the telecommunications business. Unlike many of the newly rich in China, Yidong does not smoke, drink, or show off his success. He is soft-spoken, reserved, and intensely private. With his nondescript clothing and glasses—he is extremely nearsighted—he looks unassuming.

Born into a family shattered by Mao's revolution, He Yidong did not have his father's luxury of a wandering youth. His childhood was surrounded by certain secrets. In 1966, when the family lost their home for the first time, Yidong was three years old and, in time, he thought their temporary housing was his home. As his parents harbored no hope of reclaiming the house, they never talked with the children about their own home, which was only a few doors away. When Yidong started school, which was in the neighborhood, he befriended two classmates and played at their homes at 330 Huangpi Nan Road. There he was questioned by curious residents whether he was from the He family. He learned from adult gossip that this chaotic compound where his friends lived with many other households might belong to his family. Confused, he came home for an answer but learned little. Indeed, how does one explain to a child the seemingly inexplicable nature of this nightmare?

Then, there was his grandfather's sudden death in 1968 at the hands of the Red Guards. In any politically "black"—"reactionary" or "antirevolutionary"—family of the time, there was no talk of such deaths and no open mourning. The adults only whispered among themselves about the causes of his death and quietly appealed to the authorities for years to have his name cleared, which finally resulted in a decent funeral given by the sewing machine factory in 1979. A sensitive child, Yidong felt the tension in the air that engulfed the family yet he learned to keep his apprehension to himself. In the 1970s, since his father worked three shifts and his mother, although a union cadre, was condemned to labor in the suburbs, Yidong spent most of his time with his grandmother and sisters at home reading—he loved reading and is well versed in Western literature. It was through reading a biography that the teenage Yidong discovered the African American scientist and inventor George Washington Carver, who became his lifelong hero. Like his hero, Yidong is grounded in what he considers to be substantial: knowledge, skills, and social justice, instead of what he sees as superficial: fame, status, and money.

In 1980, he attended a well-known, professional accounting school in Shanghai. Upon graduation, he was assigned by the school to work as an accountant at an automobile company. At the time, China was about to open up and establish a market economy. But government-assigned jobs still represented the safest and often the only option, and thus were sought after by many. Two things happened that changed his views about this safety net and pushed him into the emerging market economy. A successful accountant, He Yidong was promoted to head the accounting department at the company. But at the last minute, one of the officials at the company made his own son the head instead. When Yidong tried to enlist the support of an administrator to dispute that promotion, the administrator in turn asked for a favor as a condition. He wanted Yidong's mother, who had returned to a position in the Municipal General Workers' Union, to use her influence to help change his own son's work from the graveyard shift to the day shift. Those two instances made Yidong realize how CCP officials were in it to promote their own interests. He quit his job and decided to explore his future on his own. The gradually widening post-Mao reform allowed him to do so.

In the following years, He Yidong stumbled on a series of odd jobs: restaurant owner, accountant, construction worker, and handyman. Finally, in the early 1990s, he settled in the telecommunications business, representing foreign companies selling telecommunications facilities and technology to the Chinese. "Like my great-grandfather, I also became a comprador," Yidong declared, mindful of his family's history. Indeed, after forty years under Mao, China, opening its doors to joint ventures and outside capital and technology, has once again become a fertile ground for "compradors" like Yidong. China's rapid economic development has created a massive market and high demand for telecommunications equipment and technology all over the country. The business boomed and he did very well indeed financially.

He Yidong's business, plus his two sisters' earnings, provided the family with a decent financial base and enabled them to renovate their family house in 1997. But Yidong also experienced the dark side of economic development where personal connections, bribery, corruption, and the abuse of power were the norm. Shortly after 1999, when they lost their home, Yidong quit his job. He was married in 2000 and had a son the next year. He now only works intermittently, spending most of his time with his family while also trying to reclaim the house, which, he believes, is his duty as the eldest and only son of the family.

Legal Battles

The first action the Hes took was legal; they sued the district. In April 1999, two months after being forced out and still in the temporary lodging, the Hes brought an administrative lawsuit in the district court against the district government. They accused the district of violating their personal and property rights. They demanded that the district withdraw its administrative compulsory rulings and the eviction notice and compensate them for the loss of their property. At the heart of their case was the illegality of the eviction. Three months later, in July 1999, the court held a hearing and then handed down its judgment.

In a five-page verdict, the court found that the two administrative compulsory rulings and eviction notice were based on "clear facts, ample evidence, and the correct application of the law." Central to those "facts, evidence, and law" that justified the eviction, according to the court, was the very permit the district granted for the demolition of Lot 109. The court confirmed that the district had followed due procedures by issuing the administrative rulings and eviction notice when the family did not leave "on their own." The court also found that the district had followed the proper procedures on the day of the eviction by recording the contents in the Hes' home before the "demolition" and having that record "notarized." Indeed, relevant official documents did require demolition squads to record and archive the process of demolition and relocation.[22] Therefore, the district, the verdict stated, had done everything "objectively and legally." The court found the He family at fault, because they "refused to move out to meet the deadline" with no "justifiable reasons," thereby "making the compulsory administrative rulings and eviction necessary." The court thus declared the government the victor. It ordered the Hes, as the loser in this case, to pay the court's costs. The presiding judge then told Yidong that he could never win the case and, moreover, that his family could no longer afford to live in that house anyway. It was only after the luxurious Xintiandi project took shape that Yidong understood what the judge meant.

Despite the defeat, Yidong decided to press on. That the district judges ruled in favor of the same district officials who appointed them was entirely expected. Yidong now wanted to see if the higher courts, where the judges were not cronies of the district officials, would be less prejudiced. He was not so naïve as to be really hopeful. But he thought that the injustice in his case was so obvious that perhaps moving up the legal ladder would help. That the government in the post–Cultural Revolution era did the honest thing by returning their home also played a role in the Hes' decision to follow legal procedures. Yidong thus immediately appealed to the Shanghai First Intermediate People's Court, which denied his appeal. He then took the case to the Shanghai Higher People's Court, which, too, rejected his claim and upheld the verdicts by the two lower courts. The rejections by the latter two courts, in their routine legal wording and prolixity, made the same key arguments as those by the district court. Therefore, after the Hes lost their home, they also lost their court case—three times in a row.

The Hes' case demonstrates once again why China has a long way to go to become a society ruled by law. The fatal flaw in this and countless other cases, including those documented in other chapters, is that the court—as well as the district government itself—equated the demolition permits with proof of legality. Indeed, the district government had the power to hand out the demolition permit, but that does not necessarily mean that the district followed the due process of law or that the permit was automatically legitimate. In many cases, various district governments in Shanghai have used pretexts and lies in issuing such permits, as the Luwan District did in the Xintiandi case, which was certainly against regulations and the law. Also, housing regulations explicitly disallowed government administrators, such as those in the Luwan District government and its housing bureau, to participate in demolition, but they were actively involved in it anyway. Moreover, municipal regulations about urban housing reform at the time, as mentioned earlier, required a signed contract between the two parties involved before the demolition could take place, yet the Hes never agreed to surrender their house nor did they sign any contract, which alone should have made the eviction illegal. However, as long as the legitimacy of a permit is taken as a given, any actions the government and its hired demolition squad take to implement the permit, including domicide, become justified. By the same token, any actions the residents take to resist demolition and object to the permit become illegal. As such, this almighty permit has trumped the law and become little more than window dressing for corrupt official behavior. In Shanghai, many laws and regulations that residents have cited to protect their property have been ignored. But a demolition permit, once issued, has often been implemented, no matter how much evidence points to its fraud. The development of Shanghai has marched on because of such permits.

In the meantime, the district court assumed that the Hes' house was demolished, while the house, located only four blocks from the very courtroom where the verdict was handed down, was in fact still standing. The court never questioned the district why it evicted the Hes without demolishing it as it initially stated. Then, in 2001, when the Hes took their appeal to the higher court, their home had already been turned into a restaurant. The Hes argued that it was illegal for anyone to turn their home into a business without their consent. The higher court responded that the issue of the Hes' home becoming someone else's enterprise was irrelevant to the case, since it was an administrative lawsuit. The higher court thus ignored the fact that it was the demolition permit issued by the district administration that led to the transformation of the Hes' home from a private property into a business entity. Clearly, for the court, the permit as enacted *became* the law at the expense of codified law.

Also darkly comic was the way the Hes found out the true fate of their house. In late 1999, when the Hes' case was with the intermediate court, He Yidong got a call from a former neighbor who had relocated elsewhere, inquiring curiously what the Hes' were doing with their home: "Are you renovating your house?" "No!" a surprised Yidong responded, "What do you mean?" It turned out that the neighbor just happened to pass their home and saw construction workers fixing it up. He wondered why the Hes were doing this since he, like all the other residents, had been told that the houses there would all be knocked down. Yidong rushed to his home and was speechless to discover that the house, instead of being torn down, was being fixed up. The workers there could not tell him anything except that they were sent to "renovate" the house. Yidong told them that this was his home, that his case was in the court, and that they must stop what they were doing. His words must have been passed onto the district, which temporarily halted the work on the house. But the "renovation" was resumed as soon as the intermediate court ruled against the Hes.

In January 2001, three years after the He family was driven out, their home was opened as a restaurant in a chain with a cheerful name, Xinjishi, the New Lucky Gentleman, which claims to feature authentic Shanghainese cuisine. The Hes' home-turned-restaurant is right next to Vincent Lo's clubhouse, where he wines and dines his prestigious guests. The renovation of the house included tearing down the walls between the two wings on the first and second floors to open the place up for tables. The third floor is used as an office. The back courtyard opening to Xintiandi is now the entrance and the front courtyard facing the street is used for dish washing. The interior was redecorated and a new screened porch was added on the side to accommodate more patrons. But the main structure of the house with its original walls, windows, and the marble floor on the ground level remains intact. Apparently, because the Hes' house was representative of Shanghai's high-end shikumen housing and was in good shape, it fit readily into the overall architectural style of Xintiandi, which was meant to capture the feeling of the lost alleyway neighborhoods in Shanghai. For that reason the house was spared demolition.

Media Reaction

Because of the high profile of Xintiandi and the unusually fine condition of the Hes' house the conflict over the house caught the attention of the Chinese media. In February 1999, Shanghai Oriental Television covered the story as it was unfolding, calling it "The Eviction of a Nail Household." The report praised the district for forcing the Hes out. But later, the media took a different tack as pervasive corruption became exposed. On May 16, 2002, the outspoken and popular *Nanfang zhoumo* (Southern Weekend) devoted an entire page to the case with a picture of the house in the center. Under a provocative title, "Who Seized My Ancestral Shikumen [Home]?" the article recounted the history of the house based on interviews with He Liming and his wife and the process leading to their eviction. According to the report, rental rate in Xintiandi at the time was about US$1 per square meter per day, which meant the restaurant was paying Shui On Land Ltd. about US$112,000 annually in rent. When a reporter interviewed the director of public relations in Shui On's Shanghai office about the issue of property rights, the director responded that that was handled by the district government and thus was irrelevant to his company. Less than a week later, on May

22, *Zhongguo qingnian bao* (China Youth Daily) published a piece with an equally sharp title: "Who Has the Right to Touch My Shikumen [Home]?" This was more of an opinion piece than an original report as the author was so "boiling with anger" after reading the report in *Nanfang zhoumo* that he had a "sleepless night."

Both articles unequivocally condemned the Luwan District for robbing the Hes of their home. They pointed out that it was the huge profit that led the district government, on the pretext of urban development, to seize the Hes' home and then transfer it to the Hong Kong company. The article in *Zhongguo qingnian bao* estimated that the value of the Hes' home as a business site was in the millions of yuan. Both articles made clear that the government has the power to obtain, by force when necessary, private property for public projects but absolutely not for private business interests. They believed that the government should have taken itself out of the equation and the issue should have been negotiated between the two parties—Shui On and the He family— and whatever the Hes decided should have been respected because, according to the Chinese Civil Law, the two parties have equal rights in such a dispute. At that time, the much-talked-about Chinese property rights law was still being debated, but both articles argued that protecting private property is universally recognized and is almost a natural law. They concluded that what the Luwan District did to the Hes was not only wrong, but also illegal. In light of the Hes' lost lawsuit, the article in *Zhongguo qingnian bao* further argued that the Hes' case pointed to the alienation of the government from the people and the abuse of citizens' rights.

The relative freedom the Chinese media now enjoys to openly criticize local governments is one of the most remarkable changes brought about by the reform era. But that very freedom is perhaps also proof of a debased media. The media cannot hold officials accountable for any corruption, even with incontrovertible evidence. If Chinese officials are above the law, they are certainly above the media and public opinion. That they got away with their handling of such cases as the Hes only encourages them to continue their wrongdoing. This vicious circle shows the snowball effect of institutional corruption and the limited impact of the media in China.

The Human Toll

A decade has passed since the Hes relocated to the suburbs. On the surface, their daily life has little to do with their original home anymore. The family has tried to adjust their own mind-set so that the injustice they suffered does not continue to consume and mar their lives. They have tried to depersonalize their suffering to comfort themselves and to "think big" and carry on—keeping in mind that they still have each other; that they are not the only family that has been made to "sacrifice" because of the reform; and that maybe there is light at the end of the tunnel, just like what happened after the Cultural Revolution. Even though their experience defies reason, He Yidong's mother has tried to find some meaning to their loss: "We contributed to the revolution when we were young. Maybe this [the house] is our contribution to the economic reform?" Asked whether she believed in the revolution then, her reply was most affirmative: "Of course. We fought for justice." "But what are you 'contributing' to this time around?" She struggled to come up with words and finally said in resignation, "I don't know; I haven't thought about that."

Two events in 2007, however, brought a renewed poignancy to the family about just how much the house meant to them and how much they had lost. That fall, Yidong's son, the fifth generation of the family and the first generation of the Hes who was not born in and would not grow up in the family house, had reached school age. Because of the poor quality of schools in the new suburbs, Yidong wanted his son to attend a better grade school in downtown and also to get to know the neighborhood that he grew up in. Since the He family's household registration remains in Luwan District with their original address, Yidong enrolled his son at a school two blocks away from his home.[23]

The problem with his son's attending school downtown, however, was that the Hes' current apartment was 20 kilometers away and a daily commute for the boy was impossible. As a solution, Yidong moved back to the city with his wife and their son. The three of them now live in a one-bedroom rental of 12 square meters, sharing a kitchen in the hallway with a neighbor and using a chamber pot. His living conditions have been reduced to the worst in the pre-reform era of the 1970s. All the while, he watches someone else profiting from his family house nearby.

Just as the young were growing up, the elders were getting weaker. Not long after Yidong's nuclear family moved back downtown in the fall of 2007, his seventy-nine-year-old father, He Liming, was diagnosed with lung cancer, a devastating shock to the family. Until then he seemed to be the very picture of good health for someone his age. Since they relocated to the suburbs where gated high-rises often meant isolation, Liming had developed a new routine. He had been riding his bicycle twice a week downtown where he could be with a community he felt he belonged to—his friends, old neighbors, and colleagues, all retired—to have tea, play chess and cards, and have a meal and chat. It was so enjoyable that some days Liming did not come home until midnight. Such bicycle trips and gatherings were probably his way of keeping himself occupied and soothing his nostalgia for the past. After they settled in the suburbs, his wife went to visit their original home on many occasions, walking around it, but Liming never did. His gathering point in the city, however, was not far from his home. Perhaps he wanted to be close to the home he knew he might never return to yet could not bear actually seeing it.

His family, knowing that the bicycle trips and gatherings were good for him physically and mentally, supported him. But they also worried about his long hours on the road. The round-trip was 40 kilometers, and there is no shortage of reckless drivers on Chinese roads who take traffic signs casually. At one point Liming promised that he would quit once he reached the age of seventy-five. But then he insisted on continuing. He never skipped his ride, rain or shine. It was when he lost a great deal of weight and could no longer manage the bicycle trip in early fall that the family thought something must be seriously wrong. By then the cancer was already at a late stage; Liming did not stand a chance. His family tried to keep the seriousness of his condition from him. But, after less than three months of futile treatment, He Liming, his roving youth having supplied him with a lifetime of wisdom, refused to continue; he passed away just before the Chinese New Year in 2008.

His funeral was somewhat unusual: he spoke to family members, relatives, and friends gathered in the hall about his life in a characteristically understated manner from a television screen —I interviewed He Liming in his apartment on a rainy day on June 28, 2007, just two months before the cancer was diagnosed, and videotaped the interview. During his illness his family asked for a copy of the interview, which became the last testament to a remarkable life. The biggest elephant at the funeral hall was the shared sorrow that Liming left the world without seeing his home once more, a home that he had longed to reach on his bicycle for almost a decade.

If traditional Chinese medical theory is to be believed, then the mind-and-body connection to health further cast a shadow over Liming's family: how much might the eviction have contributed to his fatal illness? The Chinese believe that the lungs, of all the organs, are the most susceptible to emotional stress. A common Chinese expression about the reaction to extreme anger is that "My lungs have exploded!" The loss of his home was no doubt traumatic to Liming. Benjamin Wood still remembers how distressed Liming was when they talked. "He told me that the house was from his ancestors and that they had lived there for sixty years. He didn't want money or [to] move elsewhere." In the 2002 interview with the *Nanfang zhoumo* reporter, Liming described the eviction as "a disaster that befell my family." And he was deeply troubled by the fact that "we were able to protect this ancestral house through war and the socialist reform. But we lost it when China began to become a society [ruled] by law." In the same interview, he also expressed his guilt over having "let down" his ancestors since the house that had passed on through two generations was lost when he was the patriarch. Chinese culture renders such a person an unfilial son. Perhaps to defend or otherwise comfort himself, at one point he told his children, "It wasn't that I had lost the house, but that the house was practically grabbed from me and I was helpless."

Therefore, Liming's high-minded perspective on the eviction was perhaps more of an attempt to help his family deal with it, not that his own pain was any less profound. Through all of the ordeals under Mao, even during the Cultural Revolution, Liming managed to maintain a certain innocence, always believing the best of the government. After he lost his home for the second time, Liming initially thought that the injustice would surely be corrected. But as time went on, his hope faded away; he hardly mentioned the house anymore. When Yidong reported his experience after a court appearance or petition trip, Liming simply sighed deeply and then fell silent. As one of his daughters said, "He kept it all inside him to the very end."

Indeed, the loss of the house had become a mood killer for the Hes. Whenever the topic was brought up in the midst of even a happy gathering, a sudden deadly stillness would engulf them. In time, the children tried to avoid the topic so as not to upset their aged parents. Did Liming's repressed anger and sorrow feed the cancer? Was he ashamed in the final hours of his life when he was about to face his ancestors? Did he imagine a conversation with his grandfather, who had unequivocally dictated that the house never be put up for "pawn, sale, or rent" about the other possibility of losing it by government seizure? While the family cannot answer these questions, they do believe that the polluted air Liming breathed along his long and frequent bicycle rides to the city was certainly a health hazard. All this has made his death difficult to accept.

The Search for the Truth

His father's death and his young son's education, which has only just begun, have imbued He Yidong with a renewed sense of urgency in dealing with the housing issue. During and after the court cases, Yidong, like all other residents involved in housing disputes, also started petitioning. Of all the petitioners I have met, Yidong is one of the lonely few who recognizes the pitfalls facing a full-time petitioner and refuses to let it take over his life. He does not perpetually write petition letters. He believes that his case is clear-cut—the fact that his family owned the house, which is now used as a business by someone else, is simply not in dispute. Yidong does not make frequent petition trips to Beijing either. Having seen the ugliness in the government up close, he does not believe such trips are useful. He does go to the municipal petition office once a week and to Beijing occasionally, just to remind the authorities that his case is not going away; of that he is certain.

A source of particular frustration for Yidong has been that he was kept in the dark about how his home became a restaurant. He has found no one to account for what happened to his home. Yidong did go to the restaurant to see who exactly was in charge of the place. But all he learned was that the restaurant only rented the place from Shui On. Yet Shui On was another phantom; it simply defers to the district when it comes to all issues concerning the property.

Yidong has insisted on probing into the legal basis for the property transfer. To find this out, in 2005 Yidong requested that the municipal planning bureau release the documents that authorized the construction of the Xintiandi project that involved his property. After a month-long delay, the municipal planning bureau denied his request on the grounds that such documents were still being processed and thus it was premature to make them available. But how could it be that the Xintiandi project, which was clearly planned before 1998 and had since been completed, was still being processed in 2005? Finally, after more than six months of stonewalling, the municipal planning bureau gave in and provided a copy of the Luwan District Taipingqiao Area Specific Plan dated December 1996 and the bureau's written approval of the plan, which we discussed earlier. Yidong realized that his family never stood a chance. The government that returned their home once was capable of waving another magic wand and taking it away again.

In the meantime, several of the Hes' former neighbors who were also forced out of their homes to make way for the Taipingqiao project have embarked on a similar path in search of information and documentation to answer the root question: exactly how and when was their property transferred and who was ultimately responsible for their dispossession? While they do have a general picture of the corruption and backdoor dealings, they nevertheless want to uncover every skeleton in the closet—the problem with keeping secrets is that people can become obsessed with exposing them. They also hope to strengthen their own cases by identifying specific loopholes in those documents. It has been through years of dogged effort, through lawsuits for some of them and petitions for others, that they have managed to cobble together a considerable amount of evidence that has begun to help them piece the picture together.

During lunch time on a Wednesday in June 2007 I met Yidong and four of his former neighbors in a KFC off Huaihai Zhong Road next to Lot 108, where a high-rise was under construction. It was a routine meeting of this group that usually goes to the municipal petition office on Wednesdays and then gets together to exchange information afterward. On that particular Wednesday they brought various documents they had obtained, which included one that transferred the land use rights of Lot 108, signed by the municipal housing bureau and Shui On in 1997, and the contract Shui On signed with the Luwan District government in 2001 to commission the latter to handle the demolition and relocation of Lot 114, two documents we discussed earlier. They compared the information in the documents with what they were told at the time and discovered that the district had lied to them on many counts.

The documents made it clear that the district was a partner to the developer all along. Though the Xintiandi project was initiated a decade ago, these residents have only just begun to learn about the process by which they lost their homes. Still, the full truth has not yet been revealed. For instance, they still have not found out how Lot 109, where He Yidong's house is located and where the centerpiece of Xintiandi is built, was transferred to Shui On and at what price, though documents regarding the transfer of Lot 108 give an idea of what happened to other lots.

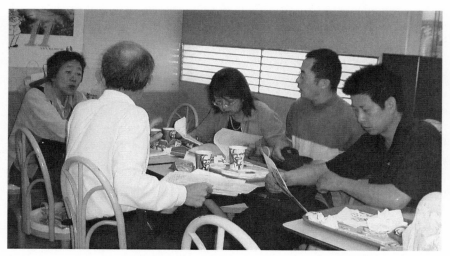

Figure 2.5. On a Wednesday in June 2007, this group of five former residents of the Taipingqiao and its surrounding area who were petitioning the government for their lost homes gathered at a KFC restaurant next to Xintiandi to exchange documents and information about their cases. He Yidong is the second from the right and the woman next to him is Zhang Xiaoqiu, daughter-in-law of Zhu Guangze.

With more information in hand and with his father's death, Yidong has explored a different approach to recovering his home. Since the Shanghai government has stonewalled him, Yidong decided to pursue justice in Hong Kong where the Shui On company is based. Hong Kong's colonial past has left a legal legacy that has given him a sense of hope. Although it is unlikely that Yidong will prevail against the real estate giant, since 2008 he has made three trips to Hong Kong to explore the possibility of pursuing his case there. Clearly, he needs the help of legal professionals in Hong Kong, but he can hardly afford them. During the first trip he learned that Hong Kong had a legal aid program to help those who cannot afford a lawyer. Yidong went through the process of applying for legal aid, but recently a Hong Kong court has denied his eligibility, which means that he must look for other channels of support.

He Yidong himself is acutely aware that going against a power structure of immense strength is an uphill battle, but giving up is not an option. In his words, the eviction was like "a piece of fish bone stuck in the throat—you can't swallow it and can't spit it out either." There was something stirring in his voice. Yidong wondered aloud when this constant irritation was going to become a damaging infection. Despite his usual calm, his anger sometimes spills out. Twice he has brought dozens of his friends to the restaurant to sit in and demand the return of his home. Twice he was brought before the neighborhood committee. He has not gotten into any serious trouble with local officials yet because the people at the committee know about his situation and sympathize with him. But they are powerless to help. At one point, a district official asked him what he would do if his house were destroyed now, which was a threat. In other words, he was implying that if Yidong kept this up, Shui On could destroy his house and build another one there so that he would not have anything to protest about. Yidong's answer was equally unsettling: "Since Shui On now owns all the property in Xintiandi except the CCP's First Congress [Museum], if they have the right to demolish my house, I'll assert my right to damage any and all the properties in Xintiandi except the CCP's Museum." "You can't show fear," Yidong told me, "or you'll be overcome by fear." It remains to be seen what this stuck fish bone will eventually turn into.

But Yidong is also realistic. Asked what exactly his expectations are since it is unlikely that he will get his house back soon, he answered, first, the district must acknowledge its mistake in forcing his family out and apologize for it. His sentiment is similar to that of Zhou Youlan and many others in their position: "What frustrates me most is that the officials clearly know about their wrongdoing but simply refuse to admit it. If only they could admit their mistakes!" Second, the district must provide information about the deal made for his house. Third, the government must restore the ownership of the house to the Hes. He fully understands that Xintiandi is now a commercial district and accepts that his family will not be able to reside there any time soon. He is therefore willing to allow the status quo—the restaurant—to continue but the family's ownership must be recognized. Related to that, Yidong believes that the parties involved—the Hes and Shui On and the district—should meet to work out terms as to when this status quo will end so that his family can plan on their return. Fourth, Yidong wants the district to compensate him for his material and emotional loss since the eviction more than a decade ago. In short, he wants to hold the district government accountable for its actions.

Can his requests be met? When? Yidong is prepared for a long fight. His family waited for a quarter of a century to get the house back the first time. He has purchased a scooter to negotiate the traffic as he appeals the family's case. His safety, especially because of his extreme nearsightedness—he can barely see traffic signs at night—is a constant concern of the family, just as they were worried about his father on his bicycle rides. Yidong expects the scooter to serve him on his long road to justice. He has also been lifting weights and exercising regularly to build up his physical strength. Yidong has seen enough of rough, even violent treatment of petitioners by the authorities. He does not know exactly what challenges may await him. But he does know that so long as he keeps seeking justice, he is a target of the authorities. He wants to be physically prepared for any possible confrontation in the future.

In light of the prolonged battle, history has once again confronted the Hes with the challenge of making the next generation understand the issues about their home. Like his father, Yidong has also faced the question of whether and how to tell his young son the truth. Unlike his father, who kept the facts from him, Yidong has taken his son to see the house from the outside and made sure that he remembers it as their family home. That his son now attends school nearby will only strengthen that memory so that Yidong's own childhood experience of mistaking a rental as his home will not be repeated. The difference between the way Yidong and his father have handled the situation stems from the fact that his father gave up the hope of returning to the house, while Yidong feels he can never lose that hope. He also understands that it may be up to the next generation to finally recover the house. As the burden of the son may be passed on, so may the sorrow of the father.

"You Destroyed My Home and You Now Own Me"

On a 2005 trip to a Forbes conference in Sydney, Vincent Lo spoke about his development in the Xintiandi area and gave an example about the patience required in doing business in China. Lo's example, according to the reporter, was about "the only [one] family still living on the site and refusing to move unless they are paid $4 million for the relocation. The issue has been going for the last two years and still hasn't been [re]solved." The reporter told the "one funny thing" Lo saw in this case, "That the very family [that] remains on the site doesn't actually have any title to the land they are living on; the local government doesn't want to vacate them because they want to have a 'harmonious' social environment and would never seek violence."[24]

Vincent Lo could qualify as the best spokesman for the Chinese government and its commitment to a "harmonious society." In reality, however, building such an ideal society is far less important than building a seven-star hotel complex for the profit-driven Luwan District government. The only truth in Lo's statement is that the family in question had indeed been holding out and their house was indeed the last one still standing by late 2005. But the rest of what he said is false—the family did have title to their property; they preferred to keep their house and, when being forced to relocate, they looked for a reasonable settlement without asking anything remotely close to $4 million; and finally, the government in Shanghai and elsewhere routinely drove residents out of their homes with force and, in this case, evicted the family by kidnapping its matriarch and her daughter in their sleep and then carried out domicide.

This family in question in Lot 108, just one block north of Xintiandi, had a matriarch named Zhu Guangze, who was in her eighties at the time. The story of how the Zhu family lost their home is similar to that of the Hes. But the two cases are also different in a number of ways that enrich our understanding of the complexities in housing conflicts.

The redevelopment of Lot 108 did not start until fall 2002. According to the Taipingqiao development plan, Lot 108 was to be the site of a seven-star hotel complex, which required the leveling of all the houses on the lot instead of the partial preservation seen in Lot 109 for the Xintiandi project. The district housing bureau expected the demolition of Lot 108 to go as swiftly as that of Lot 109. The plan initially allowed three months, from September 5 to November 30, 2002, to remove all of the families. By December, however, the district housing bureau had to extend the deadline to September 2003. But Lot 108 was not cleared until the end of 2005, when the Zhus, the last residents, were evicted. In other words, because of resistance, the planned three-month period for the demolition dragged on for three years, which apparently caused Vincent Lo great frustration, as he vented in Sydney.

The reasons for the difficulty with Lot 108 are many. First of all, more than 13 percent of the housing units there were privately owned and nearly 22 percent were new-style alleyway houses. Many of these families were unwilling to relocate. Also, the hike in the real estate market widened the gap between residents' expectations and the district's plans for compensation, which made the negotiations difficult. The big picture had also changed since 1998 when the Xintiandi project started. Cases such as the Hes and the media's exposure of corruption fast eroded whatever initial trust Shanghai's residents had in the municipal government's urban renewal program. Real estate development in Shanghai had reached a new height as it had become the main engine for GDP growth. The government moved from demolishing slums to destroying neighborhoods with decent housing. This large-scale and indiscriminate destruction of neighborhoods inevitably broadened the targets, causing more residents, especially those with private properties and better houses in the most desirable locations, to resist. Many residents also learned more about their rights and began to network with each other to strategize their struggle. All this led to much broader and more determined resistance. In 1998, after only four months of holding out, the Hes were labeled a "nail household," a label considered degrading. In the ensuing years, families had to hold out for years to earn that label and then they wore it as a hero's badge. Zhu Guangze's family, which on the surface was not even among the toughest "nail households," provides a case in point.

The Zhus' home, numbered 162, 164, 166, and 168 on Taichang Road, immediately south of Huaihai Zhong Road, was part of a four-unit property. It was constructed in the early 1900s and bought in 1925 at the cost of 40,000 silver yuan by Zhu Guangze's father, Zhu Hongnan, a Zhejiang native who built a thriving paper business in Shanghai. These four three-story units, independent from the neighboring alleyway housing, were what Shanghainese called Western-style garden houses, and were complete with multiple bathrooms, living rooms, bedrooms, balconies, gardens, courtyards, maids' quarters, and garages. Zhu Hongnan's paper shop was on the first floor of one of these street-front units. Zhu had two wives and children by each. The four units were divided between the two families.

Zhu Guangze (born 1922), one of Zhu Hongnan's daughters, attended a missionary women's middle school, and then St. John's University in the mid-1940s, majoring in education. Upon graduation she worked as a clerk in the Shanghai Municipal Bureau of Finance. In 1947, Zhu married Lu Hong-you (1916–1989), an official at the bureau and a graduate of the prestigious Dongwu University. By then Zhu Guangze's father had passed away and her mother invited the newlyweds to live with her in the two units she owned, 162 and 164, about 800 square meters in total, so that they could take care of each other. Our story here mainly concerns these two units.

During the war with Japan (1937–1945), Lu Hongyou served as a special commissioner in the GMD's Ministry of Finance. In 1946 he was appointed head of a tax department in a Shanghai district. His various diplomas and appointment letters were signed by Chiang Kai-shek, the head of the GMD and president of the Republic of China, H. H. Kung (Kong Xiangxi), Chiang's minister of finance, and Wu Guozhen, Shanghai's mayor in the late 1940s. Among his classmates at Dongwu University was one of Chiang Kai-shek's sons. His sister-in-law became Mme. Chiang's private dentist and her husband, Zhou Hongtao, was once Chiang Kai-shek's secretary. With deep roots in the GMD government, Lu and his family planned on going to Taiwan at the end of the 1940s, just as his sister-in-law and many of his colleagues had done. But the family eventually stayed put for the sake of Lu's mother because she had to take care of her younger son who was too ill to join them on the journey.

This random occurrence in life sealed their fate. Soon enough the family found out the price they had to pay for staying. During the regime transition of late 1949 and early 1950, Zhu Guangze's mother rented out the first floor of the two units to supplement their income. In the mid-1950s, that floor, a rental, became a target of the socialist reform and was taken over by the government. And the family expanded—Zhu gave birth to a daughter and a son in the early 1950s. Lu Hongyou got a job at a hardware factory and Zhu Guangze became a high school English teacher. Her mother passed away in 1965, barely missing the height of the Cultural Revolution during which time the family of four—Lu, Zhu, and their two children—were driven out of the home into a loft of eleven square meters where they lived for more than a decade. The Red Guards from both Lu's and Zhu's work units set up a stage in their neighborhood to attack them, accusing Lu of being a GMD spy and Zhu a "slave" of the capitalist West because of her English skills. Zhu and Lu were locked up in separate "cowsheds"—the CCP classified its enemies as "monsters and demons" and called the places to keep them as *niupeng*, cowsheds—for more than a year. Like the Hes, the Zhu family did not return to their home until a decade after the Cultural Revolution ended.

In the fall of 1966, when the Cultural Revolution was most out of control, the "revolutionary rebels," as they called themselves, from Lu's hardware factory searched his home seven times. They seized plenty of booty, which they catalogued in a sixty-page list of "Lu Hongyou's Evidence of Criminality and Possessions." This list of thousands of items is not only a rare source for studying the material culture of the upper-middle class in Shanghai that survived the 1949 regime change only to be destroyed during the Cultural Revolution, it is also a revealing mirror of the madness of that era. Granted that the list includes several suitcases full of "reactionary documents" and evidence of their bourgeois lifestyle—Lu Hongyou's many official titles, diplomas, seals, badges, and correspondence under the GMD; hundreds of various kinds of fur and leather coats and other clothing; a large amount of jewelry, gold bars, and other gold items; multiple sets of silverware; bolts of silk, wool, and cotton; bankbooks for dozens of accounts, bonds, old Chinese currency, American dollars, and life insurance policies; a house-full of rosewood, marble, and leather furniture; a few bullets; scores of paintings, calligraphy, china, and antiques from the Ming and Qing dynasties; and imported items such as cameras and watches from the Japanese "devils" to American and German "imperialists," all of which could be construed as the legacy of a past that was under assault. But the list also contains trivial items such as locks, envelopes, and small toys, all of which were declared to be "evidence of criminality." The Red Guards immediately consigned some of the items for sale at commission shops.

Before 1949, in addition to their residences in Lot 108, the Zhus possessed five other properties in some of the best locations in Shanghai, which they rented out. In August 1958 at the height of the CCP's socialist reform those five properties were taken over by the government without any compensation. The government did issue the Zhus a property certificate that allowed them to collect "fixed rent," 23.37 yuan a month, from the nationalized first floor of units 162 and 164, through the government. This "rent" was a token compensation for a limited period, provided as a way to ease the transition to full nationalization. Each month the Zhus carried this certificate to a designated government office to collect the rent and the office would date and stamp the transaction. This certificate, which the family has kept for all those years, shows a stamp for every month from 1963 to November 1965, the onset of the Cultural Revolution. It was then that the payments came to a halt.

Thus by 2002 when the Wuxin Co. started the demolition on Lot 108, Zhu Guangze—her husband had died years earlier—lived together with her daughter and son, both married and each with a child, on the upper two floors of the two units. The three-year struggle from 2002 to 2005 over their relocation could have been much shorter and less traumatic if the district had accommodated their initial request, as they were forced to move for the government's "urban renewal" project. The question, as in many other cases, was where and how.

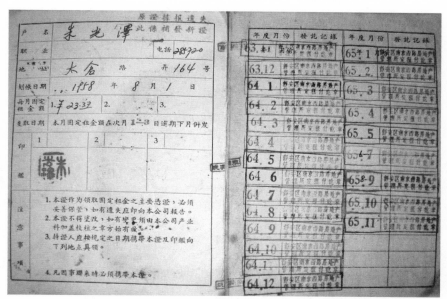

Figure 2.6. During the 1950s socialist reform, the government nationalized several of Zhu Guangze's properties. In token compensation, it issued Zhu a certificate to collect "fixed rent," 23.37 yuan a month, for one of her properties, through the government, which was now the new manager of her properties. This certificate shows a stamp for every month from 1963 to November 1965, the onset of the Cultural Revolution, when the payments came to a halt.

Zhu Guangze asked for three apartments within Luwan District, one for herself, the other two for her daughter and son respectively. The district rejected the request and instead, following its usual practice, assigned them to apartments in the suburbs. The family then was willing to accept a cash settlement so that they could purchase a house nearby. The amount of cash compensation therefore became a point of contention. The district employed a number of schemes to drive down the value of their house, which led to a series of conflicts. First, the district tried to deny that the Zhus owned the house, a fabrication that Vincent Lo continued to perpetrate in 2005. Then the district considered the Zhu house as a new-style alleyway type instead of an independent house—the government assigned a different amount of compensation for the two types of housing, with the latter being of higher value. In addition, it insisted the house was smaller than the Zhus had claimed, yet refused the family's request to actually measure the house. Finally, although Zhu and her daughter and son lived together, they were in fact three families—Zhu Guangze herself, her daughter and her family, and her son and his family—each of which had its own, separate household registration. This was an important detail in the calculation of the compensation because, according to relevant regulations, each family was entitled to an independent settlement. But the district tried to shove Zhu's children, especially her daughter, aside and focused its attention on Zhu Guangze who, in her eighties, was considered the weakest link.

The district almost succeeded. At midnight one night in June 2003, the district demolition office, after exerting much pressure, was able to compel an exhausted Zhu to sign a contract for a cash settlement. But the contract offered little for Zhu's daughter, who naturally protested. At one point, the daughter was willing to compromise if only the district would add 30,000 yuan to the package, which would allow her to purchase her own apartment. The demolition office, with Zhu's signature in hand, refused her daughter's request out of hand, losing a rare opportunity to settle the matter. Under pressure from the family and frustrated with the district, Zhu declared that she was rescinding the contract, for which the district demolition office took her to court, which caused even more bad blood with the family. The case stalled, and the swelling real estate market over the next two years only made the family more adamant in their position and diminished the possibility of reaching a settlement. In fact, the rising market had made the amount of compensation a moving target. Initially, the district offered about 4,600 yuan per square meter, more than it offered to the Hes four years earlier but not enough for the Zhus to purchase a comparable home downtown. By 2005, with the rapid rise in the market, the district agreed to pay 10,000 yuan per square meter for the Zhu house, but the family wanted 50,000 yuan, the current market price so that they could afford to buy their own apartments. The district refused to bridge the gap of 40, 000 yuan.

The family tried to rally their relatives across the Taiwan Strait for help. While such connections spelled trouble under Mao, they could be an advantage in the reform era because of the increased economic and other ties between Taiwan and mainland China. In December 2002, Zhou Hongtao, the brother-in-law of Zhu Guangze and onetime secretary of Chiang Kai-shek, wrote a letter on his private stationery addressed to the director of Luwan District on behalf of Zhu. The letter pleaded with the district to reconsider its action of "depriving Zhu Guangze of the home she had inherited from her mother." But the age of reform also prioritized economic growth above all else. The district told the Zhu family that there was nothing they could do to save their house: "You can even appeal to the United Nations—no matter where you go, your matter is in our hands."

In the meantime, the district kept the pressure on. Throughout the three years of contention, the district issued three administrative rulings, each with a deadline for the family to get out. The district court subpoenaed Zhu twice for revoking the contract, which she insisted she had been tricked into signing in the first place. The Wuxin Co. demolition squad also employed what the family claimed was a series of "abnormal, despicable, mean and dirty tricks," to "torture" them and "threatened" their "property rights and personal safety." The team stole their iron doors in the front and broke their windows. When the family called the emergency number for help, the police told them to "just move out." The Wuxin Co. also destroyed the sewer system and gas supply to the house. The family had to find friends in the gas company for help. But the broken sewer was beyond repair; the family resorted to using a chamber pot. The demolition squad tried to set fire to their roof, a known scheme employed by local governments in Shanghai and elsewhere to force residents out. It also used another common "dirty trick," literally—for a period of time the demolition squad sent its members daily to use the Zhu's courtyard, which was exposed after the front doors were stolen, as a toilet. The family photographed the human waste and included those photographs in some of their protest letters. It became a nerve-racking, full-time job for the family to struggle with and document all these abuses.

The climax of this sustained harassment came in the morning of November 18, 2005. By then, Lot 108 had been cleared except for the Zhus' house and the construction of the hotel complex had already started but could not go full speed with the house in the way. The district lost patience. The last round of threats came on October 25, 2005, when the district issued yet another eviction notice, this time ordering the family to move out within fifteen days. In response, the family restated its earlier request, which the district again rejected. Yet the district did not carry out the eviction on the designated date. The family interpreted that to mean the deadline was yet another empty threat. Just as the family thought it could relax a bit, suddenly on the morning of November 18 after most of the family members had gone to work, dozens of men from the Wuxin Co. broke into the Zhus' house. They first got hold of Zhu's daughter, who screamed "help" to warn her mother, who was still asleep in her bedroom on the third floor. The demolition squad threw both of them into a parked van and drove them away. Within hours, the Zhus' house became another victim of domicide—it was knocked down and reduced to a pile of debris.

Zhu Guangze recounted the "barbaric kidnapping and eviction" of her and her daughter that morning:

> A group of frightening scoundrels broke into my house. Without showing any identification cards, they rushed into my bedroom, tied my hands, and rolled me up in my blanket. I tried to resist but I could hardly move. They dragged

me down from the third floor and, in the struggle, I suffered multiple bruises. When they brought me out to the van, I tried to scream "help" in English because there are often foreigners around Huaihai Road, but my voice was too weak to be heard. They then drove my daughter and me to a basement and locked us up. I realized that I'd been kidnapped and was now homeless. "How am I going to live like this? Why am I still alive?" I asked myself. I took off my gold ring and swallowed it; I no longer wanted to live.

Zhu's life was spared that day because a guard saw her desperately swallowing something and took her to the hospital. She was so traumatized by the violence that she lost sight in her left eye overnight and was hospitalized for a week. But her life as a homeless person and her family's anguish over the eviction had only just begun. That afternoon on November 18, when Zhang Xiaoqiu, Zhu's daughter-in-law, returned home, she witnessed the site of domicide: the house was gone, and so were her mother-in-law and sister-in-law. She cried and collapsed to the ground, which was littered with broken but still familiar pieces of her home-no-more: caved stairway rails, stained window glass, and a French bathtub for which an antique dealer had once offered 10,000 yuan. She contacted her husband and son. They frantically went out to search for their missing family members, only to learn that their mother had tried to commit suicide.

Zhu Guangze's daughter and son have since found their own apartments, but not Zhu Guangze herself. She was so deeply offended by the domicide that she was willing to use herself as leverage to compel the district to solve the conflict. She refused to move in with her son and insisted on staying in the basement to which she had been brought on the day of kidnapping. She told the demolition team, "You destroyed my home and you now own me. You are responsible for taking care of me." More than once, the demolition squad threatened to carry Zhu Guangze to her son's home, for which they have contacted her son's current neighborhood committee and his work unit for support, but have received none from either place. The district then arranged for Zhu Guangze to stay in a small, temporary apartment with a maid about an hour's bicycle ride away from her son's new home. Her son, whom the district has accused of being unfilial, visits her daily. In early April 2007, Zhu Guangze fell down in the apartment and broke her hip while the maid was away. She crawled to the door to call a neighbor for help. When I visited her in July, she had been confined to bed for three months and had not been able to take a bath. Her son and daughter-in-law came daily to help clean her and bring her food. No more than 70 pounds and suffering from heart diseases, her body seemed to have disappeared under the blanket. But she had no intention of ending her self-imposed bondage. She talked to me for an hour, as I captured our conversation on my camcorder, about her ordeal and her resolve, pledging her life to "seek justice according to the law: return my home and compensate me for the damage done to my family."

As of 2010, Zhu's son still worked as a middle school teacher. Zhang Xiaoqiu, Zhu's daughter-in-law, a retiree, had emerged as the family representative in petitioning their case. She has made numerous petition trips to Beijing and has written many petition letters. In those letters the family has accused the district demolition squad of many crimes—distorting the type of their house; refusing a fair evaluation of its value; evicting them in a barbaric fashion; and failing in its duty at every twist and turn. They pointed out,

> Generations of our family have been law-abiding citizens. Though we are deeply attached to our family home, we understand the importance of development and we were willing to part with the house we treasured. But the district first failed to act sincerely and to follow the law and then it shockingly resorted to kidnapping us. All this has caused bitter hatred. How could such a scandal

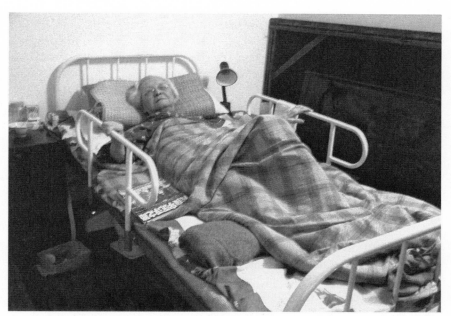

Figure 2.7. Zhu Guangze (1922–), since her eviction in late 2005, has become a self-imposed hostage—she has insisted on staying in a Spartan apartment provided by the district government until her housing dispute is resolved. She had been bedridden after a fall for three months when this picture was taken in July 2007.

happen at this time when the party promotes a harmonious society? Isn't the district too corrupt? We demand the central government investigate the scandal, uphold justice and the law, thoroughly rectify the district's mistakes, and protect citizens' property rights and personal safety, so that the wrong done to us can be righted!

All the family's petition letters have ended with these two lines: "Return our property! Compensate us for the damage!"

This new and final round of property seizures has brought to the surface the family's past grievances. After all, their home was not the only one, albeit the final one, of the properties they lost to the CCP. In the 1950s the government had taken over a number of their properties scattered in the city; all of them had now been leveled. Gone, too, are thousands of items confiscated during the Cultural Revolution and the family has not seen any of them since. The family has reopened dusty boxes to inventory their past and lost possessions. In their petition letters now they also ask about those other properties and possessions that the family was entitled to. In fact, the 2002 letter from Zhou Hongtao, Zhu's brother-in-law in Taiwan, explicitly demanded that the Luwan District government look into the Zhus' "property lost during the Cultural Revolution, forcibly taken by the government without any compensation" and "rectify the mistakes." While the family is not really hopeful that the past wrongs committed under Mao will be corrected, they nevertheless feel compelled to bring up the issue of the CCP's consistent disregard for private property and for citizens' rights. The family, however, believes the current injustice will be addressed someday. Like others who have suffered from domicide, Zhu Guangze and her family simply cannot accept that their loss, so unjust, will be permanent; they want someone to take responsibility.

Dream Team and Nightmares

When Vincent Lo and Benjamin Wood first met in 1998, Lo reportedly told Wood that the Xintiandi project would change both of their lives, and it has.

First of all, true to Wood's promise, Xintiandi has been a commercial hit. As mentioned earlier, in 1997 Shui On acquired the land use rights of Lot 108 at about $612 per square meter for forty years. If the company's acquisition of the other lots in the Taipingqiao area was made in a similar deal, then it was a steal, considering that as of 2009 commercial units in the area were priced at around $9,000 per square meter, almost fifteen times what Lo's company paid the district government. Shui On's commercial rentals in

Xintiandi, which had a 100 percent occupancy rate and a waiting list, were priced at 30 to 100 yuan per square meter per day, depending on the size of the property.[25] Movie stars from Taiwan to Hong Kong, whom Lo counts among his friends, have opened businesses there.[26] Luwan District, while investing 2 percent of the capital, is taking a 10 percent cut of the profits made in Xintiandi. In addition to profiting from rentals and leases, Vincent Lo himself directly owns some of properties there. With all this success, in October 2006, Vincent Lo took Shui On public in the Hong Kong stock exchange, raising billions of Hong Kong dollars.[27]

The success of Xintiandi goes beyond money. As a cultural and commercial icon for the new Shanghai, Xintiandi has become a name brand for the dream team of Vincent Lo and Benjamin Wood. It represents a seemingly magic formula for combining the development of highly profitable commercial projects with historic preservation. This image has certainly contributed to Shui On's subsequent success in China, as major cities across the country have lined up to retain its services. Most of those projects include "Tiandi" in their title as a reference to Shui On and Wood's phenomenal success in Shanghai. Little wonder, therefore, that the company's business milestones listed on its website were all about the name brand Xintiandi, from its initial proposal in 1996 to its official opening in 2002.[28]

Through Xintiandi, Wood has made "the ordinary extraordinary" and has "breathed life" into the Taipingqiao area where people now "eat, drink, and enjoy themselves," just as he had envisioned. But it is also about the definition of life. The "magic of the place," with its "whole litany of human experience," that had "blown" Wood away in 1998 has vanished—there is no neighborhood life sustained on a daily basis. In fact, the gentrification of Xintiandi was realized by driving the residents out and destroying the neighborhood and community life there. Very few former residents of the area can even afford a cup of coffee in Xintiandi, supposedly a re-creation of a traditional neighborhood in Shanghai.

In this regard, Xintiandi is an absolute betrayal of the model of Italian hill towns such as Siena that inspired both Lo and Wood. The "adaptive re-use" that Wood so admires in Siena allowed small, traditional, family grocery shops and residential homes to coexist with expensive and world-renowned stores. In July 2009, I took a trip to Siena to examine what Wood and Lo had seen there. My first sight upon arriving at one of the tourist entrances was an old lady in her pink nightgown chatting with neighbors on the street corner. There was laundry hanging between windows on second floor homes; a young woman was sitting on the windowsill having a cigarette while tourists walked by; mothers and children were having a picnic in the park; and the local communities were holding their twice-a-year Palio, a bareback horse race in one of Europe's oldest medieval squares, with the winning district celebrating its victory on the narrow streets dotted with its flag, a tradition dating back to the Middle Ages. The development in Siena has preserved this organic, wholesome community life which gives the town its unique historic charm and depth.

The Xintiandi project, on the other hand, has sucked out the vitality of the neighborhood life and left it soulless—deep into the night when all the businesses are closed, Xintiandi is a ghost town. As one scholar points out, if every alleyway in Shanghai is "renovated to serve a solely commercial purpose like Xintiandi, the city will soon become lifeless because of the diminishing of [mixed use] programme[s] and diversity of urban activities."[29] Wood himself recognizes both the difference between Xintiandi and Siena and the difficulty in Shanghai at the time to develop a Siena-type mixed community that preserves its traditional character.[30]

It is to Wood's credit that he does not present Xintiandi as a historic preservation project. Regardless, the project has been branded a model of historic preservation and has been fast "replicated around China."[31] This kind of misguided "preservation," as Rem Koolhaas points out, is a "new form of historical amnesia." It destroys the history of our cities, contributes to gentrification, and widens the gap between the rich and the poor by displacing local residents for the rich to take over their spaces to get richer still.[32]

This is at the heart of our stories here. After all, the huge profits from projects such as Xintiandi and the high value of downtown real estate are the root cause of the nightmare inflicted on families such as the Hes and the Zhus. Downtown Shanghai has become too expensive to allow even the original homeowners to remain there. They must be driven out to create space for the government and developers to make a profit, which has become today's top priority.

In 2006 Vincent Lo "brushe[d] aside" concerns about Shanghai residents who held out but admitted that "relocation is a huge hassle," not because of developers like him, of course, but because of the locals, some of them—"squatters" in his words—who were costing him "big money." He complained about the cost of seizing private property but was unfazed because of his faith in the Chinese government: "if they are important projects, the government will push them through."[33] Time and again, that is indeed what the Chinese government has done—it judges the importance of any project based on its profit margin instead of human values. The two cases examined here are especially telling, because one family is Muslim and the other has deep connections to high-level GMD officials. In the past, these factors could have served as leverage since the Chinese government wishes to be seen as the protector of the so-called minority nationalities and as the champion of China's reunification with Taiwan. But in post-Mao China, economic development has replaced all other considerations: it has become an overriding force that stops at nothing and respects no one.

A company with a strict "Code of Conduct & Business Ethics" from a well-regulated society such as Hong Kong is part of that force, regardless what it preaches. Shui On's website indicates that the company "strives to conduct all business affairs in accordance with the highest business ethics standards, acting as a socially responsible company and a good corporate citizen . . . All directors and employees must respect and obey the laws, rules and regulations of the cities, provinces and countries in which we operate."[34] But what happens if the government itself breaks its own laws?

And what happens if the international community is dazzled by a star performer and turns a blind eye to the context in which the star rises? Vincent Lo has received a number of honors, including "Justice of the Peace" in 1999 by the government of the Hong Kong Special Administrative Region, the 2001 Businessman of the Year in Hong Kong, and other awards from France and elsewhere. He has also held a few political and business leadership positions in Hong Kong and the central Chinese government.[35] Lo has been rewarded because of his business success, which in part has been achieved by being in bed with corrupt Chinese officials and robbing people such as the Hes and the Zhus of their homes. Such behavior is a far cry from Shui On's claimed "highest business ethics standards."

If Xintiandi is indeed the best place to appreciate "the history and modern life" in Shanghai where "yesterday and tomorrow meet,"[36] then let's recognize that it is also where the nightmares of the old and the new converge.

Notes

1. http://www.shanghai.gov.cn/shanghai/node2314/node2318/node2376/node2393/index.html, accessed 6 April 2009. In 2011, Luwan District merged into Huangpu District.

2. http://www.shanghai.gov.cn/shanghai/node2314/node2318/node2376/node2393/index.html, accessed 6 April 2009.

3. Unless otherwise indicated, this and the following paragraphs on the history of the Taiping Bridge area and the French Concession are based on Luo Xiaowei, et al., eds., *Shanghai Xintiandi: jiuqu gaizao de jianzhu lishi, renwen lishi yu kaifa moshi de yanjiu* (Shanghai Xintiandi: A Study of Architectural and Human History and Developmental Models in Urban Renewal) (Nanjing: Dongnan daxue chubanshe, 2002), 12–71.

4. Hanchao Lu, "'The Seventy-two Tenants': Residence and Commerce in Shanghai's *Shikumen* Houses, 1871–1951," in *Inventing Nanjing Road: Commercial Culture in Shanghai, 1900–1945*, ed. Sherman Cochran (Ithaca, NY: Cornell University Press, 1999), 174–75.

5. http://www.forbes.com/lists/2009/10/billionaires-2009-richest-people_Vincent-Lo_FRL6.html, accessed 22 April 2009.

6. http://www.sfgate.com/cgi-bin/article.cgi?file=/c/a/2006/01/01/BUGJCG-DH4P1.DTL; http://en.wikipedia.org/wiki/Vincent_Lo, accessed 22 April 2009.

7. http://www.citymayors.com/mayors/shanghai-mayor.html, accessed 1 May 2009.

8. http://edition.cnn.com/2007/BUSINESS/04/09/boardroom.lo/, accessed 23 April 2009.

9. http://www.shuionland.com/sol/tabid/904/Default.aspx, accessed, 23 April 2009.

10. http://www.gluckilometersan.com/XinTianDi.html, accessed 23 April 2009.

11. Benjamin Wood provided me with part of his proposal and I also interviewed him in May 2009 and June 2010.

12. http://www.gluckilometersan.com/XinTianDi.html, accessed 23 April 2009.

13. Lu, "'The Seventy-two Tenants,'" 134–47.

14. Lu, "'The Seventy-two Tenants,'" 140–42. For the best study of the history of shikumen houses and neighborhood life in Shanghai, see Hanchao Lu, *Beyond the Neon Lights: Everyday Shanghai in the Early Twentieth Century* (Berkeley: University of California Press, 1999).

15. For a recent study of Zheng He's life and experience, see Dolors Folch, "Els mars de Zheng He (The Seas of Zheng He)," in *Els grans viatges de Zheng He*, ed. Dolors Folch (Barcelona: Angle Editorial, 2008). According to Folch, while the Ming court prohibited eunuchs from adopting sons, it likely granted Zheng He an exception because of his prestige. That is why Zheng He's adoption of his nephew came late in his life (email message to author, 26 April 2009).

16. See a discussion of the GMD's postwar effort in Okinawa in http://www.drnh.gov.tw/www/page/c_book/ab19/2-%B7%A8%A4l%BE_(72dpi)-%A4%BA%A4%E5.pdf, esp. 68–69, accessed 18 May 2009.

17. The Anti-Rightist movement was one of the many mass campaigns the CCP launched under Mao to attack those who criticized the party. Jonathan Spence, *The Search for Modern China* (New York: W. W. Norton, 1999), 542–43.

18. Spence, *Search for Modern China*, 577–78.

19. For a brief mention of the revival of the Chinese teahouse in post-Mao China, see Qin Shao, "Tempest over Teapots: The Vilification of Teahouse Culture in Early Republican China," *Journal of Asian Studies* 57.4 (Nov. 1998): 1036.

20. Falü chubanshe fagui zhongxin (The Center of Law and Regulations at the Law Press), ed., *Fangwu chaiqian fugui zizhu* (Self-help in Laws and Regulations on Housing Demolition and Relocation) (Beijing: Falü chubanshe, 2004), 107.

21. http://www.madaboutshanghai.com/2005/09/meet_vincent_lo.html, accessed 23 April 2009.

22. Falü chubanshe fagui zhongxin, ed., *Fangwu chaiqian fugui zizhu*, 108.

23. The household registration system in urban China, known in Chinese as *hukou*, was used to control the urban population. It is also a basis for providing services to city residents, from housing to schools. For a detailed study of the household registration system in urban China, see Fei-Ling Wang, *Organizing through Division and Exclusion: China's Hukou System* (Stanford: Stanford University Press, 2005).

24. http://www.madaboutshanghai.com/2005/09/meet_vincent_lo.html, accessed 23 April 2009.

25. Telephone interview with Miss Taylor Xia, Shui On Property Leasing in Shanghai, 23 April 2009 (10:15 a.m. Shanghai time).

26. http://www.xici.net/b271373/d13894439.htm, accessed 16 March 2009.

27. http://www.shuionland.com/sol/tabid/919/Default.aspx, accessed 20 May 2009.

28. http://www.shuionland.com/sol/tabid/904/Default.aspx, accessed, 23 April 2009.

29. Non Arkaraprasertkul, "Towards Modern Urban Housing: Redefining Shanghai's Lilong," *Journal of Urbanism: International Research on Placemaking and Urban Sustainability* 2.1 (2009): 28.

30. In June 2010 I gave a talk at a conference at East China Normal University in Shanghai on Xintiandi and Siena. Benjamin Wood was kind enough to come to the talk and we discussed the comparison.

31. http://www.gluckilometersan.com/XinTianDi.html, accessed 23 April 2009.

32. http://www.nytimes.com/2011/05/24/arts/design/cronocaos-by-rem-koolhaas-at-the-new-museum.html?emc=eta1, accessed 25 May 2011.

33. http://www.sfgate.com/cgi-bin/article.cgi?file=/c/a/2006/01/01/BUGJCG-DH4P1.DTL, accessed 22 April 2009.

34. http://www.shuionland.com/sol/Portals/0/materials/code_eng.pdf, accessed 24 April 2009.

35. See a detailed list of Vincent Lo's awards and positions in: http://www.wharton hongkong07.com/bio-s-lo2.html, accessed 23 April 2009.

36. http://english.eastday.com/e/xx/userobject1ai4026435.html, accessed 9 April 2009.

CHAPTER THREE

~

Waving the Red Flag

It's about nothing but Costs, now. We are always appearing, and disappearing, swearing, and interrogating, and filing, and cross-filing, and arguing, and sealing, and motioning, and referring, and reporting, and revolving about the Lord Chancellor and all his satellites, and equitably waltzing ourselves off to dusty death, about Costs. That is the great question. All the rest, by some extraordinary means, has melted away.

—Charles Dickens, *Bleak House*

In June 2004, a group of residents gathered in downtown Shanghai and collectively sang "The Internationale" to support one of their neighbors who was being evicted by a government relocation squad. They also chanted, "Forced Demolition, Against the Law!" and cheered when the neighbor clutched the bars covering his apartment window and refused to be dragged out. Collective resistance like this was common in this neighborhood from spring 2003 to fall 2004 when it was under siege, facing demolition.

The neighborhood in question is known as the East Eight Lots (*dongba kuai*). This case, perhaps the best known and highest profile in the recent history of housing disputes in Shanghai, had attracted broad media coverage at the time.[1] It implicated a business tycoon whose stunning rise and fall in part contributed to the political demise of Chen Liangyu, Shanghai's party head, in 2006. It involved a Christian lawyer who was imprisoned for representing the families there facing eviction. The case also turned a former resident and a clothing retailer in Hong Kong into a onetime popular author

145

who wrote about her family's ordeal in the demolition. It produced other most intriguing figures, one of whom was a worker whose ability to play hardball in an understated manner got him exactly what he wanted. The case locked the authorities and the residents in a battle of willpower and resourcefulness and led to some surprising results. It has changed not only lives but also the cityscape.

What happened in the East Eight Lots is a textbook case of what has gone wrong in real estate development and urban renewal in Shanghai. It illustrates some of the most important characteristics of urban grassroots protest. The residents' resistance, both individually and collectively, was open, persistent, resourceful, and inventive. In fighting for their interests, they launched a "total war," so to speak, in the legal, administrative, and media domains and in the symbolic universe across China's long history from ancient times to Mao's Cultural Revolution.

The Deceit

The East Eight Lots was in Jing'an District. Jing'an, like Luwan, where Xintiandi is located, is one of the most prosperous districts in Shanghai. It included a portion of West Nanjing Road, the densely populated heart of downtown—crowded in it are on average 50,000 people per square kilometer.[2] The East Eight Lots, located between West Beijing Road to the south and the banks of Suzhou Creek to the north, covered eight neighborhoods numbered from Lot 56 to 63, hence the name. Its residences were a mix of old-style and new-style alleyway apartments. This difference in housing quality proved to be a problem later. The property status was just as mixed. Most residents were tenants renting from the district housing bureau or their work units, although some had owned their apartments since before the Communist takeover in 1949.

In 2001, Jing'an District proposed this area for demolition to make space for new apartment buildings as part of the second phase of urban renewal in Shanghai. On July 9, 2001, the municipal housing bureau issued Document 347, approving the proposal. Due to both its central location and size, this project was one of the largest and most ambitious urban renewal projects in Shanghai. Document 347 indicated that the plan was to first demolish four lots starting from the corner of West Beijing Road and Second Shimen Road as an experiment. While Lot 56 was located right at that corner, a sheet attached to Document 347 confirmed the specific area was limited to Lots 57, 58, 59, and 60 only; there was no mention of Lot 56. This bureaucratic oversight, too, would later become a point of contention. The four lots together covered about 121,226 square meters and were home to more than 5,000 households.

The chosen developer for the East Eight Lots was none other than Zhou Zhengyi, once a legendary tycoon in the Chinese world of the newly rich. Born into a slum in Yangpu District in the northeastern part of the city, Zhou opened a small wonton noodle shop in his home district in 1978 after junior high school. In the mid-1980s, he labored in Japan and returned in 1989 to invest in restaurants, a karaoke bar, and other businesses. In the 1990s he made a fortune in the stock market and then, in 1997 established Nong Kai Development Group and set out to conquer the rising real estate market in both Shanghai and Hong Kong. In 2001, at the age of forty, Zhou was ranked the ninety-fourth richest Chinese by Forbes Global.[3] He made the list again the next year, and advanced his rank to eleventh among the 400 richest Chinese.[4]

In late May 2003, however, his fortunes took a fateful downward turn as an official investigation launched by Beijing one year earlier was made public. At that time, Zhou reportedly had assets of around $312 million. As the chairman of the Board of the Shanghai Real Estate Company, Zhou allegedly owned 75 percent of the real estate in Shanghai and controlled thirty-nine companies.[5] Various banks, including the Bank of China, allegedly had lent Zhou 100 billion yuan.[6]

Zhou's final downfall quickly followed. In early June, officials openly acknowledged that Zhou was under investigation and that he had already been put in detention.[7] All this sent a wave of panic through business circles in Shanghai and Hong Kong. As the shares of Zhou's companies plunged and his companies became paralyzed, the Chinese media had a field day in early June, reporting on the collapse of Zhou's "Shanghai Kingdom."[8] A year later, in June 2004, a Shanghai court sentenced Zhou to three years in prison on some vague charges of irregular financial dealings.[9] All this was only window dressing: the court could hardly hide the fact that China suffered from systematic corruption and alarmingly bad loan practices. Also, the CCP often uses corruption charges as a weapon to attack political opponents. In this case, the downfall of Zhou Zhengyi was a prelude for Beijing to remove his friend in a higher place, the Shanghai party boss Chen Liangyu. Chen was part of the Shanghai clique built up by the former CCP head Jiang Zemin.[10]

But the real victims caught in the Zhou Zhengyi scandal were the residents of the East Eight Lots. While details about the dealings between Zhou and Jing'an District, which had granted Zhou the land use rights of the East Eight Lots, remain murky to this day, at least three crucial, interrelated pieces of information have become clear as the media and residents probed into the scandal.

First, in May 2002, the Jing'an District government signed a contract—known as Contract 19—with Zhou, handing him the land use rights of the East Eight Lots, a prime piece of property worth at least $32 million, for zero cost.[11] Zhou was not the only developer to enjoy that kind of preferential policy. At the time, the reason given for this policy was that urban renewal that involved the relocation of residents, especially in the densely populated central districts, was prohibitively costly. The Shanghai government thus sought to create an incentive for developers to take on the task of "improving people's lives" by building affordable housing.[12] But by then, the meaning of "urban renewal" had begun to change: its target was no longer the eradication of slums but instead commercial redevelopment leading to gentrification. What had not changed is that the government continued to use that now misleading term "urban renewal" for all its demolition projects. It was widely suspected that this "zero" cost land use rights policy was just a cover for corruption—developers were paying millions bribing local governments for "free" land use rights. On paper, however, any developer who enjoyed this policy was expected to follow through with his commitment to building low-cost housing.

This leads to the second piece in the story—the development in the East Eight Lots was thus supposedly not a for-profit commercial project, but a project to build affordable housing. This is relevant to the third piece. According to Document 68 issued by four Shanghai municipal bureaus in 2001,[13] residents whose houses were demolished for urban renewal were allowed to take a third option for settlement other than cash compensation and re-housing: return to the previous location with additional payments once the new houses were built there. This return policy was implemented in past urban renewal projects when slums were redeveloped. To most of the residents, the third option was the most appealing, since cash compensation would quickly lose its value with the soaring real estate market, and since they preferred to live in their familiar downtown neighborhoods instead of in the suburbs.[14] This return policy was meant to ease the opposition to demolition and speed up urban renewal. According to Document 347, the East Eight Lots project qualified for urban renewal specifically based on Document 68. Furthermore, Contract 19 specifically referred to Document 68 as the basis for granting Zhou the land use rights at no cost.[15] In short, the area was meant for residential housing development and the residents who would be displaced had the right to return.

However, the district never informed the residents of any of these crucial pieces of information, especially not the return policy. The reason, as we will see shortly, is that the East Eight Lots project was not exactly urban renewal but a patent case of gentrification and commercial development. As such, the district turned to Document 111, issued in October 2001, seven months after Document 68, as a guideline for the development in the East Eight Lots. Compared with previous urban renewal regulations, Document 111, as discussed in the introduction, practically allowed local governments and developers to do whatever they wanted. Furthermore, it contained a typical case of regulatory loopholes. Document 111 specifically invalidated three other relevant regulations issued before 1997, which did not include Document 68; yet it made no mention at all of the return policy that was authorized by Document 68. This ambiguity and disparity between the two documents regarding the return policy became a major source of contention.

In September 2002, the Jing'an District demolition office and its hired squad started its work in earnest, first on three lots, 56, 57, and 58—about 4,300 households, although Document 347 omitted Lot 56 from the project. Propaganda followed: large, red banners with slogans such as "Renew the Old District, Benefit the People!" and "Salute Residents Who Support Urban Renewal!" were hung in the neighborhood. Again, these slogans were misleading, capitalizing on the goodwill that had infused the urban renewal effort early on while this time the reality was that the residents were being betrayed. In the case of the East Eight Lots, urban renewal was not undertaken to "benefit the people" but rather, as we will see shortly, it was to drive the people out, gentrify their neighborhood, and benefit the powerful.

The demolition office sent an open letter to the residents which referred to Document 111 only. The letter included information on several sites of relocation for those who chose re-housing, which were all in the suburbs, including Pudong. It also indicated the value of their current apartments, which was based on the demolition office's estimate of 4,000 yuan per square meter, said to be the market value then. To encourage the residents to accept these conditions and to relocate quickly, the demolition office offered some cash incentives. Compensation was a zero-sum game between the demolition office and the residents. Zhou was supposed to provide the demolition office with the funds. If the demolition office could move the residents out for less, it could pocket the difference, thus creating an incentive to pay as little as possible. In Shanghai and elsewhere, most of the disputes over compensation in demolitions have resulted from this sort of zero-sum game.

In the first six months, demolition and relocation went swiftly and about 4,000 families moved out. A number of factors contributed to this initial success. First, most residents were convinced that urban renewal as a government project would be implemented anyway and the demolition of their apartments was inevitable. Also, in terms of their living space and conditions, many residents apparently stood to gain a great deal, mainly due to the price difference between downtown and the suburbs. Apartments in the suburbs, due to their remoteness, were less than half the price of those downtown. Residents could more than double their living space by relocating to the suburbs. Moreover, the suburban apartments were newer, independent units with basic modern amenities. This was appealing to many families who had lived for decades in the old, crowded alleyway apartments and had to deal with chamber pots, shared kitchen space, and coal stoves. Some multi-generational families with pending marriages or other such situations to consider saw the possibility of affording more than one apartment unit in the suburbs—something that was impossible downtown. Furthermore, these tenants could become apartment owners in the suburbs. What they sacrificed was the prime location. But many residents did not know about or understand the return option. As such, they considered the sacrifice to be the only choice and moved out—a decision some of them came to regret. As those families moved out, the demolition squad came in to tear down their apartments. By late spring 2003, for the most part, the three lots had been reduced to rubble.

But a bitter fight soon started that reversed the swiftness of the early stage. Scattered in that rubble in April 2003 were about 300 remaining families. That number was reduced to 138 by July 2003, to about 70 by May 2004, and to 30 by July. The last group of families was not cleared out until October 2004. In other words, it took nineteen months for the demolition office to deal with this small group of "nail households" in a process full of strife that threatened both the political and moral authority of the district government and the physical and emotional health of the residents—the removal of each and every remaining family after spring 2003 often meant exhausting negotiations punctuated by lawsuits, petitions, protests, and even violent clashes. Though in the end some of those families reached an agreement with the government, others were violently evicted and have to this very day refused to sign a contract with the government. What happened?

Initially, some of the remaining families had specific issues that dissuaded them from joining the early wave of relocation. For instance, one family had elderly parents who were gravely ill. It was imperative for them to stay downtown, with the best and familiar medical facilities close by. Several families had physically disabled members whose requests for special housing accommodations were denied. Others, especially those who lived in new-style alleyway apartments or owned their properties, were not eager to move out. Still others were relatively well informed about government policy and savvy as to their rights; they referred to other cases where residents were able to return to their former locations after redevelopment and insisted on the right of return as a condition for relocating—this the demolition office rejected. But most of them demanded compensation according to the market value of their apartments, which was much higher than what the demolition office offered.

Indeed, one of the main reasons for this holding out was that the Shanghai real estate market had begun to skyrocket in fall 2002, especially in the downtown area. By spring 2003, second-hand apartments downtown were fast disappearing,[16] and in private transactions their price had reached 10,000 yuan per square meter. It became clear to the residents that the value of their apartments was rising. In the meantime, the media, especially some finance magazines, had advertisements that offered tips for residents on how to take financial advantage of the relocation. They published articles with alluring titles such as "Demolition and Relocation Is Gold."[17] Some of the residents believed that the relocation was an once-in-a-lifetime opportunity to gain financial freedom, and that they should grab it and be set for life. As such, they had little incentive to move out on official terms; instead they used their apartments as leverage for the best settlement they could wangle.

The Initial Conflict

If the reasons for the residents' holding out were benign in the beginning, the unfolding of events in April 2003 changed all that. In mid-March, Shen Ting, a Hong Kong resident who grew up in Lot 58, returned to Shanghai at her mother's urgent plea because the family was in eminent danger of being evicted. The reason was apparently a 20,000 yuan difference, irresolvable after six months of negotiations: the family asked for 300,000 yuan to settle for their apartment of 47.59 square meters but the demolition office would only pay 280,000 yuan, while the market value of the apartment was said to be around 1,300,000 yuan. Initially, Shen did not understand what the demolition and relocation were all about but was convinced that the demolition office was unreasonable to threaten her family with eviction. On April 4, 2003, she helped her mother, Mo Zhujie, bring an administrative lawsuit against the Jing'an District Housing Bureau at the district court, demanding the bureau withdraw its "Permit for Demolition and Relocation" of Lot 58.

Her main argument was technical—the permit for the demolition, issued early on and in expectation of a quick result, with the effective dates from September 10, 2002, to February 18, 2003, had expired by April 2003. The demolition office warned that such a lawsuit had zero chance of winning because the development in the East Eight Lots involved both Zhou Zhengyi and the brother of Chen Liangyu, the Shanghai party chief.

Undeterred, Shen Ting searched for legal representation. To her surprise, she was turned down by more than twenty law firms and, in the process, got a crash course on the impact of political intimidation on the Chinese legal profession—no sensible lawyer dared to take such a case if she or he wanted to keep his/her job. She also realized that her parents understood little about their circumstances, especially the return policy, and much less about the law; the situation did not look promising. In the meantime, the defendant, the district housing bureau, had handed to the court a set of documents to prove the legality of the demolition. The court, perhaps considering this to be just another doomed case, gave Shen Ting a copy of the documents. Those documents were in fact problematic and would eventually came back to haunt the bureau. But at the time, Shen Ting lacked the knowledge to identify the problems in what were apparently legitimate documents.

Exhausted physically and emotionally, on April 21, the family, failing to get the housing bureau to cancel its demolition permit, withdrew its lawsuit and chose compromise as the only way to avoid eviction. On April 28, the Shen family came to the demolition office to accept the 280,000 yuan offer. But at the last minute the offer was reduced to 220,000 yuan. The family left in rage and was evicted two days later.[18]

That was the last straw: it turned Shen Ting into a committed protester. Her family had had the apartment for three generations over a span of seventy years. In the late 1930s, her maternal grandfather, who was a manager in a foreign firm, bought the apartment. In the socialist reform of the 1950s, the government turned Shen's apartment into a rental, and the Shen family became tenants in their own home. But for the Shens, their apartment was the only home they knew. The grandparents died there and Shen's mother was born, married, and gave birth to her only daughter there.[19]

Shen Ting's childhood bore the mark of the era in which she was born. In 1966, the year of her birth, the Cultural Revolution was gaining steam. Both her parents were engineers. In 1966 her father was sent to work in a factory in Guizhou Province in the southwest for fifteen years. Three years later, Shen's mother, Mo Zhujie, was accused of being a counterrevolutionary because of her casual remarks about Lin Biao, a high-ranking CCP official, being shorter than Mao.[20] Mo was forced into labor reform, and toiled twelve hours a day.

Shen Ting spent most of her childhood as a "little counterrevolutionary" with her grandmother. She was routinely bullied, discriminated against, and often left to fend for herself. Shen Ting was known to the neighbors as stubborn and fearless. Once, in junior high, to defend her grandmother, she got into a fight with a man. After suffering a broken nose, she took out a kitchen knife and chased the man down the street; both ended up in a neighborhood police station where she continued to argue her case.

After junior high, Shen Ting entered a telecommunications school and, upon graduation in 1985, became an accountant at a telecommunications bureau in Shanghai. In the early 1990s, when the opening and reform was widening, Shen Ting, like many other Chinese, went to Shenzhen, in South China, a special zone that pioneered economic reform, to be a clothing retailer. At the peak of her business, she had five shops and sometimes made 60,000 yuan a month. It was in Shenzhen that she met her future husband, who was from Hong Kong. She was married in 1993 and moved to Hong Kong in 1995. At the beginning of the conflict, some of the neighbors warned the demolition office not to provoke Shen Ting for fear of her reaction. The demolition officials took it in the wrong way and retorted: "We'll even evict families who have members in America. What's the big deal if she's in Hong Kong?"[21]

On the morning of April 30, dozens of district officials, policemen, members of the neighborhood committee, and the demolition squad broke into the Shen's home. They loaded the family's belongings onto a truck and hauled everything to an apartment 50 kilometers away that had been assigned to but rejected by the family. They then leveled the place. Shen Ting moved her parents out beforehand to protect them but set up a video recording device that captured the entire process of domicide. She did not waste much time before taking the next step as, when watching the videotape, she resolved that the district was going to pay for what it did to her family.[22] "Why should I be afraid of anything at all now that I have lost my home?" she said.[23]

Shen Ting was determined to find a lawyer. Through friends in Hong Kong, Shen identified a fifty-three-year-old Christian lawyer named Zheng Enchong in Shanghai, who had by then represented some five hundred families in similar situations and had been described as a "human rights lawyer" by the Hong Kong media. Zheng had not won a single case out of the five hundred, however, and was already under great pressure from the authorities, who had refused to renew his lawyer's license. He could no longer represent anyone in court but could still use his expertise to help prepare lawsuits. On May 1, 2003, when Shen Ting and her mother came and presented him with the court papers produced by the district housing bureau from their aborted lawsuit in early April, he decided to help them. Zheng, intimately familiar with the corruption in the Shanghai real estate market, immediately detected problems in the documents. His decision to take the case finally sealed his own fate, which he accurately predicted on that very day to Shen Ting: "Something will happen to me if I get involved. You'll have to rescue me. This will likely be my last case."[24]

The court papers in Shen Ting's possession turned out to be a powerful weapon against the district housing bureau. They included the contract between Zhou Zhengyi and the district government which indicated the zero cost to Zhou for the land use rights, Document 68 and the return policy, and the official "Application for Demolition and Relocation Permit" which revealed that the area was actually meant for luxurious commercial high-rises ranging from residential to office spaces, not urban renewal for affordable residential housing at all. In short, an expert reading of these materials validated Shen Ting's initial accusation that the district demolition permit for the East Eight Lots was indeed illegal; the Shen family had a case after all.

On May 8, the Shens and five other evicted families who were said to have represented more than a thousand neighbors, including those that had already moved out, filed a complaint with the district court against the district housing bureau. The court initially insisted on a closed session with an audience of no more than five, but the plaintiffs demanded an open session. After much negotiation and complaint, the court began an open hearing on the morning of May 28. More than 250 residents from all over Shanghai, most of whom were Zheng's former clients, came not just to witness but also to participate in the case. The case was symbolically and practically important to all of them. At the time, rumors about Zhou Zhengyi's problematic dealings involving high-level officials in Shanghai had been rife. In a country where unofficial, "small-channel" news is often more credible than the controlled official media reports, the residents believed this lawsuit could help galvanize the fight against corruption in Shanghai and possibly help their own cases in the process. Also, they were aware of the pressure on Zheng Enchong and came to show their support. The case was thus tried both inside and outside the court. While the courtroom was packed to capacity with 100 people, outside the court on the street more than 150 residents gathered to protest, holding banners that read, "Return My Human Rights! Return My House! No Justice without Judicial Independence!"[25]

In the courtroom, Shen Ting's mother, Mo Zhujie, coached by Zheng Enchong, read the charge prepared by Zheng, who was not present. The main accusation was that the permit issued by the district housing bureau for demolition in the East Eight Lots was not only illegal, but also criminal, because it allowed Zhou, contrary to his contract, to misuse state property, the land, for a for-profit commercial development but deprived the residents of the right to return as granted in Document 68. It pointed out the deceitful and illegal means by which the district tried to clear out the neighborhood. It further indicated the lack of legal and administrative grounds for the district housing bureau and other officials as well as the police to be involved in de-molition, and for the establishment of the district demolition office for that matter: "Government should be separated from business; the former can't act as both referee and athlete." The complaint also revealed that the district presiding judge for administrative lawsuits actually had a "bad record" of participating in demolitions. All of these accusations must have been devas-tating to the authorities. Three times the judge tried to interrupt Mo Zhujie: "Enough! Enough! Just submit the paper!" But Mo read the complaint out loud to its conclusion.[26]

The court case was only part of the plan that Shen Ting and Zheng Enchong made for that day. The other part was to inform the media with the hope of winning support. At noon, as soon as the court session con-cluded, they issued a prepared open letter to Hu Jintao and Wen Jiabao signed by twelve people accusing Zhou Zhengyi of being the biggest grafter supported by corrupt top officials in Shanghai, and demanding an official investigation. Zheng Enchong, through a human rights organization, sent the material to the Western media. A few days later, some residents were said to have heard a Voice of America broadcast on the lawsuit.[27] On June 5, Shen Ting returned to Hong Kong with all the court papers to inform the media there.

By then, Shen Ting's lawsuit, which was initiated in early April over a mere 20,000 yuan difference, had evolved into a major case that implicated Zhou Zhengyi and top officials in Shanghai. It had also attracted intense domestic and international media coverage. In light of all this, Shen Ting and the residents in the East Eight Lots felt they had won the case. But their victory was only recognized in public opinion; no official action of any kind to rectify the wrongdoing was in sight.

Instead, on June 6, a week after the May 28 court hearing, the Shanghai Public Security Bureau arrested Zheng Enchong on charges of "revealing state secrets." He was later sentenced to three years in prison. True to Zheng's own prediction, the Shen Ting case not only ended his legal career, but also his personal freedom. Finally, on August 19, the district court handed down its ruling: Zhou Zhengyi had obtained the East Eight Lots legally and the resi-dents had no recourse.[28]

As shocking and discouraging as all this was, the lawsuit was not a total loss. Vigilantly probing into Zhou's dealings through the lawsuit and the media, the residents learned the indisputable facts that Zhou was handed the land use rights at no cost, that they were entitled to return as specified in Document 68, and that Zhou actually intended to build a luxury complex on the East Eight Lots which would mainly target foreigners and thus be priced far beyond their reach. The residents also found out that Lot 56 was not even listed for demolition yet most of the apartments on the lot were knocked down anyway.

These revelations caused outrage among the residents, including those who had already relocated. They also changed the nature of the conflict—it was no longer about the amount of compensation, but about whether the demolition was legal in the first place, and, if not, who was responsible. To the residents, the answers to these questions were clear-cut: the demolition was illegal and even criminal and the district government must be held accountable. The residents believed that they had firm legal and moral grounds for negotiating with and protesting against the district government. All this set into motion a chain of events in the following months.

The Negotiations

In light of the residents' determined resistance, the disastrous result of the Shen Ting lawsuit, and the Zhou scandal, the district housing bureau and demolition office, now under close media scrutiny, began to change their strategy. For one thing, if the discrepancy in compensation was within 50,000 yuan, the demolition office simply conceded, a costly lesson learned from the Shen Ting case. This change proved to be effective, especially for families who considered 50,000 yuan to be a deal maker or breaker. By early July, more than 170 families took that opening and moved out, leaving 138 families that either insisted on the right to return or demanded higher compensation.

To figure out how to deal with this small but adamant group, on July 2, 2003, district officials, through the neighborhood committee, arranged a meeting with the residents. At the meeting were the deputy district director and several representatives from the demolition office. They wanted the meeting to "better communicate with the residents and move the demolition and relocation forward." But the exchange between the officials and the residents was tension-charged. In a single-spaced five-page minutes document the residents produced according to a recording they made secretly, they gave a different title to the meeting: "Residents in the East Eight Lots demand an open media report on their case; demand the use of public opinion to check and stop the district government's unjustifiable action." This was followed by five demands: the government must follow the law, and there must be a judicial explanation of Document 68, an investigation of the official behavior in the demolition and relocation, an open review of the planned luxurious high-rises in the East Eight Lots, and an investigation of Zhou Zhengyi's fraud.

The meeting was dominated by the residents, including those who had been evicted. Other than the opening and closing sections, when two officials spoke briefly, the residents took this opportunity to lodge their complaints and make demands. They mainly focused on three aspects: the harassment they suffered, the district government's relationship with Zhou Zhengyi, and the return policy in Document 68.

One evictee invoked the Cultural Revolution to protest the handling of his case: "A man on the demolition squad broke into my home without presenting any identification. When I asked for his identification, he manhandled me and threatened me instead . . . He acted like the Cultural Revolution rebels." He demanded an investigation into this "uncivilized behavior." Another resident accused the demolition office of "illegally and unreasonably" detaining him for a week after his eviction. There were complaints from the remaining families as well. The demolition office had cut off the utilities of several families. Some had suffered without gas for months. Their repeated appeals to restore their utilities went unanswered. Safety was also a major concern with these "nail households" as the demolition squad had destroyed their doors and windows. Surrounded by debris with exposed wires, broken glass and bricks, decomposed trash, and rats and insects, the residents were vulnerable to potential fire, disease, injury, and theft. Political intimidation was another issue. One resident said that when he came to the meeting, he was not sure if he could go home for dinner: "We were asked to come with our residential identification card. Why?" He thought the meeting could be a trap to arrest them. These complaints reflected some of the common tactics—cutting utilities, destroying property, and intimidation—that the government and developers used to drive residents out.

One of the most contentious issues was the district government's relationship with Zhou Zhengyi. The residents criticized the district for siding with Zhou at the expense of the residents: "If you force people out to promote Zhou's interests, then where do you stand?" They emphasized the illegality in the way the district handled their cases. Mr. C, a middle-aged man whom we will discuss in detail below, was particularly effective at the meeting. He said: "Everyone has to obey the law. The municipal and district governments both have to obey the law . . . Governing by law is the priority . . . How are we going to understand all this if the government involves itself in business development on the one hand and tries to deal with the conflict [between the developer and the residents] on the other?" Echoing these points another resident stated: "This is all very confusing. When we sue the developer, the government jumps in and messes things up. Then whom are we suing? The government? The developer?" Indeed, just like in the Xintiandi case, what residents most objected to, and what Beijing's regulations clearly forbade, was the conflict of interest created when local governments that administrated demolition also participated in demolition.

But the more practical issue was about return. The key question the residents repeatedly asked was why they could not return. "Give us a reason!" one resident demanded. He also questioned the so-called urban renewal: "Is this urban renewal or commercial development? Which one is it?" They insisted that if the return policy had been abandoned, then the government should announce it openly. Since no such announcement was ever made, then, as Mr. C argued, "we believe we still have the right to return." The residents were clearly well prepared for this meeting. When an official mentioned that Document 111 was the guideline, implying that Document 68 was no longer applicable, a resident immediately cited Contract 19, which granted the zero-land-use cost to Zhou precisely based on Document 68. They wanted to know if the developer got free land while denying the residents from returning, then where the profits generated from the free land would go: "People must ask: who'll benefit from the profits?" To make sure that the district government would not take this small group lightly, Mr. C emphasized that even if there was only one family left, the government should still follow the law and be fair. He further elaborated: "This is a chance for people to learn how to use the law to protect their rights. Those who moved out earlier didn't learn that. It's a painful lesson."

The officials at the meeting also made a few points. One was that the land and the apartments the residents lived in were all state property, and if the state decided to transfer the land, no one should argue about it. That of course did not address the residents' concerns whether the land transaction was illegal. Another was that since there was not even a blueprint for the future buildings yet, it was unreasonable for the residents to ask to return. The residents considered this to be an excuse because in previous cases where return had been allowed in other neighborhoods, temporary housing arrangements were made for the future returnees during the construction of their new apartments. As for Document 68, the officials admitted that it had not been officially abandoned: "Frankly speaking, if it doesn't contradict

[Document 111], then it's valid; but if it contradicts [Document 111], then it's invalid." Such a cynical answer could hardly satisfy the residents. The district officials were put on the defensive yet found themselves defenseless.

Cultural Resistance

The government soon broke off the negotiations. For the next year there was a stalemate as the district demolition office stopped evictions and told the residents that it was developing a "new strategy." This change was in part because of the local resistance and the Zhou scandal, but also because of pressure from Beijing.

Responding to the intense conflict generated in urban housing reform and rural land seizures throughout China, various agencies of the central government delivered a series of directives to address the situation. In August 2003, the Ministry of Construction issued an "Urgent Notice" on "Seriously Managing Demolition and Relocation and Maintaining Social Stability," which directly linked the two aspects. In February 2004, one month before the annual two meetings in Beijing, which attract large numbers of petitioners, the Bureau of National Land Resources sent out an "Urgent Notice" on "Better Handling Petition Work Regarding National Land Resources during the Two Meetings." In early June 2004, in response to heightened tension nationwide, the State Council published a document on how to "Control the Scale and Strictly Manage Urban Housing Demolition and Relocation."[29] It denounced violence against residents and emphasized the importance of protecting their interests. The official media, from the Xinhua News Agency to *Renmin ribao*, published editorials openly acknowledging the violation of residents' rights in urban development and criticized so-called "bully contracts"—the kind of contracts residents were forced to sign because of harassment, intimidation, and even beatings.[30] All this gave the residents the impression that the central government supported their "rightful resistance."

Beijing's criticism of violent demolition was stern, but only on paper. Such criticism reflects the highest hypocrisy of the Chinese state, because it was Document 305 issued by the State Council that legitimatized violence and domicide in the first place. On the other hand, what really affected the fate of the residents was district policy. In this case, a ruined neighborhood in the heart of downtown was an eyesore that the district could not ignore. In spring 2004, the district housing bureau revealed its "new strategy," which designated the East Eight Lots as a "green land." Environmental projects as a politically correct move have been manipulated by both officials and residents in disputes over property and development.[31] In this case, this "green land" scheme was clearly meant to justify the eviction of the remaining families and to silence any request for a future return. Soon the demolition office sent migrant workers to build a wall that blocked the neighborhood from street view and planted trees. This caused a clash as the residents tried to stop them; some were injured. Some residents believed that the demolition office meant to provoke the residents so as to create an excuse to arrest them. Those who were wearied by the conflict took the district's offer and moved out, reducing the remaining families to about seventy by spring 2004.

At this point, the remaining residents clearly saw how the legal and administrative system had failed them. They harbored no illusion that they would be allowed to return in the future. Their plan was simply to gain the highest payment, making it easier to purchase an apartment downtown. In one resident's words, they aimed at a "five-star" luxury hotel price. That "relocation is gold" seemed to ring especially true in early 2004 as the Shanghai real estate market shot up by more than 28 percent, and the potential to go still higher looked infinite. Residents believed that time was on their side, and that what they wanted could be achieved by waiting, not too passively, though, so as to be construed as giving up, but also not acting too radically, so as to be arrested, which would be counterproductive.

As such, they began to explore the cultural domain and especially Maoist practices and symbols as a new tactic to deal with the authorities. They formed a "Legal Study Forum" in the fashion of the CCP's small study groups used for mass organizations, sang "The Internationale" in front of the authorities, raised the red, national flag on their property, and composed couplets criticizing injustice. All this was a continuation of their struggle to delay the final eviction, gain the largest payment possible, and also protect themselves in the process.

First of all, through their Legal Study Forum the residents became more organized. Unlike residents of newly built urban neighborhoods who have various forms of homeowners' associations that often act as self-governance organizations,[32] these residents had no legitimate mechanism for collective action; they had to be inventive. In spring 2004, coordinated by the resourceful Mr. C, the residents established their Legal Study Forum as a platform to openly organize themselves. The study group was meant to learn how to apply the law to their advantage. They gathered at a large, first-floor room in an empty, partially demolished apartment building, without a door and with shattered windows and wires dangling from the ceiling. It had no electricity either; but the residents pirated it from street lamps. They arranged two old coffee tables in the center and surrounded them with abandoned sofas, chairs, and benches.[33]

One of the walls was decorated with four large characters, *Xue Fa Yuan Di* (Legal Study Forum), and with dozens of newspaper and magazine clippings. These articles—collected, contributed, and pasted up by the residents—were all critical of violent demolition. The opposite wall was covered with quotes from official speeches and publications that condemned corruption. On the tables were a dozen copies of two pamphlets: a bulletin of the Shanghai municipal government with policies on real estate, and "The Internationale," the song of the Paris Commune of 1871. The two pamphlets, like the furniture, remained in the room when the residents left at the end of a session.

Much thought was put into this crudely equipped "meeting room." First, the room had no owner, and therefore no one could be held responsible for providing the gathering place or organizing the forum.[34] The place was also open—it had no doors or locks, showing that the residents had nothing to hide. Furthermore, the materials they put in that room were all legitimate. But collective action of any kind among the neighbors was bad news for the demolition office, which more than once tried to seal the place. When that happened, the residents simply broke in and continued their study sessions.

Figure 3.1.   In summer 2004, the remaining residents in East Eight Lots formed a Legal Study Forum in an abandoned apartment. They met every Saturday evening to study the law and strategize their resistance.

They welcomed the officials to check out the place, especially to read the materials there. "They should study them—they have to study them to understand the wrong they have done to us," one resident proclaimed. In fact, the Legal Study Forum was an open message to the demolition office of the residents' determination to use the law to hold out.

While the residents created an open, legitimate façade for this Legal Study Forum, what happened there did not exactly thrill the authorities. Every Saturday at 8 p.m., forty to sixty men and women would gather there, often in their pajamas and slippers since it was summer. Among them was a blind man, a man on crutches, a woman who suffered from bone cancer, and also an elderly man accompanied by his son-in-law, a Chinese American from Seattle who returned to support his father-in-law. Like the small study sessions under Mao, this one also had its own ritual. It started with the group singing two songs: "Unity Is Strength," a Chinese song, and "The Internationale."

These meetings, though, did not have a chairperson or a stated agenda, since the overall agenda—resisting the demolition to gain the best compensation—was clear to everyone. After a rousing group sing, the residents took turns announcing relevant news, which included new policies, recent media reports of troubled demolition elsewhere, recent petition trips some of them made, and the demolition office's new moves. They also chatted among themselves in small groups. Some discussions, especially about how they confronted and ridiculed officials, would spark laughter, and others would bring silence and tears, such as when Mrs. Jiang, the cancer patient, rolled up her pants to show the bruises she suffered from being beaten by the demolition squad. Before the meeting ended, they identified tasks for the next step: they were to go to certain government offices to obtain needed information or clarify a certain policy pertaining to their cases, make more copies of newspaper articles to circulate, and initiate contact with other neighborhoods for networking. All this was done on a strictly volunteer basis and in a casual atmosphere.

In some ways, this Legal Study Forum was a replay of scenes from small study sessions the CCP had systematically employed as a political ritual to organize and mobilize the masses since its early years. Such group sessions were meant for the study of the CCP's doctrines; criticism and self-criticism, a fundamental technique—almost a ritual—of the Maoist era; and mutual help and group pressure to produce "attitude change and behavioral compliance" in the interests of the CCP.[35] The study-group type of mass organization reached its peak during the Cultural Revolution. With the CCP's imposed politicization of daily life, the Chinese were forced into study groups where they met at a designated time, weekly or even daily, to read Mao's directives and to struggle against each other, primarily to reinforce the Mao cult.[36]

With the retreat of mass political movements in post-Mao China, such officially organized, mass-based political ritual has disappeared. But now the residents initiated this group to indeed study, criticize, and help one another; except all this was to serve their own interests. Thus the study group, a form of social control, had been turned into a form of social resistance. The participants were fully aware of this irony. In fact, they were quite pleased with themselves, and thought they were brilliant to have come up with this scheme. "Our government wants China to become a society governed by law. How can anyone oppose our study of the law?" a middle-aged man asked cleverly.

Also intriguing was their choice of songs. As the number of families dwindled, fear became a real issue. One resident stated that one of the purposes of organizing the study forum was to embolden (zhuangdan) themselves. Under Mao, the song "Unity Is Strength" was sung to reinforce solidarity among the Chinese people in the hostile Cold War–era world. With such lyrics as "strength is steel, strength is iron," the song reminded the residents that they were all in the struggle together. The song was also a direct response to the demolition office, which often employed a divide and rule strategy by spreading rumors and pitting one neighbor against another to weaken their solidarity.

"The Internationale," however, is a much grander symbol. The song is known for its solemn melody and stirring lyrics: "Arise, all suffering people of the world . . . Smashing the old world into pieces . . . We will be masters under heaven . . . There has never been a Savior, nor should we rely on gods and emperors . . . This is the last struggle. Get united for tomorrow."[37] These lyrics help the powerless imagine a world in which they will gain freedom and equality, and control of their own destiny.[38] Not surprisingly, "The Internationale," introduced to China in the early 1920s, occupied a special place in the CCP's mythology.[39] Many of the revolution's martyrs were said to have sung this song when facing a heroic death. Moreover, during the Cultural Revolution, which Mao hoped would regenerate a revolutionary spirit among the youth, "The Internationale" was among the most invoked songs, often sung by large crowds in public gatherings. The residents in the East Eight Lots, most of whom were in their forties and fifties, grew up in that culture.

In post-Mao China, "The Internationale" has largely faded from public consciousness. Even in the recent vogue of reviving the "red classics"—music, songs, and plays that were popular under Mao—on stage and screen, this particular song is rarely heard. But it has not disappeared altogether; it has become a song sung for opposite purposes by mainly three groups: the CCP, rock and roll musicians, and protesters. "The Internationale" is something of a CCP anthem, sung collectively by members at the opening and closing sessions of the CCP's National Congress. It is a novel song for young Chinese rock and roll musicians. Perhaps to carry out the rock and roll protest tradition,[40] an all-male band called Tang Dynasty transformed "The Internationale" into a rock song and included it in a 2002 CD titled *Red Rock*, which ignited a debate among bloggers.[41]

Of course, neither rock musicians nor the CCP are the oppressed of society that "The Internationale" is meant to give voice to. In fact, in light of the rampant corruption and popular grievances, the song is a misfit for the CCP since it invokes irony more than inspiration. Of the three groups who continue to sing "The Internationale" in China, the most revealing and fitting one is the protesters. The song was a staple feature in the student movement for democracy throughout the 1980s.[42] While Chinese students have largely retreated from the political theater of democratic demonstration after the 1989 crackdown, "The Internationale" has found new enthusiasts among popular protesters.

In the East Eight Lots, the residents gathered to sing the song every time during domicide and other violent conflicts. They also sang it after being rounded up from petition trips to Beijing and sent back to Shanghai. Overtaken by mixed feelings of anger, fear, apprehension, and defiance, they sang "The Internationale" at the very moment they got off the train upon arrival in Shanghai. As they did with the Legal Study Forum, the residents turned this song into a weapon against the CCP. Indeed, the connection between politics and music is a two-way street. Musical traditions are often remade to inspire new social movements, and social movements are central to the reconstruction of music.[43] The invoking of "The Internationale" in popular protest in China has rendered a new and subversive sensibility to the Communist anthem, a reminder that the CCP has betrayed its original mission and become an oppressor itself.

More than "The Internationale," it is the red, national flag that is the symbol of Communist China. An ultimate icon to rally Chinese nationalism, the red flag was said to have been dyed by the blood of the martyrs and thus is a sacred object.[44] Its unquestionable political and moral authority was reinforced when the semimonthly *Hong qi* (Red Flag) was launched by the CCP's Central Committee as its main propaganda organ in 1958, the beginning of Mao's ill-conceived Great Leap Forward to disaster. During the Cultural Revolution, when the word was often mightier than the sword, *Hong qi*, together with *Renmin ribao*, launched many of the major political campaigns with lethal articles that defined "heroes" and "villains" overnight.[45]

Imbued with so much revolutionary myth and rhetoric, the red flag was bound to become a contested object. During the Cultural Revolution, "waving the red flag to oppose the red flag" was a charge frequently leveled by Mao's faction as an attack on its perceived enemies.[46] The post-Mao reform created an identity crisis for the CCP as it struggled to reconcile its claimed socialist ideology and its capitalist market economy. Eager to rise from Mao's shadow, the new party leadership debated the fate of *Hong qi*.[47] In June 1988, it killed the journal, without a proper obituary.[48] Mao's brutal rule had tainted *Hong qi* and turned it into a symbol of attack and disunity from which the new party leadership tried to distance itself.

After a quarter century of reform and the depoliticization of public and personal life in China, the presence of the red flag, still prominent at major political and ceremonial occasions, has become obsolete in the daily life of the Chinese people. Also, as China does not have a national flag day, the purposeful display of the red flag in residential areas certainly creates an anachronistic spectacle and thus generates curiosity.

Spectacle and curiosity were exactly what the residents found useful in the red flag—a legitimate but also distant, contested emblem to support their struggle and to get attention. Indeed, waving the flag has become a new ritual for nail households across China to carry their message and express their contempt, especially where the houses under siege are visible to the public—the meaning of such staging is generated only when there is a public audience, for the public will judge.[49] In late April 2004, on a petition trip to Beijing, a group of residents from the East Eight Lots, like many petitioners often do, had their pictures taken on Tiananmen Square with a red flag in their hands. Upon their return, they decided to put out larger red flags on their roofs, windows, and balconies.

For them, flying the red flag held a number of meanings. At one level, it underscored their claim to their apartments—that they were occupied and thus off limits. In this regard, the red flag functioned like any other flag at a contested site, as on a battleground or disputed land. Moreover, they used the red flag facetiously as a sacred object to claim a high moral ground. "Would they [the demolition squad] dare to level my house with the red flag flying in front? Go ahead, and that will make them anti-revolutionary!" one resident reasoned. As the tension built up, they were acutely aware that they were at risk of being thrown out of their homes or arrested. They wanted the red flag to provide them with a legitimate cover. "How could we possibly be wrong if we wave the red flag?" another resident said with a wink.

In addition, as mentioned, the residents raised the red flag to attract attention. It has been a common strategy for protesters in housing disputes to appeal to the public and media to pressure their opponents.[50] While both the Chinese and foreign media had reported on the East Eight Lots case in connection with the Zhou Zhengyi scandal and raised the public's awareness of the residents' plight, such attention was usually short lived. The residents understood that public opinion might deter the district government from openly crushing them. Waving the red flag in their neighborhood was a way to keep their case in the spotlight, since they had the benefit of an open site. In doing so, they effectively reconstructed their broken neighborhood into a "spatial agency" to their advantage.[51] The message this reconstructed space communicated was highly contentious and damaging to the authorities—a physically ruined neighborhood in glittering downtown with dozens of bright red flags eerily sticking out begged the question why and how such a mess was created under a CCP that claimed to represent the people.

However, the residents did not have any true faith in the flag nor in the CCP. As a resident said, "If the red flag is really meaningful, how could the district dismiss the law to the extent it did? But what about us? We have to do something. We have to treat the dead horse [the flag] as a live one and see what happens." The residents wasted no time mourning the death of the red flag as what they stood to gain in the housing reform was unthinkable in the Mao era; they only used the red flag to borrow some time so that they could cash in on the rising real estate market.

The antithetical couplet—a unique Chinese genre that can be traced back to the eighth century—was yet another cultural form the residents employed in their protest.[52] With two lines of four or more characters and sometimes also a horizontal phrase above to highlight the meaning, couplets are easy to compose and popular among Chinese regardless their social status. In fact, during the Chinese New Year every family used to paste couplets on its doors, carrying auspicious messages to pray for good fortune and ward off evil spirits. Such couplets have also traditionally been used for political purposes by both the powerful and the powerless to convey their respective messages.[53]

In the East Eight Lots, at least three sets of couplets stood out. One was composed by Mr. C and spread orally. It reads: "The developer enjoys zero cost; the residents suffer from eviction," with "one country, two systems" as the horizontal phrase. The couplet compares the marked differences in the way the district treated Zhou Zhengyi and the residents with the "one country, two systems" relationship between Hong Kong and mainland China. Its message is simple but vivid: the residents suffered a huge injustice.

The other two couplets were posted outside an apartment building. One family targeted for eviction framed the district's "Administrative Compulsory

Demolition and Relocation Notice" on their door with a couplet. It read: "Maintaining [my] rights led to eviction; today the Constitution looks hopeless," and the horizontal phrase gets to the point quickly: "Illegal Demolition." The couplet is stylistically imperfect. But its meaning is unmistakable. First of all, by framing the official eviction notice, the couplet was a direct response to that threat. Second, it points out that the residents' holding out was a matter of exercising their rights as guaranteed by the law. Furthermore, it criticizes the weakness of the constitution in comparison to the power of corrupt local officials. Thus in this couplet the residents at once justified their resistance by

Figure 3.2. An evicted family left an antithetical couplet on their door. It reads: "Maintaining [my] rights led to eviction; today the Constitution looks hopeless"; and the horizontal phrase gets to the point: "Illegal Demolition." The couplet was framed outside a district government's "Administrative Compulsory Demolition and Relocation Notice."

invoking the law and highlighted a well-known gap between the many written laws and the plain fact that they were not enforced.

The other couplet, pasted next to a government document obtained by the residents showing that Lot 56 was not even designated for demolition, describes the fact: "This Neighborhood of Lot 56 does not Belong to the Demolition Plans," which is followed by another line: "This 90-Year-Old Anti-Japanese Man Suffers from Forced Relocation." While this pair of lines seems to be unconnected with each other, they do help expose the absurdity of the pending domicide in this case—the district demolished a neighborhood by mistake and, as a result, a ninety-year-old man became a victim. This ninety-year-old man happened to be an Anti-Japanese War hero. He was once interviewed by a Shanghai television station about how he spied on the Japanese during the 1930s. But even to outsiders who did not know his story, the reference to the Anti-Japanese War is still potent—this man who survived the fight against the Japanese invasion was now going to have his home taken from him by his own government.

These pointed messages in the couplets were accented by the brush writing style, namely *weibei*, the residents employed. Weibei is a style of calligraphy associated with stone inscriptions of the northern Wei dynasty (fourth through sixth centuries). Its lines are arranged artistically and architecturally, resulting in elegant characters.[54] As the Chinese brush has been imbued with political and moral meanings since ancient times and has been used by the ruling class and the ruled alike to serve their respective interests,[55] weibei invokes a sense of strength, steadiness, character, and defiance, and is often used in writings of a serious nature. Not surprisingly, Kang Youwei, one of the initiators of the Hundred Days Reform in 1898 and an accomplished calligrapher himself, was said to be partial to weibei for its spirit and beauty.[56]

While the residents used traditional Chinese cultural forms, such as the couplet and calligraphy, effectively, their manipulation of the red flag, "The Internationale," and the study forum is what stands out. On the surface, these symbols are examples of what Michael Herzfeld has called "cultural intimacy"—"broadly shared *cultural engagement*" by the public.[57] But not all public culture is equally intimate. In this case, while these Maoist symbols remain part of public culture, the reform has rendered them not only largely irrelevant, out of sync, so to speak, but also unstable, and in fact contested. The struggle over these symbols, especially the red flag, reflects the compromised, split identity of the CCP, which the party has tried to deny and conceal. The residents, playing with this disjunction between the apparently transparent legitimacy and intimacy of these cultural symbols and their actual irony and alienation, put the CCP's schizophrenic identity on open display.

Mr. C

To the authorities, the cultural resistance the residents staged was indeed "naughty but not dangerous";[58] it did not save the residents from ultimately being evicted. In early June 2004, the district demolition office became determined to clear up this eyesore. Not surprisingly, it started with Mr. C in Lot 56.

If the early protest in the East Eight Lots was represented by Shen Ting and her lawsuit, the protest from spring 2004 on was marked by Mr. C's leadership. Mr. C was one of the most intriguing and articulate residents I have met. Born in 1950, he was the oldest of four siblings. His working-class parents, initially from rural Zhejiang Province, joined the CCP in the mid-1950s. In 1956, his father was awarded a prize by the Shanghai Public Security Bureau because he helped capture a gang of bandits on the run from his hometown. Yet later he was expelled from the party due to an intra-party struggle. Because of his father's experience, Mr. C grew up politically attuned but also politically inactive.

Mr. C channeled his energy and sought fulfillment elsewhere. In 1968, two years after graduating from junior high school, Mr. C entered a state-owned factory that made screws. Bright, curious, and mechanically inclined, he invested his talent in developing new technology for the factory and stood out as a gifted inventor. By the age of thirty his hair had all turned gray, said to be a result of many sleepless nights working on his inventions.

As accomplished and recognized as he was at the factory, he was struggling with his housing situation. Initially, the C family, six of them, shared a small apartment in downtown Shanghai. When Mr. C got married to a teacher in 1981, he moved in to live with his wife and in-laws and, with the birth of his son a year later, the three generations lived together in the small apartment. In 1988, his wife's school provided them with an apartment, on the southwestern edge of the city, while his factory was located on the northeastern end. That area did not have good schools either. In order for his son to go to an elite primary school, he arranged for his son to live with his mother downtown. Every morning, Mr. C commuted downtown to first take his son to school and then cross the city to work. The daily commute of two hours each way proved to be too much for him, and he quit his job after his repeated request for a more reasonable housing arrangement from his factory was denied. Mr. C was also frustrated by the blatant inequality in the way housing welfare was carried out—his work unit gave party officials the best apartments. But his time came. In 1990, the factory faced a tough technical challenge in a joint venture project with a foreign company that required the kind of skills Mr. C was known for. To secure his return, the factory provided him with a third floor apartment in the East Eight Lots.

This apartment was no ordinary deal for Mr. C and his family. As far as they were concerned, it immediately solved all their problems. The apartment, in the new-style alleyway structure, was equipped with modern amenities, even a bathtub, a rare luxury then. At the time, Shanghai was on the eve of a determined housing reform to improve its long-standing poor record of an average living space of 4 square meters per person. Mr. C's family of three with an apartment of 35 square meters was about ten years ahead of the time. In Mr. C's own words, his living conditions instantly reached the level of "small comfort," a developmental goal the CCP set early in the reform as a departure from the Spartan life under Mao. Moreover, this downtown area was surrounded by some of the best schools, hospitals, public transportation services, and other facilities. Mr. C could now bring his son back to live at home and to go to school nearby.

The apartment, however, meant much more to Mr. C than all its practical conveniences. At the time, such housing was usually only granted to section or department heads in a work unit. Mr. C was aware how status mattered as he had been watching with envy when officials in his factory were given better and better housing as they moved up the hierarchy. He also realized how his own talent and effort had now separated him from millions of his fellow workers and elevated him to a higher rank—his apartment was proof of his distinction and his personal worth. He often mentioned that among his neighbors were some department heads, an indication of his status by association. He was immensely proud of himself, believing himself to be not only equal but superior to those officials because he earned his distinction through his own talent and perseverance. Now that he had made it back from the outskirts of the city, where he had suffered from not only the long commute but also the separation from his young son, to downtown Shanghai, he had no plans to ever return to the periphery.

In 1998, with the economic reform deepening, many state-owned enterprises were in trouble because of increased competition. Mr. C's factory no longer operated regularly. Like millions of other urban workers, he was laid off and became a full-time househusband. His son was an excellent student, entering an elite college in Shanghai in 1999 and then a graduate program in 2004. Mr. C took great pride in his son and believed their downtown location and his being a caretaker contributed to his son's success.

When the demolition started in the East Eight Lots in 2002, Mr. C asked for 290,000 yuan for his apartment, which at the time would allow him to purchase another apartment downtown. But the demolition office rejected his proposal. A year later, the demolition office offered him 590,000 yuan, and this time Mr. C rejected it. A quick learner, Mr. C believed his apartment was now worth more than a million yuan—the difference a year had made in this fast-moving city. The rising real estate market also taught Mr. C that monetary compensation would soon lose its value. Better informed than most of his neighbors, Mr. C thus insisted on the right to return and refused to negotiate for anything else.

On June 9, 2003, the district housing bureau issued an administrative compulsory ruling that ordered Mr. C's family to relocate within five days to a new suburb on the very margins of Pudong across the river, about a two-and-a-half hour bus ride away. But because of the Zhou Zhengyi scandal, the district refrained from carrying out that ruling, which gave Mr. C time to contemplate his response.

In September, Mr. C brought an administrative lawsuit against the district housing bureau in the district court. In a concise, one-page statement, Mr. C demanded the bureau withdraw its administrative ruling because of its illegality. The statement charged the bureau with violating state regulations and concealing the return policy. It asked the court for a judgment "to protect tenants' legal rights as granted to citizens in the Constitution." In the ten days following the filing of the lawsuit, Mr. C sent the court seven additional letters with various requests and arguments. He insisted that the government should be "faithfully dedicated to its duty of implementing the law," and declared that if the district government's ruling was not based on law, "I can ignore it!" Mr. C ended his appeal with two slogans: "The Constitution is absolute! The interest of the people is absolute!" As expected, Mr. C lost his case.

The demolition office also frequently harassed Mr. C's family. Its staff paid five visits to his wife's school, asking the officials there to pressure her, and also contacted the head of the labor union in Mr. C's previous work unit. To force him out, the demolition office tried to literally undermine his apartment. After the families in the floors below moved out, the district demolition squad did its best to damage the apartment building, including removing its ceiling beams. As a result, Mr. C's third floor unit swayed and wobbled, and its windows were knocked out. "It was like a war movie," Mr. C said. But Mr. C never gave up his demand to return, nor did he stop his criticism of the district government. In his own words, "If you kick me off the [Document] 68 return 'train,' I'll take you down with me."

A number of factors accounted for Mr. C's uncompromising approach to the right to return. One was of course his sense of his entitlement as stipulated by Document 68. "Return was allowed by law . . . but what is legal has now become illegal. It's just unfair," he said. He also saw the officials' mistake in failing to include Lot 56 where his apartment was located in its demolition document as a great opening for protest. Also, at the time, both Mr. C's father, who had cancer and his mother-in-law, who had heart disease, ended up in the hospital. Mr. C was the main caregiver, delivering meals to them daily. He treasured the convenience of his location, with the hospital only five minutes away: "What are you going to do in an emergency in the suburbs? How are you going to get transportation at midnight? The patient would have been long dead by the time the ambulance arrives." In one of his letters to the court, Mr. C insisted that the financial assessment of his apartment take into consideration the abundant facilities in the surrounding area.

Mr. C also refused to accept the economic injustice that resulted from the government's unfair treatment of residents and abuse of power. According to him, his apartment was worth more than a million yuan while the apartment he was offered in the suburbs, although much bigger, was only worth half that, so the deal was unfair: "I'm losing money," he complained. He witnessed the tremendous wealth generated in the reform and also its uneven distribution that has led to an ever-widening gap between the rich and poor. What happened in the East Eight Lots is an example of how that redistribution has taken place—the residents with one of the most valuable addresses in Shanghai were chased to the margins of the city so that the rich developer, with the help of the district government, could get even richer by building profitable luxury high-rises. But the socialist rhetoric still spouted by the CCP places the interests of the people as its top priority. As such, Mr. C asked why the people could not share in the wealth by being allowed to return. In his case, since he believed he was already living in "small comfort," relocating to the suburbs would be a step backward. He thus demanded his status to at least be maintained, but absolutely not lowered, and the best way to do that, as far as he was concerned, was to insist on the right to return.

Mr. C's awareness of his distinction as a worker who had achieved the status of an official in housing also figured largely in his arguments. To him, that distinction was associated with and validated by the downtown location of his apartment. Mr. C saw an absolute hierarchy between downtown and the suburbs. "One must know one's political, economic, and cultural status. Those who have relocated to the suburbs didn't know their status; those families, generation after generation, have now become permanent country bumpkins. That's a huge deal. I know my status and want to protect it," he declared.

To be sure, Mr. C's adamant discrimination against the suburbs reflects a long-standing gap, both in reality and perception, between urban and rural China. Other than the obvious material backwardness, rural China suffered from the lasting damage to its reputation wrought by the Mao era.

China's strict urban household registration system practically deprived the rural population of any public services and welfare such as urban residents enjoyed and left peasants to fend for themselves. Mao's incessant political campaigns had also sent "down" millions of political and social outcasts—students, intellectuals, and cadres— to the countryside as punishment. The countryside, therefore, was "a trash dump for the unwanted urban dregs of society."[59] Though the suburbs in the reform era are a stark contrast to the bleak villages they once were, Mr. C could not quite imagine exchanging his hard-earned downtown location for a place in the remote suburbs recently built on farm land.

After the demolition and relocation started in the East Eight Lots, Mr. C, as a househusband, devoted his spare time to studying the law, regulations, media reports, and the many ins and outs of the process. A few times a week he went to a local library to read through various publications. He also took notes on important matters such as policies on land use and urban renewal. All along he insisted that he was only asking for what was sanctioned by the state. In a sense, he is a model protester with a strong "rule consciousness."[60] To play by the rules, he became knowledgeable of them, which he purposely highlighted in one of his letters to the court: "I can recite Document 68 from memory."Indeed, he has almost a photographic memory, often quoting various materials with ease. Mr. C's purpose was not so much to confirm the rules but to use them to serve his own interests.

Mr. C was also able to convey his knowledge effectively because of his superb communication skills, reasoning ability, and use of metaphors. For instance, studying the law, Mr. C said, was like "doing homework," which could be a group activity, and applying the law to defend oneself was like "taking an exam," which had to be done on one's own. He also came up with the metaphor of "one country, two systems" in one of the couplets. What the district government did in the East Eight Lots, according to Mr. C, was an "international joke." While his criticism of the district officials was razor sharp, he opposed violent protests. Perhaps because of his father's past, and certainly because of the political intimidation by the district, Mr. C insisted that dialogue, not confrontation, was the way to go. It was meaningless, Mr. C said, if you got yourself arrested.

Because of his knowledge, skills, and discipline, he emerged as a community leader. On more than one occasion when dealing with officials, his neighbors asked Mr. C to be the group contact or to speak first. But Mr. C was wise enough to see the limits of collective action and the conflicts it might lead to. He said that they could do "homework"—studying the law—together, but there should not be any "cheating" when it came to the "exam"—each resident should decide how to negotiate a settlement on his or her own.

In late spring 2004, as the Zhou Zhengyi scandal faded and the district officials decided to make a final push to clear out the neighborhood, they chose Mr. C to mark the occasion.

The Eviction of Mr. C

On May 24, 2004, the demolition office posted an eviction notice outside Mr. C's partially demolished apartment building. It stated: "The Jing'an district government will commission the district housing bureau and the district police to carry out the eviction within fifteen days of the issuing of this notice." The notice did offer an option: "We hope your family will move out on your own within the fifteen days." The demolition office followed up with another attempt at negotiations and hoped that Mr. C, faced with imminent eviction, would yield. Mr. C was convinced that this time the district meant business: "I'm ranked number one [among the protesting residents]; they had to get rid of me first in order to remove the rest." He refused to move out on his own and decided to face the consequences on June 9, the deadline.

To prepare for the inevitable, the family started packing and making plans. Mr. C took off the address plate of his apartment for safe keeping, for it was another piece of tangible evidence that he once lived there and it could be used in future protests. On June 9, his wife and his son also stayed home to face the eviction together as a family. Mr. C's brother came to support them.

The remaining neighbors were also involved in the preparation. They were all aware that the district was evicting Mr. C to intimidate them all, as expressed in the Chinese saying "Killing the chicken to warn the monkey," and that they were the next target. But the neighbors also saw this as an opportunity to counter that pressure and display their own resolve by a strong show of support for Mr. C. Because of the Zhou Zhengyi scandal, the residents realized that the officials also had much to lose and thus were fearful of an open conflict. Accordingly, they worked out a loose plan for June 9. The night before they provided Mr. C with a dozen copies of the front page of the June 5 issue of *Renmin ribao*, which had a critical editorial on forced demolition. The plan was for Mr. C to throw them from his third floor balcony during the eviction. They also prepared firecrackers. The Chinese use firecrackers for both celebrations and mourning, and the residents thought the eviction of Mr. C was an appropriate occasion for their use.

What happened on the morning of June 9 was an open political theater in its full glory. Both parties involved, the district government and the residents, tried to take advantage of this opportunity to exert pressure on each other. The morning air was filled with intense anxiety, especially because of what happened the night before. The district housing bureau was concerned about what Mr. C might do at the last minute, how the neighbors would react, and also the further negative publicity the eviction could generate. It sent guards to watch him at night and tried once again to persuade him to move out quietly. But Mr. C, in his characteristically stubborn and ironic manner, insisted that since it had finally come to this, then he must "enjoy" the "privilege" of eviction.

This "privilege" began to take shape around 7 a.m. when various actors representing the district government entered the scene around Mr. C's building. They included dozens of officials and staff from the district housing bureau and demolition office with a cameraman, also a squad of policemen, workers from a moving company, and members of the demolition squad: a total of more than a hundred. Except for the movers and policemen, the rest of them, including the demolition squad, wore identification cards bearing their names. While the main task of the demolition squad was to level Mr. C's apartment once it was empty, the officials also entrusted its members to act as "safety guards," as their red arm bands indicated. The irony is that the job of these "safety guards" was not only to destroy the property, but also to attack anyone who dared to resist.

The arrival of the district teams added a variety of institutional colors to the site: policemen were in blue uniforms; the movers in blue shirts and orange pants; the demolition squad in camouflage jackets. The authorities also brought in two huge orange trucks, waiting to be loaded with Mr. C's belongings. Prominent in this mixture of colors was red—about a dozen red flags flying from above, invoking a peculiar question: was the unfolding eviction an act of the red vs. the rest, or was the red part of the rest?

As the police were placing a cordon around Mr. C's building, the "safety guards" armed with iron bars were walking around, and the officials and staffs were setting up the place for action, the residents also gradually appeared on the scene, scattering in front of Mr. C's apartment building. A few of them brought out their sling chairs, in anticipation of an involving event. The authorities had closed the two gates to the site to prevent outsiders from coming in. Nevertheless, more than a dozen passersby looked on from outside the wall. Gradually, a large group of residents gathered at the left corner of the cordon, across from Mr. C's apartment, which happened to be on the path to one of the gates where those who were on the way to work stopped to chat.

Most visible among this crowd was the cancer patient Jiang we mentioned above. With one leg of her pants rolled up to expose her bruises, she banged on a makeshift gong—a wash basin—and shouted, almost chanted, alternatively,

Figure 3.3. In the morning of June 9, 2004, neighbors watched as the authorities cordoned off Mr. C's apartment building and got ready to evict his family. Among the crowd were members of the police force and demolition squad. Passersby looked on from outside the wall. Red flags were flying in the remaining buildings in the background.

"The Japanese devils have entered the village!" and "The campaign has begun!" The chanting was then echoed by the crowd. After a while the group switched to singing "The Internationale" repeatedly. Often someone or a few residents started singing, and the rest joined them and raised the volume.

Both slogans, "The Japanese devils have entered the village," and "The campaign has begun," were from Chinese movies. The first one was from a number of movies on the Anti-Japanese War (1937–1945) where night lookouts would warn the villagers if they detected the approach of Japanese troops. It conveys a sense of urgency and danger. The latter phrase was from *Furong zhen* (Hibiscus Town), an acclaimed 1986 film. The film dramatized the devastating impact of the Cultural Revolution on a poverty-stricken village in Hunan Province. When the Cultural Revolution, marked by one campaign after another, ended, one of the main characters, an idler-turned-rebel who wielded a great deal of power during that chaotic period, was consumed by madness. He wandered through the village like a ghost, beating on a broken gong and chanting, in a hoarse voice, "The campaign has begun; the campaign has begun."[61] The story is a potent condemnation of Mao's revolution for its destruction of human life and spirit. Because the phrase was uttered by a mad man in the film in a sluggish, remote, fading tone, it is filled with despair and soulful mourning. The residents mimicked that tone to highlight these sentiments.

These two slogans—one suggesting a pressing threat and the other profound sorrow—seemed to be appropriate for this occasion. But in this case, the "Japanese devils" were not just coming; they were already on the site, and a few of the policemen—mute and indifferent to the performance—were standing among the crowd. The slogan was thus intended as a provocation instead of a warning. While these slogans from China's disastrous past were clearly transposable symbols, the residents did find something comic and amusing in using them here and now, especially with the mute policemen standing nearby. In between chanting and singing, they were also laughing. At one point, they also repeatedly shouted, "Forced Demolition, Against the Law!"

All this was recorded on video and in still photos, by a resident, an amateur videographer, and by the official videographer. The scene was similar to one described by Nicholas D. Kristof, a *New York Times* columnist, who tried to test the boundaries of political freedom in China during the 2008 Olympics by applying for a permit at a Beijing Public Security Bureau, where the *Times* videographer and "a police videographer busily videoed each other." In that case, "the police explained that under the rules they could video us but we couldn't video them."[62] The officials at the East Eight Lots site would have preferred to shut out the resident videographer as well but they could not, because it was in an open space under the watchful eye of the public.

While the residents were staging their show on the ground, the protagonist, Mr. C, emerged periodically on his balcony to respond to the crowd. They understood each other tacitly. Mr. C was calm, and even smiled. The first time he appeared, the crowd applauded and he waved to them. To show they were not afraid of eviction, one of them even playfully shouted "Bring me along [with you in the eviction]." At another time, Mr. C came out with a stack of the *Renmin ribao* copies and waved, shouting "*Renmin ribao, Renmin ribao!*" The crowd urged him on: "Toss them down! Toss them down!" Mr. C did make an attempt to do so but, after some hesitation, placed them on the air conditioner unit outside the balcony instead. Later he explained that he did not want to drop anything within the yellow cordon, which could be construed as disrupting public order, a charge the police could use to jail people. He then held one copy with both hands above his head, shifting to face one side and then another, in a gesture of display and protest. At another point, he was on his mobile phone, calling the emergency police number in Beijing and reporting a pending robbery. But he was told to contact the Shanghai police instead. He then dialed the emergency number in Shanghai. Apparently, he was not the first evictee to use this scheme, and he was told that he must be responsible for what he was reporting. From time to time Mr. C's brother joined him on the balcony, and his wife and son were standing by the window and looking down.

The display on the balcony and the gong-beating, chanting, singing, and laughing on the ground, on and off for about two hours, were a three-dimensional prelude to the main act of domicide. During the two hours, the authorities were positioning their entourage and equipment, including the two trucks, at appropriate points. One thing clear was that the officials, staff, and policemen were strategically placed among the residents for a quick response should any confrontation arise. The authorities were also negotiating with Mr. C on the phone in the hope he would open the door downstairs for them, despite his refusal the day before: "Bring your own iron bars—you'll have to break in if you want to evict me," he declared. But the district officials were concerned about the crowd's reaction if they broke in. They hoped for the best, but were prepared for the worst. Shortly before 9 a.m., one of the trucks

Figure 3.4. Mr. C on his balcony, holding a page of the Renmin ribao *to protest, while the movers and their truck, arranged by the authorities, were ready to take away his family's belongings. Notice the red flag on his balcony and also on the window of the apartment across from Mr. C's from which I took this picture.*

was driven to the front of Mr. C's apartment and a few officials and demolition workers broke in. Soon two officials appeared on the balcony with Mr. C, with him pointing to the *Renmin ribao* and arguing with them.

Regardless, the movers had begun to bring out Mr. C's belongings and load them on to the trucks. The moving part itself was uneventful. The family's possessions filled the two trucks. But the protest on the ground went on. Jiang continued to beat the gong and the crowd sang "The Internationale." In between they watched and commented on the happening and chatted with each other. They were clearly upset. Perhaps stirred by the scene, a few residents got into an argument with an official, pointing at him and waving their arms in frustration. Overall, the officials and staff, while nervously walking around, tried to remain calm. But they were obviously concerned. The members of the demolition squad constantly walked around with iron bars in hand and the official cameraman was video recording the process, perhaps to both intimidate and capture on film anyone who might initiate a confrontation. Also, when Mr. C tried to sit on the windowsill, one of the officials immediately motioned him to step down, as if to prevent him from jumping out the window. Mr. C and his family remained inside the apartment and watched their belongings being carried out. As if there was too much heat in the air, Mr. C and his family had a popsicle, the last thing they ate in the place they had called home for more than a decade.

The climax came when the apartment was emptied and the last two items, the air conditioner unit and the red flag, both on the balcony, were taken down, the latter, tellingly, by an official. Mr. C had been near the window most of the time during the move where the neighbors could see him. Now, he positioned himself for the "final struggle," as "The Internationale" has it, sitting next to the window with both hands holding the window bars—he knew the officials were going to take him out and he was not going to make it easy for them. Immediately, a group of officials and staff surrounded him to persuade him to give up. Mr. C shook his head in refusal. For a moment the two sides were locked in a stalemate. The neighbors were applauding and cheering him from the ground. In the end, the officials had to break his grip and drag him out.

Realizing Mr. C was being brought out from the back door of the apartment building, all the people on the ground, including the police, rushed to the back alleyway where he was put in a white van and driven away. The residents applauded for the last time, though they could not see Mr. C in the van because of its dark windows. As the "safety guards" went into Mr. C's apartment to knock it down, the firecrackers went off, as if to mourn the loss of another neighbor and also to celebrate the neighborhood's spirit. It was 12:30 p.m.

Figure 3.5. At the end of the five-hour eviction, Mr. C grasped the bars on the window of his apartment as a last act of resistance. The authorities tried to persuade him to leave; unsuccessful, they finally dragged him out. They sent the family and their two truckloads of belongings to an apartment in Pudong, which the family was forced to accept.

If the firecrackers symbolized the grand finale of the five-hour eviction, another episode of the drama continued in Mr. C's new apartment. The housing bureau brought Mr. C's family and their possessions to the new apartment in Pudong, which Mr. C never agreed to accept. But the family now had to have a place to live. Local governments and developers often used this situation to present a fait accompli to force residents into signing an agreement, or something that can be construed as such, which will end their responsibility for the residents. At the new apartment the officials from the district housing bureau asked Mr. C to sign a receipt for his belongings and the apartment. But such a receipt could in the future be used as evidence that Mr. C accepted the apartment as a final settlement, thus he refused and told the officials, "You can break my fingers, but you can't make me sign the paper." The officials then threatened to throw the family and its possessions into the street. But Mr. C was unmoved. He said that would just be fine with him, and he would be happy to transport everything back to the East Eight Lots and have the family sleep on the street there. The authorities would not mind so much if Mr. C's family slept on the street in this new suburb where there was hardly anyone, much less foreigners, around, but for them to do so downtown was a completely different story.

In the end, the officials gave in, but before that they tried one last time: they handed the apartment key to Mr. C and expected him to take it with his hand, which, again, could be considered an act of accepting the apartment as a settlement. But Mr. C said, "If you'd like, you could leave the key on the table, and if I feel like it, I might use it; or else I won't." That he was careful every step of the way demonstrated a profound distrust that underlined the relationship between the residents and the district. The residents were alert to the possible traps set by the officials. In this case, the official cameraman was recording the process, mainly to show that it did settle the family and their possessions in this new apartment safely, which, by a stretch, could prove that it had accomplished the task of relocation. Had Mr. C extended his hand for the key, it would also have been caught by the camcorder.

The eviction of Mr. C's family boosted the district demolition office's confidence and weakened the collective defense of the neighbors. The demolition office was initially nervous since this was the first eviction after a year-long interval. Moreover, this time the target was a community leader. Yet while Mr. C's eviction was eventful, it was largely non-threatening. The demolition office then pushed through the process of clearing out the remaining families there, evicting the diehard nail households and making concessions to those who were open to negotiations. Up until October 2004 when the last holdouts were cleared, the residents still came out to show their support when an eviction took place, but most of them accepted the inevitability of their own imminent relocation and were engaged in aggressive last-minute negotiations. In the end, many of them did reach a settlement close to their demands, which was much better than that received by those who moved out earlier, a continuous source of grievance among the latter group.

A Mixed Ending

The protest in the East Eight Lots has produced mixed results. Some of the former residents continue to petition, while a few have achieved tangible, surprising gains. The struggle has also changed the downtown cityscape.

On February 28, 2006, almost three years after she and her family first suffered from domicide, Shen Ting reached a settlement with the district. Her persistent appealing and her overseas contacts convinced the district government to pay her 2,630,000 yuan, ten times more than its earlier offer, which the Shen family accepted. But Shen Ting also paid a stiff personal price. Under constant stress, her marriage unraveled and she lost custody of her two young children. Her business suffered and now she barely supports herself with one clothing shop. Shen wrote a book about her family's experience and the corruption in the Zhou Zhengyi case, which was a popular seller in Hong Kong in late 2007 and early 2008 but was banned in other parts of China.[63] She then had to battle the authorities again because they had confiscated the documents necessary for her to travel between Hong Kong and Shanghai to visit her aged parents. Even the limited justice came with twisted, destructive results that perpetuated conflict.

Compared to Shen, Mr. C is even a bigger winner, though he had to wait longer, until 2010, on the eve of the Shanghai Expo. Mr. C's refusal to sign any paper on the day of his eviction indicated his determination to pursue the issue in the future. For the time being, though, he and his family stayed in the apartment and endured all the inconveniences, as the area had no market and other facilities yet. The apartment, like most new buildings in China, was a cement shell. Families usually spend months and thousands of yuan to transform such a space into a livable home. Mr. C did none of it and let the authorities know that he would not settle down there and that his heart was set on returning downtown.

A patient, foresighted man with unflappable calm and determination, Mr. C planned to wait until new apartments were constructed in the East Eight Lots, and then come back with his old address plate, pictures of his old apartment, and a rocking chair, to camp out in front of the new building to protest. "Don't they care about China's international image?" He banked on the 2010 World Expo in Shanghai to make his case. What if no apartments were ever built in that location? "Then it's up to my son to bring the family back downtown. And I'll want my ashes to be spread there."

It turns out that Mr. C would triumphantly return to his beloved downtown in the flesh. He achieved that in his own way. Most of his fellow evictees continued to petition to the municipal and central government agencies, sometimes as a group and in radical ways, which caused the district government endless trouble. Mr. C gradually distanced himself from the group. Convinced that a settlement, if one were to come, would only be on a case-by-case basis, and that negotiations for a settlement were thus an "exam" one had to take on one's own, he changed his strategy and began a quiet but determined pursuit of closure. He kept in touch with the district authorities without embarrassing them. Whenever there was a new policy or speech from Beijing that urged the diffusion of tension for the sake of promoting social harmony, Mr. C let the district know that he was encouraged—he was playing by the rules to win and his message was consistent and firm: he wanted his housing issue to be resolved before the 2010 World Expo . . . or else. The authorities understood that this "else" meant Mr. C's squatting at the site of his previous apartment and making a scene during the Expo. Moreover, since the district officials had got a taste of his leadership skills during the demolition, they were concerned he might again lead other evictees in squatting. In the meantime, in light of the upcoming Expo, the Shanghai government was especially sensitive to the issue of social stability. To defuse some tension, it relaxed its policy in dealing with some of what the authorities considered to be solvable housing disputes. All this gave an opening for Mr. C and the district to pursue a deal.

Timing is everything. The Shanghai Expo was due to open on May 1, 2010. In February, Mr. C intensified his pressure while expressing his will-ingness to work with the district. But he was adamant about a May deadline and an apartment downtown. Soon negotiations started in earnest. By the end of April, on the eve of the opening of the Expo, a plan acceptable to both sides emerged: the district would purchase a three million yuan apart-ment downtown for Mr. C, while also allowing him to keep the apartment in Pudong. As luck had it, in early May, an apartment close to the former East Eight Lots in that price range came on the market; Mr. C checked it out and liked it. The district and Mr. C then signed the final contract and the district purchased the apartment for Mr. C. Case closed.

Mr. C and his wife now live exactly where they wanted, in the heart of downtown. The new apartment is larger than his original one—116 square meters—and has three bedrooms. It is located on the twelfth floor of a 28-story building and has a view of the city. They also own the apartment of 111 square meters in Pudong, now their "country" home. Their son is study-ing abroad for a doctoral degree. Mr. C said he could have asked for a more expensive apartment but decided to compromise when he realized this time that the district was sincere in dealing with his case. He is pleased with the result but does not flaunt it. In fact, the district instructed him not to reveal the details of the deal, so as to prevent others from referring to this case, a sign that the authorities are not ready to solve all pending cases.

Mr. C contemplated his success:

> I'm the only one among my neighbors who has returned to a downtown apart-
> ment. It was a complicated process. I was very patient and also low profile

without openly challenging the district. I never doubted that I would return downtown in the end, though I didn't expect to keep the Pudong apartment as well. It's a bonus, as if it were a punishment for the district and a reward for me because of the eviction.

Some people don't know their own rights and interests, and also the law. They either think that the government is all dark or they make impossible demands . . . It's also about endurance and mental balance. Some people got so angry at an eviction that they died of a heart attack soon after. I was waiting for my opportunity and tried to reach my goal without exhausting myself . . . In the end, it was the wisdom on both sides that led to the solution in my case. If I demanded more, I would corner myself. What's the use of that? Now I can enjoy the apartment when I'm still healthy.

I've planned everything. I've nothing else to worry now. If my son comes back after graduation, the downtown apartment will be my gift to him, a gift that is better than money. The value of real estate downtown will last, and the quality of life is also better here. In the future his children can attend school downtown, just like he did.

Society is making progress, so is the government. During the demolition, the government, without knowing the strength of residents' resistance, thought it could do whatever it wanted and push us around. Now it knows better; that's progress.

But the ultimate and surprising winner in this story is perhaps the city of Shanghai—the residents' protest has changed part of the cityscape permanently. Because the evicted families had threatened to move back and squat if and when new apartments were built in their former neighborhoods, this prime piece of property in the heart of Shanghai remained an eerie wasteland for nearly three years following the removal of all the families in late 2004. One part the officials fenced off as "green land" was once claimed by rank growth. Clearly, the authorities did not quite know what to do with this highly contested space. The development plans Zhou Zhengyi made certainly had to go. The district could sell this land to another developer. But whoever took the land would also have to inherit its tainted history and ongoing tension, as the former residents threatened to return. With the pending World Expo in 2010, the authorities certainly did not want to see agitated former East Eight Lots' residents squatting downtown. In the end, the authorities completely abandoned the idea of any commercial development on the property and made it a park instead, turning what had been a temporary strategy in responding to resident protest into a permanent project. At the park opening ceremony in early 2008, Mr. C and other evicted families, who had kept a close eye on the site, joined the ceremony as unexpected and certainly unwelcome guests. Again, they waved the red flag to remind the authorities of their special affinity for this location and to keep their struggle alive.

Then, as part of the large-scale cosmetic makeover and infrastructure development to prepare for the World Expo, the park was expanded into a major, 30,000-square-meter sculpture garden. Beautifully landscaped with ponds, fountains, manicured lawns, well-maintained shrubs and flowers, and numerous mature trees, the garden has quickly emerged as one of the city's gems, an oasis in the crowded downtown.[64] The tall trees especially give the impression that the garden has been there for decades. As of summer 2010, an image of Haibao, the mascot of the Shanghai Expo, was prominently displayed in front of the garden together with a sign on which was written the Expo theme, "Better City, Better Life." Any trace of the lives of thousands of people who called this place home and of the domicide that took place there only six years before had all but vanished. Only the supporting frames for the trees betrayed that they had been recently transplanted from elsewhere, which perhaps raised the question among mindful visitors of what was here before.

One frequent visitor is more than mindful. Mr. C's new apartment is next to the garden, which he can actually see from his balcony. His favorite point in the garden is a flower-draped pergola. Mr. C often sits there, gazing at a Barbara Edelstein sculpture in front the pergola, *Elemental Spring: Harmony*, made of copper, bronze, and water; it is on the spot of his former bedroom.

Notes

1. See the BBC News, 10 June 2003 and again 21 January 2007 (http://news.bbc.co.uk); *Huanqiu ribao*, 6 June 2003: 12; *Xibeifeng* 9 June 2003: 1, 12, 14; *Caijing ribao*, 7 June 2003: 1; *Minzhu yu fazhi*, 17 June 2003: 13; *Shanghai Daily*, 2 June 2004: 1. It was also mentioned in Zhang, "Forced from Home," 273–74.

2. *Wenhui bao* (Wenhui Daily), 10 July 2003.

3. http://www.forbes.com/global/2001/1112/032_99.html, accessed 29 August 2012.

4. http://www.atimes.com/atimes/China_Business/IC01Cb03.html, accessed 29 August 2012; Shen Ting, *Shen Ting chuanqi: tiaozhan Shanghai bang* (The Story of Shen Ting: Challenging the Shanghai Clique), unpublished manuscript, 2007, chapter 1: 5–6.

5. Ouyang Yifei, *Shanghai shoufu: Zhou Zhengyi wenti diaocha* (An Investigation of Zhou Zhengyi: The Richest Person in Shanghai) (Urumqi: Xinjiang renmin chubanshe, 2004), 1–142; *Caijing shibao* (Financial Times), 7 June 2003.

6. Lu Sheng, "Zhou Zhengyi zhimi, heshi neng jiedi?" (When Will the Zhou Zhengyi Puzzle Be Solved?) *Minzhu yu fazhi* (Democracy and the Legal System), 17 June 2003: 13.

7. *Caijing shibao*, 7 June 2003; Shen, *Shen Ting chuanqi*, chapter 2: 9–12.

8. *Caijing shibao*, 7 June 2003.

9. Ouyang, *Shanghai shoufu: Zhou Zhengyi*, 122–44; Michael Sheridan, "Tycoon's Fall Gives Hope to China's Poor," *Sunday Times* (London), 6 June 2004.

10. http://www.nytimes.com/2006/09/25/world/asia/25china.html; http://news.xinhuanet.com/english/2008-04/11/content_7959627.htm, accessed 29 August 2011.

11. Shen, *Shen Ting chuanqi*, chapter 1: 10; Sheridan, "Tycoon's Fall Gives Hope to China's Poor."

12. *Wenhui bao*, 10 July 2003.

13. On February 9, 2001, the four bureaus—Shanghai Municipal Construction and Management, Urban Planning, Real Estate and Land Resources, and Housing Development—issued Document 68, titled "On Trial Implementation of Encouraging Residents to Return and Promoting a New Wave of Urban Renewal."

14. On city residents' resistance to relocating to the suburbs, also see Yongshun Cai, "Civil Resistance and Rule of Law in China: The Defense of Homeowners' Rights," in *Grassroots Political Reform in Contemporary China*, ed. by Elizabeth J. Perry and Merle Goldman (Cambridge, MA: Harvard University Press, 2007), 179.

15. Shen, *Shen Ting chuanqi*, chapter 1: 10–11.

16. *Xinmin wanbao* (Xinmin Evening News), 11 March 2003.

17. *Licai zhoukan* (Money Weekly), 21 January 2002: 17.

18. Shen, *Shen Ting chuanqi*, chapter 1: 11–12; Telephone interview, 24 October 2007.

19. Shen, *Shen Ting chuanqi*, chapter 1: 2.

20. Lin Biao was Mao's chosen successor until his death in 1971. See Spence, *The Search for Modern China*, 584–85.

21. Shen, *Shen Ting chuanqi*, preface: 1, chapter 1: 2–3; Telephone interview, 24 October 2007.

22. Shen, *Shen Ting chuanqi*, chapter 1: 12–13.

23. Telephone interview with Shen Ting, 6 November 2007.

24. Telephone interview with Shen Ting, 6 November 2007.

25. Sheridan, "Tycoon's Fall Gives Hope to China's Poor"; *Caijing shibao*, 7 June 2003; Telephone interview with Shen Ting, 6 November 2007.

26. Shen, *Shen Ting chuanqi*, chapter 2: 1–5.

27. In early June 2003, the Voice of America made at least six reports on the Zhou Zhengyi scandal, lawyer Zheng Enchong, and the East Eight Lots case. See http://www.voanews.com/chinese/archive, accessed 28 February 2008.

28. Shen, *Shen Ting chuanqi*, chapter 3: 1.

29. Zhongguo fazhi chubanshe, ed., "*Xinfang tiaoli*" *yibentong*, 278–79.

30. *Xinmin wanbao*, 15 September 2003; *Renmin ribao* (People's Daily), 5 June 2004: 1.

31. In Guangzhou a neighborhood tried to plant trees to block a road project. See Yongshun Cai, "China's Moderate Middle Class: The Case of Homeowners' Resistance," *Asian Survey* 45 (2005): 787–89.

32. Cai, "China's Moderate Middle Class," 782–83.

33. The description of the Legal Study Forum and its activities is based on my own visit to one of the sessions in June 2004.

34. The Chinese government often punishes leaders of group protests to dismantle collective actions. Cai, "China's Moderate Middle Class," 786–87.

35. Martin K. Whyte, *Small Groups and Political Rituals in China* (Berkeley: University of California Press, 1974), 5.

36. For an example of such a study group in rural China during the Cultural Revolution in the mid-1960s, see Zhang Letian, *Gaobie lixiang: Renmin gongshe zhidu yanjiu* (Farewell to an Ideal: A Study of the People's Commune System) (Shanghai: Shanghai renmin chubanshe, 2005), 121.

37. Craig Calhoun, *Neither Gods nor Emperors: Students and the Struggle for Democracy in China* (Berkeley: University of California Press, 1994), 238.

38. Ian Christopher Fletcher, "The Internationale" (review), *Radical History Review* 82 (Winter 2002): 187–90.

39. http://qingdaowangyin.blogchina.com/5215128.html, accessed 24 May 2009.

40. On rock music and social protest, see Deena Weinstein, "Rock Protest Songs: So Many and So Few," in *The Resisting Muse: Popular Music and Social Protest*, ed. Ian Peddie (Aldershot: Ashgate, 2006), 3–15.

41. http://post.baidu.com/f?kz=7108219, accessed 22April 2008.

42. Elizabeth J. Perry, *Patrolling the Revolution: Worker Militias, Citizenship, and the Modern Chinese State* (Lanham, MD: Rowman & Littlefield, 2005), 292.

43. Ron Eyerman and Andrew Jamison, *Music and Social Movements: Mobilizing Traditions in the Twentieth Century* (Cambridge: Cambridge University Press, 1998), 2, 6, 138.

44. In *A Chinese-English Dictionary* published in 1979, one of the exemplary sentences for the use of the word "dye" is "Our standard is dyed with the blood of our martyrs" (Beijing: Shangwu yinshuguan), 568.

45. See such examples in Geremie R. Barmé, *In the Red: On Contemporary Chinese Culture* (New York: Columbia University Press, 1999), 337–38; Joseph W. Esherick, Paul G. Pickowicz, and Andrew G. Walder, eds., *The Chinese Cultural Revolution as History* (Stanford, CA: Stanford University Press, 2006), 52, 73, 224.

46. A search of the *Renmin ribao* database alone yields 240 uses of the phrase. The phrase was coined in an authoritative *Renmin ribao* editorial, on what proved to be an ominous date: June 4, in the year 1966, the onset of the ten years of the chaotic Cultural Revolution. The date June 4 is now best known for the CCP's crackdown on the student protest in Tiananmen Square in 1989.

47. Zong Fengming, *Zhao Ziyang ruanjin zhongde tanhua* (Zhao Ziyang: Captive Conversations) (Hong Kong: Kaifang chubanshe, 2007), 366.

48. It was replaced by a new journal entitled *Qiu Shi*, which means "seeking truth," a guiding principle in Deng Xiaoping's stated early reform effort.

49. See other such examples in *New York Times*, March 27, 2007, http://affordable-housinginstitute.org/blogs/us/2007/04/china_property.html, accessed 28 March 2007.

50. Cai, "China's Moderate Middle Class," 777.

51. William H. Sewell, Jr., "Space in Contentious Politics," in *Silence and Voice in the Study of Contentious Politics*, ed. Ronald R. Aminzade et al. (New York: Cambridge University Press, 2001), 55.

52. Ma Guangzhong, ed., *Zhongguo duilian daguan* (An Overview of Chinese Antithetical Couplets) (Shenzhen: Haitian chubanshe, 2006), 1.

53. Qin Shao, *Culturing Modernity: The Nantong Model, 1890–1930* (Stanford, CA: Stanford University Press, 2004), 80–83.

54. He Xuesheng, *Shufa wuqiannian* (Five Thousand Years of Chinese Calligraphy) (Changchun: Shida wenyi chubanshe, 2007), 182–83.

55. Richard Curt Kraus, *Brushes with Power: Modern Politics and the Chinese Art of Calligraphy* (Berkeley: University of California Press, 1991).

56. Liu Tao, *Zhongguo shufa* (Chinese Calligraphy) (Shenzhen: Haitian chubanshe, 2006), 73.

57. Michael Herzfeld, *Cultural Intimacy: Social Poetics in the Nation-State* (New York: Routledge, 2005), 3.

58. Geremie R. Barmé used the description in an essay on the Chinese artist Ai Weiwei, http://www.chinaheritagequarterly.org/articles.php?searchterm=026_aiweiwei .inc&issue=026, accessed 12 January 2012.

59. Kang Zhengguo, *Confessions: An Innocent Life in Communist China*, trans. Susan Wilf (New York: W. W. Norton, 2007), 343.

60. Elizabeth J. Perry, "Popular Protest in China: Playing by the Rules," in *China Today, China Tomorrow: Domestic Politics, Economy, and Society*, edited by Joseph Fewsmith (Lanham, MD: Rowman & Littlefield, 2010), 13.

61. http://www.huaxia.com/20031209/00155057.html, accessed November 18, 2007.

62. http://www.nytimes.com/2008/08/17/opinion/17kristof.html?th&emc=th, accessed 17 August 2008.

63. Shen Ting. *Shui yinbao Zhou Zhengyi an: Shen Ting, Zheng Enchong tiaozhan Shanghai bang shiji* (Who Exposed Zhou Zhengyi? A True Record of Shen Ting and Zheng Enchong's Challenge to the Shanghai Clique) (Hong Kong: Kaifang zazhi chubanshe, 2007). What I have cited in this book is the unpublished manuscript in a different title Shen Ting sent me. See some reports about Shen's book: http://www .zonghexinwen.net/news/1010000932/accessed 18 August 2009; http://www.epoch weekly.com/gb/053/4146.htm, accessed 18 August 2009.

64. http://live.shanghaidaily.com/directory_detail.asp?type=venues&id=3197, accessed 22 July 2011.

CHAPTER FOUR

~

A Barrack-room Lawyer

Jarndyce and Jarndyce has stretched forth its unwholesome hand to spoil and corrupt . . . From the master, upon whose impaling files reams of dusty warrants in Jarndyce and Jarndyce have grimly writhed into many shapes . . . no man's nature has been made the better by it. In trickery, evasion, procrastination, spoliation, botheration, under false pretences of all sorts, there are influences that can never come to good.

—Charles Dickens, *Bleak House*

He walks around greeting his neighbors with such commanding ease that one might think he owned the streets, and in a sense he does. Of medium build, with a friendly face, disarmingly boisterous and effervescent at times, and extremely shrewd and calculating at others, Shi Lin, a descendent of gangsters and squatters, is almost an urban legend, a legend partially constructed by Shi himself.

Among the residents-turned-protesters in Shanghai, Shi Lin is known as "Teacher Shi," not because he is in the teaching profession, but because his extensive knowledge of housing issues has earned him this generic title of respect in Chinese culture. Shi's is one of the toughest nail households in Shanghai, having held out in his home for more than a decade. During that time his old neighborhood has mostly disappeared, leaving his home like an outpost in a dense zone of nondescript high-rises. But Shi is confident that his largely homemade shack initially of mud and straw in what was once the worst shantytown of the city is worth millions. He is in no rush to cash in yet, not until, as he anticipates, the further rise of the market will add more zeros to its value. Shi celebrates the demolition and relocation while also struggling against it. With a tenacious squatter mentality bolstered by up-to-date legal concepts, Shi is just about the best student produced in the largest seminar of Chinese society where a deeply flawed system has taught its people to maneuver within the system and beat it at its own game, perversely or otherwise.

A more appropriate title for Shi Lin is perhaps barrack-room lawyer. It is a testament to the lack of legal services for dispossessed people that Shi Lin and many others in his position have turned to study the law themselves. Shi has filled the legal vacuum and become a gainfully employed amateur lawyer. He represents the underrepresented with his apparently encyclopedic knowledge of the law and regulations concerning housing reform and his ability to twist them to suit his needs. For more than a decade, he has invested thousands of yuan in books, magazines, and government documents on redevelopment and housing conflicts—they now constitute an impressive collection in his home library. He has spent countless hours studying them so diligently that he can recite relevant legal provisions with ease, not always accurately, though—precision does not concern Shi; he is known not merely for his knowledge of the law but perhaps even more for his ability to stretch it.

The determination to pursue the potential financial gains in the housing reform has turned Shi into a politically active policy entrepreneur. He has made contact with human rights activists in China and has led group petitioning and street protests in Shanghai, Beijing, and even Hong Kong. He has also engaged in political and legal debates and lobbied for policy change. In his political activities, Shi Lin has used his masterful skills in theatrics. He has invented tricks and gimmicks to expose corruption, and is good at throwing verbal darts at officials, all of which reflect both his insight into the nature of property issues and his street smarts that spring from his family's rough roots. Shi Lin's story is unique and at the same time representative of the pulse of the cataclysmic change in the reform era and its impact on people from all walks in life.

Squatting in Shanghai

Born in 1954, Shi Lin is the third generation of a migrant family from Jiangbei, that part of Jiangsu Province north of the Yangzi River and south of the Huai River. Due to chronic famine, floods, and a host of other problems, Jiangbei, unlike Jiangnan, which lies south of the Yangzi River, has since late imperial times been notorious for its poverty and its emigrants, most of whom gravitated to Shanghai where they formed an underclass. Jiangbei migrants consistently occupied the lowest rungs of unskilled labor that served the city: "the majority of rickshaw pullers, dock workers, construction workers, nightsoil and refuse collectors, barbers and bath-house attendants."[1] As such, Jiangbei people have suffered a deeply rooted prejudice born of their image as the poorest, dirtiest, most uncouth group in Shanghai well into the last years of the twentieth century when the reform burst open the floodgates to a new massive wave of peasants migrating from all over China into the cities.

The family of Shi Lin's biological father, the Lis, came from Yancheng, among the poorest districts in Jiangbei. But one of Shi Lin's forebears gave the family history a colorful twist. One of the brothers of Shi Lin's maternal grandfather, who pioneered the family's entrance to Shanghai in the 1920s, became a "snake in its old haunts," that is, a minor hoodlum (or, as the Chinese put it, a local bully). His name was Xu Laosan. Xu's turf was in the Dapuqiao area, which in the 1940s was still on the southeastern margin of the city, where he was influential among street peddlers, small merchants, rickshaw pullers, pedicab drivers, and especially nightsoil collectors. The area was close to Rihuigang, a dock on one of the tributaries of the Huangpu River that was used mainly for disposing of the city's human waste and other refuse. Xu Laosan controlled the dock and had his own boats, which shipped the collected nightsoil out to the countryside where it was sold as fertilizer. Appropriately enough, he was known as *Fenba*, literally "nightsoil bully." Xu also collected a fee from other boats and businesses that used his dock. With Xu Laosan's help, some of his relatives, including Shi Lin's maternal uncle, came to Shanghai and became rickshaw pullers.

By 1958 Shi Lin's family could no longer get by on the small piece of land they worked in Yancheng. The year 1958 was the beginning of Mao's Great Leap Forward, which would cause nationwide starvation and death, even in traditionally prosperous areas such as Jiangnan. Jiangbei was hit especially hard.[2] Shi Lin's family was eating carrots mixed with tree bark and grass and suffering from body swelling. Also at the time, Shi Lin's uncle got married and moved out of Xu Laosan's house. The uncle wanted his sister to take his place in Xu's home and wrote to ask her to "come south," to Shanghai, to escape starvation. Shi Lin's mother took his advice and fled with her son to Shanghai. His father, who suffered from tuberculosis, was left behind.

While the socialist reform movement in the 1950s ended Xu Laosan's nightsoil monopoly, it did not completely put him out of business. Shi Lin's mother helped Xu clean toilets and wash nightsoil buckets in exchange for a place to stay and Xu's support of her son's education. In the early 1960s, two things happened that pushed the family to the verge of breaking up. In

1962, Shi Lin's father joined his family in Shanghai but died two years later, on the eve of the Cultural Revolution. By then, Xu Laosan, who sensed the gathering political storm that would likely sweep him away, asked Shi Lin's mother to move out.

Shi Lin's mother survived by doing odd jobs, mending clothes for workers and selling popsicles on the street. Barely earning her keep, she quickly married another Jiangbei native, named Shi, who became Shi Lin's stepfather. In the late 1940s while still a peasant back home in Jiangbei, the older Shi had been drafted by the CCP to serve as a stretcher-bearer in the civil war between the CCP and the GMD. The exploding of artillery shells permanently damaged the older Shi's hearing. Deaf and unskilled, he was taken in by a small bean-curd shop where he was not paid but was at least fed. His job was to push the millstones round and round for hours grinding soy beans. Because the job requires getting up before dawn to prepare fresh bean curd for morning shoppers and is boring and backbreaking, a Chinese proverb couples it with iron smithing and boat towing as the three hardest occupations under the sun.

When it came to housing, the Shi family was in an especially dire situation. Like many other immigrants from Jiangbei, the family settled near Zhaojiabang, one of the city's worst shantytowns. Shantytowns began to appear in Shanghai in the first decades of the twentieth century, and by the late 1940s, they virtually surrounded it. They appeared on the periphery of the city because that was where the factories were concentrated, and on the border of the International Settlement, because that was where the control of the Chinese authorities was weakest. The largest slum covered 130,000 square meters and had 16,000 residents in 4,000 mostly straw shacks.[3] The inhabitants there were left to the "art of not being governed"[4]—surviving in dark, muddy, and filthy hovels, with no utilities of any sort nor any other social or public services. But this was considered to be a step up from the villages from which they had fled.

The slums in Zhaojiabang were typical. The area was located on the southern boundary of the French Concession. It was named after the creek that flowed through it: Zhaojiabang—"bang" here means creek—which until 1937 carried water and flowed into the Huangpu River. The deterioration of this "picturesque waterway" into a stagnant sewer was a direct result of the Japanese invasion of the city in 1937. The Japanese constructed military roads at the creek's upper reaches and thus cut off its flow. Hanchao Lu writes about Zhaojiabang's devastating descent to shantytown:

> The creek finally silted up after the Japanese occupied the city . . . It gradually became a trash dump for factories and residences along its banks. Stagnant

water in the creek joined by polluted water from nearby factories plus a daily in-pouring of garbage soon made Zhaojiabang a stinking sewer. At the end of the Sino-Japanese War, the silted-up creek became home to thousands of migrants who swarmed into the city from the countryside because of the Civil War (1946–49). After 1945, the central stretch of the creek, about 2 miles long, quickly became crowded with poor people. During 1946–48, the numbers of households along Zhaojiabang rapidly increased from several dozens to 2,000, with a population of about 8,000, making Zhaojiabang one of the largest slums of Shanghai.[5]

After the CCP takeover in 1949, Zhaojiabang became a poster child for the new government's slum clearance policy. By the mid-1950s, the squatter settlements on and around Zhaojiabang were gradually removed and the creek was filled in to build a road. Appropriately named Zhaojiabang Road, it became a major east-west artery in the southern part of the city.[6] But this change was only visible in the immediate area of the road and was partially cosmetic. Barely half a mile from the road, the slums continued to exist, and in fact to expand. They were simply an economic imperative: the government lacked both the determination and the resources to eliminate them, even well into the twenty-first century,[7] testifying to the impact of the stagnant economy under Mao and the tenacity of the squatters.

The Shi family is a case in point. When in late 1964 Shi Lin's mother married his stepfather, the family rented a shed in Zhaojiabang. But the monthly rent was five yuan while Shi Lin's mother only made eight yuan a month. The family soon had two more children, Shi Lin's stepsisters. Unable to pay the rent, the Shis were induced by a friend to squat in a cemetery half a mile north of the middle section of Zhaojiabang Road, which until 1966 was still unregulated by the city and avoided by superstitious people. In the late 1950s and early 1960s many families of mostly Jiangbei origin, like the Shis, moved into the cemetery and expanded the slum settlement. The Shis leveled a piece of ground and put up a nineteen-square-meter shack with a straw roof and wattle walls mixed with mud. There was no distinction between its walls and roof—the shack was in the shape of a triangle with straw and wattles extending from the top all the way to the ground, without windows or ceilings. The shack leaked and everything in it was often mildewed and rotten. The family's coal briquette stove filled the hovel with fumes and smoke. The hundreds of people in this slum shared a public water station and a couple of public toilets. The Shis' shack, like all the rest, did not have an address. Shacks were put up helter-skelter wherever people could find a scrap of land and there were no streets. But they were rent free.

From such a low point things could only go up for the Shi family, and they did. Beginning in 1965 the municipal government started to develop the area by building factories, schools, and apartments. The development put an end to new squatter settlements but left the old slums intact. Although the Shi family still lived in the same shack, the surrounding area began to improve. Also, because of the socialist reform of the 1950s, the small, private bean curd shop where the older Shi worked joined a factory making pickled vegetables, which in turn soon merged with a state-owned seafood production company. As such, the older Shi became a full-fledged state worker with access to precious seafood, which, like almost everything else, was rationed at the time.

The Shi family was on especially good terms with a neighborhood briquette shop, giving its staff seafood as gifts. In 1966, when the shop closed its doors, it returned the Shi family the favor by giving them its electric meter, a luxury most squatters could not afford then. With this meter the Shi family managed to get electricity for their home, something the rest of their neighborhood did not get until the 1970s. Then, in the early 1970s, the Shis borrowed a street address from a friend and applied for the installation of indoor running water. The doorman of the water company happened to be a distant cousin of Shi Lin's mother and helped speed the process by connecting the family shack with a public water station nearby, while most families in the settlement continued to depend on the neighborhood water station well into the late 1980s. Though the Shi family used a briquette stove until 1985 and a public toilet until 2002, when they were finally fitted with a flush toilet at home, Shi Lin remembers, more than four decades later, how getting basic utilities made him feel special: "Our shack was like a regular apartment flat; we had our own electric meter and running water right there in the house, which was extremely rare then."

Further progress was on the way. The older Shi became a union member and union benefits in a socialist state soon came to have an impact on the family. On weekends the union mobilized its members and brought material to fix up the Shi's home, which not only suffered from a leaking roof but also a sinking foundation. As more quality apartments were constructed on higher ground nearby, their house became more vulnerable to water. On rainy days it was as muddy inside as outside.

Over time, the shack underwent a transformation. First, the wattle walls were replaced with bamboo and finally, in 1968, with bricks. The family, with the help of the older Shi's union and many neighbors, managed to elevate the house, add a loft, where Shi slept, and put up a tile roof. In stark contrast to members of the propertied class, like the Hes and Zhus discussed in the preceding chapter, whose lives were perceptively deteriorating after 1949, the Shi family, among the poorest in the city, was benefiting from the Communist takeover. The shack, though, remained the same size, nineteen square meters, for the family of five now with three growing children—improving the house had exhausted both the family's resources and the union's goodwill.

In 1973, Shi Lin graduated from junior high and, after three years of training, he was sent in 1976 to work in a machinery factory in a desolate county in Anhui Province, north of Shanghai, where he became a skilled welder. In 1979, a new opportunity opened up for him. At the onset of the economic reform, the Jinshan Petrochemical Factory, in a distant southwestern suburb of Shanghai close to Hangzhou Bay, was expanding and especially needed skilled welders. Shi Lin was among the first group of workers "lent" by Anhui to Jinshan, with his personal registration remaining in Anhui. Still, Jinshan is more than 60 kilometers away from the city and Shi Lin could only return home on weekends. He gradually managed to move closer to the city, changing to a job with a gas company in Pudong and, finally, in 1988, to a rubber plant near his home in the city. With this last job transfer, he was no longer someone being "borrowed" from Anhui and temporarily stationed in Shanghai; instead his household registration was transferred to Shanghai. In other words, by 1988 Shi became a Shanghai resident again. His mother, who had lived with her two daughters after his stepfather passed away, was delighted with Shi's return to Shanghai, because now there was once again a man in the house. Shi Lin himself is very proud of this achievement—and it was indeed an achievement considering how tight control of the household registration system was then: "It [returning to Shanghai] was rare then for anyone. Very few could achieve this. Many of my co-workers are still in Anhui to this day," Shi said.

Through it all, Shi Lin has carried with him the profound imprint of his upbringing. Growing up in a Jiangbei immigrant family suffering from economic hardship and discrimination, Shi is inherently insecure. But instead of bowing to his fate, Shi compensates with a strong, aggressive yet adaptable personality, inflated optimism, and a strong work ethic. His insecurity is only revealed when he comes across as too self-confident about his own achievements; he routinely brags about them and considers himself superior to others. But Shi also grew up with a role model. Xu Laosan, the "nightsoil bully," who passed away in 1965, was Shi's boyhood hero and remains so to this day. As a little boy new to Shanghai, Shi was shocked to discover that he could eat white rice at Xu's home, something so rare and luxurious that he had hardly seen it back in the countryside. Xu immediately became the richest and most powerful man in the child's eyes. Because Shi could pack away an unusual amount of food, Xu predicted that he would grow up to be a strong man with great promise, which has been an inspiration for Shi.

Shi Lin has since internalized some of Xu's qualities. Xu came to Shanghai with nothing but built a business and life for himself and his clan, which taught Shi that people can turn even profound disadvantages around and come out on top, if only they work hard, are determined, and cultivate good relationships with others. Shi is thus eager to help people and routinely performs good deeds. Once, as we finished a dinner in a restaurant near his home, Shi took the time to write in the "Customer Review" book about how great the waitress who served us was. Shi explained to me, "Most of the waitresses here come from the countryside and are poor. Good customer reviews are important for them to get a bonus and a promotion. Every time I come here I write down my praise of the waitresses. It costs me nothing but a few minutes but it may really help the waitresses."

But doing good deeds for others, even in the most benevolent and enlightened Buddhist tradition, often implies an investment in one's own interest—the return of a favor when needed. Such a reciprocal, mutual beneficial relationship is at the heart of *guanxi*, connections, that dominate every aspect of Chinese life. It is an especially valuable resource for people in poverty. Indeed, Shi was most impressed with Xu's human skills. In Shi's words, "Xu maneuvered through the system and settled problems for people in trouble, because he had connections." Shi Lin's parents were apparently also good students of human relationships. It was not by accident that the Shi family had benefited from special connections every time they most needed them, such as in getting electricity and upgrading their home.

Shi has certainly taken this lesson to heart. His decade-long march from a remote corner in Anhui Province back home to Shanghai was in part made possible by many of the relationships he built along the way. In fact, his final return to the city was through his connections as a union leader with a cadre in the personnel department of the rubber plant. Not surprisingly, from the mid-1980s onward, Shi Lin had held various leadership positions in his work units, from head of a workshop to union official in charge of propaganda and workers' welfare.

Shi is also comfortable in the area of propaganda. He was active at school in poetry recitation, editing wall newspapers, and writing stylized calligraphy. As a union cadre, Shi used his talent to identify among the workers "good people and good deeds," and featured them in wall newspapers, a standard propaganda tool to manipulate mass behavior under the CCP. Shi helped solve union members' issues ranging from property disputes, traffic accidents, and marital problems, to housing assignments. His work often involved dealing with local government, law enforcement officials, the courts, neighborhood committees, and cadres in other work units. Like the "nightsoil bully" Xu Laosan, Shi became the point man who settled issues for his workers where reasoning, arguing, hassling, bribing, and bullying were all useful skills that could lead to solutions.

With years of such experience, Shi not only became a problem solver and skilled negotiator, but also learned much about government policy and the workings of the system, both its loopholes and its limits. More specifically, since the late 1980s the transformation of welfare housing into a commercial housing market created many problems for the workers and their families, which became a large part of Shi's work. Helping his co-workers deal with property issues proved to be an invaluable asset in the ensuing decades when Shi emerged as a deal maker in housing disputes.

The Transformation of a Shack

When Shi Lin returned to Shanghai in 1979 he brought with him a girlfriend whom he intended to marry. But housing was a problem since Shi felt the family shack simply could not accommodate a married couple. However, he was not discouraged. Just like his parents, who made their first shelter with their bare hands, he decided to put a separate kitchen in a small space next to the house. In this housing-shortage era, it was common for families to move their stoves outside into whatever space they could manage to find, on the street, the backyard, the courtyard, or the hallway. All of this was another form of squatting.

At the time, construction materials were controlled by the government and, to get any, a person had to apply for a permit at the district housing bureau. Shi Lin's application resulted in an allowance of two bags of cement, not enough to do much. However, he managed to use that and scraped together other material to build a 14-square-meter kitchen. When he married in 1982, that kitchen became the newlyweds' bedroom at night. At the time, both Shi Lin and his wife worked in Jinshan and stayed in separate factory-provided dormitories for male and female workers on weekdays. They only used the "bedroom" when they returned home on weekends.

Shi understood that any significant improvement of his home would inevitably require expanding the foundation. Luckily, there was a 52-square-meter empty lot next to the house, which for years remained an unclaimed space. In time, conflict arose over the use of that space. Because the shacks routinely suffered from leaking roofs and poorly sealed walls, families had to sun dry their clothes and other household contents after a rainy day. They competed for outdoor space, including the empty lot next to the Shi's house, blocking its entrance. After some confrontations with neighbors, the Shi family fenced in the space to claim it as their own so that they could build an addition.

Several things happened in 1988 that made the Shis' plan possible. That year Shi's transfer to a job in the city spared him a long commute, allowing him more time and energy to work on the addition. His family had now grown to include his daughter and the need for space became more desperate. With this difficult housing situation, Shi became eligible to apply for the use of that empty lot and for the purchase of building materials.

Moreover, his years as a union cadre dealing with the housing problems of his co-workers gave Shi exceptional insight and foresight. In August 1988, the State Council held its first national conference to plan for commercialization of the housing market. To people like Shi who followed the news, it was clear that housing was facing a profound change: it would become a commodity for anyone with the means to purchase it. Shi understood that expanding and improving his home would certainly increase its value in the future market. Also, he gradually learned from the district that his neighborhood, like many other shantytowns, would be targeted for demolition. Unlike most people, who would simply give up on any renovation plans because of the pending demolition, Shi moved forward. His experience taught him that his house was a most important investment; a bigger and better house would yield more compensation in the future. He also understood that once the government formally designated his neighborhood for demolition, it would not allow any changes to the houses there. In other words, if he wanted to set up his house for a future payoff, he had to race against time.

With all that in mind, in the late 1980s Shi Lin laid the foundation on the empty lot next to his home for the addition. He gradually put together what appeared to be a temporary shelter, mostly made of reeds and bamboo. The addition was crudely built because of both his limited financial means and his strategic concerns. Since the Shis did not legally possess the adjacent lot nor did they have a government permit to use it yet, it was questionable whether it was legal for them to build there. In fact, it was certainly illegal unless he had an official permit. But Shi did not want to apply for a permit since if it was denied it would tie his hands. Instead, he wanted to present a fait accompli and see what happened before doing any elaborate work. The history of this squatter settlement, which spread willy-nilly, also played a role in Shi Lin's sense of entitlement to the adjacent space: "This used to be a free place. No one who lived in this slum ever purchased the land. Everyone just built their own homes," he declared.

Leaving nothing to chance, Shi worked at securing a land use permit for his new addition by researching the process and, more important, by identifying the crucial officials in charge of such permits. It all worked out, partly because of his connections. Needless to say, Shi presented the district with a compelling case of his extremely difficult living conditions. By 1992 Shi had succeeded in obtaining a certificate granted by the municipal housing bureau for the land use rights of the 52 square meters. He registered the 52 square meters and the addition he built on it in his own name and his original home together with the kitchen—which now added up to 33 square meters—under his mother's name. Combined, the two parts of the house had a land area of 85 square meters.

Shi was among the last few lucky ones who obtained land use rights for free. With the development of a real estate market, the city banned any applications for such rights in 1996. This land use certificate became invaluable to Shi Lin. He always keeps a copy of it in his briefcase and by his desk so that he can produce it quickly whenever the situation calls for it. Shi learned the importance of land use certificates from his years of union experience: "You can't just go by your words and expect others to believe you; you have to have the hard evidence of this certificate. Then you're protected by law and no one can deny it."

Shi Lin then focused on improving the addition. Once again, the union provided him with some much-needed building materials free of charge, leaves of absence, and helping hands. Step by step, he was able to replace the initial reed and bamboo structure with bricks and a tile roof. And by the end of 1992, Shi had added about 60 square meters of living space to his part of the house.

In 1994, his neighborhood was designated for demolition and the freeze rule—all the property there was to stay as it was without any expansion, renovation, rental, or sale—took effect. But Shi was used to pushing the limits and manipulating the system. He added a story to his part of the house in 2000 and another one to his mother's part in 2002. Shi also built a flat roof top on his portion where he has planted flowers. Since such work was a clear violation of the rules, the government tried to stop him. On one occasion, more than a hundred people from the municipal and the district governments arrived on trucks to halt his project. But he was able to make a strong enough case to avoid any punishment.

Also in violation of the freeze rule, in 1998 Shi rented the first floor of his house on the street side at 2,000 yuan per month to three peasant migrants from Fuyang, Anhui, a notoriously poor area that, like Jiangbei, was known for its refugees. The renters opened a store selling glass and some grocery items there. The other side of the house faces an alleyway across from a newly built neighborhood. Shi Lin built a stairway leading to the family's living space on the upper level. Next to the stairway was a basement that Shi rented to a couple of migrant workers who sell milk and newspapers. The monthly rental of 1,500 yuan for that space goes to Shi's mother.

The payback of Shi's hard work is significant. While the expanded house was visibly hand-built and patched together, it provided the family with a much more spacious and comfortable living space. The size of the house considerably enhanced the value of the property. Furthermore, the rental space, as we will see later, also supplied Shi not only with extra income, but also leverage in his negotiations with the government over the value of his home.

Because of his tireless effort and his ability to "think ahead," in his words, Shi Lin and his mother are now the owners of a house with two stories and two sections, with a total living space of more than 300 square meters, that is, according to Shi, on top of the 85 square meters of land to which they hold use rights. The size of his house has been an issue in dispute, as we will see: Shi counts the flat roof as part of the living space, but the district disagrees.

Furthermore, Zhaojiabang is no longer the "stinking sewer" on the periphery of the city that it used to be. The sprawling growth of the city has incorporated Zhaojiabang into its extended downtown and made it a highly desirable area. Zhaojiabang Road was widened and dotted with numerous shops, restaurants, and hotels, some of which are high-end. A newly constructed 20-story hotel on Zhaojiabang Road with hundreds of rooms and dozens of executive rooms and a 500-seat restaurant is located right next to Shi's alleyway. Xujiahui, a bustling business, entertainment, and cultural center with renowned universities and upscale malls is only fifteen minutes by car west of Shi's house. In fact, the area has gone through such a drastic change that one can no longer locate Shi's house according to its original address. His alleyway now has a new name and his house a new number. To reaffirm the identity of his house, Shi made an address plaque to install on the street-front of the house above the small shop which states both its previous address and a crucial claim: "Private House."

The Shi family, the owners of this private house who were once among the downtrodden peasant migrants, has become a patron and landlord of a new generation of migrant workers in this sought-after area of the city. Their little muddy shack has been transformed into a hugely valuable concrete and brick house almost twenty times larger than its original size, mainly because of the sheer will, hard work, and smarts of Shi Lin.

Figure 4.1. Shi Lin's home. He rents the street-front of the house to peasant workers for a glass shop. Shi made a plaque with the previous street address of the house and a claim, "Private House" and installed it below the roof at the right corner behind the telephone lines.

A Nail Household

Shi Lin would need all those qualities and then some to deal with the demolition and relocation. Shi's neighborhood of two clusters of slum dwellings was located on either side of the public toilet it shared. In 1993, as part of the "365 Project" to clear out the city's slums, the Xuhui District Housing Bureau made plans to develop Shi Lin's neighborhood. Shi Lin's house was among the more than two hundred in both clusters targeted for demolition. But Shi refused to move out, which also encouraged his immediate next-door neighbor and a few dozen other families in the other cluster to stay. In the end, 188 families were relocated, which made it possible in 1998 for the district to build a group of nine high-rise residential apartment buildings. Still, the district was responsible for clearing up the slums and tried to force the remaining families out. By 2007 about ten families in the two clusters were still holding out.

Like most other residents in the early stage of the reform, Shi Lin was also prepared to relocate. But he had his own terms and was convinced that his negotiating skills would prevail. But the gap between Shi Lin's demands and the government's offers proved to be too great to bridge. The key dispute was about the land use rights. Shi Lin's neighbors who relocated to the suburbs now owned their apartments there, but they did not have the land use rights: this is the standard policy since all land is state property. Yet those residents, despite, and in fact because of their history as squatters, actually had land use rights to the land on which their shacks were built—in a sense, acquisition by adverse possession—which they gave up when they moved.

While land use rights were not of much concern to most of Shi's neighbors since such rights never in any way had contributed to the quality of their lives in the past, they were important to Shi Lin, who recognized the value of land use rights in a market economy. He demanded that wherever he moved, the land use rights also had to be transferred to the new location. "It should be an exchange of private property—a house for a house and a piece of land for a piece of land. I should be compensated with private ownership of both the house and the land since they want to demolish my private home. What's so wrong with that?" Shi Lin explains the relationship between state-owned land and its occupants, demonstrating the mentality of a true squatter who has become familiar with legal terminology: "Though the land originally belongs to the state, if I've occupied it for decades, then it becomes mine. With the land use rights certificate that I have, the land is legally mine." Shi Lin's argument is essentially similar to the concept of adverse possession in English common law. He also sees land use rights and land ownership rights as one and the same thing and on that basis has tried to push through a settlement on his terms.

As such, Shi will not give up his existing land use rights certificate unless the government issues him another one for his new location. Yet it is impossible to grant land use rights to apartment owners in a high-rise as hundreds of them live on top of each other. Shi also wanted to relocate nearby and was unwilling to move to the suburbs: "If I wanted to live in the suburbs, I could have had a nice apartment there in the 1980s. Why should I change my mind now that I've transformed my house into a comfortable home?" But the dispute over the land use rights is a key in Shi Lin's housing conflict, a subject we will come back to later.

As in other such cases, monetary compensation was another option that would have bypassed the thorny issue of land use rights altogether. Shi Lin was willing to consider it: he initially asked for 700,000 yuan. In 1993, the real estate market, while on the verge of taking off, was still grossly undervalued. A two-bedroom apartment in his area cost about 150,000 yuan: thus Shi could have purchased four such apartments with 700,000 yuan. That was a huge amount of money at the time; most of Shi Lin's neighbors who took the cash option were satisfied with less than 200,000 yuan. Still, if only the district housing bureau knew then what Shi would come up with later, they might have happily settled on that amount and celebrated it as a smart move. But predictably, the district was also out to maximize its own profit by minimizing the compensation. The housing bureau offered 620,000 yuan instead, in part due to the dispute over the size of Shi's house, namely, whether or not the flat roof should be counted as part of the floor space. Shi insisted on 700,000 yuan. In any event, a difference of 80,000 yuan kept the two parties from reaching a deal.

The district thought that this difference could be easily overcome by exerting pressure. The housing bureau started what Shi termed a "wheel war"—continuous high pressure meetings at his home, at and with the neighborhood committee, with the neighborhood public security office, the district office, and his work unit, all involving threats and assaults. Shi pushed back accordingly. He warned his work unit to stay out of the dispute: "It's a social issue, not a work unit issue. If my work unit gets involved, I'll hold it responsible for the result, whatever that may be." This veiled threat was heightened by the unpredictability of the vague term "whatever." But Shi did not really think his work unit should be impartial in this matter so long as it was partial to him. He was just concerned that the work unit might possibly support the demolition office. In keeping with the traditional role of the union, he said that "The work unit and the union should help their own workers, not the demolition office." Shi also threatened the district, claiming that if it dared to evict him, he would ship all of his belongings to Beijing and squat in Tiananmen Square for good.

By then the district officials had begun to realize, albeit slowly, that Shi Lin was more of a troublemaker than they had anticipated. In the early stage of the housing reform, there were relatively few people like Shi who hassled endlessly and officials had yet to gain experience dealing with them. The district took care to check with his work unit to see if he was indeed someone who might squat in Tiananmen Square and got a full confirmation. Given that among his relatives was a "nightsoil bully," a piece of information which Shi freely shared with pride, his self-identity as a true "proletarian" as he put it, his tough-minded and sometimes boisterous demeanor, and his well-known gift of gab, the officials got a clear sense that Shi was someone to be taken seriously if not outright feared. In the end, the district conceded and spared Shi Lin's house. As Shi watched the high-rises being erected, he began his decade-long marathon of holding out for the highest possible payoff.

The issue of land is of course not just about abstract rights, but about concrete interests. Property rights, even more than the right to freedom of speech, are intertwined with practical economic interests. In the case of Shi Lin, he firmly believes that the value of land in the city will rise indefinitely, which so far has largely been true. In the summer of 2007, he said,

> The potential value of the land will always increase faster than the value of the renminbi [the currency]. Since the reform, housing prices have risen by 10 percent, but land values have increased 100 percent. I'm the only one in my neighborhood who understands the value of the land. No one else here thought about gaining this certificate of their land use rights. They moved out without realizing the huge loss they suffered by giving up their rights to the land. They never asked for a separate payment for their land. Yet land is an unrenewable resource and thus is priceless.

His point is right on target, especially as available urban land is diminishing at a fast pace. Also, as always, Shi never misses a chance to distinguish himself from his fellow residents. That his house still stands today seems to give him bragging rights.

Of course, Shi Lin's position reflects what he has learned about real estate development in China since 1994. He is almost gleeful that the district refused to meet his demand for 700,000 yuan at the time, since he would have missed a potential windfall. According to the more educated Shi Lin in 2007, his house was worth about 9,500,000 yuan, ten times more than his original asking price. His new estimate is based on a mathematical formula, bulletproof in his own logic, which involves figuring both the market price per square meter for housing and for land. Shi estimates the value of the house, about 300 square meters according to him, at 6,000,000 yuan, and the land use rights at 3,000,000 yuan, and the two rentals—the glass shop and the basement, which Shi Lin considers as his business since it supplies the family's income—at another 1,000,000 yuan. He is willing, however, to cut the last item, the rentals, to half their value. These numbers add up to the 9,500,000 yuan that Shi Lin now demands. This is an astronomical amount for a cobbled-together house. Shi understands that the district is unlikely to agree with his calculations. Privately, he says he is willing to start the negotiations at 6,000,000 yuan. But he is confident that the final settlement will be close to what he is asking, because of the information he possesses and his ability to negotiate and to game the system.

The Education of Shi Lin

In 1993, before the start of the demolition in his neighborhood, Shi Lin might have been considered a street-smart college freshman with regard to housing policy, while the majority of the Shanghai residents had no clue whatsoever. By 2007, however, he had become a shrewd doctoral student majoring in housing policy. Shi's self-education has been a decade-long, consistent, and purposeful process. His best teachers are not only government policies and regulations and the media, but also the take-no-prisoners behavior of local officials and developers ranging from cutting corners to outright corruption and crime in the pursuit of profit. Shi has taken all of this in from the biggest, most complex classroom of Chinese society and has reinvented himself accordingly.

I did not get to know Shi until the summer of 2007. Whenever I had a question about an official term or policy issue during my interviews with residents, they would uniformly refer me to Shi Lin, "Ask Teacher Shi. He knows everything." One resident also said, "Teacher Shi has collected all the government housing policies and regulations. You should check with him." Initially, I did not pay too much attention to such referrals, because most government documents are readily available and because all the residents I have studied have a special interest in policy. But the awe in their voices did raise my curiosity. Little did I know that Shi was already an urban legend. As one resident told me, "You can't find anyone else in Shanghai like Teacher Shi; he's unique and you must meet him."

When I learned that it is not just his library, but his practice as an amateur lawyer and broker that has gained him such fame, I knew that I indeed had to meet him. Our first meeting at his house lasted six hours. This meeting, like all the subsequent meetings, was frequently interrupted by phone calls from people consulting with him or making an appointment with him for their next round of negotiations or their next court appearance. Sometimes he spoke slowly about a specific regulation and its meaning so that the person on the other end of the line could take notes. People also dropped in and out to update Shi on their cases and strategize the next move. Some of them would stay and join our conversation, while others would just listen and smoke. Clearly, this was routine for them and they were all comfortable with it.

Shi exudes confidence and provides a periodic push to keep his often skeptical and distressed clients going: "This is not the time to give up, not yet. You're on the right side of the law. Keep pushing and they [the officials] will have to give in." Shi gets something akin to an adrenaline rush when talking about the topic of housing disputes. The difficulty was not to get him to talk, but to get him to take a break. Often he would call at 9 p.m. and ask me to see him, because someone had just stopped by his home after an eventful petition trip to Beijing with stories to share. Observing his interaction with visitors and on the phone, it was immediately clear to me that Shi was a man in demand and in his element. He reminded me of a general in his headquarters giving orders and encouraging his soldiers on the battleground, which in his case could be a courtroom, a petition office, or a negotiating table. He was also like a retailer of government policy and regulations with his own brand of interpretation.

But Shi understands that one has to know the law in order to maneuver. Since the early 1990s he has systematically gathered and studied housing regulations. The deepening of the economic reform in general and the housing reform in particular left previous knowledge of economic norms in limbo. Both the government and the people were "feeling [for] the stones while crossing the river." The government has often issued experimental, short-lived, and even contradictory regulations, leading to confusion and disorientation. Since the housing reform has been a massive undertaking affecting every family in urban China, there has been a widespread demand for information, direction, and clarification. This demand only intensified as local officials arbitrarily applied the law at the expense of the people. Information about housing reform began to fill the airways, the printed media, and the Internet—that wave has not receded.

In the process Shi has become a news junkie. In the early 1990s, an educational television station in Shanghai had a daily one-hour program on housing policy, especially on demolition and relocation policy. The station invited experts to lecture and explain policy issues. Also, a Shanghai radio station hosted an hour-long program titled "Everyone Talks about Real Estate" (*Dajia tan fangchan*) daily that welcomed call-ins. Shi was among the loyal followers of both shows but not a passive listener: "I listened to those shows every day. Then I wanted to learn more about the original government regulations. What exactly did the government say?" Shi started to browse bookstores. The municipal housing bureau has since the late 1990s published a yearbook that includes housing and land policy and regulations from every level of the government. These yearbooks, in hardcopy, are about 400 pages each and cost nearly 100 yuan. Such an expensive publication is mostly intended for government records, libraries, and other institutions; few copies are available in bookstores. Not many individuals, even researchers, own a complete set of the yearbooks. But Shi has ordered a copy from the municipal housing bureau every year and has thus collected a complete set of the yearbooks. They serve as the main source of his knowledge and authority on policy issues.

The mushrooming growth in the number of magazines and newspaper sections on economic and housing issues was a feast for Shi. He is a long-time subscriber to two daily newspapers in Shanghai. He also frequents a nearby newsstand and buys issues that he considers particularly important. Like the residents in East Eight Lots, Shi was most pleased with the magazine article entitled "Demolition and Relocation Is Gold." He also took to heart an article with the title "A Humble Room Is Worth Thousands of [pieces of] Gold,"[8] which seemed to directly speak to his particular situation. Part of the agenda during his petition trips to Beijing was to visit bookstores. Shi believes in a conspiracy theory that the Shanghai government prevents certain books published by state agencies on housing policy from reaching the local market. He has thus made a point of purchasing books in various central government offices in Beijing. If he sees something relevant there but absent from Shanghai's bookstores, he gets multiple copies to share with others back home.

Shi keeps a book cabinet in his bedroom. The bedroom is separated by a curtain from his living room, which doubles as a dining room. If a visitor has a question about a policy, he disappears behind the curtain and, in no time, reappears with a book in hand, most likely one of the thick yearbooks, and points to the relevant pages for an answer. In time Shi has become intimately familiar with the material. He is a careful reader, using a poker card both as a bookmark and a ruler to underline important passages. While he may not know everything in those publications, he is certainly familiar with the most common issues. He underlines important passages with a straight line, thanks to the poker card, most of the time in blue ink. He marks some especially important passages in both blue and red and emphasizes key phrases with red dots. His well-thumbed books testify to both his determination to study the law and his mistrust of the government's interpretation of the law.

What Shi has taken away from all his studying of both government policy and the corrupt behavior of the powerful are a few fundamental principles. One is that residents have rights. Those who own private property have ownership rights and no one can take away their property without their consent and adequate compensation. Tenants also have rights: to a fair settlement, a settlement that should improve, not worsen, their housing situation, a point Shi takes for granted. "That," he argues, "is what the reform is all about. If the compensation lowers one's standard of living, one should reject it outright. Just read Deng Xiaoping's speech on reform." Indeed, Deng, the architect of China's opening and reform, encouraged a few to get rich first but also expected the majority of Chinese to benefit from the reform and reach the level of "small comfort" in living standards. Shi Lin wants the government to deliver the economic justice it has promised. The other principle Shi believes in is that forced demolition and relocation for commercial development is simply illegal and unjust, and that the National People's Congress, China's legislature, has never endorsed it.

The key to Shi's understanding is the issue of people's rights, a seemingly simple but revolutionary idea for people who grew up under Mao. It is simultaneously a familiar, novel, slippery, and confusing concept. After all, according to the prevailing rhetoric of the Mao era, the people were the masters and owners of the state and thus enjoyed every possible right. However, these rights were so all-encompassing and abstract that they granted nothing specific to the individual and became an empty promise, leaving people defenseless against the state's encroachment on their lives. In the Mao era, that people could use their rights to actually protect their own interests against the state and officials was unheard of. Therefore, in the reform era, the rhetoric of people's rights was nothing new, but the idea that their rights actually meant something tangible was novel. It took a long time for people to recognize the fundamental difference between rights as rhetoric and rights as individual interests.

Shi Lin is among those residents who have stubbornly insisted on exercising and realizing their rights. He does everything, including "causing trouble" if necessary, to protect what he considers rightfully his or his clients' in his position as a barrack-room lawyer.

The Formula

Shi's knowledge of housing policy and his ability to negotiate and maneuver have become his most prized capital. They have served him well in many ways. First, he has kept holding out in his own home since 1994, which has enabled him to demand a multimillion yuan payment. It has also secured his reputation as an amateur lawyer. That reputation itself has become leverage in Shi's protracted negotiations with the district over his own house. Moreover, Shi has represented a dozen clients and, in some instances, he has been able to negotiate a significantly better compensation package than initially offered. He also drafts petitions for them, writes appeals, and represents them in court. His clients often express their gratitude in the form of gifts, meals, and monetary payment, which has varied from a few hundred yuan to thousands. Shi's lawyering has become a source of income.

Shi has not had a regular job since 1998 when he was laid off with severance pay of 700 yuan a month. His wife quit her job before that. His daughter is the only one in the family with a regular job. Thanks to the demolition and relocation, the family has not had to pay for any utility bills since 1994, courtesy of the district housing bureau—its demolition office covers the cost of utilities once a neighborhood is designated for demolition, with the expectation that such coverage is temporary. But in Shi's case, it has been fifteen years and counting. The Shis thus use their air conditioner and heater generously, without concern for the cost. The family is not rich, but comfortable, living as it does on Shi Lin's severance pay, the two rentals, and the extra income from Shi's informal consulting.

Whether it is negotiating about his own house or representing another resident, Shi brings a deceptively simple formula to the table, which he calls "plus and minus":

> I use a pen and paper when I negotiate. It's just math. The math I do is plus—adding everything that should be included in the value of the house. I understand officials and developers are in [it] to make money, so I ask my opponents to do the minus if they dispute my numbers, and then see if we can come up with an agreement.

But of course what is involved is much more than mathematics. Shi goes into negotiations armed with the history of housing policy. In his words:

> You must understand the law so that you can reason with officials. The better your brain is, the bigger your wallet will be. The most important inequality at the beginning of the housing reform was in knowledge capital. Ordinary people simply didn't understand government policy and their own rights; they were being hopelessly manipulated by the government and developers.

Shi in fact calls the essence of his formula "policy plus"—pluses according to policy, which most people are not aware of and which officials are all too eager to conceal. But some of the officials themselves are ignorant of the details of many policies, especially since they often change and contradict each other. Shi has a list of such details that can benefit residents. Generally, housing compensation is based on the number of people in the house—in other words, the larger the family, the more the compensation. The government uses compensation to support some of its public policies. For instance, before 2001, housing compensation policy allowed a bonus for families with one child to promote the one-child policy. Also, many residents often assume that the estimated value of their houses as determined by an appraisal company is final. But that estimate is just a reference. Residents can contest it if they believe the appraisal is unfair, especially because local officials often try to influence appraisal companies. Another major issue in compensation is the price gap for different locations—downtown, for instance, is much more expensive than the suburbs, and compensation for those who relocate from the city to the suburbs should reflect the price difference. But, as Shi points out, many residents either do not know about such policies or fail to figure out how to apply to them: "There's a lot of room in the policy to maneuver. My job is to squeeze out sufficient benefit from the policy for those residents."

Shi has engaged in some tough negotiations. In one case, a family was initially offered 850,000 yuan by the district for their house. In an intense three-month negotiation, Shi had twenty-some meetings with the demolition office. There were times when even the family was discouraged and ready to give up. But Shi "squeezed" harder. In the end, the family received 2,100,000 yuan. But in other cases, residents wanted more than Shi could deliver. In 2006, an evicted family insisted on 1,200,000 yuan to settle their case, while the district was only willing to pay 500,000 yuan. At that point the family asked for Shi's help. After many rounds of negotiations in a year-long marathon, the district agreed to pay 1,800,000 yuan, a much better deal than the earlier one. But by then, the animosity between the family and the demolition office had become intractable. The family's expectations rose and they demanded 2,300,000 yuan, which included not only the initial value of its property, but also court fees, petition fees, the rent they paid, lost wages, the rise in the real estate market, and emotional suffering. In the end, Shi was able to reach a compromise and get 2,100,000 yuan for the family.

Some of the people who have come to Shi for assistance have been referred by friends, neighbors, and clients, who in turn have served as brokers. Shi does not openly ask for a fee, but there is a mutual, unspoken understanding that he is to be paid for his services. Sometimes the fees are explicitly agreed upon, often by those go-betweens. As an informal lawyer, his fees are often arbitrary and he is willing to take less than he asks. In the case mentioned above, where the family received 2,100,000 yuan, the initially agreed fee for Shi was 100,000 yuan. Once the settlement was reached, the family had second thoughts and asked the broker to renegotiate. In the end, Shi took 26,000 yuan instead, a significant cut from the original deal. "It's all right," Shi said. "The family had difficulty in dividing the settlement among their members and couldn't spare 100,000 yuan; I understand." The fact is that making money off his service to other residents was not part of Shi's grand plan for getting rich; it just happened because of the lack of legitimate help for dispossessed residents. For Shi, this income is a bonus and he can be flexible about it. His grand plan to make a windfall is through his own home in the final settlement he has been orchestrating.

Shi has applied his "plus and minus" formula to his sister-in-law's case. In 2003, Shi's sister-in-law in Putuo District, in the northwest part of the city, faced demolition. Her neighborhood was another shantytown where many residents had private but poorly built homes. The district offered about the lowest market price at the time, 3,500 yuan per square meter, to resettle the families there. By the summer of 2006, most families, including Shi's sister-in-law, were being forced out. Shi's sister-in-law was paid 107,055 yuan as a settlement for her 25-square-meter home.

But to Shi, that amount was way off the mark. His sister-in-law filed a lawsuit against the Putuo District Housing Bureau two weeks after her eviction. Shi, who represents his sister-in-law in court, made several arguments in a fifteen-page court document with eleven appendixes that demanded the district pay 1,329,083.41 yuan, twelve times more than its offer. Shi provides a series of calculations that adds up to the final amount. This sum includes a 15-square-meter addition to the house which the district excluded from the compensation on the grounds that the addition was built in violation of housing regulations, the land value of the main house and the addition, renovation costs over the years when the family lived there, and cost of rent and real estate broker's fees since his sister-in-law's family had been renting after the eviction. For each of the items and its value that Shi listed—the house, the land, and the cost of renovations—Shi's court paper provided "Facts and Reasons"—the facts of the size of the house, for instance, and the reasons why it was worth what Shi asked for—to substantiate his claim. Six years have passed and Shi's meticulous calculations in this case have not resulted in a settlement, while the rent his sister-in-law pays has increased dramatically, which Shi has made sure to include in his ensuing petition and lawsuit.

Because some other families in that neighborhood were in the same situation as Shi's sister-in-law, at least a dozen of them have decided to put their fate in Shi's hands. They were all encouraged and convinced by Shi Lin's formula and expect a large payout in the end. Shi has become the group's ring leader, taking them to Beijing to petition, leading them in street protests and in sit-ins at the municipal petition office in Shanghai. As of October 2011, when I once again interviewed Shi, his sister-in-law's case is still being negotiated; Shi is confident it will be resolved soon.

Clearly, Shi's main purpose in all these negotiations is to gain the maximum monetary compensation for the families involved. While this is commonsensical, Shi has taken it to a new level. He is among the few who have really taken the idea of "demolition and relocation is gold" to heart and tried to turn it into a reality. Shi expects a windfall that will make his family wealthy for life. With that in mind, he not only looks at the current market value of the property in question and its anticipated future increases, but also the amount the family would need to be financially secure for life, and he sets the bar as to what constitutes that security rather high. Once he told a resident who was in the midst of intense negotiations with local officials:

> This is your once and only chance in life and you have to grab it if you want to live in comfort for the rest of your life. Make sure that the final payment is large enough to settle everything for your future—your wife can quit her job; your son's college education will be covered; and you can get him an apartment for his marriage.

The resident was in his mid-forties and his son barely a junior high student. But Shi insisted on looking forward, for he understood that the opportunity to make hundreds of thousands of yuan in a single whack will be hard to come by once the wave of housing reform has crested.

For Shi, his involvement in the Putuo neighborhood and in cases elsewhere is a mixed blessing. He has been harassed by local officials, Public Security personnel, and demolition squads, warning him not to "meddle" in others' business. Sometimes they call to threaten him, "Be careful if you go out!" He usually does not go out at night and when he does go out, even during the day, he is indeed careful. Once when he was consulting with a family, the demolition squad came to beat up the family and trash their home. Shi was among those injured, but he was far from an unintended casualty. The demolition squad blamed Shi for the family's adamant demands and meant to teach him a lesson. Shi ended up in the hospital. In another case, a demolition squad burst into a home where Shi and the family were discussing strategies. The family called the emergency number for help and the police brought all of them, including Shi, to its station for questioning.

But Shi's reputation can also work in his favor. The Xuhui District government was particularly concerned with Shi's influence among his immediate neighbors. It is in that sense that Shi owned his street—if Shi stays, so will some of his neighbors. Given the local officials' understanding of his leadership capacity, they would rather deal with a single Shi Lin than a group of neighbors all looking to Shi for guidance. So they have tried to contain and isolate him. When the district required that he stop "meddling" in his neighbors' housing cases in exchange for its promise not to evict him, he agreed. In October 2005, the district housing bureau issued Shi a letter with a key statement: "The demolition and relocation involving your house must be based on mutual consultation and agreement between the demolition company and the residents. If your family disagrees with the settlement, the company cannot force you to accept it." The letter means that Shi most probably will not be evicted. It places the initiative to decide when or even whether to relocate in his hands, which is exactly what Shi was looking for.

Needless to say, Shi was overjoyed with the letter. Leaving nothing to chance, he called the district afterward and made the official on the phone repeat the key statement while Shi recorded it on tape—he wanted to have the statement in both writing and on tape. "Now when my neighbors come to me with questions, I just present them with government policy, which is public knowledge and no one can stop me from sharing it. But I try to withhold my own opinion and interpretation." In Shi's mind, however, his deal with the district only applies to his immediate neighbors in the district. He thus continues to "meddle" in cases in other districts.

The Political Arena

If early on Shi considered a substantial monetary compensation to be the only purpose of his work, in time he has grown to become more politically active. He has moved from the small, number-driven negotiating table to the larger and politically charged arena of public protest in Shanghai, Beijing, and even Hong Kong. He has engaged in policy debates and demanded changes in demolition and relocation policy from Beijing, in the blogosphere and in person.[9] In that sense, he has become one of many policy entrepreneurs among the concerned Chinese who have campaigned for their preferred ideas.[10] He understands that the arbitrariness and complexity of negotiations defeats most residents and believes that policy change is one way to rein in the rich, the developers in this case, and to give residents a fair settlement. Born into poverty and growing up on the social and cultural margins of society, his innate sense of justice is with the deprived. Having benefited from political changes under Mao and being a long-term union cadre, his political awareness is never far from the surface. His self-education with regard to the law and policy and his experience in the housing reform have helped him recognize the acute gap between the written law and the lawless reality. Shi's thinking is informed by a combination of a squatter's mentality of entitlement, commonsense justice, Mao's socialist welfare culture, and a market-driven capitalistic logic. All of this eventually led him into the political arena.

Shi did not take his first petition trip to Beijing until November 2006, when he was representing his sister-in-law and her neighbors. "All the formal channels for us to appeal their cases were obstructed—the district evicted the families; the court ruled in the favor of the developer; and the petition submitted to offices in Shanghai fell on deaf ears. We had no way to go but Beijing," Shi recalls. He went to Beijing with ten residents from his sister-in-law's neighborhood. After some setbacks because of the Shanghai government's attempt to intercept them, Shi eventually had a chance to visit the petition office of the State Council. He made the most out of the opportunity and managed to have a detailed talk with the officials there. The material Shi had prepared and the points he made went beyond the specific cases of the residents whom he represented.

Shi's focus was to lobby for the abolition of Document 305, which he saw as the root cause of all the wrongdoing in demolition. As discussed previously, Document 305 allowed the issuance of a demolition permit to trump the law. Most damaging of all, it legitimized domicide and was responsible for much of the violence in demolition and relocation.

Shi offered an analogy to the unchecked power of the demolition permit granted by Document 305:

> Issuing such a permit is like issuing someone a driver's license. The person now has the right to drive, but he doesn't have the right to ignore a red light or kill someone. If he makes a mistake and gets into a crash, he'll be punished according to the law and may even lose his driver's license. But how come those with a demolition permit are allowed to break the law by invading private property and violently throwing people out without any consequences? Does this make sense? Where is protection for the people? It's completely against [the] law for a demolition squad to evict people.

Using the same analogy of driving, Shi declared that the relationship between residents and developers should be like that between two drivers. If two drivers get into a collision, both should be examined for their responsibility and no one should be automatically exempted. Shi argued: "Why do we not see developers petitioning? Why are the majority of petitioners residents? If someday developers are also petitioning, that'll be a welcome change."

Shi was not alone in opposing Document 305. He was part of a nationwide and sustained movement among assorted policy entrepreneurs—urban residents, legal experts, political activists, and other concerned citizens—that fought to have Document 305 abolished. In July 2002, barely one year after it was issued, a retired teacher in Hangzhou, the capital of Zhejiang Province, initiated a petition asking the Standing Committee of the National People's Congress to investigate Document 305. The petition was eventually signed by 116 people whose main charge was that the document simply violated the constitution and that, as the legislative branch of the government, the National People's Congress was obligated to take action. Because of the broiling conflict generated in the housing reform, popular opposition to Document 305 continued. The passing of the Property Law in 2007 reaffirmed the government's legal and theoretical commitment to the protection of private property rights, which, as Item 4 of the Law indicates, "no units or individuals can violate." The Property Law emphasizes that where the development of public projects involves private property, the parties involved must follow legal procedures. The key here is public projects and the law. It does not allow commercial development and business interests to infringe upon private property. In theory, the Property Law effectively invalidated Document 305. But local governments have continued to hold fast to Document 305, thus causing much confusion and misunderstanding. In fact, with Document 305 and many similar local regulations still in place, the Property Law was a sham.[11]

Regardless, the passing of the Property Law was encouraging to protesters. They renewed their call for the elimination of Document 305. In Shanghai, Shi became a leader of this effort. In June 2007, he drafted a petition letter to the State Council and started a signature drive to build momentum for their demand. In the petition, Shi stated that because of the "unconstitutional Document 305, numerous people in Shanghai lost their homes, jobs, and even freedom—they were thrown into jail or sent to labor camps." He pointed out the fatal flaw of Item 16 in the document, which gives local government the authority to carry out demolition even during the three-month period when residents are allowed to appeal their case. "How absurd!" Shi's letter declares. Item 16, according to the petition letter, is especially a "devil's law."

Shi's petition is a damning indictment not only of Document 305, but also of the collapse of the justice system in protecting people's rights and interests:

> When residents call 110 for help after being beaten in an eviction, the security bureaus and police stations in Shanghai refuse to help. According to them, forced demolition and relocation is not a public security issue. But when a demolition squad comes to evict residents, the security personnel and police are all on site to protect the squad against the residents. . . . As a result, residents have suffered tremendously.

The petition especially highlights the consequences of Document 305: "Thousands of people have no homes to return to and enter the hopeless process of petitioning. . . . Yet the powerful keep breaking the law and leave the powerless to deal with the consequences." The petition ends with a number of demands that are "shared by all those who signed their names below": "Document [305] must be abolished immediately; the government must recognize the suffering of evictees and provide a solution; officials involved in breaking the law and abetting forced evictions must be brought to justice."

Shi's signature drive gained more than five hundred supporters, who signed with both their names and phone numbers. Shi then sent the petition by registered mail to the State Council. In mid-June, 2007, Shi made a third trip to Beijing because of the momentum that was building up for abolishing Document 305. At the State Council's petition office Shi's main talking point was how, in issuing Document 305, the State Council overstepped its authority, since the National People's Congress never passed a law permitting violent eviction. He emphasized that it was time for "administrative authorities to retreat from demolition and relocation and allow residents and developers to conduct their negotiations as equal parties protected by law." Indeed, the key to the anti-Document 305 campaign was to end the collusion between government and business and thus free residents from the oppressive threat of domicide and jail time. Such a demand, as we have seen in the previous chapters, was shared by other protesters. Document 305, as pointed out in the introduction, was finally abolished in spring 2011.

The anti-Document 305 campaign is significant in many ways. Most important is that it reflects heightened popular awareness about the boundary between law and policy and the law's precedence over policy. In the past, anything issued by the government or even spoken by a CCP leader was considered official policy and law—there was no distinction between policy, regulations, law, and high-ranking officials' statements.[12] This is accepted as normal in a society ruled by man and in a party-controlled judicial system. The uproar against Document 305 thus reflects a popular demand for judicial independence, a key to justice. Because of Shi's understanding of the constitution, which he deems to be fundamentally just, he is an ardent supporter of judicial independence. His calls for justice, the reform of policy, and the punishment of abusive officials in the anti-Document 305 campaign all indicate his venturing out of the singular focus on monetary compensation into an active role in the political arena.

Shi's political activism was intensified when he established a connection with the human rights lawyer Zheng Enchong. Zheng, as documented in the preceding chapter, was imprisoned in 2004 for his involvement in the Shen Ting case in East Eight Lots. His release in summer 2007 energized housing protesters in Shanghai. The news of his release rapidly spread on the Internet and by word of mouth. Shi identified with Zheng's struggle and was eager to contact him. But Zheng's influence, even though mostly symbolic by then, continued to make him a government target. He was put under house arrest, with security guards screening his visitors. After some setbacks, Shi managed to contact Zheng and even hosted a banquet to celebrate his freedom.

Zheng's release had emboldened Shi to take more risks. Like Zhou Youlan, Shi became an event petitioner. When he and a group of petitioners arrived in Beijing on the eve of the CCP's seventeenth National Congress in October 2007, he was among the lucky ones who escaped a police roundup. Shi immediately started writing online to report that almost everyone in the Shanghai petition "army" was "being arrested." "I must speak out. If no one speaks out, how can people have any hope?" he said.

Due to the danger of protesting in mainland China, Shi Lin and some other Shanghai housing protesters looked to Hong Kong as a place for public demonstrations. In 2008, on December 9, the eve of the international Human Rights Day, a group of more than forty residents left Shanghai for Hong Kong at separate times and by separate routes. The trip was not spontaneous since everyone had to apply in advance for a special document to enter Hong Kong and to show up on the same day. No one, though, would admit to having organized the trip and the subsequent activities in Hong Kong. On December 10, all of them gathered in front of the Hong Kong Police headquarters to stage a sit-in protest. They held various signs. Shi's read "Demolition leads to poverty; we protest to express our grievances." They also sat in by the United Nations Refugee Center in Hong Kong. Shi stayed in Hong Kong for three days. Shen Ting, the former resident of East Eight Lots whom Zheng Enchong represented, was their "legal advisor" in Hong Kong. It does not take much to figure out the connection among Shen Ting, Zheng Enchong, and Shi Lin that led to this group protest in Hong Kong. Apparently, the Chinese authorities figured that out as well and promptly confiscated their entrance documents to Hong Kong upon their return.

The star event in the media on this 2008 Human Rights Day regarding China was the publishing of an open letter, known as Charter 08, signed by 303 Chinese intellectuals, lawyers, writers, journalists, and people from other walks of life. Liu Xiaobo, its lead signatory, was the Nobel Peace Prize winner in 2010.[13] But the forty-some residents-turned-protesters on the streets of Hong Kong, nameless to the outside world, are nevertheless part of the same movement in China where people are breaking free of the CCP's control and demanding an open society ruled by law.

The Hong Kong trip was educational for Shi. He was particularly impressed with the orderly public behavior there and by the openness of society: "So long as you don't break the law, you can protest freely. We could even use the bathrooms at the Hong Kong police headquarters and get tea there. That is what a society governed by law is all about."

Whether on the streets of Hong Kong or Shanghai, Shi has used the considerable propaganda skills he learned at school and as a union cadre to theatrically stage protests. Since residents' petitions and demands often fall on deaf ears, Shi has come up with a number of ways to grab attention. During street protests, he often carries a piece of cardboard, about 14" x 17", with a hole in the upper end as a handgrip. The messages Shi Lin writes on these cardboard signs are often brief and blunt, highlighting his point that most of the real estate development in Shanghai is not for wartime needs or public projects and that it is therefore unjust to evict people in order to line the pockets of developers and officials.

Shi once had someone take a picture of himself with eight residents from his sister-in-law's neighborhood. The nine people, seven women ranging from their mid-thirties to a gray-haired grandmother, and two middle-aged men, are arranged in two rows against a bright, flowery background that evokes the image of a rural home in some remote time. The people in the front are holding a horizontal paper scroll consisting of five pieces of paper. The words on the scroll are a bit melodramatic: "O! Party: We are suffering and helpless; evictees are searching for you." The scroll, with its characters

Figure 4.2.   Shi Lin made several cardboard signs to carry in street protests. On this one, the circled word is "not," followed by "public interest," meaning "if it is not for public projects," then "forced relocation [allows] business [interest to] harm people; the party and government [should] uphold justice."

in a formal style of calligraphy, is large enough to dominate the image, especially because it is in white while most of the nine people are in dark clothing. Each of the four people in the back row also holds a piece of white paper that together read "Return my house" and "Protesting for my property rights." Most interesting is their body language. All the nine people, looking uniformly solemn and determined, have raised their right hands as if they were taking an oath.

The combination of this oath-taking gesture and the apparent search for the party by the evictees as expressed in the scroll makes the picture highly revealing, especially if it is understood in a historical context. It is common knowledge in China that the CCP conducts a ceremony to admit new members by having them raise their right hand and take an oath of loyalty. That is the gesture the nine people mimicked in the picture, though none of them is a party member.

The main theme of the picture, however, is on the melancholic scroll about the evictees' search for the party, which implies that the party is missing. This theme invokes a particularly difficult time in the CCP's history

Figure 4.3. Shi Lin assisted these eight residents with their cases. They took this picture together to appeal for help. The characters in the front scroll read: "O! Party: We are suffering and helpless; evictees are searching for you." Shi instructed the eight people to attach a copy of the picture to every petition letter they sent out, in the hope that it might catch the eye of those in power.

back in the late 1920s and 1930s. In the spring of 1927, the fragile united front between the CCP and the GMD, which had been formed to defeat the regional warlords, was broken when Chiang Kai-shek crushed the CCP's organizations in Shanghai, in what was characterized as the "white terror." The CCP suffered a tremendous blow as many of its members and activists were arrested, murdered, or driven into hiding, and largely retreated from China's major cities to remote rural areas. To the extent the CCP continued to be present in the cities it was as an underground organization. The members of the CCP who remained in urban areas were scattered and had a difficult time reconnecting with the party.

It is one thing that the CCP was missing, so to speak, during that "white terror." But it is quite another matter that the CCP as a ruling party in today's China is invisible. The plea on the scroll thus poses some intriguing questions. Why is the ruling party missing when the people need it the most? Has the party been blind to the abuse of power and the suffering of the people? The purpose of the oath-taking gesture was not so much to convey their loyalty to the party—their loyalty was to their own interests—as it was to highlight the party's betrayal of the people. These residents included this picture in their petition letters, in the hopes of catching the eye of those in a position to respond to their plea.

Shi's masterpiece of propaganda is a special envelope he designed. In brown paper, the 9" x 12.5" envelope seems like a regular large Chinese envelope. Like any Chinese envelope, the front has designated spaces for the zip codes of the sender and recipient. On the back, a small space on the lower right corner indicates that the Bureau of the Post Office in Hebei Province supervised its making and that a local print shop in Hebei turned out 20,000 copies in February 2006; it was completed with a certified number and type code. Indeed, the envelope looks to be officially produced.

The genius of the envelope, however, is all on its back, which is covered by a chart consisting of seventeen rectangles of various sizes that are connected to each other by lines. The chart features three groups of people: the developers, the government, and the residents. The contents in each of the rectangles are mostly words, but occasionally images, all of which indicate the relationship among the three groups and their positions in the housing reform. Its content is so rich that it qualifies as an outline of a dissertation on the ins and outs of housing reform in China.

At the center of the chart is a long and narrow rectangle depicting two hands with their index fingers extended into each other so that they become one. The caption beneath the image reads, "Closely holding hands." But who is holding hands with whom? The caption next to the left hand states "the developer," and next to the right hand, "government offers land at discounted prices." This is followed by two small rectangles in one square box that reads: "Big profit is used for bribery; state property suffers a loss." In other words, the material points to the fact that the government and developers are closely connected in housing reform for their mutual benefit—the government provides land to developers at low cost, which allows the latter to make a huge profit and in turn to bribe officials. The rest of the content on the envelope reinforces that central point. It indicates that developers often distort official policy and illegally evict people; that the government issues demolition permits in violation of the law; that demolition officers act like Cultural Revolution rebels by threatening and beating people; and that local public security bureaus and neighborhood committees have all been bought off by developers.

This characterization of developers and the government leads to the third group in the chart—residents—which the chart presents as the victims of abuse by the other two groups. Several rectangles are allocated to present their predicament: that they take their cases to court without results; that they petition over grievances for years without relief; and that they wonder when the government will come to their aid. The chart ends with four phrases: "the people are in pain; [they] have no home to return to; [they] plead with the central government; [they] expect a just and fair compensation and settlement."

The chart thus vividly and insightfully summarizes the nature of housing development, the means by which both developers and the government profit from the process and, as a consequence, how the residents suffer the loss of both their property and the protection of the law. A quick glance at the envelope is all that is needed to take in its contents, which is precisely what Shi intended.

This envelope was all Shi's making. He composed the chart and had a print shop in his neighborhood print it on the back. He made about fifty copies of the envelope and distributed them to some of the petitioners he knew. But this politically loaded envelope was too radical for some of them. Shi himself certainly used the envelope to send letters to Hu Jintao and Wen Jiabao with his name and home address clearly written on it. Those letters were sent by registered mail with return receipts signed by the receivers so Shi is certain that they reached the offices he intended. His hope is that even if higher-level officials do not open his letter or read it carefully, the envelope will grab their attention. In fact, the envelope has to go through the hands of many people, from the post office in Shanghai to that in Beijing, and its form and message are bound to catch someone's eyes. Shi is very proud of his creation: "You can't find in all of Shanghai an envelope of this kind."

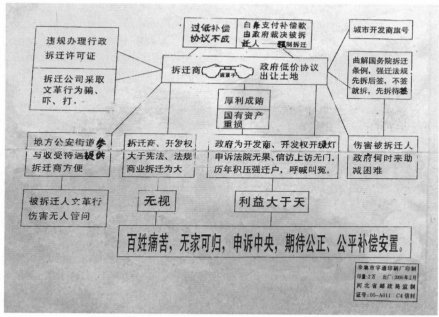

Figure 4.4. Shi Lin created this chart and printed it on the backs of the envelopes in which he sends petition letters to Beijing. The chart demonstrates the combined force of political power and business money that advances itself at the expense of the people. The second rectangle at the center from the top depicts two hands—one represents the developer and the other government—with their index fingers extended into each other. The caption beneath the image reads, "Closely holding hands." The last line reads, "The people are in pain; [they] have no home to return to; [they] plead with the central government; [they] expect a just and fair compensation and settlement."

As one would expect, Shi's role in protests and other politically charged activities and his apparent influence among petitioners have earned him special attention from the security forces in Shanghai. Shi has been confined against his will in his home, under surveillance. This has usually happened after he has been rounded up and sent home from a petition trip to Beijing. Though so far he has never been formally arrested, a recent encounter is reason for concern. In late May 2009, on the eve of the highly sensitive twentieth anniversary of the suppression of the Tiananmen Square protest on June 4, 1989, the Putuo District Public Security Bureau took him away from his home and put him in a hotel for eighteen days. This was largely because of his involvement in his sister-in-law's and her neighbors' cases in Putuo, which had often led to group petitioning in Beijing. He was told that his home had become a gathering point for malcontents, which spelled trouble, especially at an unsettling time like the June 4 Tiananmen anniversary, and that removing him from his home would ensure social stability. The police never called it detention, though, but told him instead that "we would like you to spend a few days in a hotel room." Shi understood the government's position perfectly but wanted to make sure that he was not in any danger. A consummate negotiator, he reached a deal for his detention: that he could bring his own clothing and books; that he could use his cell phone to contact home, though not anyone else; that in case something happened at home, he could come back. Shi needed the officials to meet those terms to have a sense of connection to his family and also to feel distinguished from other detainees, even though he lost his freedom of movement for the eighteen days.

During the eighteen days, a team of twelve people divided into two shifts guarded him and delivered his meals. He had to stay in the room without any contact with the outside world, except phone calls to his family. All he was allowed to do was watch television. Always resourceful, Shi made use of his time there to do two things: in his words, "to clear my own thoughts and to provide the government with some suggestions." He wrote about his views on policy issues, especially land use rights and petitioners' requests and settlements.

When he was released, he refused to be taken into the car provided by the public security bureau and sent home: "They must tell me once again why they put me there in the first place. I'm not a piece of wood that you can move around. I didn't do anything wrong. What they did to me is illegal. It's Cultural Revolution–type behavior. What if I deprived you of your freedom for eighteen days?" The truth is that Shi wanted to use his detention as leverage to compel the Putuo District to solve his sister-in-law's case, which the district was said to have promised to do. So Shi did not consider his detention to be a complete waste: "I'm willing to sacrifice myself if my sister-in-law's case gets resolved." As usual, he appreciated every bit of the special treatment: "They were polite to me. Most of [the] petitioners are put under house arrest in the countryside," Shi said.

Although many of the issues Shi has raised in petitions are critical of the CCP, Shi himself insists that his intention is not to oppose the government but to improve it. As always, Shi has a ready justification for his position. The government, he says, is not the enemy but developers are. According to Shi, residents cannot possibly fight against developers and win, and therefore they must enlist the government's help. The first step, Shi believes, is to stop the government from supporting developers so that each resident will have a fair chance to negotiate a settlement based on the law. That is why he has tried to lobby for policy change and especially for judicial independence.

Also, Shi points out that people can help the government to change its policy and push it in the right direction, much like what he has been doing, especially in the anti-Document 305 campaign.

But Shi Lin will not back down from his demand for compensation for his own home. On the contrary, he has set his mark even higher because of the rise of the market: "I'm happy to just wait for a while," he said. All that remains of the former slum in which Shi lives is Shi's house and that of his immediate neighbor—the rest of the area has all been built on. The small lots of the two houses cannot be of much use for any major development and thus their value is questionable. "What if the district decides to let you stay so that it doesn't have to meet your demands?" I asked. Shi is not worried about that. For one thing, he believes that shacks like his are an embarrassment that the government must get rid of, as it promised to do in the early 1990s. Shi needs to believe in that promise as leverage to make his bid. Besides, he trusts the value of his location to increase without limit. According to Shi, the 9,500,000 yuan he now asks for his home is only a negotiation price, not even the market price, "The real market price could be much higher. If I auction the house with the land, it could go for as much as 20,000,000 yuan. In time, it could go up even more." Shi emphasizes that "time + land = money." As far as he is concerned, his house is a magic money tree that grows on its own.

Waiting for Nirvana

Shi's story indicates among other things the toll that oppressive poverty took on the urban poor. Long after the CCP's takeover and its claim to have cleaned up squatters in Shanghai, squatter settlements continued to exist and even expand, as in the Zhaojiabang area. Various forms of squatting, such as Shi's appropriation of the space for a kitchen, were even more prevalent; it was simply life's imperative for the poor. As such, the squatter mentality of toughness, entitlement, and the value of human relationships that Shi personifies has continued to thrive. The socialist welfare system and the workers' union only reinforced that sense of entitlement. But that sense has been crushed by the advent of the market economy and the retreat of the state welfare system. Even though Shi is an astute student of the capitalist market, his discontent and frustration nevertheless reflect the yawning chasm between the socialist state and the market reform.

Clearly, Shi is not complaining about the reform per se. On the contrary, he embraces it enthusiastically. After all, it is the market economy that has potentially turned Shi's homemade shack into a multimillion yuan property and Shi into a very rich man, a dramatic upward mobility he could never have imagined under Mao. Accordingly, his sense of entitlement has also evolved—not just what a socialist state should offer to the people as it has promised, but also what market forces and the law dictate. Shi's "plus and minus" formula and his appeal for judicial independence reflect his understanding of economic justice in the capitalist market. He believes he is as entitled as those in power to capitalize on the reform and to realize that upward mobility; he demands nothing less.

While China's weak legal system has provided a niche for Shi to thrive as a barrack-room lawyer, in many ways that role is an extension of a family tradition, as evidenced both in his belief in good human relationships and by his efforts to take care of the less fortunate. Shi is fundamentally decent and his sympathy is with the disadvantaged. He believes that the vulnerability of the poor can be overcome to some extent by mutual help, and he is well aware of his own ability to secure justice. In the end, Shi, just like his childhood hero Xu Laosan, uses his skills in reasoning and hassling in the hope of settling matters for not only his own family, but also for others in a similar plight.

Shi also remembers his roots in other ways. He came from nothing, and therefore he has little to lose. When he is cornered, he often taps into this ancestral impulse to fight back, as in his threat to squat in Tiananmen Square. Shi wants to pass on this survival impulse to the next generation. During the struggle over his house, he has taken his daughter with him to negotiations with officials so that she could learn how to be strong and tenacious.

This survival instinct and official corruption in the housing conflict have also allowed Shi to unapologetically exploit the many loopholes in the law and game the system for his own gain. Despite his knowledge of government policies and his emphasis on following the law, some of his arguments and actions point in the other direction. His refusal, for instance, to acknowledge the difference between land use rights and land ownership rights is problematic to say the least. The fact that he continued to expand his house and even rents out part of it, years after his neighborhood was subject to the freeze policy, is a clear-cut case of the violation of government policy.

Shi understands very well what he is doing. But he also understands that the law in China is malleable. Those who are powerful or otherwise resourceful can twist it to suit their own needs. In negotiations, Shi sometimes just pushes through on his terms, regardless of the exact meaning of the relevant policies. Indeed, if for the government and developers the law is only optional and abuse of the law is the norm, then why should people like Shi, who happen to have the ability to twist the law, follow it either, especially when following it often means to simply roll over and play dead? As the proverb goes, "As you sow, so shall you reap." The Chinese government is getting exactly what it has planted, in its paradoxical teaching of both the importance of the law and the rewards for breaking it.

As far as Shi is concerned, his life is all set. Sitting on a pile of gold, he has already planned his post-relocation life—he is nothing if not foresighted. With the millions of yuan he counts on, he will first purchase three apartments: one each for himself and his wife, his daughter, and his mother. Then he will buy two middle-size vans to start a rental business. His research shows that with China's improved living standards, more and more families now rent a van not only for weddings, birthdays, and other special occasions, but also for tours and vacations. Shi hopes his daughter will manage the rental business.

Once his family's future financial well-being is secure, he will go on to pursue his other ambitions. He has already mapped out plans for the rest of his life. His experience highlights his ability to overcome life's challenges, to learn from and articulate complex issues, and to motivate and inspire others. He is convinced that these talents can be put to good use in other ways. Shi envisions himself becoming a motivational speaker to young people, especially to those from poor families. He is willing to travel around the country giving lectures: "By then I won't have anything to worry about; I'll devote myself to encouraging children to succeed in life." Shi looks forward to that day with pure joy: then he will indeed become "Teacher Shi," mentoring a new generation of the vulnerable.

Notes

1. Emily Honig, "Invisible Inequalities: The Status of Subei People in Contemporary Shanghai," China Quarterly 122 (June 1990): 273; also see Antonia Finnane, "The Origins of Prejudice: The Malintegration of Subei in Late Imperial China," Comparative Studies in Society and History 35.2 (1993): 211–38.

2. On the famine, see Jasper Becker, Hungry Ghosts: Mao's Secret Famine (New York: Henry Holt, 1998); Frank Dikötter, Mao's Great Famine: The History of China's Most Devastating Catastrophe, 1958–1962 (New York: Walker, 2010).

3. Lu, Beyond the Neon Lights, 118; also Hanchao Lu, "Creating Urban Outcasts: Shantytowns in Shanghai, 1920–1950," Journal of Urban History 21.5 (July 1995): 563–96.

4. These Chinese immigrants were victims of a dysfunctional state. In this sense, they differ from the people in Zomia of Southeast Asia, who deliberately tried to escape the state in pursuit of self-determination. See James C. Scott, The Art of Not Being Governed: An Anarchist History of Upland Southeast Asia (New Haven, CT: Yale University Press, 2009).

5. Lu, *Beyond the Neon Lights*, 125.

6. Lu, *Beyond the Neon Lights*, 126.

7. A headline in the newspaper *Shanghai shangbao* (Shanghai Business News) dated 11 September 2001 stated that "The map of Shanghai will not have slum dwellings."

8. *Licai zhoukan* (Money Weekly), 21 January 2002: 17.

9. One of Shi Lin's blog entries appeared at http://news.boxun/com/news/gb/yuanqing/2010/10/201010201832.shtml, accessed 20 November 2010.

10. See a discussion on policy entrepreneurs and their practice in China in Andrew C. Mertha, *China's Water Warriors: Citizen Action and Policy Change* (Ithaca, NY: Cornell University Press, 2008), 6–12.

11. http://www.jsmedia.tv/bbs/viewthread.php?tid=44901, accessed 20 August 2009. There are many essays and blogs criticizing Document 305 and demanding its termination; see a sample at http://www.chaiqian315.com/C1/A6/200710/454.html; http://wangcailiang.blshe.com/post/559/32478, accessed 20 August 2009.

12. Kevin J. O'Brien and Lianjiang Li, *Rightful Resistance in Rural China* (New York: Cambridge University Press, 2006), 5–6.

13. Charter 08 makes a number of recommendations to implement democracy. See its English translation at www.foreignpolicy.com/articles/2010/10/08/charter_08, accessed 26 December 2011.

CHAPTER FIVE

~

Mr. Lincoln's Lane

Jarndyce and Jarndyce drones on. This scarecrow of a suit has, in course
of time, become so complicated, that no man alive knows what it means.

—Charles Dickens, *Bleak House*

"Mr. Mayor of Springfield, how are you?" reads the opening of an urgent letter
dated July 20, 2003, from a Shanghai neighborhood to the mayor of Springfield, Illinois, the hometown of President Abraham Lincoln. It appealed for
the mayor and the people of Springfield to protect "Lincoln's spirit" as well
as Sino-US friendship, which, the letter emphasized, was uniquely embedded
in their neighborhood but was in imminent danger.

This neighborhood was named Linken fang (hereafter, Lincoln Lane),
in the Hongkou District, northeast of downtown Shanghai. It was said to
be the only place in this world city named after an American president. At
risk was not exactly "Lincoln's spirit" or Sino-US relations, but the lane
and the neighborhood that had been facing demolition since fall 2002. The
letter was part of a concerted campaign the residents launched to save their
neighborhood.

Built in the 1920s on a 5,650-square-meter lot by a young man who had
studied in the United States, reportedly an admirer of President Lincoln,
this group of twenty-five units of three-storied, red-brick row houses, each
equipped with modern amenities and a small garden, was by any measure
an ideal residential area. Tucked away from the traffic of a main circular,
with the historic Hongkou (now Lu Xun) Park established in 1896, a

new subway station, the Hongkou Football Stadium, a renowned antique market in Duolun Road around which China's giant literary and political figures once lived,[1] and numerous shops along the famous Sichuan Road, all within walking distance, it was also a prime piece of property that tempted developers.

In late 2002, the residents in Lincoln Lane learned that their neighborhood was to be demolished for a government-sponsored project, the Metro Line 8 subway (hereafter, M8 line). But the residents' own investigations soon revealed that instead of the M8 line, their neighborhood was to be replaced by two 28-story commercial buildings—they were simply being lied to by the district, and they started a campaign to protest against the district and to preserve their neighborhood.

Like the East Eight Lots, this was yet another case in which the district used a public project as a pretext to clear out the residents for a commercial development. Also like East Eight Lots, residents in Lincoln Lane collectively resisted domicide. But the resistance there had its own characteristics. Unlike the East Eight Lots, which was large and open to the downtown public, Lincoln Lane was small and secluded. This geographic and spatial difference meant that for the residents to put out red flags to attract public attention was futile. Instead, they aggressively reached out for support and waged a propaganda war against the district government on a battlefield that stretched from the walls surrounding the lane to China Central Television (CCTV), and even reached overseas, taking full advantage of the globalizing age.

Also, they defined a noble cause for their campaign. Instead of opposing demolition for their own sake, they framed their resistance in terms of historic preservation. They argued that, as "excellent historic architecture" and a rare piece of history of the city, their lane should be preserved. They extensively researched their lane and unearthed its past to validate their argument. Some renowned preservation experts in Shanghai initially supported the residents' effort but in the end contributed to its collapse. This case illustrates the economics and politics of historic preservation in an era driven by growth and profit.

The Pretext

Lincoln Lane, with the official address of Lane 264 Xijiangwan Road, was a gated neighborhood with semidetached, three-story, red brick row houses. The neighborhood was secluded—an 80-meter-long and 5-meter-wide pathway shielded it from the outside street. Each of the houses there had an arched entrance, a garden in the front and back, a fireplace, a chimney, and modern amenities. With its secluded, quiet location and decent quality of housing, the lane retained an aura of a middle class and cosmopolitan lifestyle that existed in Republican Shanghai. There was also a more pronounced gap among the residents in their economic and living conditions than that of neighborhoods with workers' apartments and the old-style alleyway houses because of the CCP's takeover in 1949 and its many social reform movements that broke down the initial ownership rights of the residents there.

Each of the units in the lane ranged from roughly 174 to 200 square meters in area. In 2002, about six of the approximately one hundred households there owned their three-story units. One such unit belonged to a Chinese American in Florida who let her relatives live there, another was co-owned by several siblings, one of whom was a Chinese Australian, and still another was an empty nest with only an old couple. But most of the units were rented from the Hongkou District Housing Bureau and shared by four to seven families each, which also meant that they shared kitchens and bathroom facilities. Nonetheless, even many of the tenants there were attracted to the lane's environment and were not eager to move out.

Among the residents were an art professor at a major university in Shanghai, a man with a Japanese mother and a Chinese father, lower-level CCP officials, retirees, workers, retailers, single mothers, the unemployed, and the elderly. The residents believed that the tranquil surroundings of the lane contributed to their longevity. On the eve of the demolition in 2002, seven people were in their nineties and sixty people were in their seventies. Some families had lived there for three generations, while a few others had purchased their flats only in the late 1990s after the opening of the housing market. The long-term residents and newcomers were nevertheless respectful of each other. With a touch of a civility and a polite culture, such a neighborhood was certainly not a source of rabble-rousers.

In October 2002, the Hongkou District government made plans for the construction of a subway station at the Hongkou Football Stadium as part of the M8 line. The Shanghai metro is one of the fastest expanding urban rail systems in the world. It started in 1995 and, by the end of 2007 had expanded to eight lines stretching for 227 kilometers, reaching the sprawling suburbs where millions of newly relocated residents depended on public transportation. The M8 line was a municipal initiative that provided a north-south line to connect the growing northeastern part of the city directly with downtown and also the Minhang District in the south.[2] The project had a clear mandate.

The Hongkou District's responsibility was to support the construction of the portion of the M8 line that went through the district and, in the process, to build a local system with the football stadium station as a hub to coordinate among various modes of transportation, reduce traffic congestion, and improve efficiency. This local system would include more and widened roads, parking lots, taxi stands, and separate lanes for buses, non-motor vehicles, and pedestrians, all to accommodate the ever increasing traffic in the area. All this required a lot of land. Since the stadium itself was not to be touched and since Lu Xun Park was located immediately east of the stadium, the project had to be located on the southwest side of the stadium. Lincoln Lane was on the south margin of the area.

In fall 2002, relevant Hongkou District and municipal agencies in charge of housing, land, urban planning, and development engaged in an intense exchange of documents. They involved the district's definition of the scope and function of the M8 project and its applications for permits to demolish the neighborhoods and relocate the residents in order to free up the land for construction. This exchange finally led to the approval by the municipal housing bureau, in its Document 141, of the M8 line project and of the demolition permit, which the Hongkou District Housing Bureau issued on January 3, 2003.

Both the district's applications and the municipal approval indicated that the project was centered on the M8 line and its accessory road expansion, with no mention of constructing any high-rise buildings, commercial or otherwise. The designated area covered more than five hectares with about two thousand households. Lincoln Lane, on the south end of the area, was not part of the land needed for the construction of the station itself but was included in the road expansion. But the lane was flanked by a high-rise building and another construction site for an already planned commercial project without through traffic, and thus was cut off from the area for the road projects. Of all the official documents regarding the M8 line, none explained why, or, more importantly, how, the lane could be part of the road expansion project for the M8 line. Regardless, Document 141 allowed two months starting from January 3, 2003, for the district to complete the demolition of the neighborhoods, including Lincoln Lane, and relocation of the residents, which by any means was a gross underestimate of the time it would take to accomplish what was to be a difficult process.

The Issue of Preservation

The residents of Lincoln Lane became aware of the possibility of demolition as early as 1994, and so had been on the lookout and contemplating their options. On the left side of the pathway that connected the lane with the outside street and separated by a wall was a rubber products plant. In 1994, the early stage of Shanghai's overall renewal and large-scale construction,

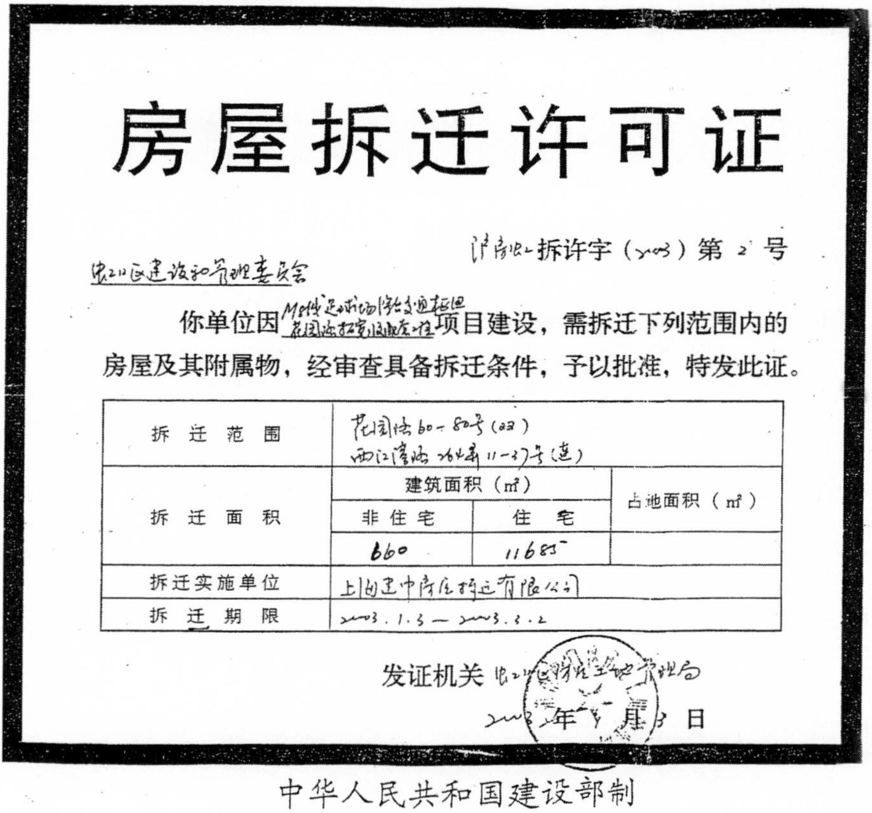

房屋拆迁许可证

拆许字（ ）第 号

你单位因 项目建设，需拆迁下列范围内的房屋及其附属物，经审查具备拆迁条件，予以批准，特发此证。

拆迁范围			
拆迁面积	建筑面积（m²）		占地面积（m²）
	非住宅	住宅	
	660	11685	
拆迁实施单位			
拆迁期限			

发证机关

年 月 日

中华人民共和国建设部制

Figure 5.1. This "Housing Demolition and Relocation Permit," issued by the Hongkou District Housing Bureau and dated January 3, 2003, listed Lane 264, Xijiangwan Road (Lincoln Lane) and another neighborhood as part of the M8 line road extension project and scheduled the demolition to be completed in two months.

the municipal government decided that all the factories within the inner city would gradually be relocated to the suburbs because of concerns for the environment and the high property values in the city. In time, the residents also heard rumors, which unfortunately turned out to be true, that if the rubber products plant was to go, Lincoln Lane would be lost as well. The reason was that it would be more attractive and profitable for a developer if the plant and the lane were combined into one property.

The rubber products plant was removed in October 2002. Soon after, a construction company came to clean up the property and, by early 2003 it started to construct what later turned out to be a 28-story commercial building. But the residents in Lincoln Lane were never told that their lane was also part of this package deal for another 28-story building—a twin-tower project. This they discovered on their own later. Instead, they were informed that their neighborhood was to be sacrificed for the M8 line. Unlike some other neighborhoods that were ambushed by a governmental decision for demolition without any forewarning, the residents in Lincoln Lane, facing uncertainty for years, had been discussing how to best protect their homes. Their strategy was to appeal to the relevant authorities by proving that Lincoln Lane was a historic neighborhood worthy of preservation.

The preservation of historically significant and excellent construction in Shanghai in the post-Mao era started in 1991, on the eve of the rapid development that was going to remap the city. That year, Mayor Huang Ju issued a directive on "Methods to Preserve and Manage Excellent Modern Construction in Shanghai." It stated that buildings constructed between 1840 and 1949 with the following four characteristics qualified as excellent modern structures: representative of Chinese urban architecture and by famous architects; uniquely artistic in architectural style; unique in architectural technique; and representative of traditional architectural styles and landmarks in Shanghai. The emphasis was on architecture itself. The document placed the responsibility for identifying, preserving, and managing such structures on three relevant government bureaus: the municipal housing bureau, the municipal planning bureau, and the municipal cultural relics management bureau. The document also stipulated that the functions of such structures were not to be casually changed, and any changes, either by the owners or users, had to be reported to and approved by the above-mentioned government agencies.[3] But the inevitability of the destruction of historic buildings became immediately evident as large-scale development started in 1992. Two years later, the municipal housing bureau was compelled to reissue the mayor's 1991 directive and reemphasize the importance of preservation because "damage to preserved buildings has caused broad attention and reaction."[4]

Preservation, however, was a low priority in an era obsessed with growth and profits. Historic buildings and projects continued to disappear in Shanghai at an alarming rate amid public outrage. In July 2002, the Standing Committee of the Shanghai Municipal People's Congress issued Document 70, titled "Regulations on the Protection of Historic, Cultural, and Scenic Districts and Excellent Historic Architecture in Shanghai," with the most detailed instructions to date on preservation. By "excellent historic architecture" the document meant any structure more than thirty years old with one or more of the following groups of characteristics: technologically, artistically, and scientifically unique and valuable; of an architectural style representative of the history and culture of the city and the city's industrial development; by famous architects; and/or with other historic and cultural significance.[5]

Most encouraging is that Document 70 included citizen participation in historic preservation. Namely, it allowed owners and users of such buildings to submit recommendations. Then the municipal housing and planning bureaus would research the building and, in consultation with the municipal cultural relics management bureau and local governments, they would make a proposal. The proposal would be reviewed by an expert committee, and a final decision would be made by the municipal government.

While most regulations in the document pertained to buildings that had already been preserved, Item 13 pointed out that for valuable structures that had not been listed for protection, the municipal housing and planning bureaus should identify and protect them first, and then follow the procedures to apply for preservation status. This item gave rise to citizen preservation in Shanghai and almost spared Lincoln Lane from demolition.

Finally, Document 70 specified the punishment to be meted out to those who violated the regulations, which ranged from fines, compensation to be paid for damaged buildings, restoration of protected properties should they be demolished, administrative disciplinary measures, and even criminal charges. Document 70 was to take effective on January 1, 2003.[6]

There were some unresolved issues with the document. First, its criteria for excellent historic architecture were vague and thus open to interpretation. Also, it did not define the scope of authority of any of the agencies nor their relationship with one another, which proved to be a problem in the case of Lincoln Lane.

Still, the residents in Lincoln Lane, who had been paying close attention to both municipal policies and local maneuvering, saw an opening in Document 70 for them to take initiative to protect the lane. But they were compelled to act quickly. In fall 2002, a month before the M8 line expansion project was even approved, the neighborhood committee had inquired whether one of the residents would rent out his unit as an office for the use of the district demolition office, an unmistakable sign that the lane was targeted for demolition. And then in October 2002 the relocation of the rubber products plant became the latest warning that the lane was in danger. The same month, the residents sent a letter with more than sixty signatures to both the Hongkou District and municipal governments, requesting the preservation of this eighty-year-old neighborhood, based on Document 70. They hoped that their case would be among the first citizen preservation projects to be considered under the new document as soon as it took effect in January 2003. This letter began a two-year long campaign that traversed many hills and valleys.

A Community Leader

The letter was drafted by Dai Lixiang, who was most responsible for coming up with the idea of preservation as a way of resisting the demolition. He emerged as a community leader in the struggle that followed. Dai Lixiang (1947–) came from a large family and grew up relatively privileged. Both his parents were from rural Zhejiang Province, without much education beyond primary school. But like many self-made men in Republican Shanghai, his father became a successful industrialist and businessman. He had a silk mill in Shanghai and an import and export company in Guangzhou. As did many other wealthy Chinese men of the time, he had more than one wife—in fact he had three, and a total of fifteen children. Dai's mother was the first wife and had seven children; Dai Lixiang was the second youngest. His mother helped his father establish his business and one of her brothers, Dai Lixiang's maternal uncle, had successful businesses in various parts of southeastern Asia.

In the 1940s Dai Lixiang's father purchased a unit in Lincoln Lane for his first wife and her children while he himself lived with the third wife and their children in downtown Shanghai. In the late 1940s the unit was used by a group of radical students and CCP members for underground activities, thanks to the intercession of Dai Lixiang's oldest brother, a student activist. During the Great Leap Forward and the famine in the late 1950s and early 1960s, the family was spared much suffering because Dai Lixiang's maternal uncle in Cambodia frequently sent them food and money. The uncle also had a residence in Hong Kong, and traveled between Cambodia, Hong Kong, and Guangzhou on business. His help allowed Dai to grow up comfortably and to feel special.

After senior high school in 1967, Dai Lixiang was initially assigned a job in a factory in Shanghai. During that radical phase of the Cultural Revolution, with most of the urban youth having no job prospects in the city, his was a dream job. But someone with better connections snatched his position by "back door" dealing, a common practice in China. Because of his father's capitalist background, which was a huge liability at the time, Dai could not fight to regain that position and, in 1970, left for a poverty-stricken county in northern Anhui Province where he joined countless other sent-down urban youth.

Articulate, persuasive, enthusiastic, and enterprising, Dai Lixiang was a natural leader and often distinguished himself from his peers. Like Shi Lin,

Dai as a student was also involved in propaganda—one of the most common and important political enterprises under Mao—in the student association, where he wrote, edited, and published a student wall newspaper. Also like Shi Lin, Dai later made good use of such skills in the housing protest, especially in the media campaign he and his neighbors launched.

In the countryside, Dai was lucky to obtain a teaching position at a village middle school instead of tilling the fields. But he did more than teach. Having inherited the family's entrepreneurial and innovative spirit, Dai started a factory at the school to produce educational equipment and sell it to other schools. His mother initially offered to send him five yuan per month, an enviable sum for many of the sent-down students whose parents made on average 30 yuan a month. But he declined it—in a year he had accumulated 300 yuan in savings, which he brought back to Shanghai to purchase material for his school. While other students ate poorly, Dai could afford the best. Once again, that he fared better than others reaffirmed his confidence that he could succeed under any circumstances.

Dai's once enviable teaching position and his entrepreneurship proved to be a disadvantage by the mid-1970s as the Cultural Revolution was winding down and colleges and factories gradually began to recruit from among the sent-down urban youth. Dai stood no chance as he was considered to already have a good job. Years later, in 1979, he finally returned to Shanghai when the sent-down policy was being systematically reversed under Deng Xiaoping. Because no jobs were readily awaiting the massive number of returned students, Dai did odd jobs in neighborhood enterprises, from working in a hardware factory to repairing televisions.

A turning point came in 1987 when he visited his uncle in Hong Kong for three months. At the time, the market reform had just started in China. In Hong Kong, Dai experienced a full-fledged capitalist economy and completely embraced it. He took the opportunity to work in Hong Kong as a handyman, fixing beds and other furniture in a hotel, making 10,000 Hong Kong dollars each month, the kind of money he could never have dreamed of making in mainland China despite all his hard work and entrepreneurship. According to the government's policy then, he was allowed to bring one "big item"—selected from a list of durable consumer goods—back to Shanghai. He chose a motorcycle, which proved to be one of his best and most useful investments—the motorcycle later became indispensable in the numerous trips he took to petition and network during the housing dispute. Upon his return to Shanghai, he started a factory back in his ancestral hometown in Zhejiang Province to produce toys based on the Taiwan-made toys he brought back from Hong Kong. Dai later closed the factory and engaged in retail businesses, with a flexible schedule which was again helpful during the housing dispute.

Like other privately owned units in Lincoln Lane, the Dais' house also suffered during the Cultural Revolution. Six families moved in and consigned the Dai family to the third floor. In 1982, when Dai Lixiang was getting married, the family contemplated exchanging the third floor with two rooms elsewhere so that the newlyweds could have their own place. But Dai, who never accepted the chaos of the Cultural Revolution as the norm or the occupation of their house as permanent, believed that order would be restored in China and their housing situation would improve, which became a reality in the late 1980s with the return of the entire unit to the Dai family.

Because of his complicated family relationships, the demolition of his unit could lead to a bitter dispute within the family and deprive him of his comfortable housing. At issue was the ownership of the unit. In theory, his father's fifteen children could all claim a share of the property. But his father gave this unit to his first wife, who also worked with her husband to build the family fortune. Before she passed away in 1987, she explicitly instructed her children to maintain the unit as the family home for her own seven children and indicated that the house was never to be sold or divided, a situation most beneficial to Dai. At the time, Dai's six siblings were all scattered in other parts of China and also overseas. They came to stay only when visiting Shanghai; otherwise Dai's family of three—his wife and a daughter—had the house all to themselves. When the demolition was announced, Dai, while making preservation plan A, nevertheless thought about plan B, which was to sell the unit in order to buy another house elsewhere as the family's home: his nuclear family would continue to live in that family home and his siblings would still have a place to return to when they visited. However, his half-siblings saw an opportunity in the demolition for them to lay claim to the unit. They preferred to divide the monetary compensation among all of them, which of course would severely disadvantage Dai, since his share of the proceeds would not be enough to purchase a comparable place.

Concerned about the thorny family dynamics and his father's advanced age, Dai initially did not tell his father about the pending demolition of Lincoln Lane. But the district officials realized that his family situation was a weakness to be exploited. They went directly to his father and informed him of the demolition, because if the father and his other children agreed on a settlement, Dai's resistance alone would be futile. That was when the other wife and her children raised the issue of their entitlement to the Lincoln Lane unit. His father, feeling helpless in dealing with the family conflict and the pressure from the district, began to spit blood and died within ten days of learning the news of demolition. Dai continued to resist the demolition, now with added resentment against the district authorities, whom he held responsible for his father's death. Finally, in summer 2004, his family was violently evicted without reaching a settlement, which in turn also denied his half-siblings any payment. The dispute between Dai and his half-siblings has since evolved into a lawsuit, while Dai has also been involved in petitioning and suing the district.

But back in 2002, the best option for Dai to hold on to his unit, avert an ugly family fight, and also help his neighbors was to argue for preservation. With abundant confidence and optimism, he believed it was possible to fight off the district and to keep the lane intact if the neighbors were united. It was this belief that led him, in October 2002, to write that initial letter and gather dozens of signatures from his neighbors.

Discovering a Usable Past

Three months later, in January 2003, the residents received a mostly inept reply from the municipal petition office: their letter was being passed on to the Hongkou District office, which would address their concerns. It never did. The district, determined to tear down Lincoln Lane, simply ignored the residents' appeal. By then, several things were happening simultaneously. First, Document 141—issued by the municipal housing bureau that approved the M8 project and the demolition permit for that project—was being implemented. The Hongkou District Housing Bureau was about to start demolition of Lincoln Lane in order to meet the March 2 deadline for completing the process. Also, Document 70 on preservation became effective, which encouraged the residents to continue their struggle. But with demolition about to take place, the residents were pressed for time. In addition, the residents learned, after some investigation and poking around, that their lane was not really going to be used for the M8 line road project, but rather for the construction of another 28-story commercial building. In fact, the residents located a blueprint of the area with the twin towers clearly marked, one of which was where the lane stood. This discovery confirmed their earlier suspicions and further outraged them, and also gave them hope in the fight against the district since they now had tangible evidence of its scheme.

The residents started their campaign on several fronts: researching the history of their lane; writing letters to relevant government agencies, especially the three municipal bureaus which played a key role in identifying preservation targets, and even to the mayor of Springfield; lobbying both the media and experts; resorting to legal channels; and networking for support.

They often used these activities to reinforce each other. For instance, they provided their research on the history of the lane to the media and, when media reported on it, they used that as evidence of public support for their cause. Or, when a newspaper covered their case, they used that to get other media outlets to report as well. Their research and media reports were also frequently cited in their lawsuits. All throughout 2003 and 2004 they waged this kind of constant, evolving battle against the district's attempt to demolish the lane.

Research proved to be key as they argued the value of their lane. What was the history of the lane? Did anything important or interesting happen there in the past? Were there any famous people among their former neighbors? Dai Lixiang took advantage of his flexible schedule and made countless trips on his motorcycle to various libraries, bookstores, and archives. If he found a promising clue that needed further research, he would share the task with his neighbors. They were all in it together. Residents with regular jobs went door to door in the evening, interviewing older neighbors and family members. Retirees and the unemployed helped make phone calls, sort out interview notes, cut newspaper clippings, and piece information together. They met almost daily in the evening at one or another of the neighbors' homes to exchange information and figure out the next step. These efforts were meant to dig out a usable past to strengthen their case. Gradually, they compiled an annotated chronicle of the lane with highlights of significant events and people.

According to the chronicle, Lincoln Lane was nothing ordinary indeed. Its survival was itself a miracle as its strange numbering system demonstrated—it started with unit number 11 instead of 1. On January 28, 1932, Japanese troops began to bomb Shanghai. The war caused tremendous loss of Chinese lives and destroyed numerous properties.[7] The first ten units of Lincoln Lane were among the casualties, but the rest of the lane was spared only because, perhaps inspired by its name, the foreign residents there put out an American flag on its roof. That was why the units numbered 1 to 10 were missing. In the following decade, the Japanese occupied some of the units in Lincoln Lane, as some Japanese settled in Hongkou. After Japan's defeat, those units fell into the hands of Nationalist officials, and the American Naval Rescue Headquarters was housed in four units, which were later transferred to the CCP. In the early 1950s, three units there housed a branch of the Central People's Bank.

Although Lincoln Lane, like Shanghai as a whole, was spared much damage in the Civil War of the late 1940s, it suffered new trauma under Mao. In the Great Leap Forward, the two big carved iron doors at the entrance of the lane became casualties of the mad rush into neighborhood backyard steelmaking. During the Cultural Revolution, the name Lincoln was seen as pro-Western and redolent of the capitalism that the revolution was intent on wiping out, so the Red Guards changed it to "Miezi Lane"—literally meaning "destroying capitalism." The original name was restored only after the Cultural Revolution ended. Clearly, the lane was not only a material witness to but also a survivor of modern China's tumultuous history.

The residents also detailed the lane's direct contribution to the CCP's own history, since, as we have noted, Dai Lixiang's home was used in the late 1940s by CCP activists and students for underground publishing and networking. Their activities were documented in a book about the CCP's history, the cover of which is graced with Jiang Zemin's calligraphy. Indeed, as Hanchao Lu has pointed out, the alleyway compounds in Shanghai were a fertile ground for the CCP's subversive activities because of the density of the residents, their assorted occupations, and their anonymity. As noted in chapter 3, in 1921 the CCP held its First National Congress in a residential neighborhood which is now known as Xintiandi, and its official publication, *Hong qi*, was once printed in an alleyway house.[8] Since the CCP had preserved and restored as relics some of those sites that played a part in its history, the residents hoped that Lincoln Lane would get the same treatment because of its tangible connection—limited though it was—with the history of the party.

According to the residents, their lane also had rich human interest. The residents presented some notable former and current neighbors. They included an American doctor known for reattaching severed limbs; a ninety-two-year-old man who was once the secretary of Wang Daohan, former mayor of Shanghai; a teacher of Zhu Rongji, former premier of China; and the ancestral house of Tang Yingnian, a high-ranking official of Hong Kong. Among the current residents, as mentioned above, were a famed young artist and university professor and a former soldier at the People's Liberation Army. In addition, since the late 1980s some Japanese who had spent their childhoods in Lincoln Lane had returned to visit and photograph themselves together with the residents.

Of these materials, some are confirmed by independent sources and others are based on single accounts. The Japanese bombing of the lane, for instance, was verified by both oral and written history. The suffering of the lane during the Cultural Revolution was a lived experience for most of the residents. But other information, such as whether big shots like Tang Yingnian were once connected to the lane, was less clear. The vaguest was the name of the lane, as much of the information was transmitted only orally. Did the name "Linken" in Chinese mean the American president Lincoln, whose name also happened to be translated into the same Chinese characters, Linken? Did it reflect the architect's admiration of Lincoln? The residents' research did not yield specific answers to these questions. In the end, they settled on what made sense to them—that the name of their lane was a reference to the American president. Indeed, the name became their most important capital as it allowed them to claim the uniqueness of the lane. This claim was contested later.

Based on these materials—which the residents, working like researchers, historians, anthropologists, archivists, and writers, documented as meticulously as possible by including dates, names, eyewitnesses, addresses, phone numbers, articles, and books, often in appendixes—they made their case for preservation. They argued that the lane should be preserved as a valuable witness to the city's past and also celebrated for its survival through enemy attacks and other turmoil. "Could anything be more destructive than the 1932 Japanese bombing?" they asked. What they implied was that this icon of survival should not be lost in peacetime at the hands of China's own government. They also suggested that, in terms of its connection to the CCP, the lane should be kept as an educational site for future generations to learn about the CCP's history—typical CCP rhetoric. Furthermore, they argued that the lane, imbued with so much human interest in and outside China, should be protected for Chinese and foreigners who want to search for their past. "Standing in front of it, one can feel the history of Shanghai come alive. . . . Once this piece of history is destroyed, it can never be restored, and we will be left to regret it for thousands of years to come," they wrote in their recommendation for preservation of the lane. Of course, they also referred to the relevant items in Document 70 and insisted on three most obvious points: the lane's eighty-year history; its well-preserved condition; and its unique name, mysteriously linked to an American president. All of them, they argued, made the lane a unique candidate for preservation.

Letter Writing

The residents made those arguments in many of the letters they sent out. On January 10, 2003, soon after the residents learned about the impending demolition, an "Urgent Appeal" signed by an "old CCP member who engaged in underground party activities day and night in Lincoln Lane prior to Shanghai's liberation," namely Dai Lixiang's oldest brother, was sent to Mayor Han Zheng. Befitting the author's status, the letter emphasized that the survival of Lincoln Lane through the late 1940s Civil War reflected the wise decision of the People's Liberation Army to preserve Shanghai in its entirety. To destroy the lane would be to mock the revolutionary martyrs who died liberating Shanghai. Dai Lixiang's younger brother, on the other hand, was sending letters from Australia to various government agencies, including the State Council. In the meantime, many letters signed simply as "Lincoln Lane residents," individually and collectively, were sent to the mayor's office, the three municipal bureaus, and also across the Pacific to America.

Though many of the letters to the Chinese authorities were similar, the letter to America was different. It was specifically designed to appeal to an American audience. The letter, dated July 20, 2003, and addressed to the mayor of Springfield, Illinois, begins by introducing its authors as the residents of a lane named after the sixteenth American president: "We very much understand you are the hometown of Abraham Lincoln and we are proud of you." To show how knowledgeable they were about the American president, the letter listed his major political achievements, including the Emancipation Proclamation. It stated that "it was out of Chinese people's admiration of Lincoln" that their neighborhood was named after him in the 1920s. Clearly, the residents turned the vague meaning of the lane's name into an advantage—they imagined the missing historical links and ran with them: "It shows the Chinese people's support of justice in the world and the long and deep friendship between the Chinese and American peoples." The lane, the letter emphasizes, is thus a "monument that commemorates a world-renowned hero." In other words, to preserve the lane was to preserve this monument and, in that sense, the residents were not only protecting their own homes but also doing Lincoln's hometown a favor. The letter thus tried to invent and impose a shared interest between the lane and Springfield.

The letter then turns to the reality that "some profit-driven developers now want to demolish Lincoln Lane and build a 28-story cement building. We the residents have firmly resisted the attempt to destroy this historical witness of the lasting friendship between our two peoples." In the shadow of a not-so-distant past when simply writing overseas, much less telling about the wrongdoing in China, could be treasonous, the residents took pains to make sure their letter was politically correct in the eyes of the Chinese authorities. It carefully emphasizes that the Shanghai government was keen on historic preservation and that at fault were the greedy developers. "To protect this precious history of Sino-US friendship, we very much need help from Lincoln's hometown friends. We propose that Shanghai and Springfield become sister cities." The residents had heard about a Lincoln foundation in America. Mindful of the possible financial help a foundation might provide to preserve and renovate the lane, the letter states:

> We wish to convey through you to the friends at the Lincoln Foundation that we are struggling resolutely to prevent Lincoln Lane from disappearing from the map of Shanghai. We hope someday the history of Shanghai Lincoln Lane will be included in the Lincoln Library and the Lincoln Museum in America. The lane will forever prove Shanghai people's sincere support of the Lincoln spirit in promoting social progress.

The letter suggests that Shanghai as an international city should have a statue of Lincoln to advance Sino-US friendship. Finally, it returns to the urgent message that "We are pleading that Lincoln Lane be preserved as a great historical footprint!"

The letter, from perhaps a partially invented past to a promised friendship, never clearly stated what exactly was expected of its recipient. But any specific request was not necessary since what the residents looked for, above all else at this point, was some response, any response, from Springfield to serve as a tangible connection so as to validate their rather elusive claim. Such a validation would then strengthen their case. The main purpose of the letter, of course, was to call attention to their situation and to put pressure on the district, and they believed that pressure from overseas was more consequential than that from within China. Unfortunately for them, although they tried to send the letter through multiple channels, no reply ever came.

A Propaganda War

The same strategy to raise the profile of their case also led the residents to aggressively reach out to the media. They not only wrote and made phone calls to the various news outlets in Shanghai, but also visited them in person to present their case. Preservation, while not as important an issue as development, was nevertheless a legitimate, morally superior, and popular topic for the media to cover, but only to a degree. Preservation is ultimately at odds with development. Still, there have been a number of Shanghai reporters who are genuinely interested in history and have been reporting sympathetically on endangered historic buildings. The residents, who had been following the media, identified those reporters as allies and approached them. In time, some of the reporters became their supporters, but were intimidated by the officials, and at least one of them lost her job over her reporting.

In late July 2003, when it seemed that the district demolition office might provoke violence in the lane, the residents immediately called the Shanghai Oriental Television station, which came to cover their case. In the ensuing months, some newspapers began reporting on the Lincoln Lane case.[9] *Shanghai Daily*, an English-language newspaper, also printed an article titled "'Unique' Houses in Jeopardy,"[10] which was followed by an essay in an architecture magazine about the lane.[11] By then, the residents had succeeded in convincing the media that their lane was indeed named after the American president Lincoln as the latter began to report as such.

The earliest report on Lincoln Lane, however, appeared in an Australian Chinese newspaper, *Moerben ribao* (The Chinese Melbourne Daily), on July 3, 2003, the eve of America's Independence Day.[12] The author, on the surface an innocent tourist and observer, gave the essay a deceptively plain but eye-catching title, "Shanghai Has a Lincoln Lane." It described how impressed he was on his recent visit to Shanghai by the history and architecture of Lincoln Lane. Then he asked a pointed question: "Is this significant and valuable old Lane among those historic buildings being protected in Shanghai?" Not to be too subtle about his own position, he pointed out that since the lane had survived nearly a century of war and chaos, "It will certainly again show its graceful bearing in the forward-looking Shanghai." This was a direct message to pressure Shanghai's officials with the weight of history. This report, it turned out, was initiated in the lane. A female neighbor had a brother working in the Melbourne media and, after some discussion, the residents decided to take this opportunity to publicize their case overseas. Later, the demolition office learned about the story and harassed the woman, forcing her family out earlier than most of her neighbors.

The residents also took advantage of the age of multimedia. In spring 2004, for months the battle of Lincoln Lane was also waged in cyberspace. As one of the residents put out a series of "SOS" messages and appealed to the cyber crowd to "rescue the old houses," a blogger argued that the lane was just another ordinary alleyway and not worth preservation. Immediately, the resident listed the gardens and fireplaces and also the media reports to argue to the contrary and then asked: "Are you from the demolition squad? Ha ha! Even if you are, you can't deny the facts." The resident then put out the address of the lane and invited the blogger to visit before making a judgment.[13] This case was discussed among the residents who were convinced that the blogger was a stooge of the demolition office assigned to discredit their campaign. In early 2004, as soon as the demolition squad began to tear down the lane, a resident put photos and articles online to document the destruction and the resistance.[14] Another person, who had apparently spent her childhood in the lane, started a photo diary to record the lane from its pre-demolition days to its final ruin and also her own memory of neighborhood life there, a subject to which we will return.[15]

The wall surrounding the lane was another arena where the propaganda war was waged. If the media and online outlets were mainly to rally public support and pressure the municipal agencies, the wall space was local, targeting the district demolition office. The residents claimed a space for displaying their propaganda on an enclosing wall at the end of the 80-meter-long walkway and the beginning of the units. They posted dozens of copies there of the article "Shanghai Has a Lincoln Lane" from *Moerben ribao*. In March 2004 when the two annual meetings of the People's Congress were taking place in Beijing, which raised the issue of protecting private property, the residents immediately posted newspaper pages that reported on the topic. They also wrote a long headline on the wall that demanded, "[Those behind] the illegal construction of the 28-story building must respond to society," and placed underneath many newspaper clippings and documents that condemned illegal and violent demolition. In many ways, such use of the wall space is not that different from the wall newspaper propaganda Dai Lixiang engaged in as a student. The residents essentially used what they learned under Mao in this new round of propaganda warfare against the authorities.

One thing stood out among the material the residents posted on their doors and the wall: an open letter addressed to "the demolishers." In the demolition process, the norm was for officials and developers to inform the residents in the form of an open letter, not the other way around. But in this letter, the residents argued that in order to prove that the district and the developers were acting legally regarding the Lincoln Lane case, the government needed to produce eleven documents, including bank statements showing the relocation fees, permits for land use rights and for construction, construction plans, and special municipal approval for demolishing new-style alleyway houses. This list of documents demonstrated the residents' knowledge of government regulations as some of them had studied them in depth. It also challenged the district to prove that the demolition of the lane was indeed for the purpose of constructing the M8 line road project, which the residents knew was impossible since the only existing construction plan for the area, concealed from the public, was for the twin towers. Furthermore, the open letter reaffirmed the status of the lane as a type of new-style alleyway housing, which required special procedures if it was to be demolished. The letter concluded by stating, "If you provide all the documents listed above, we will actively cooperate with your legal demolition and relocation work; otherwise we refuse to deal with you." The letter itself was clearly an embarrassment to the district, because it could not produce all of these documents. But more importantly, in posting the letter, the residents assumed the position of an equal partner with the government—by asserting that they had the right to demand all of these documents or otherwise to ignore the district's order if it failed to produce them.

Figure 5.2. The residents used the wall space in Lincoln Lane to campaign for their cause. This headline reads, "[Those behind] the illegal construction of the 28-story building must respond to society." Underneath are newspaper clippings condemning violent demolition and supporting their case. March 16, 2004.

The most deliberate and attention-grabbing sign the residents put out was a custom-made plaque that cost 180 yuan, paid for by contributions, placed at the lane's entrance right below its address plate. It was titled "A Brief Introduction of Lincoln Lane." This special plaque, eight times larger than the regular address plate, with President Lincoln's well-known profile in the background, states the key information about the lane that the residents wanted to convey: that the lane was built in the 1920s; that it is the only place in Shanghai named after an American president; that CCP underground activities took place there, with a connection to Jiang Zemin; and that its name was changed during the Cultural Revolution and restored thereafter, which, the residents claimed, "sufficiently demonstrated the Shanghai people's admiration of this world-class politician."

This plaque, placed outside the lane, served several purposes. By presenting to the public as a fact the significance of the lane, the residents hoped to legitimize their claim that it qualified for preservation. Usually, the municipal government would issue a plaque as a certificate to structures officially identified as "excellent historic buildings" for preservation. But now the residents took the initiative in putting up this plaque to challenge the authorities over the status of the lane.

Perhaps more importantly, the plaque was a way to extend their propaganda war from within the lane to the outside—to overcome their geographic

264弄 8-37号
西江湾路

林肯坊简介

林肯坊始建于上世纪二十年代初，是上海唯一一处以美国总统林肯冠名的近代优秀建筑。由二十五幢联体别墅组成，环境优美，人文气息浓郁。

在迎接上海解放的日子里，这里活动着一支优秀的中共地下党组织，江泽民同志题字《火红的青春》一书中出现了其中的部分人物。

在文革中曾易名，但很快又恢复原名。这充分体现了上海人民海纳百川敬仰世界公认的杰出政治家—亚伯拉罕·林肯。

Figure 5.3. The residents placed this custom-made plaque at the entrance of Lincoln Lane to rally public support for the preservation of their lane. The plaque is titled "A Brief Introduction of Lincoln Lane." With President Lincoln's well-known profile in the background, it states the key information about the historic significance of the lane. March 16, 2004.

isolation and to alert the public. The seclusion from the outside streets guaranteed by the long pathway had once provided the residents with a sense of tranquility and community, but since early 2003, the demolition squad had taken this spatial isolation as a natural cover for its abuse and harassment of the residents; it tried to intimidate this small neighborhood while counting on the absence of public scrutiny.

In July 2003, on two separate occasions without any warning, the demolition office overwhelmed the lane with an army of nearly three hundred—policemen, demolition workers, neighborhood committee members, and developers and construction workers—to seal the entrance of the lane, its only outlet, and force the residents to use a temporary, narrow exit leading to the construction site of the M8 project. The new outlet and the construction site were full of debris and equipment and thus hazardous, especially for the elderly and children. The residents rose to protest. On one such occasion, as the demolition squad began to build a wall to block the regular entrance, the residents, including a seventy-year-old woman, threw themselves on the ground to defend it. Held by four policemen, the woman cried out for help. A young mother, trying to free the seventy-year-old, ended up being grabbed by her hair and dragged on the ground, losing her toenails and hair. Her husband and other neighbors jumped into the fight and the violence escalated. In the end, several residents sustained injuries and were detained by the police for hours. They were released only after their repeated pleas for medical attention. The authorities were forced to reopen the entrance after the residents contacted Shanghai Oriental Television, which came to report the incident and appealed for consideration of the residents' needs.

The officials' blocking the only outlet of the lane and attacking an old woman would not likely have taken place in the daylight in a neighborhood like the East Eight Lots that was open to public view. Also, while residents in the East Eight Lots could take pictures and videotape the conflict in front of the demolition squad, those in Lincoln Lane could not. In this fight over the lane's entrance and instances of domicide, officials had smashed residents' cameras and forbidden them from recording such contentious scenes. The residents still tried to use cameras, but only surreptitiously. In a way, the custom-made plaque at the lane's entrance was to inform the public about the confrontation within. It invited passersby to stop, check out, and support this neighborhood.

The propaganda campaign around the lane was like a guerrilla war. Whatever the residents posted on the walls the demolition squad often tore down and destroyed over night; the next morning the battle resumed, with the residents putting up more material. The space underneath the long banner on the enclosing wall was often empty, with only dark marks of paste as evidence that something had been posted there and removed. The demolition office also persistently pressured the residents, especially Dai Lixiang, to take down the plaque. The government's argument was that only officials could place such a sign on the entrance. What happened between the residents and the district over this plaque is a typical case where public space becomes an arena contested by competing forces. In late spring 2004, not long before Dai was threatened with eviction, he gave in to the pressure and took down the plaque, a step some of his neighbors considered to be a sign of weakness.

The Involvement of Experts

By closely following the media, the residents finally came in contact with a group of experts on urban planning and preservation at Shanghai's Tongji University, known for its architecture program. On September 1, 2003,

Xinmin wanbao (Xinmin Evening News), a popular newspaper in Shanghai, in a page-long article titled "The Guardians of the City's Cultural Pulse," featured four preservation experts who represented different generations. They included Ruan Yisan, a senior professor and renowned preservationist at Tongji University, whom we will return to later, and Wu Jiang, a middle-aged Tongji professor who had recently been promoted to the position of deputy director of the municipal planning bureau, a key position in preservation. The youngest of the experts was Lin Weihang, a doctoral student at Tongji, who, supported by some of the faculty and working with a group of Tongji students, launched a Historic Preservation Hotline as part of an effort to inventory valuable buildings by mobilizing Shanghai residents for recommendations. Lin and his group had spent the preceding summer and weekends investigating and researching Shanghai's neighborhoods. They interviewed residents, photographed buildings, and archived their findings.

A more specific purpose for their activities was to identify possible buildings for the fourth batch of preservation projects that the municipal government was undertaking. Since 1989 the municipal government had launched three such projects, which had identified a total of 398 buildings and structures for protection.[16] The Tongji student group led by Lin Weihang was helping the relevant agencies with the task of selecting candidates for the fourth batch of preservation projects by thoroughly inventorying old buildings. The phone number of their Historic Preservation Hotline, printed at the end of the *Xinmin wanbao* article, was meant to tap into the pool of the city's most enthusiastic preservationists—the residents—whose participation was legitimated by Document 70.

Indeed, for many residents and communities, getting their properties recognized as "excellent historic buildings" was the best and often only way to preserve them. At the time, many residents anxiously hoped their buildings would be included in the fourth batch of preservation projects. Not surprisingly, on the same day when the *Xinmin wanbao* article was published, the hotline rang nonstop, overwhelming the Tongji team. Residents in Lincoln Lane were among those who called. A month later, in October, Lin Weihang and some of the faculty, including Ruan Yisan, held a meeting at Tongji University with the residents who responded to the hotline to discuss issues concerning preservation, a meeting to which Lincoln Lane also sent representatives. The residents registered their respective properties and left their contact information, which later was compiled together with the meeting minutes. This meeting helped build a community of citizen preservationists and also put the citizens in touch with professionals.

All of this provided much hope for the residents. Through the hotline, Lin Weihang became directly involved in the Lincoln Lane case, which also brought about more media attention. Upon his on-site investigation, Lin concluded that the lane belonged to the new-style alleyway type, and that it was very well preserved, rare in Shanghai, and thus worth protection. He photographed the lane for record keeping and spoke to the media about its significance: "Lincoln Lane is an extraordinary heritage construction, like a living fossil among the city's old lanes. . . . The lane's building materials and layout are of great research value for today's architecture."[17] A group of students majoring in communications at Fudan University in Shanghai also came to conduct interviews and to film the site. In the meantime, in May, the municipal government issued another document, numbered 162, that further tightened up its preservation policy. It stipulated that the demolition of new-style alleyway apartments and houses—houses, such as those in Lincoln Lane, with modern amenities—in principle was not allowed unless it was for municipal, public projects and, should that be the case, the relevant agencies must report to the municipal housing bureau with sufficient justification which would then be subject to special review and approval.[18] All of this renewed the residents' hope and prompted them into another wave of intense letter writing, petitions, and negotiations with the municipal and district governments.

More good news seemed to be on the way. On November 5, 2003, a reporter from *Qingnian bao* who had been following the Lincoln Lane case published a full-page article, "Delaying the Demolition of Lincoln Lane: Eighty-year-old American-Style Residential Housing Will Apply for Excellent Historic Building Status." The title, as hopeful as it was, was actually a twist on reality. What happened was that the demolition of Lincoln Lane, which was supposed to be completed by March, did not go as officials had planned. In fact, throughout 2003, only about a dozen families moved out, some due to retirement. This was followed by the Severe Acute Respiratory Syndrome (SARS) outbreak, which slowed down the process.[19] With the expiration of the March deadline and SARS in the summer, the district renewed the demolition permit and extended it to January 2004, which was meant to continue the demolition, not to change the course. But the reporter and her editor, eager to help preserve Lincoln Lane, decided to put a spin on the situation by implying the reason for delaying the demolition as being prompted by the district's decision to consider the residents' application for preservation. This was not meant to give empty hope to the residents but to publicly pressure the officials to protect Lincoln Lane. The residents and their supporters, seizing the opportunity presented with this report, intensified their lobbying.

A Ghost Document

As it turned out, the *Qingnian bao* report partially and unknowingly foretold what was to come in the Lincoln Lane case. Both the best and the worst days lay ahead for the residents and their supporters. The residents' persistent campaign was not in vain. Their case had gained the support of both the media and experts, who had a certain influence on government decisions. In December 2003, the municipal planning bureau called a meeting to compile a provisional list of candidates for the fourth batch of preservation projects. The case of Lincoln Lane came up. The consensus at the meeting was to include the lane on the list. Both the municipal planning bureau and the municipal housing bureau then rendered their decision in February 2004, in Document 107. It stated that a preliminary investigation confirmed Lincoln Lane's qualification and the two bureaus had recommended it to be among the fourth batch of preservation projects, pending final municipal approval. Document 107 also indicated that according to relevant regulations, which in fact was Item 13 of Document 70 as discussed earlier, once the building was recommended for preservation, the local government, Hongkou District in this case, should take steps to protect it as the procedure to finalize its status was taking place.

This document was exactly what the residents had been fighting for. Ironically, though, they were kept in the dark about it. Document 107 was directly issued to the Hongkou District government, supposedly to halt the demolition and protect the lane. The district, however, not only ignored the document but, contrary to what the document required, began to intensify its destruction of the lane. It sent the demolition squad to tear down some of the vacant units that initially had only suffered minor damage. Its purpose was to damage the lane beyond repair so as to render Document 107 meaningless: one could not possibly argue to preserve something that was already lost. The residents, without knowing what was going on behind their backs, least of all Document 107, were bewildered by the sudden intensity of this "terrorist" destruction, which, in their words, plunged the lane into an "urgent life-or-death situation." Desperate to rescue the lane, they started another round of letter-writing, but this time following a new approach: they agreed to move out but pleaded that the lane nevertheless be protected. "Residents can relocate, Lincoln Lane can't be demolished!" was the title of one of the letters they sent out in February, in which they promised to give up their "small homes for the big home [the city]," which was an official propaganda slogan for urban renewal. But the residents provided a new meaning—the "big home" was not just what the authorities defined as the city's immediate need for development but also what the residents understood as something more profound and long term, which was the city's history and heritage. They agreed to move elsewhere "under reasonable conditions." "Please protect for future generations this irreplaceable history! Please stop the demolition and destruction!" they pleaded. To appeal to the district's thirst for profit, they suggested that once they moved out, the district could turn the lane into a tourist destination, unique because of its "American style of row houses." Considering the other tourist attractions such as the Hongkou Stadium, Lu Xun Park, and the popular antique market on Duolun Road, all in the vicinity, such a commercial development project could be feasible.

But the residents were also clearly frustrated and angry. In another letter, sent in March 2004 to the chairman of the Standing Committee of the Municipal People's Congress and titled "Historic Buildings Suffer Terror and Destruction," the residents enclosed pictures of the damaged units and wrote,

> Such beautiful houses were torn down! We people are heartbroken! We have worked for more than a year to try to protect them. But now some of the units have been completely destroyed . . . We have petitioned numerous times. But every time our petition letters were forwarded to the district officials who caused our misery and whom we petitioned against. As a result, nothing was resolved and those officials have intimidated us and forced some of our neighbors to leave.

Although they got no response from the chairman, a reporter from *Xinmin wanbao* investigated the case and contacted the municipal planning bureau, only to learn about Document 107 and the preservation status of the lane. In fact, the reporter was told not to believe the residents who, according to the bureau officials, must be mistaken—the officials assumed that the Hongkou District had acted on Document 107 and protected the lane. Confused, the reporter came to Lincoln Lane and witnessed the destruction himself. By then, though, the issue of whether to preserve the lane had become a controversy between the officials at the municipal planning bureau and those at the Hongkou District. But, to preserve a façade of strength and unity, an authoritative government will conceal its internal conflicts as much as possible. The reporter was only able to publish the story in an internal government reference journal to which the public had no access.

Part of the problem, as indicated earlier, is China's decentralized decision-making structure and the involvement of multiple agencies without clear lines of authority. While the two municipal bureaus in charge of housing and planning are responsible for identifying preservation objects in all the districts, each district government nevertheless has jurisdiction over the use of land under its control. Even if in theory the municipal government has the final say in granting preservation status, in practice such decisions are made through negotiations between municipal agencies and the district governments; the two parties often have conflicting interests. In any case, the former is powerless if the latter resists its decisions. This is what happened to Lincoln Lane—the Hongkou District government, which had already committed to the 28-story commercial building, simply rejected the two bureaus' decision to preserve the lane.

While the municipal and district governments tried to resolve their conflict, the residents, through their connections and some helpful hints from reporters, sensed that their lane was designated for protection but were still kept in dark about the existence of Document 107. Their repeated requests for both the district government and the municipal planning bureau to issue a ruling on their preservation application were met with silence. In fact, to cover the internal conflict and figure out the next step, each of the offices tried to shift the responsibility and pass the buck to the other and in the process to stall off the residents.

Frustrated with the lack of information and fearing the loss of the lane, the residents turned a largely defensive strategy—appealing for preservation—into an offensive one. First, they wrote a letter demanding an investigation: "The demolition here was for a for-profit commercial construction project under the pretext of a municipal project. It severely violated the law and regulations. We demand an investigation of the case." They also expressed their anger: "We can no longer tolerate this anymore after being under intense pressure for more than a year!" They castigated the officials for their failure to follow and implement the preservation regulations: "Why couldn't the municipal planning bureau stop the demolition in Lincoln Lane? Where is the authority of government regulations? What is the point of all the talk about preservation?" In another letter, the residents simply stated that they would never accept illegal demolition. In fact, the district's concealment of Document 107 was itself a violation of government policy, because since May 1, 2004, the municipal government had started an "open information" campaign and promised broader public access to official documents and greater government transparency.

The Peak and the Valley

The residents' boldest and most expensive action in this offensive strategy, however, was taken in secret—they hired a middle-aged, big-name lawyer, Wang Cailiang, in Beijing for help. Wang Cailiang is one of the many miracles brought by China's rapid economic development. He is a self-made lawyer that only the early post-Mao reform could have produced. In 1988, Wang, then thirty-four years old, was a low-level manager at an insignificant state-owned enterprise in his hometown, Jingdezhen, in Jiangxi Province, the historically renowned capital of China's porcelain industry. But the reform had already generated sufficient conflict that there was a demand for experts in the law, namely lawyers, a profession that did not exist in Mao's China. The CCP heads at Wang's enterprise thus appointed some of its cadres to provide legal advice, and Wang was among them. He found himself right at home with the job. In 1989, Wang formally transferred to a state-controlled law firm and quickly became its lead lawyer.[20] Six years later, in 1995, when private law firms were emerging in China, Wang established his own law office, specializing in civil law, contracts, construction, property transactions, and housing disputes, booming areas in the growth-driven economy that were also full of confusion and conflict. He and his firm won some high-profile cases in Jiangxi that were covered by the national media, which put Wang in the national spotlight.[21]

A key moment came in 2004 when Wang Cailiang moved his law firm to Beijing. It quickly became known as one of the best firms dealing with rural land seizures and urban demolition. By then Wang was a rising star in the still nascent Chinese legal profession. He was involved in several projects in the establishment and interpretation of laws related to his field and also served in the National Lawyers Association.[22] Unlike most lawyers, Wang Cailiang is also a prolific writer, authoring dozens of articles and several books. Two of the books specifically on urban housing reform and construction are highly critical of violent demolition. On the cover of one of them are two statements in alarming red: "Stop illegal and brutal demolition and relocation; truly protect the legal rights and interests of evictees."[23] It was these books that made his name known among the residents who were most eager readers of such publications.

By the time the residents in Lincoln Lane contacted him in 2004, Wang had become a nationally recognized legal authority and appeared on television as a legal commentator for an investigative CCTV program *Oriental Horizon (Dongfang shikong)*, which aspired to be the *60 Minutes* of China.

Oriental Horizon often exposes corruption and thus was very popular among its viewers.[24] Wang projected other attractions as well. The fact that he can get away with sharply criticizing the government while maintaining a thriving legal career in the nation's capital has led many people to speculate on his likely connection to top-ranking party officials. All this has made him highly sought after by those who are fortunate enough to persuade him to represent them—and who can also afford his steep fees.

In late May 2004, some of the Lincoln Lane residents saw Wang on *Oriental Horizon* in a program on a high-profile case of violent demolition in Hunan Province. That case eventually compelled a central government investigation and led to front-page coverage in *Renmin ribao* on June 5—it was that page that Mr. C at East Eight Lots showed on the day of his eviction. The television screen also flashed a phone number of the program's legal office. The residents immediately made the call and asked to be put in touch with Wang Cailiang. Soon after, they arranged to meet Wang in Shanghai on one of his book tours to the south. The residents brought all the material they had collected to present their case. Wang, experienced with such cases, quickly pointed out that the local government was at fault and that they indeed had a case. But he charged 60,000 yuan for representing them.

The residents then held a meeting to discuss the matter. The key was whether to hire Wang and how to pay him. They were running out of options with the loss of more neighbors and the imminent total destruction of their lane. Since early 2004 the district demolition office had gradually become ruthless. It first targeted the weakest links among the residents, such as a single mother and the elderly, with dire consequences. Once it summoned an eighty-year-old man to a meeting and threatened to evict him. The man suffered a heart attack and died shortly after. Many of the grief-stricken neighbors who attended his funeral were convinced that the demolition office was directly responsible for his death. The early belief that the tranquil atmosphere of their lane had contributed to longevity was shattered. The Lu family, an elderly couple, was harassed by the demolition office, which tried to deliver letters and "negotiate" with them by constantly phoning them and knocking on the door during meal times. The Lus became prisoners in their own home—they kept the house dark at night and asked family and friends not to call at certain hours so that they could screen the calls from the demolition office and ignore them. But Mr. Lu had high blood pressure and heart disease, which had worsened because of the stress. After the heart attack of the eighty-year-old neighbor, Mrs. Lu called a family meeting and decided to give in and move out, because "our lives are more valuable than our home."

It was through such harassment and intimidation that the district succeeded in reducing the numbers of the residents in the lane. It also started issuing administrative compulsory rulings and eviction notices to more and more families. In fact, the demolition office was able to relocate eight families in one week in May and, in late May around the time the residents were contacting lawyer Wang Cailiang, Mr. W, who was a volunteer handyman in his spare time and thus a popular figure among the neighbors, was evicted. He and his family, refusing to take the assigned apartment in the suburbs because his work unit was only a few minutes away from the lane, became homeless. They depended on the generosity of neighbors, who took turns inviting them in for meals and providing temporary housing. But this could only be a short-term solution and Mr. W was making plans to petition in Beijing. Also, Dai Lixiang, the community leader, was getting an unmistakable warning of pending eviction as well. He and his family were in fact packing to prepare for the inevitable. With merely thirty-some families left it was only a matter of time before they would all suffer domicide unless they took some drastic actions.

The residents decided to hire Wang Cailiang as a last resort. The thirty-some families put together 60,000 yuan with contributions that ranged from 60 to 20,000 yuan per family. In early June, four residents, including Mr. W and Dai Lixiang's wife, representing the lane, took a secret train ride to Beijing to meet with Wang.

For that 60,000 yuan, Wang did two things for the residents. First, through the Ministry of Construction in Beijing, he quickly obtained a copy of Document 107, which, as mentioned above, was from the municipal planning and housing bureaus to Hongkou District with instructions to provisionally protect Lincoln Lane. When he presented the four residents with the document, the latter were overwhelmed with bittersweet feelings; Mr. W broke down crying. After all, this was what they had being fighting for. They believed that Document 107 had finally validated their effort and had the power to rescue them from eviction—they desperately needed to believe that.

Apparently, lawyer Wang had the same high opinion of this piece of paper and told the residents that their homes were now safe if they just went back and showed the document to the demolition office. Eager to return to share this wonderful news, they flew back to Shanghai and made a copy of Document 107 for each of the remaining families. From that point on, they showed the paper every time the demolition officials came to pressure them.

The next move Wang pulled off was actually initiated by Mrs. Dai. After securing Document 107, she asked if Wang could have *Oriental Horizon* dispatch its reporters to investigate the Lincoln Lane case on site. Wang, not in a position to directly suggest that to the TV program, nevertheless orchestrated a plan with her to make it happen—Mrs. Dai went to the *Oriental Horizon* studios to deliver the Lincoln Lane material to lawyer Wang so that, in the process, the program's staff would be alerted to the case, which in turn provided Wang with the opportunity to evaluate the case together with the TV program and raise the issue of an investigation.

Only days after the four-resident delegation returned from Beijing, Li Juan, a well-known reporter for *Horizon Link (Shikong lianxian)*, an investigative news unit with *Oriental Horizon* that specialized in scrutinizing cases of illegal and violent demolition and relocation, arrived with her camera crew to interview Lincoln Lane residents.[25] Just like they saw on television when the program exposed outrageous corruption elsewhere, which seemed to always lead to the punishment of corrupt officials and justice for the people, the Lincoln Lane residents prayed that Li Juan would be their savior. In a sense, CCTV, directly controlled by the central government, is a more powerful weapon than the courts in upholding justice, but it has its limit. It steers clear of certain subjects and its critical reporting is constrained within the boundaries of official censorship. Such media actions work as a controlled check on corruption at the local level, which has boosted Beijing's image. After all, CCTV is to serve the core interest of the Chinese party state. Not surprisingly, the Chinese consider it an incarnation of the "blue sky" official who will ultimately deliver justice to them.

As soon as CCTV's crew entered the lane, residents immediately surrounded it and started airing their grievances. The gathering crowd attracted local police and members of the demolition office who had no idea what was going on. They tried to intimidate Li Juan, asking who she was and where she came from. Li's answer was to simply flash her reporter's badge and continue the interview— journalists from the CCTV can actually act as the much celebrated "king without a crown," an idealized title bestowed on journalists in a free society.

Li's crew was on site for about thirty minutes. Li also meant to interview the neighborhood committee but no one showed up as the committee members and policemen all disappeared to report back to their respective supervisors about CCTV's surprising visit. In the following days, Li interviewed some of the district officials and Ruan Yisan, the Tongji professor and preservation expert mentioned above. Ruan reportedly immediately contacted officials at the municipal planning bureau, including Wu Jiang, his former colleague at Tongji. The key to Li's investigation was whether Lincoln Lane was truly unique and worthy of preservation. To answer this question Ruan's expert testimony was crucial. But at this make-or-break moment, Ruan, aware of the conflict between the relevant municipal agencies and the Hongkou District over Lincoln Lane and the likely collapse of the case, backed off and report-edly stated instead that the lane was not unique at all and belonged to the ordinary type of alleyway style, a point he would indeed reiterate on record later, as we will see below. In other words, according to Ruan, Lincoln Lane was not worth protecting. In the meantime, municipal officials, alerted to the situation, also stepped in to prevent the CCTV investigation from dig-ging deeper into the matter.

The involvement of *Oriental Horizon* brought unprecedented excitement and hope to the residents. But their case for preservation disintegrated even before the camera crew left Shanghai. Li's visit represented both the peak and the valley of their struggle. The symbolic and political implications of the investigation went beyond Lincoln Lane; Shanghai's officials simply would not allow such a report to air. Because of *Oriental Horizon*'s reputation for busting corruption, it was public knowledge that its mere appearance at any place was bad news for local government. It is little wonder that while *Oriental Horizon* and other CCTV programs had been reporting corruption nationwide, the Lincoln Lane case was the first and only one in Shanghai in which CCTV got involved. Under then party boss Chen Liangyu, the Shanghai clique had built a powerful kingdom insulated from the central government. But by bringing *Oriental Horizon* to Shanghai, the Lincoln Lane residents broke that barrier. They were also no longer dealing with the Hongkou District, but the municipal party leaders, who saw this as a threat and an embarrassment. If the municipal agencies and the Hongkou District had conflicting views about how to handle the Lincoln Lane case before, they now could no longer afford the division.

Also, should the Lincoln Lane case be aired on CCTV, it would encour-age other Shanghai residents to contact the program and thus open a Pan-dora's Box, exposing corruption in Shanghai. At the time, neither lawyer Wang Cailiang nor the CCTV reporters seemed to have sufficiently under-stood that Shanghai was not just another city in China, nor did they appre-ciate how tightly controlled Shanghai was. But the Lincoln Lane case woke them up. Later when the residents asked for Wang's continued help, he was reluctant because "the 'water' in Shanghai is deep and the 'fish' there big." The big "fish," Shanghai's party head Chen Liangyu and his followers, who were behind many corruption cases, were not openly exposed until fall 2006.

The Last Nail

Although the municipal and district officials succeeded in killing the *Orien-tal Horizon* investigation, what happened in Lincoln Lane did shock them.

For a brief moment, the residents had out-maneuvered them. The district officials were surprised that the residents had gotten hold of a copy of Document 107, which they thought they had concealed, and that the residents had even prompted the CCTV's on-site investigation, which could have been explosive. The officials had no idea of Wang Cailiang's involvement either. The residents did all this right under their noses. It was clear to the officials that the residents would not give up. In fact, on June 18, immediately after the aborted *Oriental Horizon* investigation, the residents once again petitioned the municipal government, this time requesting it to take specific measures to implement Document 107. The residents' determination and resourcefulness were a nightmare to the authorities who believed that the ultimate damage control was to level the lane so as to finally invalidate the argument for preservation. By that time, the relevant municipal bureaus had surrendered their position and given in to the Hongkou District government. After all, they had nothing particular to gain for themselves and thus were not committed supporters of the case, while the district had much to lose and thus was ardently opposed to it. In fact, the CCTV investigation effectively united the various government agencies.

Thus emboldened, the district authorities pushed forward. As the residents put it, "The more we appeal for preservation, the faster they destroy our lane." Dai Lixiang and his family, as expected, were evicted to a nearby apartment building only two weeks after the CCTV investigation. But the eviction did not go quietly. Supported by the neighbors, Dai's wife and daughter, the latter a recent college graduate, decided to reclaim their unit. The fact that the demolition squad had cut off the utilities and destroyed some of the walls, windows, and floors did not deter them. Mr. W, the handyman, helped get electricity from another unit and, together with his family, which had been homeless for months, also joined the mother and daughter team of the Dai family in camping out in the partially demolished unit. Without screen doors and windows, the campers suffered from mosquitoes and other insects in the heat of the summer, not to mention the hazards of exposed wires and broken glass. To deal with this defiance, the demolition squad came for a second act of eviction, which was highly confrontational and violent. Dai's wife was thrown out of the unit first while his daughter was holding out in the house arguing and screaming. In the end, she was dragged out and through to the crowd of neighbors gathered outside while still screaming and crying. All this was caught by a hidden camera by a resident. After the second eviction the demolition squad came in to finish the job of domicide—it thoroughly smashed up the Dais' unit, making it impossible for anyone to return again.

Clearly, the authorities realized that the Lincoln Lane case had become a hot potato that they had to get rid of fast. Since Document 107 was now open knowledge, the officials had to backtrack on it to disqualify Lincoln Lane as a valuable historic structure, kick it off the fourth batch preservation list, and thereby justify its demolition. For that purpose they got the experts involved, since their review was required in deciding whether a structure was to be preserved.

On June 30, 2004, the municipal planning bureau convened an expert panel to review the Lincoln Lane case and determine, on the surface, whether to recommend it for preservation—but everyone involved understood it was to kill the case. Of the twelve persons on the "Experts Review Committee," four were listed as Tongji professors, and the other eight were officials, researchers, and engineers mostly associated with relevant government agencies.

Of the panelists, the best known is Ruan Yisan, professor and director of the National Research Center of Historic Cities, the man of the hour on all questions about preservation. As mentioned earlier, Ruan participated in the October 2003 meeting at Tongji where he met with the residents who came through the Historic Preservation Hotline. He also made a speech at the meeting about the importance of historic preservation. Ruan was widely credited with spearheading the preservation of Zhouzhuang, a water town in Jiangsu Province that bestraddles the several rivers that run through it, and its transformation into a commercially successful tourist destination. In 2003, the preservation of Zhouzhuang and several other water towns in the Yangzhi River region received the UNESCO Asia-Pacific Awards for Cultural Heritage Conservation.[26] Considered to be a leading champion of preservation, or even China's "Preservation God," Ruan was named by the Chinese media as one of China's fifty most influential "public intellectuals."[27]

Each of the twelve experts was required to file an evaluation form for Lincoln Lane. The form listed seven items. The first five were criteria by which the experts were asked to render their opinion. These included: whether the lane was unique in architectural style; whether it reflected the historic and cultural character of Shanghai's regional architecture; whether any of its buildings were by renowned architects; whether the lane had any other historic and cultural significance; and how well the site fit into its surroundings. Item 6 asked the experts to provide an overall evaluation and item 7 asked whether or not they would recommend the lane as "excellent historic architecture [for preservation]." The experts' answers to these questions were extremely brief, with only a couple of phrases devoted to each response, and most criteria were answered with a simple "yes" or "no." Of the twelve panelists, only three indicated that Lincoln Lane had a unique architectural style. Seven of them did not know much about the lane at all, and nearly all of them failed to see the lane as fitting well into its surroundings because, as they pointed out, the area had already suffered severe destruction, thus diminishing the significance of Lincoln Lane. Only one expert suggested the lane be partially preserved and its "historical memory" be sustained by putting out a plaque. In the end, all twelve of the experts answered "no" to the last question—they did not recommend the lane as excellent historic architecture worthy of preservation.

There were several problems with this so-called expert evaluation. First, the panelists were not required to support their views with any evidence. The explicit reason they were consulted was their supposed knowledge about such subjects. But most of them had no idea about Lincoln Lane's architect nor its value in the context of the region's architectural style, and they simply answered "no," "not known," or "no details." One expert even stated that Lincoln Lane was built in 1937, not in the 1920s, completely disregarding the well-documented fact that the lane was damaged in the 1932 Japanese bombing. Willful ignorance and stunning obliviousness were apparently accepted, in a twisted way, as signs of authority. The carelessness with which the experts handled the case was in stark contrast to the thoroughness of the residents. The latter, conducting themselves like trained experts, did their best to research their case and document their arguments with oral and printed material and with copious appendixes. But the actual, trained experts could not be bothered nor were they required to study the case and support their opinions with evidence. Furthermore, in regard to the surrounding area, the panel essentially said that since much in this area had already been destroyed, then why not also Lincoln Lane? But a counterargument could have been made: since so much had already been destroyed, what was left was all the more valuable and therefore warranted protection.

Of the experts' recommendations, Ruan Yisan's was the most troubling. Ruan had publicly expressed his dismay at the wholesale destruction of old Shanghai. He had campaigned and in fact continues to campaign for the preservation of alleyway houses, especially those in the new styles in Shanghai which he believes should be valued and protected as a world heritage for their unique architectural style, culture, and scope.[28] Even in November 2003, regarding the Lincoln Lane case specifically, Ruan was still adamantly against demolishing any new-style alleyway houses such as those in the lane. Mindful of the deceit in the Lincoln Lane case, he criticized some developers who used the pretext of municipal projects to arbitrarily demolish "quality houses that were outside the scope of a municipal project." In fact, Ruan especially warned that "Shanghai residents' enthusiasm and the municipal government's determination for preservation" would challenge such developers' schemes. One point he made was perhaps the most relevant: "If experts, residents, and the government work together, we can preserve some fast-disappearing [sites] of our cultural heritage. Our job is to serve the people and help them in recommending excellent historic buildings."[29] Ruan's statements were a godsend to the residents, who treated him as a powerful ally and admired his courage. The Lincoln Lane residents often quoted his remarks—they are many in number—in their letters arguing for preservation.

Yet at the committee meeting, Ruan dismissed Lincoln Lane without any reservation and, like the others panelists, failed to recommend it for protection. More specifically, he wrote that the lane was "ordinary alleyway [houses]" without "historical value" and "important characteristics" in its architecture and culture, "[therefore it] may not be a candidate for preservation." Although this statement was consistent with what he reportedly said in the CCTV interview, it was directly at odds with the view he had publicly expressed only a few months earlier.

But Ruan's position on the review panel is perhaps not surprising, considering the fact that he had also capitalized on his fame by establishing a contract firm to work on and profit from commercial preservation projects, which largely depended on the government's favor. In other words, he needed the officials' support or his company would fail. Ruan has built his fame with many of his highly publicized scholarly and public initiatives in the field of historic preservation. They include the National Research Center of Historic Cities at Tongji University and the Ruan Yisan Foundation for the Protection of City Heritage.[30] But the nature of these two organizations is not as clear as their titles suggest because both organizations are also tied to Ruan Yisan's for-profit business venture—the Shanghai Ruan Yisan Urban Planning and Design Company, Limited (Shanghai Run Yisan chengshi guihua sheji youxian gongsi)—a fact that is not as widely known. This company is said to be an enterprise of the National Research Center of Historic Cities.[31] As both the company and the center bear Ruan's name, the relationship between the two is murky. Did Ruan use a research center at a public university to operate his private business? Or were the company and the center both of his own creation to promote his business? It is also not clear what exactly his foundation, formed in 2006, has done beyond holding some meetings, which are also listed under the National Research

标题"先予保护建筑是否"推荐为优秀历史建筑专家评审意见

郑时龄	中科院院士，市建筑学会理事长
阮仪三	同济大学博士生导师，国家历史文化名城研究中心主任
罗小未	同济大学博士生导师
赵天佐	市建筑学会历史保护专家委员会副主任
周俭	同济大学城市规划学院副院长
谭玉峰	市文物委员会文物处处长、高工
马云安	市房地局副局长、高工
卢永毅	市建筑学会历史建筑保护分会委员，同济大学教授
苏功洲	市规划设计研究院总工
张松	同济大学教授、市建筑学会历史建筑保护分会委员
李孔三	市文物委员会委员、副研究员
王安石	市房地局改造修缮处处长、高工

1、郑时龄

1	是否在建筑样式，施工工艺和工程技术具有建筑艺术特色	否
2	是否能反映上海地域建筑历史文化特点？	否
3	是否是著名建筑师的代表作品	否
4	是否具有其他历史文化意义	否
5	是否与周边环境形成风貌特色	否
6	专家综合评定意见：	同意调查意见
7	最终意见是否推荐为优秀历史建筑：	建议不推荐为优秀历史建筑

2、阮仪三

1	是否在建筑样式，施工工艺和工程技术具有建筑艺术特色	一般联排式住宅
2	是否能反映上海地域建筑历史文化特点？	属一般上海地域新式里弄
3	是否是著名建筑师的代表作品	否
4	是否具有其他历史文化意义	经查证不具有取要意义
5	是否与周边环境形成风貌特色	周边议建，原有房屋也未形成环境风貌特色
6	专家综合评定意见：	因十一般里弄联排式住宅，终查证不属有历史价值的建筑，风貌特色也不具有重要特色，可不作为保护对象
7	最终意见是否推荐为优秀历史建筑：	否

Figure 5.4. On June 30, 2004, the authorities convened an expert panel, ostensibly to review the Lincoln Lane case but essentially to retract an earlier document that proposed to preserve it so as to allow the Hongkou District government to demolish the lane. This form indicates the twelve experts on the panel and the evaluation by two of them. The second of these is by Ruan Yisan, a professor of Tongji University and "Preservation God" in China. Ruan had previously campaigned to preserve Lincoln Lane and its likes, but here he contradicts his earlier position by recommending against the preservation of the lane.

Center of Historic Cities as part of its activities. All of them—the center, the foundation, and the company—seem to be in one family and connected by one person, Ruan Yisan.[32] Some people in Shanghai have speculated that both the research center at Tongji and Ruan's foundation are meant to serve Ruan Yisan and his company's business interest.

During the Lincoln Lane controversy, Ruan was reportedly working on a project to restore the wartime Jewish ghetto in Hongkou, a project the district government supported since the site could become a profitable tourist attraction with an international appeal. A number of government offices, both Chinese and foreign organizations, companies, and individuals have been involved in the project which has been ongoing for years. The details of Ruan's association with the project and whether and how he and his company have profited from it are unknown.[33] Still, some people, including the residents of Lincoln Lane as we will see shortly, considered it a conflict of interest for Ruan to evaluate the Lincoln Lane case while he was working on the Jewish ghetto project in Hongkou. In any event, in this case Ruan did not fulfill his self-appointed, publicly announced responsibility to help people and the city in the cause of preservation. Moreover, he contradicted his own point about the historic value of the new-style alleyway houses in Shanghai. Indeed, making bold statements in the abstract about historic preservation is one thing, acting on such statements against official will when one's own interest may be at stake is quite another. After all, "Preservation God" Ruan Yisan was himself also a developer, driven by the same pursuit of profit.

To be sure, Ruan's connections to government and hypocrisy are not unique. All of the twelve experts were appointed and invited to sit on the panel by the municipal planning bureau, which also paid each—1,000 yuan in an envelope—for their brief answers to the seven questions. The officials' trouble with the lane and their changed position from Document 107 were not a secret to the experts. If those experts wanted to be invited back for future consultations and to continue to profit from their expertise, they had to be in good standing with the officials. In other words, "public intellectuals" like Ruan Yisan were not exactly public-minded. While they spoke out openly on preservation, they looked the other way when real courage was needed. In the process they also played a hand in wiping out part of the city's history—the wholesale destruction in Shanghai could not have occurred without those experts' collaboration with the government. No wonder the frustrated lawyer Wang had reportedly said, "Those experts in Shanghai are up to no good!"

The panel's review outraged the residents. In a lawsuit the residents filed against the municipal planning bureau for failing to enforce Document 107, they contested the panel's conclusion and bitterly complained that the experts "knew nothing about history and even showed no interest in it." They questioned the fairness of the panel and called out Ruan Yisan—they had heard that Ruan contracted with the Hongkou District to undertake the Jewish ghetto project, but it remains unclear whether Ruan had a contract directly with the district or if he worked with other companies under contract with the district: "If some of them were under contract to the Hongkou district, they should have excused themselves from the panel." The residents were convinced that "those experts had betrayed themselves and their ruling was unconscionable." They ridiculed one panelist's mistake that Lincoln Lane was built in 1937. The same person also argued that the lane had no relationship to Lincoln whatsoever, to which the residents responded: "If the lane was named 'Lincoln,' then how was it not a reference to the American president? Or did the expert have any other explanation?" The residents also took their criticism, especially of Ruan Yisan, into cyberspace, since he was labeled a "public intellectual" in the blogosphere. One blogger suggested stripping Ruan of the title because "he is a politician who colluded with the Hongkou district government and sold out Lincoln Lane."[34]

In fact, "public intellectual" is a contradictory term in the Chinese context. China's imperial system produced a scholarly class whose highest calling and lifelong mission was precisely to serve the emperor. Dissenting from those in power was perilous, which has been the case throughout China's history, including during the Mao era when hundreds of thousands of intellectuals were attacked, fired, forced into labor camps, or driven to commit suicide for speaking their minds. The post-Mao reform has created some space for independent-minded intellectuals to grow, but they remain a rarity as their own interest often depends on their relationship with the government. Furthermore, despite a greater degree of freedom as a result of the market economy, China is still a one-party state and political dissidents are still at risk of relentless persecution. A truly public, independent-minded intellectual has to have the courage to take that risk, as did the 2010 Nobel Peace Prize winner Liu Xiaobo, who remains in prison today. However, among the large crowd of known intellectuals in Shanghai, lawyer Zheng Enchong has stood alone as a profile in courage in risking his life for justice and principle.

In the Lincoln Lane case, the panel served the interests of the authorities. Its unanimous decision to veto preservation of the lane was exactly what the officials expected from its invited reviewers. After orchestrating the expert evaluation, the authorities had a legitimate reason to demolish the lane. Two days later, on July 2, 2004, the municipal planning bureau and the municipal housing bureau issued Document 662 regarding the fourth batch of preservation projects. It contained a paragraph to formally retract Document 107: "Document 107 was issued to provisionally protect Lincoln Lane. Now after going through an investigation and expert review process, [it has been determined that] Lincoln Lane should not be recommended to be on the final list for preservation." In a "Report on the Preservation of Excellent Historic Structures in the District," the Hongkou District Housing Bureau repeated this point: that it had investigated each of the items on the list recommended for the fourth batch of preservation and based on expert opinion, had eliminated some unsuitable items. The example it provided was Lincoln Lane.[35]

The politics of preservation, after all, boils down to money, not unlike many of the other issues in post-Mao China. Preservation does not simply involve allowing a structure to remain; it is an expensive enterprise. There are at least two kinds of historic preservation. One is to preserve the integrity of buildings and sites for their historical value. In that case, once the government identifies a preservation project, it has to renovate and maintain it, which involves a huge expense that no agency willingly pays. In the same report by the Hongkou District Housing Bureau mentioned above, the bureau complained about a number of problems with preservation. First, because of decades of neglect, most of the old buildings were run down and needed major renovation, but the bureau had no funds for that as preservation was not a high priority. Also, other than office buildings, most of the old buildings were overcrowded residential housing; relocating the residents would be extremely expensive. Relevant regulations also stipulate that relocation compensation for residents of preserved projects should be 5 to 15 percent higher than for those in regular housing, which is clearly an additional incentive for officials to oppose preservation and for residents to support it.[36] The lack of expertise is another issue. The report provided an example of misusing paint on a preserved building which amounted to ruining it. In other words, it is a win-win game for the district to tear down old buildings to make space for profitable new high-rises; and it is a loss-loss situation to preserve them.

The other kind of preservation is essentially commercial development in the name of preservation which, according to Rem Koolhaas, is destroying our past, contributing to the gentrification of the city, and widening the gap between the rich and poor, as we discussed in the chapter on the Xintiandi project. This kind of redevelopment is driven by profit—to develop projects into a money-making machine, drawing in tourists and thus increasing local revenue. In fact, Ruan Yisan has engaged in many such commercial preservation projects in China.

In light of the politics and economics of preservation, it is little surprise that Lincoln Lane lost its fight. The case illustrates why in Shanghai old buildings have so rapidly disappeared. This is especially alarming when compared with other cities of the world. By spring 2004, Shanghai had designated 398 buildings for preservation. Yet Singapore, the city-state that is the smallest country in Southeast Asia, with a population of less than five million on an area of 271 square kilometers, has put more than 5,300 buildings under protection.[37]

A Problematic Future

As far as the officials were concerned, Document 662 closed the Lincoln Lane case and also the life of the lane itself. In reality, the case is far from over. Every step of the way, the residents have insisted on their rights and have refused to be intimidated. In the final days of the demolition, one resident shaved his head and deliberately walked shirtless in front of district officials. Asked why, he said this was to show his fearlessness, in fact, his willingness to go to jail if necessary since prisoners often have shaved heads. "If I'm not even afraid for my life, how can they intimidate me to sign anything?" he said. Another resident, who relocated to Lincoln Lane in the late 1990s from another part of Hongkou District where he had witnessed his neighbor commit suicide in protest against domicide, a tragedy the district wanted him to keep quiet, threatened to expose that case if he was denied reasonable compensation. Collective action continued in the last stage as well. In October 2004, thirty-some families, including those who had already been forced out, brought a lawsuit against the municipal planning bureau for failing to implement Document 107. After the court ruled against them, they appealed to the Shanghai Second Intermediate People's Court, which, like "people's courts" all over China when it came to housing disputes with local officials and governments as the accused, ruled against the people.

Although the residents who had already been evicted continued to use their Lincoln Lane addresses on lawsuit documents, the effort to hold on to the physical lane was crushed as the demolition squad, armed with Document 662, marched to destroy it. By the end of 2004 most of the families were bought out and fifteen of them were evicted. After the last group left in April 2005, the lane was leveled and the ruin was closed off by a wire fence.

Late 2005 witnessed the laying of the foundation for the 28-story building, the Jiahe International Building. In summer 2007 when I visited the site again, a new sign, "Sales Office," was posted at the entrance of the lane where the residents once put their plaque—the 28-story "luxury office building," as the promotional material indicated, was ready for sale with a telling price tag. When the demolition started in 2002, the residents were offered 4,500 yuan per square meter in compensation for their homes. By early 2007, despite a temporary adjustment of the Shanghai real estate market, the 28-story building was marketed at 30,000 yuan per square meter. Like

Figure 5.5. The destruction of Lincoln Lane in March 2005. Courtesy of Dai Lixiang.

the other cases documented in this book, such a price gap is what ultimately motivated the district to carry out the domicide of Lincoln Lane.

By then, the M8 line and the road extension project were also complete. The road project, as the residents accurately pointed out earlier, did not involve the Lincoln Lane location, which contradicted the district government's rationale for demolishing the lane. Both the road outside the lane and the 28-story building within attest to corruption in Shanghai and its destructive force in ruining people's lives, destroying their homes, and erasing the city's past. In 2008, however, a single one-story house was built next to the 28-story high-rise as the district government's effort to symbolically "preserve" Lincoln Lane. This house only begs the question of why the lane was leveled in the first place if it warranted an awkward new structure to remember it after all.

The evicted families are now scattered in different parts of Shanghai, living in temporary rentals. They have since become regular petitioners, going to Beijing several times a year and the municipal petition office at least one a week. They have continued to take the district to court, asking not only for adequate compensation for their homes and the ordeal afterward but also for the government to admit its mistakes. They continue to utilize cyberspace to express their determination to wage the "battle to the very end."[38]

Their struggle since 2002 has been documented by a website, "Recording Shanghai," which is managed by a non-governmental organization of the same name.[39]

Eternally optimistic, Dai Lixiang, who now works at his daughter's retail clothing shop, has demanded that the government rebuild his house. A three-page petition letter dated December 22, 2008, signed by both Dai Lixiang and his wife, was addressed to Premier Wen Jiabao and bore the title: "Expose the lie and return our livelihood." The letter, like many of the early materials the residents wrote, is filled with government regulations, numbers, and dates, and also fifteen appendixes, including the blueprint of the M8 road project, photos of their property, and eviction notices, which by now have become standard contents of Dai's petition package.

The 2008 election of Barack Obama as president of the United States and his frequent reference to President Lincoln has apparently reenergized but also further saddened Dai Lixiang. He has been forwarding me Western media reports on the connections between President Obama and President Lincoln. In one of his email notes Dai wrote that because of President Lincoln, Obama was able to become the first African American president: "Lincoln Lane attested to the Chinese people's admiration of President Lincoln and the lane had a rich history. . . . This vanished corner [the Lane] will never be forgotten." Asked whether the district will eventually restore his house, a buoyant Dai Lixiang replied without hesitation, "Absolutely! It will and it must! Since it is now proven that its demolition was a mistake and Document 70 spells out one way to correct such a mistake is to rebuild it!" He has stubbornly refused to accept the permanence of the domicide inflicted on him and his neighbors. Shortly after the 2010 Chinese New Year, Dai sent me a greeting card without a word, just an image of a gold statue of Buddha standing above a pristine lake. Dai will need to hold on to his desperate cheerfulness and the spirit of a god who endures suffering in the belief of a future enlightenment, both of which are compensatory mechanisms, in order to sustain hope in the pursuit of his lost home.

The long and costly struggle has taken a toll on the people in many ways. One family was 70,000 yuan in debt after their eviction. With the husband ill and unable to work and a son at junior high school, the wife, named Zhou, has been carrying the main burden of the struggle, both in petitioning and in taking care of the tiny rental in which they live. Initially, they borrowed money from another neighbor and hoped to pay back the loan once they were compensated for their Lincoln Lane home. But with no resolution in sight, the disappointed creditor turned on them, threatening a lawsuit. In the end, Zhou borrowed from elsewhere and repaid the initial debt, but the two neighbors are no longer on speaking terms. Zhou's relationship with her parents and siblings has also suffered because she once moved back to stay with her family after losing her own home which caused some tension in the family's already crowded living situation. "The demolition has caused me to lose home, family, friends, neighbors, and relatives; I've lost everything," Zhou lamented.

This profound sense of loss and mourning has become part of the lives of the former residents of Lincoln Lane. During the demolition, the whole neighborhood sank into a funerary mood every time a neighbor was forced out. Watching the happening in tears, they knew that the departure of each family diminished the chances for their own homes to survive.

They also mourned the death of other living things, including a cherished tree. The Lu family had had a cherry tree in its garden since 1949. Every summer for more than half a century, Mrs. Lu carried a basketful of fresh cherries to share with the neighbors; it was the joy of the lane. When the Lu family was forced out in early 2004, Lu's daughter, who was born in the house and grew up with the tree, came back to transplant it to her new home. However, Lu's garden in Lincoln Lane did not remain bare for long. Mrs. Lu had once given a young cherry tree, grown from the seeds of the old one, to a neighbor. The neighbor now returned the favor by planting a new cherry tree, the grandchild of the old one, in its place. In the summer of 2004, the young tree, one foot tall, was thriving in Lu's old garden in front of her shattered home. Unable to face her home in ruins, Mrs. Lu had not set foot in the lane for months after being forced out. But she could not let go of her home either. She came back frequently, wandering around outside the lane, hoping to get a glimpse of her lost home and garden from afar. In June 2004, a neighbor spotted her outside the lane and persuaded her to come in to see the young tree. They had a small lunch gathering for her. Mrs. Lu left with bittersweet tears—with more neighbors being pressured to move out and the whole lane facing its ultimate destruction, she knew that the life of this young tree would be cut short.

Mourning is accompanied by and, in fact, is a form of remembrance. The cyber diary mentioned earlier included eighteen photos of Lincoln Lane, documenting it from its pre-demolition days to its final destruction. The author, a woman who spent sixteen years of her childhood in Lincoln Lane, remembers the hide-and-seek game she played with other children in the lane, an old grandpa's brush pens and his desk underneath which she used to hide, the bamboo gardens, the aroma of food during dinner time, neighborhood summer parties, and a tricky corner where she once fell from her bicycle. She also remembers how her grandma could tell who was who in the lane even in the dark just by the way they walked, and how the grandmas in the lane sometimes formed their own cliques and gossiped and argued "just like children." She started her online diary by explaining why it took so long for her to post the photographs: "Perhaps they are too heavy on my heart." The last two of her photographs showed the lane in partial ruin, and she concluded that "Lincoln Lane," the address that she was so familiar with, had been "forever abandoned."[40]

In truth, the Japanese damaged Lincoln Lane, the Cultural Revolution renamed it, and the post-Mao reform destroyed it.

Notes

1. So-called Duolun Cultural Street is deemed a must see for foreign tourists; see http://www.transindus.co.uk/index.php?pg=1&rn=China&t=CCD&td=2, accessed 29 April 2008.

2. http://www.urbanrail.net/as/shan/shanghai.htm, accessed 4 March 2008.

3. Shanghai shi fangwu tudi ziyuan guanliju (Shanghai Municipal Housing and Land Resource Management Bureau), ed., *Shanghai shi youxiu lishi jianzhu baohu falü fagui wenjian huibian* (A Collection of Laws and Documents on the Preservation of Excellent Historic Architecture in Shanghai) (Shanghai: fangwu tudi ziyuan guanliju, 2005 (internal document)), 82–84.

4. http://sh.focus.cn/news/2003-03-13/42523.html, accessed 13 March 2003.

5. Shanghai shi fangwu tudi ziyuan guanliju, ed., *Shanghai shi youxiu lishi jianzhu baohu falü fagui wenjian huibian* , 4–5.

6. Shanghai shi fangwu tudi ziyuan guanliju, ed., *Shanghai shi youxiu lishi jianzhu baohu falü fagui wenjian huibian*, 5–14.

7. Donald A. Jordan, *China's Trial by Fire: The Shanghai War of 1932* (Ann Arbor: University of Michigan Press, 2001), 188–98.

8. Lu, "'The Seventy-two Tenants,'" 133–84, especially 173–77.

9. *Qingnian bao* (Youth Daily), 5 November 2003.

10. http://www.china.org.cn/english/culture/87340.htm, accessed 30 August 2012.

11. http://www.cein.gov.cn/home/ad/jssb/guanli/neirong.asp?id=7030, accessed 10 March 2008.

12. Shi Chang, "Shanghai youge Linken fang" ("Shanghai Has a Lincoln Lane") *Moerben ribao* (The Chinese Melbourne Daily), 3 July 2003.

13. http://hrb.focus.cn/msgview/4059/50850005.html, accessed 10 March 2008.

14. http://www.abbs.com.cn/bbs/actions/archive/post/2701329_0.html, accessed 18 March 2008.

15. http://littlesleeve.blogcn.com/diary, 3325901.shtml, accessed 5 March 2008.

16. *Xinmin wanbao* (Xinmin Evening News), 18 March 2004.

17. http://www.china.org.cn/english/culture/87340.htm, accessed 30 August 2012.

18. *Qingnian bao*, 5 November 2003.

19. Severe Acute Respiratory Syndrome (SARS) broke out in China in spring 2003 and caused a worldwide health scare. http://www.who.int/csr/sars/en/, accessed 27 January 2009.

20. *Falü yu shenghuo* (Law and Life), 2007, 3: 26–27.

21. http://news.sina.com.cn/c/2007-03-12/150712496404.shtml, accessed 2 September 2012.

22. http://news.sina.com.cn/c/2007-03-12/150712496404.shtml, accessed 2 September 2012.

23. Wang Cailiang, *Fangwu chaiqian shiwu* (Practical Matters Regarding Housing Demolition and Relocation) (Beijing: Falü chubanshe, 2002); *Fangwu chaiqian jiufen jiaodian shiyi* (Guide to Solving Disputes over Urban Housing Demolition and Relocation) (Beijing: Falü chubanshe, 2004).

24. See a brief introduction of the CCTV program at http://www.cctv.com/program/oriental/sklx/index.shtml, accessed 28 March 2008; http://www.cctv.com/program/oriental/01/index.shtml accessed 2 September 2012.

25. See information on *Horizon Link* at http://www.cctv.com/news/other/20040216/101246.shtml, and some of Li Juan's reporting notes at http://www.cctv.com/program/oriental/sklx/index.shtml, accessed 2 September 2012.

26. http://cms2.unescobkk.org/index.php?id=2181, accessed 8 November 2012.

27. http://business.sohu.com/20040908/n221944557.shtml, accessed 21 March 2008. For a discussion on the concept and controversy of "public intellectuals" in China, see Merle Goldman, *From Comrade to Citizen: The Struggle for Political Rights in China* (Cambridge, MA: Harvard University Press, 2005), 225–26.

28. http://info.china.alibaba.com/news/detail/v0-d1003252020.html, accessed 2 September 2012.

29. *Qingnian bao*, 5 November 2003.

30. http://www.china-mc.org/zhongxinchuanzhen/. This website also includes information on some of the preservation projects Ruan Yisan has been involved in. Accessed 24 August 2012.

31. http://www.iliyu.com/job/html/job-413714.html, accessed 22 August 2012.

32. http://www.tianzhilou.com/csl/cszz/content/2012-06/04/content_1345721.htm; http://www.china-mc.org/zhongxinchuanzhen/, accessed 24 August 2012.

33. http://www.sfgate.com/news/article/Shanghai-again-opens-its-arms-to-Jews-Once-a-2540006.php#page-2; http://www.movius.us/articles/AWSJ-tilanqiao.html; http://wenku.baidu.com/view/8b77b5ee998fcc22bcd10d5c.html; http://www.yilin.com/book.aspx?id=4594 accessed 15 August 2012.

34. http://vip.bokee.com/authorEdit/articleCommentAll.php?id=44050, accessed 20 September 2009.

35. http://www.hkrd.gov.cn/zyhy/detail.asp?ObjectID=335, accessed 5 March 2008.

36. Shanghai shi fangwu tudi ziyuan guanliju, ed., *Shanghai shi youxiu lishi jianzhu baohu falü fagui wenjian huibian*, 27; *Qingnian bao*, 5 November 2003.

37. *Wenhui bao* (Wenhui Daily), 5 February 2004.

38. http://newhouse.sh.soufun.com/housecomment_v/1210131026_zonghe.htm, accessed 10 April 2008.

39. http://ddhs.blogcn.com/diary,11415468.shtml, accessed 18 March 2008.

40. http://littlesleeve.blogcn.com/diary, 3325901.shtml, accessed 5 March 2008.

~

Conclusion

The year of 2011, like that of 1989, will go down in history as a watershed in popular protest and regime change. It started with the Arab Spring that toppled dictators in the Arab world. In early August, Hosni Mubarak, the former head of Egypt, now "the Pharaoh in the cage of the accused," was put on trial in Cairo for his years of crime against the people.[1] In October, the Libyan dictator Muammar el-Qaddafi was shot dead by rebel soldiers. In Russia, Vladimir Putin's iron fist could not prevent thousands of Russians from braving the cold in street protests.[2] Societies with Western-style democracies are not immune either. In August, the riots in London and the tent city protest in Israel seemed to have anticipated the Occupy Wall Street movement in America, which has in turn spread to other parts of the globe.

Aided by the Internet and social media that collapse the wrinkles in time and space, protest and street politics have become more pervasive and inventive. They have come in many forms: in Ukraine, defiant young women bared their breasts in public; in Russia, a radical artist painted a 210-foot penis on a St. Petersburg drawbridge; in Belarus, a group of people clapped their hands and beeped their cell phones in a protest that led to scores of arrests;[3] in China, those who were inspired by the Jasmine Revolution in Tunisia simply sang a popular folk song and took a silent stroll.[4]

These movements, large and small, are unpredictable, perturbing, and contradictory. As lived experience often does, they defy neatly formulated theoretical abstraction. The Arab Spring started with the self-immolation of a fruit vendor. Among the Occupy Wall Street protesters, some see the capitalist system as the root of all the evil and others want to fix it. The results of these movements are uncertain as well. As the political scientist John M. Owen IV points out, "a revolution's consequences need not follow from its causes"; the Arab Spring, for example, has produced "flowers of a decidedly Islamist hue" instead of "bringing secular revolutionaries to power."[5] Regardless of their origins and outcomes, however, these movements certainly indicate that more and more people worldwide have risen against the abuse of power, social injustice, repression, and humiliation. They are demanding accountability, justice, dignity, and above all else, a fairer society and a better life.

That is what has essentially inspired the protesters documented in this book. Although these Chinese protesters have been provoked by causes specific to them—domicide, the threat of it, and unjust compensation—they nevertheless have shared aspirations and determination with protesters in Tahrir Square, Zuccotti Park, and points beyond. But because China is a socialist state, we often overlook the similarity between protest in China and elsewhere in the world. China scholars have debated the nature of popular resistance in China. The issue in question is best captured in the distinction between what Elizabeth Perry terms "rights consciousness" and "rules consciousness."[6] Some scholars have identified elements of Western democracy in popular protest and other activist movements in China, especially noting a rising rights consciousness among Chinese. According to them, this rights consciousness represents a departure from the Maoist past, a challenge to the authoritarian CCP government, and a sign of fundamental transformation in Chinese society.[7] Other scholars, however, are more cautious. They point out a number of limits regarding Chinese protesters—Chinese protesters aim at economic compensation and thus can be bought by government money;[8] and they play by the rules and attempt to work within official boundaries, much like protesters and rebels throughout Chinese history have done. According to them, the post-Mao protesters have done little to undermine the Chinese state.[9]

At the center of this debate on rules consciousness or rights consciousness is the question of whether protests in China remain within a long-standing authoritarian Chinese tradition or have entered into the new domain of Western democracy. However, this question itself may be problematic. If we free ourselves from the binary oppositions of Western and Chinese, and authoritarianism and democracy, we may realize that rights consciousness and rules consciousness are not necessarily contradictory.

In most cases, as demonstrated in the book, Chinese protesters play by the rules to secure their rights. The main reason for this is that the alternatives of operating outside the system are either unavailable or too risky and thus will not help their cause. But they are by no means confined by official rules; in fact, they have challenged "evil" rules, as in their decade-long campaign to overturn Document 305. They also have a concrete conviction that their claim to their property and proper compensation is legally and morally just and it is their right to pursue such a claim—they consider monetary compensation to be inseparable from justice and their rights. Whether this sense of rights and justice is Western or Chinese is irrelevant to them. Furthermore, their demand goes beyond money. Government accountability and personal dignity have become increasingly important for Chinese protesters particularly and Chinese citizens generally. Zhou Youlan, He Yidong, and Dai Lixiang all want to hold their respective district governments accountable. They insist that the officials not only admit and apologize for their mistakes but also correct them. They are not satisfied by a mere cash payment. In fact, both Dai Lixiang and He Yidong have refused to negotiate with their respective district governments for any financial compensation unless and until their demands are met—Dai wants his home to be restored and He wants his home to be returned, nothing less. While government payment can neutralize certain conflicts, it has its limits. That China's huge budget for "Stability Maintenance" has not calmed down popular protest and defiance is a case in point.

The fact of the matter is that Chinese protesters do not act within a framework of any clear-cut binary opposition. Within their expectation that the government will take care of them, their kneeling down to petition, their sense of entitlement, their unabashed pursuit of financial self-interest, and their demand for government accountability is a mix of values drawn from the patrimonial bureaucracy dating back to the imperial past as well as from Mao's socialist welfare state, the newly legitimized capitalist ethos, and democratic ideas. Chinese society today is a hybrid. People oscillate among different, even opposing, but also interconnected worlds—socialist, capitalist, democratic, and Confucian—because of the imperative of sheer survival and competition.

In his study of ritual systems in south-central Africa, Victor Turner used the concept "betwixt and between" to describe a "liminal period" where the "passenger" separates from an early stable point to transform to the next stage. This liminal period, which is full of opposing elements, is "ambiguous," "interstructural," and "complex," because it is "neither this nor that, and yet is both." He further pointed out that in this "betwixt and between" state, the "decomposition" of the past goes along with "growth, transformation, and the reformation of old elements in new patterns."[10] According to Turner, such a liminal period should be understood on its own terms, as it does not fit into any constructed, rigid categories.

Similarly, in a recent study of contemporary Vietnam, Erik Harms challenges the binary oppositions between rural and urban, and inner and outer city.[11] He examines a district lying on the edge of Ho Chi Minh City. This district and daily life there are neither rural nor urban, but "uncomfortably both." They are on the edge of different patterns of life.[12] Harms explores the "social edginess" of this urban fringe at multiple levels—spatially, socially, culturally, and symbolically. This edginess can be both empowering and discouraging. People oscillating among various contexts can be "edged out by processes beyond their control," but also "edge their way into opportunities" by capitalizing on "different regimes of value" and crossing varied social space. Harms' emphasis is on the importance of understanding how people negotiate their daily lives in alternative modes, not on some fixed binary categories.[13]

Both concepts, Turner's "betwixt and between" and Harms' "social edginess," are instructive in understanding protest in China. Shanghai's residents-turned-protesters clearly utilize the "different regimes of value" afforded by the hybrid nature of Chinese society. They include paternalistic Confucianism, socialist welfare, the market economy, Western culture, and other threads of ideas. These protesters have multiple identities as well. Zhou Youlan is a petitioner on her knees, a homeowner, and a day trader in the fully fledged capitalist market. Shi Lin sees justice through the lens of a squatter, a Maoist worker union cadre, a capitalist enthusiast, and a policy entrepreneur. Such "edginess" in identity is a norm in this liminal period. The liminal period, as Turner has indicated, also allows the re-formation of old elements into new patterns. The residents-turned-protesters in Shanghai, for instance, have given new meaning to Maoist cultural symbols to serve their struggle for accountability and justice. Both the various values and multiple identities represent their strength, not their weakness.

As for the impact of grassroots protest in China, the dominant question among scholars has been whether popular protest reinforces or undercuts the Chinese state, with the emphasis on whether it promotes or undermines democratization. In recent years, however, some scholars have begun to suggest new ways of looking at the impact of grassroots movements in China. For instance, in his study of China's hydraulic power systems, Andrew Mertha notes the increased space in Chinese politics for previously powerless actors, such as non-governmental organizations and the media, to become "viable players" in shaping China's water policy.[14] He calls for a shift of our focus from China's democratization to its political pluralization. Mertha's study identifies significant progress China has made toward a more pluralized society in policy making. Government has sometimes had to halt or abandon altogether a dam project because of grassroots campaigns against it. In other fronts as well, popular resistance has been an ongoing force in propelling policy change.[15] Resisters recognize that they can organize and pressure the government. Some of the protesters in Shanghai certainly think that their actions have led in some ways to a more responsible government. They consider it an accomplishment of their protest and a sign of progress if their demands are met, collectively, such as in the abolishment of Document 305, and individually, such as in the case of Mr. C. Such examples give those whose cases still linger the hope that the Chinese state will become more open and accountable in the future.

The Chinese state is also at the point of "betwixt and between." Terms such as imperial China, Republican China, the Mao era, and the post-Mao era do have a temporal boundary. But these periods have significant institutional, economic, social, and cultural overlaps, regardless of the respective official rhetoric of those eras. The idea of a "harmonious society," proposed by the current CCP head Hu Jintao, for instance, has its roots in classical Confucianism, and, in this post-Mao era driven by market capitalism, both a huge portrait of Mao and his mausoleum are still prominently featured in Tiananmen Square. While the CCP state puts up a unified front, the reform has greatly diminished Beijing's control. Beijing's sacking of ambitious regional party bosses such as Chen Liangyu in Shanghai and Bo Xilai in Chongqing has done little to reverse the course of decentralization as more and more decisions are made at the local levels. Indeed, the tension and negotiation between the center and the regions is unremitting; the CCP state is in constant motion.

On the world stage, the Chinese state also projects an image of and is perceived as being a mixed package. It is at once an authoritarian state, as is evident in its prosecution of the Nobel Peace laureate Liu Xiaobo and countless other dissidents and protesters,[16] but it is also an economic powerhouse, to whom failing Western corporations and even political entities such as the troubled European Union look for rescue. Much like the oil reserves in the Middle East that have helped legitimize Arab dictatorships, the economic might in China has helped legitimize the Chinese state. This economic powerhouse, on the other hand, has been described as full of bubbles about to burst and has been blamed for threatening the environment and the cultural heritage within and without China as it hunts for resources and markets.[17] In short, within China and on the world stage, the Chinese state has multiple and contradictory identities. Perhaps a debate after the announcement of Liu Xiaobo as the 2010 Nobel Peace Prize winner has best captured the "betwixt and between" complex nature of the Chinese state. A Norwegian friend told me that some of his countrymen suggested that Liu and the Chinese government should have shared the prize—Liu for his political courage and the Chinese state for lifting millions of people out of poverty.

In short, the Chinese state is not a static authoritarian government. A Western-style, institutional democracy may not be on the horizon for China in the near future. But the Chinese state has made adjustments and concessions when under absolute pressure due to the persistent grassroots protests and campaigns scattered all over China. While some concessions may take decades to come, others are made within days, as with the mass protest on August 14, 2011, in the city of Dalian. Protesters there demanded the removal of a $1.5 billion chemical plant from the city out of a concern for safety. Almost immediately, the city authorities shut down the plant and announced its relocation. Mass incidents like this have been increasing in China—180,000 were reported in 2010—with varied results.[18]

While state and society are generally in conflict, the resolution of a specific conflict may not always result in one side's utter defeat and the other side's total victory. It is possible for both sides to gain, so to speak, if an outcome reinforces each other's strength. In the Dalian case, for instance, the citizens learned about the power of collective action and are likely to build on this experience in the future. The municipal government, on the other hand, gained credibility by its swift response. In fact, both parties in the Dalian case may have been influenced by a similar mass demonstration in 2007 in Xiamen, in southeast China, which convinced the local government to relocate a chemical plant.[19]

This pattern of mutual conditioning by demands and concessions between the state and society, punctuated by suppression and even bloodshed, has after all characterized the evolution of the capitalist West. No one can downplay the impact of the Civil Rights Movement, for instance, on the basis that it did not overthrow the American government. On the contrary, the movement strengthened the legitimacy of a political system that became more plural while also advancing the status of the disenfranchised.

In China, evidence strongly suggests that the deeply entrenched and corrupt interests of the ruling party dictate that initiative for political reform from the top will be slow and painful, if not utterly impossible. But evidence also suggests that the Chinese people are developing a penchant for taking to the street to ensure that their demands are not only heard but also met, much like the South Koreans have been doing for decades. In fact, Chinese street protest, from housing and land disputes to labor unrest, has been increasing and increasingly violent in recent years. In the United States, this ethos of street activism and its strategies and tactics, which Charles Euchner calls "extraordinary politics," have challenged the ordinary structures of democracy and set an agenda for a host of important issues, from gay rights to freedom of religion.[20] Street protest in China, too, has led to positive results, especially because of the support from the Cyber Street—four million Chinese bloggers are part of this pressure group that demands government accountability. Indeed, protests and demonstrations in China have already forced the government, for instance, to eliminate the agricultural tax in 2006 and improve environmental regulations. In the absence of a nationwide system of democratic elections, such protests help hold the Chinese government accountable and protect the people's interests, while also strengthening people's power. The Chinese party state has a choice: meet the demands of the protesters or resist them at its own peril.

Property deprivation, domicide, and corruption in China have not only destroyed homes but also patterns of life. From their ruins has risen an increasingly determined struggle for social and economic justice and human dignity. This struggle will continue not only to propel China into a more open society, but also to redefine the people in the People's Republic.

This project started as an open-ended investigation of demolition and relocation in Shanghai. Eight years later, most of the cases documented in this book, like so many others not included, remain open-ended.

Of course, Mr. C's case was an exception. Since the Shanghai government's pre–World Expo goodwill gesture led to the satisfactory closure of his housing dispute, Mr. C has shifted his focus to his son's marriage since he thinks that the downtown apartment has made his son's dating prospects all the brighter. He has joined a group of concerned parents who believe their children are inherently unprepared to date or date the right person on their own and that it is the parents' responsibility to be involved in the matter, a sad comment on the consequences of the one-child policy. Those parents meet weekly at a corner of People's Square to exchange information. Mr. C has become quite an expert on the dating market for the younger generation; he is nothing if not thorough.

In early 2011, Zhou Youlan received a letter from the district petition office announcing the dismissal of her case, which Zhou in turn dismissed. She has heard about some other petitioners whose cases were resolved after petitioning at the United Nations Headquarters in New York. Zhou is considering such a trip herself.

Shi Lin remains determined and cheerful about a satisfactory conclusion to his own housing issues. He has apparently worked with government-assigned legal aid staff and lawyers to find solutions to some of the long-standing housing disputes. He stressed that all he has told me in our interviews and conversations is true and, as such, that I can write about anything he has said with confidence. But, he emphasized, I should use the past tense—"Shi Lin once said this." Anticipating the end of his holdout, the ever-adaptive Shi Lin is planning the next chapter of his life where confrontation with the government will not play a major part.

Equally determined and cheerful is Dai Lixiang. The Hongkou District has invited Dai to "talk" about the appropriate amount of monetary compensation. But Dai is not interested. He insists on the restoration of his home in Lincoln Lane. The district's construction of the one-story "preservation" building in 2008 gave Dai much hope for achieving his own goal. To him, this building validates the lane's significance and his demand.

Of all the protesters, He Yidong is the least optimistic. As part of the Xintiandi commercial establishment, his ancestral property is unlikely to be reclaimed as a residence anytime soon. He Yidong said recently: "I don't know if there will be a good result or a bad result. But I know there will be a result in the end." There are certainly a number of ways to read his statement.

Zhu Guangze, now in her nineties, remains a self-imposed hostage and bedridden in the district-provided apartment. Her daughter-in-law continues to petition on behalf of the family. During a detention following a 2011 petition trip to Beijing, she lost most of her eyesight and has been certified as a person of disability. But she soldiers on with her bi-monthly petition trips to Beijing.

No one quits.

Notes

1. http://www.nytimes.com/2011/08/03/world/middleeast/03egypt.html?nl=todaysheadlines&emc=tha22, accessed 3 August 2011.

2. http://www.guardian.co.uk/world/2011/dec/23/kremlin-protesters-russia?newsfeed=true, accessed 23 December 2011.

3. http://www.nytimes.com/2011/07/15/world/europe/15belarus.html?pagewanted=all, accessed 1 October 2011.

4. http://www.nytimes.com/2011/02/24/world/asia/24china.html, accessed 1 October 2011.

5. http://www.nytimes.com/2012/01/07/opinion/why-islamism-is-winning.html?nl=todaysheadlines&emc=thab1, accessed 7 January 2012.

6. See Perry's concise review of the literature on the issue in Perry, "Popular Protest in China," 11–13.

7. Minxin Pei, "Rights and Resistance: The Changing Contexts of the Dissident Movement," in *Chinese Society: Change, Conflict, and Resistance*, eds. Elizabeth J. Perry and Mark Selden (New York: Routledge, 2010), 40–43; see also Minxin Pei,

"Citizens v. Mandarins," 832–62; Merle Goldman, *From Comrade to Citizen: The Struggle for Political Rights in China* (Cambridge, MA: Harvard University Press, 2005): 222–23.

8. Lee, "What Was Socialism to Chinese Workers?" 2007; Zhang Yong Hong and Ching Kwan Lee, "Zhizao tongyi: jiceng zhengfu zenyang xina minzhong kangzheng" (Creating Consensus: How the Grassroots State Absorbs Popular Unrest in China), unpublished manuscript, 2012, 10–13.

9. Perry, "Popular Protest in China," 11–13; Zhang and Lee, "Zhizao tongyi," 24.

10. Victor Turner, *The Forest of Symbols: Aspects of Ndembu Ritual* (Ithaca, NY: Cornell University Press, 1967), 93–99.

11. I thank David Strand for suggesting the relevance of the works by Turner and Harms.

12. Erik Harms, *Saigon's Edge: On the Margins of Ho Chi Minh City* (Minneapolis: University of Minnesota Press, 2010), 3.

13. Harms, *Saigon's Edge*, 4, 7, 224.

14. Mertha, *China's Water Warriors*, 5.

15. O'Brien and Li, *Rightful Resistance*, 123–24.

16. http://www.nybooks.com/articles/archives/2011/jan/13/china-famine-oslo/, accessed 1 November 2011.

17. http://www.nytimes.com/2011/11/11/business/global/government-policies-cool-china-real-estate-boom.html?nl=todaysheadlines&emc=tha25, accessed 11 November 2011.

18. http://www.nytimes.com/2011/08/16/world/asia/16dalian.html?emc=eta1; http://www.nytimes.com/2011/08/15/world/asia/15dalian.html?emc=eta1, accessed 22 August 2011; also see a list of successful bottom-up campaigns in Mertha, *China's Water Warriors*, 15.

19. http://www.nytimes.com/2011/08/16/world/asia/16dalian.html?emc=eta1, accessed 22 August 2011.

20. Charles Euchner, *Extraordinary Politics: How Protest and Dissent Are Changing American Democracy (Transforming American Politics)* (Boulder, CO: Westview, 1996).

~

Bibliography

Chinese Journals, Magazines, and Newspapers

Baokan wenzhai (Digest of Newspapers and Magazines)
Caijing shibao (Financial Times)
Caijing ribao (Financial Daily)
Falü yu shenghuo (Law and Life)
Fazhi ribao (Legal Daily)
Hong qi (Red Flag)
Huanqiu shibao (Global Times)
Jiefang ribao (Liberation Daily)
Licai zhoukan (Money Weekly)
Minzhu yu fazhi (Democracy and the Legal System)
Moerben ribao (The Chinese Melbourne Daily)
Nanfang zhoumo (Southern Weekend)
Renmin ribao (People's Daily)
Qingnian bao (Youth Daily)
Qingnian cankao (Elite Reference)
Qiu Shi (Seeking Truth)
Shanghai Daily
Shanghai shangbao (Shanghai Business News)
Wenhui bao (Wenhui Daily)
Xibeifeng (Northwest Wind)
Xinmin wanbao (Xinmin Evening News)
Xinmin zhoukan (Xinmin Weekly)
Yangzi wanbao (Yangzi Evening News)

Zhongguo jingji shibao (China Economic Times)
Zhongguo qingnian bao (China Youth Daily)
Zhongguo xinwen zhoukan (China News Week)

Selected Sources

Allison, Eric W., and Lauren Peters. *Historic Preservation and the Livable City*. Hoboken, NJ: Wiley, 2011.

Arkaraprasertkul, Non. "Towards Modern Urban Housing: Redefining Shanghai's Lilong." *Journal of Urbanism: International Research on Placemaking and Urban Sustainability* 2.1 (2009): 11–29.

Barmé, Geremie R. *In the Red: On Contemporary Chinese Culture*. New York: Columbia University Press, 1999.

Becker, Jasper. *Hungry Ghosts: Mao's Secret Famine*. New York: Henry Holt, 1998.

Benford, Robert D., and David A. Snow. "Framing Processes and Social Movements: An Overview and Assessment." *Annual Review of Sociology* 26 (2000): 611–39.

Brown, Kerry. *Struggling Giant: China in the 21st Century*. London: Anthem Press, 2007.

Burkitt, Laurie, and Loretta Chao. "Made in China: Fake Stores." *Wall Street Journal*, August 3, 2011: B1.

Cai, Yongshun. "China's Moderate Middle Class: The Case of Homeowners' Resistance." *Asian Survey* 45 (2005): 777–99.

———. "Civil Resistance and the Rule of Law in China: The Defense of Homeowners' Rights." In *Grassroots Political Reform in Contemporary China*, edited by Elizabeth J. Perry and Merle Goldman, 174–95. Cambridge, MA: Harvard University Press, 2007.

———. "Local Governments and the Suppression of Popular Resistance in China." *China Quarterly* 193 (2008): 24–42.

Calhoun, Craig. *Neither Gods nor Emperors: Students and the Struggle for Democracy in China*. Berkeley: University of California Press, 1994.

Cao Kangtai and Wang Xuejun, eds. *Xinfang taoli fudao duben* (Supplemental Reading to "Regulations on Petitioning"). Beijing: Zhongguo fazhi chubanshe, 2005.

Carpenter, Daniel. "The Petition as a Recruitment Device: Evidence from the Abolitionists' Congressional Campaign." Unpublished manuscript, http://people.hmdc.harvard.edu/~dcarpent/petition-recruit-20040112.pdf.

Chen, Feng. "Worker Leaders and Framing Factory-based Resistance." In *Popular Protest in China*, edited by Kevin J. O'Brien, 88–107. Cambridge, MA.: Harvard University Press, 2008.

Cui Zhuolan, ed. *Fangwu chaiqian weiquan zhinan* (Legal Guidelines in Rights Maintenance in Housing Demolition and Relocation). Changchun: Jilin renmin chubanshe, 2004.

Davies, David J. "Visible *Zhiqing*: The Visual Culture of Nostalgia among China's *Zhiqing* Generation." In *Re-Envisioning the Chinese Revolution: The Politicis and Poet-*

ics of Collective Memory in Reform China, edited by Ching Kwan Lee and Guobin Yang, 166–92. Stanford: Stanford University Press, 2007.

Davis, Deborah S. "From Welfare Benefit to Capitalized Asset: The Re-Commodification of Residential Space in Urban China." In Housing and Social Change, edited by Ray Forrest and James Lee, 183–96. London: Routledge, 2003.

———. "My Mother's House." In Unofficial China: Popular Culture and Thought in the People's Republic, edited by Perry Link, Richard Madsen, and Paul G. Pickowicz, 88–100. Boulder, CO: Westview Press, 1989.

Davis, Deborah S., and Hanlong Lu. "Property in Transition: Conflicts over Ownership in Post-Socialist Shanghai." European Journal of Sociology XLIV, 1 (2003): 77–99.

David, Deborah S., and Wang Feng. Creating Wealth and Poverty in Postsocialist China. Stanford: Stanford University Press, 2008.

Diao Jiecheng. Renmin xinfang shilue (A Brief History of People's Petitioning). Beijing: Beijing jingji xueyuan chubanshe, 1995.

Dikötter, Frank. Mao's Great Famine: The History of China's Most Devastating Catastrophe, 1958–1962. New York: Walker, 2010.

"Dongqian shi jin" (Demolition and relocation is gold). Licai zhoukan (Money Weekly), January 21, 2002.

Esherick, Joseph W., Paul G. Pickowicz, and Andrew G. Walder, eds. The Chinese Cultural Revolution as History. Stanford: Stanford University Press, 2006.

Euchner, Charles. Extraordinary Politics: How Protest and Dissent Are Changing American Democracy (Transforming American Politics). Boulder, CO: Westview, 1996.

Eyerman, Ron, and Andrew Jamison. Music and Social Movements: Mobilizing Traditions in the Twentieth Century. Cambridge: Cambridge University Press, 1998.

Falü chubanshe fagui zhongxin (The Center of Law and Regulations at the Law Press), ed. Fangwu chaiqian fagui zizhu (Self-help in Laws and Regulations on Housing Demolition and Relocation). Beijing: Falü chubanshe, 2004.

Fang Ke. Dangdai Beijing jiucheng gengxin, diaocha, yanjiu, tansuo (Contemporary Redevelopment in the Inner City of Beijing: Survey, Analysis, and Investigation). Beijing: Zhongguo jianzhu gongye chubanshe, 2000.

Fang, Qiang. "Hot Potatoes: Chinese Complaint Systems from Early Times to the Late Qing (1898)." Journal of Asian Studies 68.4 (November 2009): 1105–135.

Finnane, Antonia. "The Origins of Prejudice: The Malintegration of Subei in Late Imperial China." Comparative Studies in Society and History 35 (1993): 211–38.

Fletcher, Ian Christopher. "The Internationale" (review). Radical History Review 82 (2002): 187–90.

Folch, Dolors. "Els mars de Zheng He (The Seas of Zheng He)." In Els grans viatges de Zheng He, edited by Dolors Folch, 8–62. Barcelona: Angle Editorial, 2008.

French, Howard W. "Disappearing Shanghai." In China in 2008: A Year of Great Significance, edited by Kate Merkel-Hess, Kenneth L. Pomeranz, and Jeffrey N. Wasserstrom, 117–31. Lanham, MD: Rowman & Littlefield, 2009.

George, Rosemary Marangoly. *The Politics of Home: Postcolonial Relocations and Twentieth-Century Fiction*. New York: Cambridge University Press, 1996.

Girard, Greg. *Phantom Shanghai*. Toronto: Magenta Foundation, 2006.

Goldman, Merle. *From Comrade to Citizen: The Struggle for Political Rights in China*. Cambridge, MA: Harvard University Press, 2005.

Han, Chunping, and Martin King Whyte. "The Social Contours of Distributive Injustice Feelings in Contemporary China." In *Creating Wealth and Poverty in Postsocialist China*, edited by Deborah S. Davis and Wang Feng, 193–212. Stanford: Stanford University Press, 2009.

Harms, Erik. *Saigon's Edge: On the Margins of Ho Chi Minh City*. Minneapolis: University of Minnesota Press, 2010.

Harvey, David. *Paris, Capital of Modernity*. New York: Routledge, 2003.

He Xuesheng. *Shufa wuqiannian* (Five Thousand Years of Chinese Calligraphy). Changchun: Shidai wenyi chubanshe, 2007.

Herman, Judith Lewis. *Trauma and Recovery*. New York: Basic Books, 1997.

Herzfeld, Michael. *Cultural Intimacy: Social Poetics in the Nation-State*. New York: Routledge, 2005.

———. *Evicted from Eternity: The Reconstructing of Modern Rome*. Chicago: University Chicago Press, 2009.

Hill, Anita. *Reimagining Equality: Stories of Gender, Race, and Finding Home*. Boston: Beacon, 2011.

Honig, Emily. "Invisible Inequalities: The Status of Subei People in Contemporary Shanghai." *China Quarterly* 122 (1990): 273–92.

———. "Pride and Prejudice: Subei People in Contemporary Shanghai." In *Unofficial China: Popular Culture and Thought in the People's Republic*, edited by Perry Link, Richard Madsen, and Paul G. Pickowicz, 138–55. Boulder, CO: Westview, 1989.

Jianshe bu zhengce yanjiu zhongxin (The Center for Policy Research at the Ministry of Construction), ed., *Zuixin chengshi fangwu chaiqian zhinan* (Newest Guidelines on Urban Housing Demolition and Relocation). Beijing: Zhongguo jianzhu gongye chubanshe, 2004).

Johnson, Ian. *Wild Grass: Three Portraits of Change in Modern China*. New York: Vintage Books, 2004.

Jordan, Donald A. *China's Trial by Fire: The Shanghai War of 1932*. Ann Arbor: University of Michigan Press, 2001.

Kang Zhengguo. *Confessions: An Innocent Life in Communist China*. Translated by Susan Wilf. New York: W. W. Norton, 2007.

Kinkley, Jeffrey C. *Corruption and Realism in Late Socialist China: The Return of the Political Novel*. Stanford: Stanford University Press, 2007.

Kraus, Richard Curt. *Brushes with Power: Modern Politics and the Chinese Art of Calligraphy*. Berkeley: University of California Press, 1991.

Koolhaas, Rem, and Bruce Mau. *S, M, L, XL*. New York: The Monacelli Press, 1998.

Lee, Ching Kwan. "What Was Socialism to Chinese Workers? Collective Memories and Labor Politics in an Age of Reform." In *Re-Envisioning the Chinese Revolution:*

The Politicis and Poetics of Collective Memory in Reform China, edited by Ching Kwan Lee and Guobin Yang, 141–65. Stanford: Stanford University Press, 2007.

Link, Perry. *An Anatomy of Chinese: Rhythm, Metaphor, Politics*. Cambridge, MA: Harvard University Press, 2012.

Lipman, Jonathan N., and Stevan Harrell. *Violence in China: Essays in Culture and Counterculture*. Albany: State University of New York Press, 1990.

Liu Tao. *Zhongguo shufa* (Chinese Calligraphy). Shenzhen: Haitian chubanshe, 2006.

Lu, Hanchao. *Beyond the Neon Lights: Everyday Shanghai in the Early Twentieth Century*. Berkeley: University of California Press, 1999.

———. "Creating Urban Outcasts: Shantytowns in Shanghai, 1920–1950." *Journal of Urban History* 21 (1995): 563–96.

———. "'The Seventy-two Tenants': Residence and Commerce in Shanghai's *Shikumen* Houses, 1872–1951." In *Inventing Nanjing Road: Commercial Culture in Shanghai, 1900–1945*, edited by Sherman Cochran, 134–47. Ithaca, NY: Cornell University Press, 1999.

Lu Sheng. "Zhou Zhengyi zhimi, heshi neng jiedi?" ("When Will the Zhou Zhengyi Puzzle Be Solved?"). *Minzhu yu fazhi* (Democracy and the Legal System), June 17, 2003: 13.

Luo Xiaowei, Sha Yongjie, Qian Zhonghao, Zhang Xiaochun, and Lin Weihang, eds. *Shanghai Xintiandi: jiuqu gaizao de jianzhu lishi, renwen lishi yu kaifa moshi de yanjiu* (Shanghai Xintiandi: A Study of Architectural and Human History and Developmental Models in Urban Renewal). Nanjing: Dongnan daxue chubanshe, 2002.

Ma Guangzhong, ed. *Zhongguo duilian daguan* (An Overview of Chinese Antithetical Couplets). Shenzhen: Haitain chubanshe, 2006.

Maier, Charles. "A Surfeit of Memory? Reflections on History, Melancholy, and Denial." *History & Memory* 5.2 (1993): 136–52.

Manion, Melanie. *Corruption by Design: Building Clean Government in Mainland China and Hong Kong*. Cambridge, MA: Harvard University Press, 2004.

Merkel-Hess, Kate, Kenneth L. Pomeranz, and Jeffrey N. Wasserstrom, eds. *China in 2008: A Year of Great Significance*. Lanham, MD: Rowman & Littlefield, 2009.

Mertha, Andrew C. *China's Water Warriors: Citizen Action and Policy Change*. Ithaca, NY: Cornell University Press, 2008.

Michael, Franz. *China Through the Ages: History of a Civilization*. Boulder, CO: Westview, 1986.

O'Brien, Kevin J., and Lianjiang Li. *Rightful Resistance in Rural China*. New York: Cambridge University Press, 2006.

O'Connor, Thomas H. *Building a New Boston: Politics and Urban Renewal, 1950–1970*. Boston: Northeastern University Press, 1993.

Oi, Jean C., and Andrew G. Walder. *Property Rights and Economic Reform in China*. Stanford: Stanford University Press, 1999.

Ouyang Yifei. *Shanghai shoufu: Zhou Zhengyi wenti diaocha* (An Investigation of Zhou Zhengyi: The Richest Person in Shanghai). Urumqi: Xinjiang renmin chubanshe, 2004.

Pei, Minxin. "Citizens v. Mandarins: Administrative Litigation in China," *China Quarterly* 152 (1997): 832–62.

———. "Rights and Resistance: The Changing Contexts of the Dissident Movement." In *Chinese Society: Change, Conflict, and Resistance*, edited by Elizabeth J. Perry and Mark Selden, 31–56. New York: Routledge, 2010.

Perry, Elizabeth J. *Anyuan: Mining China's Revolutionary Tradition*. Berkeley: University of California Press, 2012.

———. *Challenging the Mandate of Heaven: Social Protest and State Power in China*. Armonk, NY: M. E. Sharpe, 2002.

———. *Patrolling the Revolution: Worker Militias, Citizenship, and the Modern Chinese State*. Lanham, MD: Rowman & Littlefield, 2005.

———. "Popular Protest in China: Playing by the Rules." In *China Today, China Tomorrow: Domestic Politics, Economy, and Society*, edited by Joseph Fewsmith, 11–28. Lanham, MD: Rowman & Littlefield, 2010.

———. "'To Rebel is Justified': Cultural Revolution Influences on Contemporary Chinese Protest." In *The Chinese Cultural Revolution Reconsidered: Beyond Purge and Holocaust*, edited by Kam-yee Law, 262–81. New York: Palgrave Press, 2003.

Porteous, J. Douglas, and Sandra E. Smith. *Domicide: The Global Destruction of Home*. Montreal: McGill-Queen's University Press, 2001.

Richards, Keith. *Life*. New York: Little, Brown, 2010.

Scott, James C. *The Art of Not Being Governed: An Anarchist History of Upland Southeast Asia*. New Haven, CT: Yale University, 2009.

Scribner, Charity. *Requiem for Communism*. Cambridge, MA: MIT Press, 2003.

"Seeking Gao Zhisheng." *Wall Street Journal*, January 11, 2011.

Sewell, Jr., William H. "Space in Contentious Politics." In *Silence and Voice in the Study of Contentious Politics*, edited by Ronald R. Aminzade, Jack A. Goldstone, Doug McAdam, Elizabeth J. Perry, William H. Sewell Jr., Sidney Tarrow, and Charles Tilly, 51–88. New York: Cambridge University Press, 2001.

Shanghai gaige kaifang ershi nian bianjibu (Two Decades of Opening and Reform in Shanghai Editorial Committee), ed. *Shanghai gaige kaifang ershi nian: chengjian juan* (Two Decades of Opening and Reform in Shanghai: City and Construction). Shanghai: Shanghai renmin chubanshe, 1998.

Shanghai shi fangwu tudi ziyuan guanliju (Shanghai Municipal Housing and Land Resource Management Bureau), ed. *Shanghai shi youxiu lishi jianzhu baohu falü fagui wenjian huibian* (A Collection of Laws and Documents on the Preservation of Excellent Historic Architecture in Shanghai). Shanghai: fangwu tudi ziyuan guanliju, 2005 (internal document).

Shanghai zhengda yanjiusuo (Research Institute of Shanghai Zhengda), ed. *Shanghai ren* (Shanghai People). Shanghai: Xuelin chubanshe, 2002.

Shao, Qin. "A Community of the Dispersed: The Culture of Neighborhood Stock Markets in Contemporary Shanghai." *Chinese Historical Review* 14.2 (Fall, 2007): 212–39.

———. *Culturing Modernity: The Nantong Model, 1890–1930*. Stanford: Stanford University Press, 2004.

———. "Tempest over Teapots: The Vilification of Teahouse Culture in Early Republican China." *Journal of Asian Studies* 57 (1998): 1009–41.

———. "Waving the Red Flag: Cultural Memory and Grassroots Protest in Housing Disputes in Shanghai." *Modern Chinese Literature and Culture* 22.1 (Spring, 2010): 197–232.

———. "Xi 'Minben': dui xian Qin zhi xi Han 'minben' sixiang de kaocha" ("Minben": An Investigation of the Changing Statecraft from the pre-Qin to Western Han Periods). *Lishi yanjiu* (Historical Study) 6 (1985): 3–16.

Shen Ting. *Shen Ting chuanqi: tiaozhan Shanghai bang* (The Story of Shen Ting: Challenging the Shanghai Clique). Unpublished manuscript, 2007.

Shen Ting. *Shui yinbao Zhou Zhengyi an: Shen Ting, Zheng Enchong tiaozhan Shanghai bang shiji* (Who Exposed Zhou Zhengyi? A True Record of Shen Ting and Zheng Enchong's Challenge to the Shanghai Clique). Hong Kong: Kaifang zazhi chubanshe, 2007.

Sheridan, Michael. "Tycoon's Fall Gives Hope to China's Poor." *Sunday Times* (London), June 6, 2004.

Shi Chang. "Shanghai youge Linken fang" ("Shanghai Has a Lincoln Lane") *Moerben ribao* (The Chinese Melbourne Daily), 3 July 2003.

Spence, Jonathan D. *The Search for Modern China*. New York: W. W. Norton, 1999.

Sun, Yan. *Corruption and Market in Contemporary China*. Ithaca, NY: Cornell University Press, 2004.

Tarrow, Sidney. *Power in Movement: Social Movements and Contentious Politics*. New York: Cambridge University Press, 1998.

Tilly, Charles. *The Contentious French*. Cambridge, MA.: Belknap Press of Harvard University Press, 1986.

Turner, Victor. *The Forest of Symbols: Aspects of Ndembu Ritual*. Ithaca, NY: Cornell University Press, 1967.

Vine, David. "Dying of Sorrow: Expulsion, Empire, and the People of Diego Garcia." In *The War Machine and Global Health: A Critical Medical Anthropological Examination of the Human Costs of Armed Conflict and the International Violence Industry*, edited by Merrill Singer and G. Derrick Hodge, 179–207. Plymouth, UK: AltaMira Press, 2010.

———. *Island of Shame: The Secret History of the US Military Base on Diego Garcia*. Princeton, NJ: Princeton University Press, 2009.

Wang Cailiang. *Fangwu chaiqian jiufen jiaodian shiyi* (Guide to Solving Disputes over Urban Housing Demolition and Relocation). Beijing: Falü chubanshe, 2004.

———. *Fangwu chaiqian shiwu* (Practical Matters Regarding Housing Demolition and Relocation). Beijing: Falü chubanshe, 2002.

Wang, Fei-Ling. *Organizing through Division and Exclusion: China's Hukou System*. Stanford: Stanford University Press, 2005.

Wang Jun: *Beijing Record: A Physical and Political History of Planning Modern Beijing*. Singapore: World Scientific Publishing, 2011.

Wasserstrom, Jeffrey N. *Global Shanghai, 1850–2010: A History of Fragments*. New York: Routledge, 2009.

Weinstein, Deena. "Rock Protest Songs: So Many and So Few." In *The Resisting Muse: Popular Music and Social Protest*, edited by Ian Peddie, 3–15. Aldershot, UK: Ashgate, 2006.

Whyte, Martin K. *Small Groups and Political Rituals in China*. Berkeley: University of California Press, 1974.

Wu, Duo, and Taibin Li. "The Present Situation and Prospective Development of the Shanghai Urban Community." In *The New Chinese City: Globalization and Market Reform*, edited by John R. Logan, 22–36. Oxford, UK: Blackwell, 2002.

Wu, Fulong. "Real Estate Development and the Transformation of Urban Space in China's Transitional Economy, with Special Reference to Shanghai." In *The New Chinese City: Globalization and Market Reform*, edited by John R. Logan, 153–66. Oxford, UK: Blackwell, 2002.

Wu Jiang. *Shanghai bainian jianzhu shi (1840–1949)* (A Hundred Years of Shanghai's Architectural History, 1840–1949). Shanghai: Tongji daxue chubanshe, 1997.

Xie, Zhuoyan. "Petition and Judicial Integrity." *Journal of Politics and Law* 2.1 (March 2009): 24–30.

Zang, Xiaowei, "Urban Housing Reform in China." In *China in the Reform Era*, edited by Xiaowei Zang, 53–80. Commack, NY: Nova Science Publishers, 1999.

Zhang Letian. *Gaobie lixiang: Renmin gongshe zhidu yanjiu*. (Farewell to an Ideal: A Study of the People's Commune System). Shanghai: Shanghai renmin chubanshe, 2005.

Zhang, Li. "Forced from Home: Property Rights, Civic Activism, and the Politics of Relocation in China." *Urban Anthropology* 33 (2004): 247–81.

———. *In Search of Paradise: Middle-class Living in a Chinese Metropolis*. Ithaca, NY: Cornell University Press, 2010.

Zhang, Xing Quan. "Chinese Housing Policy 1949–1978: The Development of a Welfare System." *Planning Perspectives* 12 (1997): 433–55.

Zhang Yong Hong and Ching Kwan Lee, "Zhizao tongyi: jiceng zhengfu zenyang xina minzhong kangzheng" (Creating Consensus: How the Grassroots State Absorbs Popular Unrest in China). Unpublished manuscript, 2012.

Zhongguo fazhi chubanshe (Law Press of China), ed. *Chaiqian buchang shiyong falü shouce* (Compensation in Demolition and Relocation: A Practical Legal Handbook). Beijing: Zhongguo fazhi chubanshe, 2007.

———. "*Xinfang tiaoli*" *yibentong* (Comprehensive Reading of "Regulations on Petitioning"). Beijing: Zhongguo fazhi chubanshe, 2005.

Zhou, Min, and John R. Logan. "Market Transition and the Commodification of Housing in Urban China." In *The New Chinese City: Globalization and Market Reform*, edited by John R. Logan, 137–52. Oxford, UK: Blackwell, 2002.

Zong Fengming. *Zhao Ziyang ruanjin zhongde tanhua* (Zhao Ziyang: Captive Conversations). Hong Kong: Kaifang chubanshe, 2007.

Index

Aciman, Andre, 25
"adaptive re-use," 100, 139. *See also*
    Italian hill towns; Siena
Administration Litigation Law (ALL),
    17
Ai Weiwei, 16
alleyway housing, 2, 7–8, 92–95, 100–
    103, 130, 133, 146, 150–51, 231,
    246, 251, 262–65. *See also shikumen*
American Navel Rescue Headquarters,
    240
Anhui Province, 195, 200, 236
annual "two meetings," 39–40, 43,
    70, 73, 159, 246. *See also* National
    People's Congress; People's Political
    Consultative Conference
"anti-corruption" campaign, 15–16, 20
anti-Document 305 campaign, 214–16,
    224
Anti-Japanese War, 168, 176
Anti-Rightist movement, 142n17
Arab Spring, 275–76

Baijing Ltd. (of Hong Kong). *See* Shui
    On Land Ltd

Bank of China, 147
barrack-room lawyer, 190, 205, 208,
    210–12, 225
Beijing Olympics Games (2008), 25–26,
    43, 177
Beijing Public Security Bureau, 177
Beijing South Railway Station, 43
Beijing University, 79–80, 94
"betwixt and between," 277–79
"black jails," 46. *See also* detention
Bleak House, vii, 39, 91, 145, 189, 229
"blue sky" official, 19–21, 44, 61, 85,
    258
Bo Xilai, 15, 279
Bureau of National Land Resources, 11,
    159

Cai Yutian, 96
Carnegie Endowment for International
    Peace, 15
Carpenter, Daniel, 21, 48
Chagossians of Diego Garcia, 26–27, 83
chaiqian. See demolition and relocation
Changsha, 79
chanquan. See property ownership rights

Charter 08, 217, 227n23
Chavez Ravine, Los Angeles, 26
Chen Duxiu, 94
Chen Guangcheng, 19, 46
Chen Liangyu, 15, 70, 145–47, 152,
    259, 279
Chengdu, 16
Chiang Kai-shek, 94, 131, 134, 220. See
    also Guomindang
China Central Television (CCTV), 49,
    230, 255–60, 258, 263; Horizon Link
    (Shikong lianxian), 258; Li Juan, 258;
    Oriental Horizon (Dongfang shikong),
    255–60; 60 Minutes of China, 255
China's Ministry of Health, 79
Chinese Communist Party (CCP):
    birthday of, 43, 49; confiscation of
    property, 29, 55–56, 92, 105–7, 131–
    32, 138; corruption, 15–16, 116, 147;
    First Congress, 94–95, 101, 109–10,
    127, 241; forced labor, 76; Hong qi
    (Red Flag), 164–65; housing crisis,
    5–7; identity crisis, 165; petition
    system under Mao, 19–20; small
    study groups, 160–168; Seventeenth
    National Congress, 70, 78, 217
Chinese Muslim, 28, 101, 105, 140. See
    also Hui ethnic group
Chinese New Year, 65, 111, 115, 123,
    166, 270
Chinese stock market, 66–67, 77,
    88n32, 147; gumin (people of the
    stock market), 66
"Chujin jingshe." See "Chujin's Fine
    Home"
"Chujin's Fine Home," 101–3, 108
City Temple, 23, 52, 63
Civil Rights Movement, 280
Clinton, Bill, 63
CNN, 96
Cohen, Roger, 45
Cold War, 26, 163
Communist Youth League, 95

"comprador bourgeois," 101
Confucian statecraft, 19, 35–36n79
"Consultation on the Demolition and
    Relocation of Private Homes," 110
corruption, 15–16, 116, 147; in
    demolition and relocation, 16,
    96–99, 107–8, 133–34, 146–50,
    239, 246, 252–54, 259, 263–65; in
    East Eight Lots, 146–50; in housing
    reform, 56, 119, 221, 255; in Lincoln
    Lane, 239, 246, 252–54, 259,
    263–65; in urban renewal, 12–16,
    133–34, 146–56. See also Chen
    Liangyu; demolition and relocation;
    domicide; eviction; housing reform;
    Zhou Zhengyi
couplet and calligraphy, 166–68, 167
"cowsheds" (niupeng), 131
Cultural Revolution: "big character
    posters," 55–56; confiscation of
    property, 29, 92, 105–7, 131–32,
    138; forced labor, 76; Hong qi (Red
    Flag) 164–66; Red Guards, 50, 106–
    7, 116, 131–32, 241; "revolutionary
    rebels," 131; small study group,
    160–68

Dai Lixiang, 236–72, 277, 282; Cultural
    Revolution, 238; demolition and
    relocation, 238–70; employment,
    237–38; family, 236–39; housing,
    236–39; propaganda, 242–69; youth,
    236–37. See also Lincoln Lane
dajia tan fangchan. See "Everyone Talks
    about Real Estate"
Dalian, 280
danwei. See work unit
Dapuqiao, 191
Davis, Deborah, 9
demolition and relocation: corruption
    in, 16, 96–99, 107–8, 133–34,
    146–50, 239, 246, 252–54, 259,
    263–65; courts' involvement in, 5,

13–14, 18, 118, 197, 258, 268; of
East Eight Lots, 151, 171–81; impact
on social instability, 4–5, 26–27,
30–31; of Lincoln Lane, 238–70; of
other neighborhoods, 52–56; permit
for, xiii, 13, 118–19, 152, 154, 214,
221, 239, 251; police involvement
in, 56, 62, 73, 153, 175, 248–49; in
Taipingqiao area, 110–15, 133–37;
violence in, 2, 11, 16, 48, 92, 111,
137, 157, 162, 212, 248–49; and
wholesale destruction, 12, 262, 265.
See also demolition squad; detention;
domicide; East Eight Lots; housing
policy and regulation; Lincoln Lane;
urban renewal; Zhou Youlan
"Demolition and Relocation Is Gold,"
151, 207
demolition squad: arson by, 11, 135;
evictions by, 25, 64, 114, 119,
150–53, 175, 245, 249, 252, 257,
268; harassment by, 55, 111, 135,
171, 248, 260; kidnapping by, 135;
as "safety guards," 175, 179; violence
by, 48, 92, 111, 137, 157, 162, 212.
See also domicide; eviction
Deng Xiaoping, 6, 207, 237
"Detailed Regulations on Shanghai City
Housing Demolition and Relocation
Management," 10
detention, xi, 16, 19, 39, 46, 147,
282; "black jails," 46; of Shi Lin,
222–23; of Zhou Youlan, 39–40,
59, 63, 70, 73–75, 75, 84, 147. *See
also* domicide; grassroots protest;
petitioners; petitioning; protesters
Dickens, Charles, vii, 39, 91, 145, 189,
229
Ding Ling, 94
dingzi hu. See nail households
district government (Shanghai), xii,
xiii, 11, 13, 17, 55, 95–96, 98–99,
101, 109, 111, 114, 118, 121, 126,

128–29, *137*, 138, 148, 150, 154,
156–57, 166, *167*, 171–75, 182, 199,
212, 230–31, 251–52, 254, 260, *264*,
265–66, 269, 277
District Housing and Land Management
Bureau (Shanghai), 13. *See also*
district housing bureau
district housing bureau (Shanghai), xiii,
13, 14, 55, 96, 99, 108, 110–11, 129,
146, 151–52, 154–56, 159, 171, 174–
75, 180, 197, 201, 203, 208, 211–12,
231–33, 239, 267
domicide, 4, 69, 119, 185, 214, 276,
281; causes of, 5, 10, 11–12, 24–25,
28; definition of, xviii, 2, 4–5,
24–25; in Diego Garcia, 26–27;
in East Eight Lots, 153, 168, 178,
182; and economic interest, 25–28;
and emotional damage, 27–28, 68,
83–84; everyday type of, 24–26;
extreme type of, 24–26; as global
phenomenon, 28; impact of, 24,
27–28; and lawsuits, 18; in Lincoln
Lane, 230, 249, 257, 260, 269, 270;
and memory, 25–26; as "moral
evil," 28; and petitioners, 27–28,
86, 83–84; process of, 158; reaction
to, 26–28; resistance to, 18, 29, 30,
164, 230, 249, 268; solutions to, 28;
by state policy, 10, 159, 214, 216;
in Taipingqiao are, 92, 112, 129,
135–38; threat of, 55–56, 135, 151,
216, 249, 276; two types of, 24–26;
victims of, 25–28; and Zhou Youlan,
55–56, 64, 83. *See also* demolition
squad; eviction; East Eight Lots;
Lincoln Lane; Zhu Guangze
dongba kuai. See East Eight Lots
Duolun Road, 230, 253

East Eight Lots, 146–85; corruption,
146–50; couplet and calligraphy, 166–
68, *167*; demolition and relocation,

149–51; demolition squad, 157, 162; Document 347, 146–49; "green land," 159–60, 184; land use rights, 147–48, 154, 156; Legal Study Forum, 160–62; Mr. C, 157–58, 160, 166–81, 183–84; negotiations, 156–59; return policy, 148–49, 152–58; Shen Ting, 151–56, 182

economic reform, 22, 64, 122, 153, 170, 195, 206; as cause of economic inequality, 20; impact on personal and political freedom, 20; impact on state-owned enterprises, 64, 170; as cause of violence, 10. *See also* housing reform; market reform; post-Mao reform; urban renewal

ecosystem, 27

Edelstein, Barbara, 185

el-Qaddafi, Muammar, 45, 275

energy and resource nationalism, 25

European Court of Human Rights, 27

European Union, 279

"Everyone Talks About Real Estate," 206

Evicted from Eternity, 4

eviction, 17, 20–21, 25, 27, 29, 83, 211, 268; causes of, 214–16; compensation for, 67–68; courts' defense of, 117–18; and death, 184; in East Eight Lots, 145, 151–53, 157, 159, 160, 166–67, 174–79, 180, 182, 184; of the He family, 92, 101, 112–15, 117–19, 120, 123–24, 127–28; and kidnapping, 135; in Lincoln Lane, 249, 257, 260, 270; notice of, 56, 112, 117, 174, 257, 270; and petitioners, 48, 81; resistance to, 26, 256; site of, 30, 175–79; as cause of suicide, 2, 26–27, 42, 92, 136, 268; of Zhou Youlan, 56–58, 64, 66–68, 76, 81, 84; of the Zhu family, 135–36, *137*. *See also* demolition squad; domicide

Feinberg, Kenneth, 21

Fenba. See "nightsoil bully"

First Congress (CCP), 94–95, 101, 109–10, 127

Forbes conference (2005), 129

foreign dignitaries' visits, 63

Fortune 500, 93

Freedland, Jonathan, 21

French Concession, 93, 192

Fudan University, 251

Furong zhen. See Hibiscus Town

Fuxing Construction Development Company, 96–99, 114

Fuyang, Anhui Province, 200

GDP (gross domestic product), 12, 15, 20, 130

gentrification, 4, 8, 23, 28, 92, 99, 101, 139–40, 148–49, 267

George, Rosemary Marangoly, 3

Georgetown, Washington, DC, 95

global context: domicide in, xviii, 28; economic change and market in, 5, 66; historic preservation in, 22; housing issue in, 3–4, 275–76; and local protest, 29; propaganda campaign in, 29, 230

GMD. *See* Guomindang

grassroots protest, 16–17, 21–22, 146, 278–80; in Beijing, 43–44, 190, 213; collective resistance, 145; against domicide, 12, 276, 281; about environment, 24, 280–81; in Hong Kong, 190, 213, 217; for just compensation, 17, 221–22, *222*, 276–77; in Shanghai, 62, 64, 154, 184, 189–90, 213; signature drive, 17, 49, 215–16; signs of, 217–18, *218*, *247*, 247, *248*; slogans, 73, 106, 149, 171, 176–77; on street, 60, 62, 64, 190, 211, 218, 280–81. *See also* petitioners; petitioning; protesters

Great Leap Forward, 164, 191, 236, 240

"green land," 159–60, 184
"grief syndrome," 27
Guan Hanqing, 85. *See also Injustice to Dou E*
Guanjing laoren (Well-Watching Old Gentleman), 101
Guomindang (GMD, Nationalist Party), 6, 50, 131–32, 141. *See also* Chiang Kai-shek; Zhou Hongtao

Ha Shaofu, 101–4, *104*
Han Zheng, 95, 242
Hangzhou Bay, 195
"harmonious society," 43, 74, 129, 138, 279
Harms, Erik, 278
Harvey, David, 30
Havel, Vaclav, vii
He Chujin, 101–5, *104*
He Liming, 105–7, 112–14, 122–24
He Shen, 85
He Shuhong, *104*, 104–7
He Yidong, 101, 110–28, 277, 282; careers, 116–17; childhood, 115–16; Chinese Muslim, 28, 101, 105, 140; demolition and relocation, 110–15; family, 101–8; home, 101–2, *103*, 107–11, 116, 119–20; 330 Huangpi Nan Road, 101, 110, 116; legal struggles, 117–20, 125, 127–28; media, 120–21, 123–24; petitioning, 124–26; psychological price mark, 127
Hebei Province, 220
Herman, Judith, 84
Herzfeld, Michael, 4, 168
Hibiscus Town (*Furong zhen*), 176
Hill, Anita, 3
historic preservation, 17, 22–24, 37n100; citizens' participation in, 23–24, 29, 235, 250; Document 70, 234–35, 239, 242, 250–52; Document 107, 252–54, 257, 260–61, 265–68; Document 662,

266, 268; hotline for, 250, 261; in Lincoln Lane, 230, 234–35, 240–42, 250–51, 260–67; politics and economics of, 23, 29, 267; as means of resisting demolition, 23; in Xintiandi, 94–95, 100–101, 139–40. *See also* Koolhaas, Rem; Ruan Yisan
Ho Chi Minh City, 278
home: in Cultural Revolution, 92, 106–8, 131, 238; meaning of, 3–4, 25–27; in post-Mao reform, 92, 131, 152. *See also* domicide; eviction
home lost, 4, 25–27; in East Eight Lots, 153, 168, 178, 182; in Lincoln Lane, 230, 249, 257, 260, 269, 270; in Taipingqiao area, 92, 112; 129, 135–38; Zhou Youlan, 55–56, 64, 83. *See also* domicide; eviction
Hong Kong, 29, 109, 121, 127, 147, 166, 236–37, 241; Chinese protesters in, 127, 190, 213, 217; Shen Ting of, 141, 151, 153, 155, 182; Vincent Lo and Shui On company in, 95–99, 139, 141
Hong qi (Red Flag), 164–65, 241
Hongkou District, *vi*, 229, 231–35, 239–40, 252–54, 257–68, 282
Horizon Link (*Shikong lianxian*). *See* China Central Television
household registration system (*hukou*), 143n23, 173, 195
housing issues: in 2008 financial crisis, 3; in global economy, 3–4; in global politics, 3, 275–76; as cause of social unrest, 5, 190, 211, 218, 222, 275
housing policy and regulation, 99, 118–19, 190, 205–8, 209, 211; "Detailed Regulations on Shanghai City Housing Demolition and Relocation Management" (*see* Document 111); Document 68, 148–49, 154–58, 171–73; Document 70, 234–35, 239, 242, 250–52; Document 107, 252–54,

257, 260–61, 265–68; Document 111, 10–11, 149, 158–59; Document 141, 232, 239; Document 305, 9–11, 13–14, 18, 49, 159, 214–16, 278–79; Document 347, 146–49; Document 590, 11; Document 662, 266, 268; "Regulations on Urban Housing Demolition and Relocation" (1991 Regulation), 9–10

housing reform, 6–8, 33n32, 166, 169, 203, 206, 209, 212, 213, 220; books on, 207, 255; commodification of housing, 8–9; corruption, 50, 56, 119, 220–21, 255; government intervention, 159, 203, 215; economic impact of, 4, 166, 170, 190, 206; other impact of, 4–5, 159, 206, 215; in market economy, 1, 4, 6; regulations of, 9–11, 13–14, 18, 49, 99, 118–19, 159, 190, 206, 211, 214–16, 278–79; in Shanghai, 6. 10–11, 148–49, 154–59, 171–73, 234–35, 239, 242, 250–52. *See also* urban renewal (*jiuqu gaizao*)

Hu Jintao, 155, 221, 279

Huai River, 190

Huaihai Zhong Road, 91, 93, 125, 130

Huang Ju, 234

330 Huangpi Nan Road, 101, 110, 116

Huangpu River, 12, 191–92

Hui ethnic group, 101. *See also* Chinese Muslim

hukou. See household registration system

Human Rights Day (2008), 217

"A Humble Room Is Worth Thousands of (pieces of) Gold," 207

Hundred Days Reform, 168

"Image projects," 25

Industrial Revolution, 2

Injustice to Dou E, 85. *See also* Guan Hanqing

Institute of Rural Development at the Chinese Academy of Social Sciences (CASS), 82, 85–87

International Settlement, 192

"The Internationale," 21, 73, 145, 160, 162–64, 176, 179

Internet, 8, 30, 206, 216, 245, 266, 269, 275; bloggers, 79–80, 82, 164, 281; blogosphere, 16, 79–80, 213, 266; censorship, 30, 258; email, 29, 270; microblogging, 16; netizens, 47

Israeli-Palestinian conflict, 3

Italian hill towns, 100, 139. *See also* "adaptive re-use"; Siena

Jasmine Revolution in Tunisia, 275

Jasmine song in China, 275

Jiahe International Building, 268

Jiang Zemin, 15, 57, 147, 241, 247

Jiangbei, 190–95, 200

Jiangsu Province, 79, 190, 261

Jiangxi Province, 255

Jifang. See group petitioning

Jilin, 81

Jing'an District, vi, 146–51, 174

Jingdezhen, 255

jingles, 84–85

jingshenbing. See mental health issue

Jinshan Petrochemical Factory, 195

Jiujingzhuang shelter, 50

jiuqu gaizao. See urban renewal

Kang Youwei, 168

kidnapping (*shizhong*), 45–46, 74, 77, 92, 129, 135–37

Koolhaas, Rem, 1, 23, 140, 267; generic city, 1

Kristof, Nicholas D., 177

Kung, H. H. (Kong Xiangxi), 131

land ownership rights, 202, 225

land policy and regulation, 206

land use rights: abuse of, 11–12, 16; authority over, 11, 16; East Eight Lots, 147–48, 154, 156; Lincoln Lane, 246; Shi Lin, 199, 202, 204, 223, 225; Taipingqiao area, xi, 97, 126, 138

Landton Ltd. of Hong Kong. *See* Shui On Land Ltd. *lao shangfang jingshenbing. See* long-term petitioners' mental illness

Law on Mental Health, 80

lawsuit, 18, 112, 117–19, 121, 125, 150; by residents in Lincoln Lane, 239–40, 265, 268, 270; by Mr. C, 171; by Shen Ting, 151–56, 169, 171; by Shi Lin, 211

lawyers, 17, 29, 76, 127, 145, 152, 218, 255–59, 265; as activists, 18–19, 46, 79, 153, 216, 266; barrack-room, 189, 190, 208, 210, 225; and the CCP, 18; in housing disputes, 29, 76, 145, 152, 153–55, 281; in petition process, 47, 76. *See also* Cheng Guangcheng; lawsuit; Wang Cailing; Zheng Enchong

Legal Study Forum, 160–64

legal system, 41, 69, 84, 85, 225

Li Juan. *See* China Central Television

Liberation Daily, 50

"liminal period," 277–78

Lin Biao, 152

Lin Weihang, 250–51

Lincoln, Abraham, 229, 241, 245, 247–48, 270

Lincoln Lane (Linken fang), 229–72; corruption, 239, 246, 252–54, 259, 263–65; Dai Lixiang, 236–72, 277, 282; demolition squad, 245, 248–49, 252, 256, 260, 268; Document 70, 234–35, 239, 242, 250–52; Document 107, 252–54, 257, 260–61, 265–68; Document 141, 232, 239; Document 662, 266, 268; historic preservation, 230, 234–35, 240–42, 250–51, 260–67; Japanese bombing of, 1932, 241–42, 262; land use rights, 246; lawsuit, 265–68; Metro Line 8 subway (M8 line), 230–35, 239, 246–48, 269–70; neighborhood, 229–31; psychological price mark, 270–72; scandal, 233–34

Liu Xiaobo, 217, 266, 279

Lo, Vincent (Luo Kangrui): Baijing Ltd., 98; clubhouse of, 120; "Code of Conduct & Business Ethics," 141; connections of, 96–101; on evicting residents, 114–15; honors of, 141; interviews by, 96, 129; as "King of Guanxi," 95; Landton Ltd., 96–98; as legal representative, 96, 98; as "Mr. Shanghai," 95; on residents' holdout, 129–30, 133, 140; in Shui On Group, 95. *See also* Shui On Land Ltd.; Taipingqiao project; Wood, Benjamin; Xintiandi

Longmen Cun (Dragon Village), 52

long-term petitioners' mental illness, 82–83, 85

Lu, Hanchao, 192–93, 241

Lu Hongyou, 131–32

Lu Xun Park (previously Hongkou), 229, 232, 253

Luo Kangrui. *See* Lo, Vincent

Luwan District, vi, 91, 93, 122, 133; Fuxing Construction Development Company, 96–99, 114; government, 95–98, 109–13, *113*, 118, 121, 126, 129, 138–39; Wuxin Real Estate Demolition and Relocation Company, 99, 110–11, 114–15, 132, 135

Maier, Charles, 22

mainland China, 134, 166, 217, 237

Mao Zedong, 94; Maoist cultural memory, 21; Maoist cultural remains, 24; Maoist cultural repertoires, 22, 29; Maoist cultural symbols, 22, 168, 278; Maoist era, 162; Maoist past, 276; Maoist practices and symbols, 160; Maoist values, 22; Maoist worker union, 278

Marais, Paris, 95

Market reform, 8, 224, 238

Massachusetts Institute of Technology, 99

master frames, 17

memory, vii, 2, 22, 29, 37n97, 173, 198, 245, 262; and amnesia, 5, 25, 26, 140; collective, 29, 37n96; cultural, 21–22; and domicide, 25–26; historical, 262; memoricide, 25–26

mental health issue, 79–85; China's Ministry of Health, 79

Mertha, Andrew, 278

Metro Line 8 subway (M8 line), 230–35, 239, 246–48, 269–70

middle class (China), 4, 93, 100, 105, 132, 231

"Miezi Lane," 241

minben. See Confucian statecraft

Ming dynasty, 29, 85, 104, 104. See also Zheng He

Ministry of Construction, 9, 72–73, 159, 257

Ministry of Railways, 15

Mme. Chiang, 131

Moerben ribao (Chinese Melbourne Daily), 245–46

moment of inertia, xvi, 85

Monti District of Rome, 4

Mr. C, 157–58, 160, 166–81, 183–84; childhood, 169; demolition squad, 171; eviction, 174–81; family, 169–70; home/apartment, 170; lawsuit, 171; negotiations, 170–71, 174; self-education, 173; settlement, 183–84; work unit, 169, 170–71

Mubarak, Hosni, 45, 275

Museum of the CCP's First Congress, 94–95, 101, 109, 127

nail household, 16–17, 21, 55–56, 130, 150, 157, 165, 181, 189, 201

Nanfang zhoumo (Southern Weekend), 120, 121, 123–24

Nanjing Road, 52, 62, 93, 146

Nanpu Bridge, 74

Nanshi District, vi, 52, 55, 88

Nanya Hotel, 74

National Day, October 1, 43, 58, 70, 72, 78

National Lawyers Association, 255

National People's Congress, 39, 43, 208, 214, 216. See also annual "two meetings"

nightmare: political, 43; of property deprivation, 29, 91–93, 101, 108, 116, 138, 140–41

nightsoil, 191

"nightsoil bully" (fenba), 191, 195, 197, 203

niupeng. See "cowsheds"

nongovernmental organization (NGO), 270, 278

Nong Kai Development Group, 147. See also Zhou Zhengyi

Obama, Barack, 21, 270

Occupy Wall Street, 275

Okinawa, 105–6

Olympic Games (Beijing), 25–26, 43, 177

opening and reform policy, 6–10

Opium War, 1

Oriental Horizon (Dongfang shikong). See China Central Television

Oriental Pearl Television Tower, 12
Owen, John M., 276

Pandora's Box, 69, 259
Paris Commune of 1871, 161
pedicab, 106, 191
Pei, Minxin, 18
People's Daily (*Renmin ribao*), 49
People's Liberation Army, 105, 241–42
People's Political Consultative
    Conference, 39, 43. See also annual
    "two meetings"
200 People's Square Boulevard,
    Shanghai ("Number 200"), 48–49,
    62, 71–73, 77
Perry, Elizabeth, 21–22, 276
petitions, 43, 46–47; "petition 101," 49;
    petition forms, xi, 61
petitioners: in Beijing, 41–44, 50, 80,
    217; community of, 20, 48–49,
    80, 86; "concentration camp" for,
    50; control of, 41, 44–45, 47, 50;
    death of, 46–47; diehard, 28, 42;
    evictees-turned, 27, 40, 51, 69–70;
    full-time, xv, 40, 59, 125; identity
    of, 278; long-term, 40; mental issue
    among, 79–81, 82–85; occupational,
    79; "professional," 48; punishment
    for, 20, 45–46, 48, 81, 128, 224;
    ritual for, 48; seasoned, 17, 49, 268;
    shelter for, 50; stars among, 49; Sun
    Dongdong and, 79–80; tactics of,
    42, 46, 49, 221–22; in Tiananmen
    Square, 44, 166; village of (*shangfang
    cun*), 43; Zhou Youlan as, 56–63, 67–
    78. See also detention; petitioning;
    protesters petitioning, 19–21, 40–50,
    59–61, 85–87; "abnormal," 44–45,
    50; and "black jails," 46; during
    events, 43–45, 50, 62, 217; as group
    (*jifang or qunfang*), 42–43, 50, 190,
    222; He Yidong, 124–26; in-person

(*shangfang*), 41, 59–61; by letter
    (*xinfang*), 19–21, 41, 57; log, 68;
    regulations on, 40–42, 86, 87nn1–2;
    specialists on, 40, 49; violence in ,
    45–46, 48. See also grassroots protest;
    petitioners; protesters
pipa, 50
policy entrepreneur, 17, 29, 190, 214,
    227n10, 278
post traumatic stress disorder (PTSD),
    27, 83–84
post–Cultural Revolution, 118
post-Mao reform, 255, 266, 272;
    economic opportunity, 115–16, 165,
    255, 266; media, 121
Property Law, 18, 215
property owner, 6, 95, 107–8
property ownership rights, 8, 108–10,
    115, 202, 207, 225, 231
protesters, 17, 164, 276; arrest of, 42;
    characteristics of, in China, 276–79;
    in China and elsewhere, 275–76;
    framing by, 17–24; in Hong Kong,
    127, 190, 213, 217; identity of, 278;
    and "The Internationale," 164;
    "language game" by, 21; of Occupy
    Wall Street, 275; and Property Law,
    215–16; residents-turned, 11–12,
    17–18, 21, 24, 152, 189, 217, 265,
    278; rights consciousness among,
    276; rule consciousness among, 173,
    276; strategies of, 17–24, 166; tent-
    city, 3; in Tiananmen Square, 1989,
    43, 63, 64. See also grassroots protest;
    petitioners; petitioning
provident fund, 9
psychological price mark: He Yidong,
    127; Lincoln Lane, 270–72; Zhou
    Youlan, 64–66, 68–70, 83–84;
    Zhu Guangze, 136–37. See also
    petitioners; petitioning
"public intellectuals," 261, 265

public security bureau–run mental institutions, 81
Pudong, 12, 55, 81, 149, 171, 180, 183–84, 195
Putin, Vladimir, 19, 275
Putuo District, vi, 210–11, 222, 223
Pyongyang, 105

Qian Yunhui, 47
Qing dynasty, 6, 85
qingtian. See "blue sky" official
qunfang. See petitioning

real estate development, 3, 8–9, 13–14, 93, 120, 146, 204, 218
"Recording Shanghai," 270
red flag: meaning of, 164–66; in pictures, *176, 178*; on roofs and windows, 21, 175, 179, 185, 230. *See also* nail household
Red Guards, 50, 106–7, 116, 131–32, 241
red-brick row houses, 299
reform era, 5, 16–17, 20–21, 93, 121–22, 134, 173, 190, 208
"Regulations on Petitioning," 41–47, 86–87
"Regulations on Urban Housing Demolition and Relocation," (1991 Regulations), 9–10
Renmin ribao, 49, 159, 165, 174, 177–79, 256
Republican Shanghai, 231, 236
Richards, Keith, 59
"rightful resistance," 21, 59, 159
"rights consciousness," 276
rights-protection (*weiquan*) lawyers, 18–19
Rihuigang, 261
Ruan Yisan: Foundation for the Protection of City Heritage, 263, 265; historic preservation, 261; interviews, 250, 258; National Research Center of Historic Cities,

261–67, *264*; Planning and Design Company, limited, 263, 265; "Preservation God," 261, *264*, 265; Zhouzhuang, 261. *See also* historic preservation; Tongji University
rule by man, 19–21
rule of law, 17, 22n14, 96

sagren (profound sorrow), 27–28, 83
Second Shimen Road, 146
sent-down urban youth, 92, 236–37
Severe Acute Respiratory Syndrome (SARS), 251
shangfang. See petitioning
shangfang cun. See petitioning
Shanghai, 1–2; administration in, 11, 12; alleyway housing in, 2, 7–8, 92–95, 100–3, 130, 133, 146, 150–51, 231, 246, 251; 262–65; City Temple of, 23; cityscape of, 2, 184–85; consumer culture in, 22; corruption in, 12–13, 15, 53, 70, 145–47, 152, 154–55, 259, 269, 279; downtown of, 7, 12, 29, 48, 62, 66, 91, 93, 140, 145, 169, 170, 229, 236; foreign concessions in, 93, 141n3, 192; high-rises in, 1–2, 12, 122, 154, 157, 172, 189, 203, 267; historic preservation in, 23–24, 234–35, 243–45, 249–51, 261–65, 267; history of, 1–2, 8, 241–43, 244; housing policy and regulation in, 10, 112, 119, 205; housing reform in, 5, 8–10, 170; housing shortage in, 7; Japanese bombing of (January 28, 1932), 240; land policies in, 9, 11–12, 148; library of, 78; metro system in, 231–32; Muslim community in, 102; neighborhoods in, 1, 5, 8, 11–14, 16, 23, 26–27, 29, 46, 51–52, 54–55, 59, 63, 66–67, 76–77, 94–95, 101, 108, 120, 130, 145, 149, 159–60, 166, 168, 194, 229, 249; neighborhood

committee in, 76, 78, 107, 109, 127, 153, 156, 203, 221, 235, 248, 258; neighborhood life in, 101, 139, 140, 142n14; People's Court in, 118, 268; People's Square of, 48, 62, 281; petition offices in, 48–49, 62, 211; petitioners of, 39–40, 45, 57, 63, 70–74, 78, 214–15, 217; as "phantom" city, 5; population of, 7, 102, 146; Port Office in, 51; public security apparatus in, 58, 153, 155, 169, 177; public space of, 2, 5, 29; Pudong in, 12, 55, 81, 149, 171, 180, 183–84, 195; real estate market in, 92, 102, 154, 160, 268; Shanghaiese (local language/slang), 94; shantytown in, 189, 192, 198, 210, 226n3; *shikumen* in, 92, 101–102, 105, 109, 120–21; socialist welfare housing, 7; stock market (*see* Chinese stock market); World Expo (2010), 25, 182–85, 281. *See also* Chen Liangyu; demolition and relocation; district government; domicide; eviction; petitioners; petitioning; urban renewal; Xintiandi

Shanghai Cooperation Organization Summit, 74

Shanghai Daily, 244

Shanghai First Intermediate People's Court, 118

Shanghai Foreign Correspondents' Club, 74

Shanghai Higher People's Court, 118

Shanghai Municipal Bureau of Finance, 131

Shanghai Municipal Cultural Relics Management Bureau (municipal cultural relics bureau), 234–35

Shanghai Municipal Housing and Land Resource Bureau (municipal housing bureau), 96–97, 126, 146, 199, 206, 232, 239, 252, 266

Shanghai Municipal People's Congress, 62–63, 234, 253

Shanghai Municipal Urban Planning Bureau (municipal planning bureau), 95–96, 125, 234, 250–54, 261–68

Shanghai Oriental Television, 120, 244, 249

Shanghai Public Security Bureau, 155, 169

Shanghai Real Estate Company, 147

Shanghai Second Intermediate People's Court, 268

Shanghai-Beijing railway line, 71

shangye kaifa. See real estate development

shantytowns, 43, 189, 192, 198, 210, 226n3

Shen Ting, 151–56, 182; childhood, 152–53; Cultural Revolution, 152; demolition and relocation, 151; domicide, 153; family, 152–53; home/apartment, 152–53; lawsuit, 151–55; media, 155; settlement, 182; Socialist reform, 152. *See also* Chen Liangyu; corruption; East Eight Lots; Zheng Enchong; Zhou Zhengyi

Shenzhen, 9, 153

Shi Lin, 189–226; childhood, 190–97; barrack-room lawyer, 190, 205, 208, 210–12, 225; demolition and relocation, 201–3, 208–9; demolition squads, 212; detention, 222–23; event petitioning, 217; family, 190–97; home/house, 192–200, *201*; land use rights, 199, 202, 204, 223, 225; petitioning in Beijing, 213–15, 218–22; "plus and minus" formula, 209–10, 225; policy entrepreneur, 29, 190, 278; "policy plus" formula, 209–13; protest in Hong Kong, 190, 213, 217; shantytown, 189, 198; "Teacher Shi," 189, 204–7; union

connections, 194–97, 199; "wheel war," 203; work unit, 196–97, 203
shikumen, 92, 101–2, 105, 109, 120–21. See also alleyway housing
shizhong. See kidnapping
Shui On Land Ltd., 95–101, 114, 120–21, 125–28, 138–40, 141; Baijing Ltd., 98; "Code of Conduct & Business Ethics," 141; Landton Ltd., 96–98; milestones of, 101, 139; Shui On Group, 95; Taipingqiao project, 95–101, 114–15, 120, 129–30, 138–41; Wood, Benjamin, 99–101, 114, 138–40. See also Lo, Vincent; Xintiandi
Sichuan earthquake, 15–16
Sichuan Road, 230
Siena, 100, 139, 140, 140n30. See also "adaptive re-use"; Italian hill towns
Singapore, 267
Skidmore, Owings & Merrill LLP (SOM), 99
"social edginess," 278
Socialist Reform, 20, 106, 124, 131–33, 152, 191, 194
Southern Weekend (Nanfang zhoumo), 120, 121, 123–24
Special Economic Zones, 9
Springfield, Illinois, 229, 239, 243–44
stability maintenance, 4, 277
Standing Committee of the Municipal People's Congress, 253
State Council, 9, 11, 20, 40–41, 49, 73–74, 86, 159, 198, 214–16, 243
state-owned enterprises (SOEs), 22, 64, 170
suicide, 2, 26–27, 42, 92, 136, 266, 268
Sun Dongdong, 79–82
Suzhou Creek, 146

Tahrir Square, 276
Taichang Road, 130
Taipingqiao (Peace Bridge), 93–101, 114, 125–26, 129, 138–39. See also "Taipingqiao Area Specific Plan"; Wood, Benjamin
"Taipingqiao Area Specific Plan," 95–101, 109–11, 119–20, 125; Lot 108, 94, 96–98, 97, 126, 129–35, 138; Lot 109, 95, 101, 109–11, 117, 126, 129. See also Lo, Vincent; Shui On Land Ltd.; Taipingqiao; Xintiandi
Taipingqiao project, 95–101, 114–15, 120, 129–30, 138–41. See also Lo, Vincent; Shui On Land Ltd.; Wood, Benjamin; Xintiandi
Taiwan Strait, 134
Tang Dynasty, 164
Tang Yingnian, 241
Three Gorges Dam, 13, 25
Tiananmen Square, 43–44, 63–64, 165, 203, 222, 225, 279
"tofu projects" (shoddy construction), 15
Tongji University, 104, 249–50, 263–64. See also Ruan Yisan
Turner, Victor, 277–78
"two meetings." See "annual two meetings"

UNESCO Asia-Pacific Awards for Cultural Heritage Conservation, 261
union cadre, 116, 196, 198, 213, 217, 278
United Nation's Human Rights Council, 74
United Nations Refugee Center in Hong Kong, 217
United States, 3, 20–21, 44, 48, 229, 270, 280
UN-Habitat goal, 8; "365 Project," 8, 201
urban renewal (*jiuqu gaizao*), 4–16, 109; "365 Project," 8, 201; authorities over, 11–12; confiscation of property, 26, 52, 55–56, 94–95, 109–10, 132, 146; "Control the Scale and Strictly

Manage Urban Housing Demolition and Relocation," 159; corruption, 12–16, 133–34, 146–56; Document 68, 148–49, 154–58, 171–73; Document 111, 10–11, 149, 158–59; Document 305, 9–11, 13–14, 18, 49, 159, 214–16, 277–79; Document 347, 146–49; Document 590, 11; media coverage, 120–21, 123–24, 130, 206–7; regulations, 9–11, 13; return policy, 148–49, 152–58, 171. *See also* housing policy and regulation; housing reform

Vine, David, 21, 26–27, 83
violent demolition and relocation. *See* demolition and relocation; domicide; eviction
Voice of America, 155

Wang Cailiang, 255–60
Wang Daohan, 241
Wangzhi Road, 94
weibei. *See* couplet and calligraphy
weiquan. *See* rights-protection lawyers
Wen Jiabao, 49, 155, 221, 270
West Beijing Road, 146
West Enders, Boston, 26
"wheel war," 203
"white terror," 220
wholesale destruction, 12, 262, 265
Wood, Benjamin, 99–101, 114, 138–40. *See also* Lo, Vincent; Xintiandi
work unit (*danwei*), 7, 76, 94, 146, 257; involvement in demolition and relocation, 52–53, 55, 63–65, 131, 136, 169, 170–71, 196–97, 203
World Expo (2010), 25, 182–85, 281
World Health Organization (WHO), 27
Wu Changshuo, 103
Wu Guozhen, 131
Wu Jiang, 250, 258
Wukan village, Guangdong Province, 47

Wuxin (Five Hearts) Real Estate Demolition and Relocation Company, 99, 110–11, 114–15, 132, 135

Xiamen, 280
Xijiangwan Road, 230, *233*
xinfang. *See* petitioning
Xingye Road, 94
Xinhua News Agency, 49, 80, 159
Xinjishi (New Lucky Gentleman restaurant), 119–20
xinli jiawei. *See* psychological price mark
Xinmin wanbao (Xinmin Evening News), 250, 253
Xintai County, Shandong Province, 81
Xintiandi (New World), 28–29, 92–101, 114, 118–20, 125–30, 138–40; architect for, 99–100; architectural style of, 120; architecture firm for, 99; as commercial and entertainment center, 92, 128; as concealed project, 109, 126; cost of, 101; dream team for, 138–39; as historic preservation, 100, 140; human toll of, 121–24; impact on residents and neighborhood, 101, 109, 114, 140; and Italian hilltowns, 139, 140; location of, 93; media reaction to, 120–21; models for, 95, 100; as name brand, 139; as nightmare of property deprivation, 29, 91–93, 101, 108, 116, 138, 140–41; property in, 127; real estate price at, 138–39; redevelopment of, 92; resistance to, 114; as SoHo of Shanghai, 92; success of, 139; Xinjishi (New Lucky Gentleman restaurant) in, 119–20. *See also* Lo, Vincent; Taipingqiao; Wood, Benjamin
Xu Laosan, 191–92, 195–96
Xue Fa Yuan Di. *See* Legal Study Forum
Xuhui District Housing Bureau, 201–4, 212–13
Xujiahui, 200

Yangpu District, vi, 147
Yangzi delta, 11, 101
yezhu. *See* property owner
Yonganmen, Beijing, 74
Yu Jianrong, 82, 85–87
Yuan dynasty, 85

zero-land-use cost, 158
zero-sum game, 14, 149
Zhang Xiaoqiu, *126*, 136–37
Zhao Liang, 43
Zhaojiabang, 192–93, 200. *See also*
    shantytowns
Zhejiang Province, 11–12, 47, 71, 169,
    214, 236
Zheng Enchong, 153–55, 216–17, 266
Zheng He, 28–29, *104*, 104;
    seventeenth great-grant daughter of
    (Zheng Huifang), *104*, 104. *See also*
    Ming dynasty
Zhongguo qingnian bao (China Youth
    Daily), 121
Zhou Hongtao, 131, 134, 138. *See also*
    Chiang Kai-shek; Guomindang
Zhou Youlan, 39–40, 50–78, 84, 277;
    childhood, 50–51; demolition
    squad, 55; demotion and relocation,
    52–56; detention, 39–40, 59, 63,
    70, 73–75, *75*, 84, 147; domicide,
    56; event petitioner, 62–63, 70–74,
    78; eviction, 55–56; family, 50–52,
57, 64–65, 78; full-time petitioner,
    59–62; GMD connections, 50;
    home/house, 51–52, *54*; petition-
    by-letter, 57–59; psychological price
    mark, 64–66, 68–70, 84; settlement,
    63–64, 67–70; stock market, 66–67,
    77, 88n32; surveillance, 63, 70–71,
    76–78; violence, 60, 62, 71–72, 74,
    75; work unit, 52–53, 55, 63–65
Zhou Zhengyi, 147, 152–57, 166, 171,
    174, 182, 184; Contract 19, 148. *See*
    also East Eight Lots
Zhouzhuang, 261
Zhu Guangze, 129–38, 282; attempted
    suicide, 136; Cultural Revolution,
    131–32; demolition and relocation,
    133–36; demolition squad, 135–36;
    detention, 282; domicide, 135–36;
    family, 130–32, 133–36, 282; GMD
    connections, 131–32, 134; home/
    house, 130–33, *133*; kidnapping,
    135–36; petition, 137–38;
    psychological price mark, 136–37;
    socialist reform, 131–32, *133*; work
    unit, 131, 136; Zhu Hongnan, 130–
    31. *See also* Lo, Vincent
Zhu Rongji, 241
Zinn, Howard, vii
Zongguo xinwen zhoukan (China News
    Week), 79
Zuccotti Park, 276